ROOTS OF
MENTAL ILLNESS
IN CHILDREN

ANNALS OF THE NEW YORK ACADEMY OF SCIENCES
Volume 1008

ROOTS OF MENTAL ILLNESS IN CHILDREN

*Edited by Jean A. King, Craig F. Ferris,
and Israel I. Lederhendler*

The New York Academy of Sciences
New York, New York
2003

Library of Congress Cataloging-in-Publication Data

Roots of mental illness in children / edited by Jean A. King, Craig F. Ferris, and Israel I. Lederhendler.
  p. ; cm. — (Annals of the New York Academy of Sciences ; v. 1008)
This volume is the result of a conference, held on March 15–17, 2003 in New York.
Includes bibliographical references and index.
  ISBN 1-57331-478-1 (cloth : alk. paper) — ISBN 1-57331-479-X (pbk. : alk. paper) 1. Child psychopathology—Etiology—Congresses. 2. Adolescent psychopathology—Etiology—Congresses.
  [DNLM: 1. Mental Disorders—etiology—Child—Congresses. 2. Child Psychology—Congresses. 3. Conflict (Psychology)—Child—Congresses. 4. Emotions—Child—Congresses. 5. Parent-Child Relations—Congresses. WS 350 R782 2003] I. King, Jean A. II. Ferris, Craig F. III. Lederhendler, I. Izja. IV. Series.
  Q11.N5 vol. 1008
  [RJ499]
  500 s—dc22
  [618.92/890
                                                2003025509

GYAT/PCP
Printed in the United States of America
ISBN 1-57331-478-1 (cloth)
ISBN 1-57331-479-X (paper)
ISSN 0077-8923

ANNALS OF THE NEW YORK ACADEMY OF SCIENCES
Volume 1008
December 2003

ROOTS OF MENTAL ILLNESS IN CHILDREN

Editors
JEAN A. KING, CRAIG F. FERRIS, AND ISRAEL I. LEDERHENDLER

This volume is the result of a conference entitled **Roots of Mental Illness in Children** sponsored by the New York Academy of Sciences and the National Institute of Mental Health held on March 15–17, 2003 in New York, NY.

CONTENTS

Preface. *By* JEAN A. KING ix

Introduction: Behavioral Neuroscience and Childhood Mental Illness.
  By ISRAEL I. LEDERHENDLER 1

Categories, Dimensions, and Mental Health of Children and Adolescents:
  Keynote Address. *By* MICHAEL RUTTER 11

Part I. Parent–Child Interactions

Attachment Relationship Experiences and Childhood Psychopatholgy.
  By CHARLES H. ZEANAH, ANGELA KEYES, AND LISA SETTLES 22

Social Engagement and Attachment: A Phylogenetic Perspective.
  By STEPHEN W. PORGES 31

Part II. Parent–Child Interactions: Separation

Can We Develop a Neurobiological Model of Human Social–Emotional
  Development? Integrative Thoughts on the Effects of Separation on
  Parent–Child Interactions. *By* CHARLES A. NELSON 48

Family and Community Factors that Predict Internalizing and Externalizing
  Symptoms in Low-Income, African-American Children: A Preliminary
  Report. *By* NADINE J. KASLOW, SHERYL HERON, DEBRA KIM ROBERTS,
  MARTIE THOMPSON, OMAR GUESSOUS, AND CLAUDIA JONES 55

Part III. Social Interactions: Conflict

Using an Animal Model to Assess the Long-Term Behavioral and Biological Consequences of Adolescent Abuse and Exposure to Alcohol. *By* CRAIG F. FERRIS 69

Aggressive Behavior in Abused Children. *By* DANIEL F. CONNOR, LEONARD A. DOERFLER, ADAM M. VOLUNGIS, RONALD J. STEINGARD, AND RICHARD H. MELLONI, JR. 79

Part IV. Social Interactions: Risk Assessment

The Amygdala and Development of the Social Brain. *By* DAVID SKUSE, JOHN MORRIS, AND KATE LAWRENCE 91

Experience-Dependent Affective Learning and Risk for Psychopathology in Children. *By* SETH D. POLLAK 102

Part V. Learned Fear and Anxiety: The Sense of Safety

Applying Learning Principles to the Treatment of Post-Trauma Reactions. *By* BARBARA OLASOV ROTHBAUM AND MICHAEL DAVIS 112

Developing a Sense of Safety: The Neurobiology of Neonatal Attachment. *By* REGINA M. SULLIVAN 122

Gene–Environment Interactions and the Neurobiology of Social Conflict. *By* STEPHEN J. SUOMI 132

The Policy Context for Child and Adolescent Mental Health Services: Implications for Systems Reform and Basic Science Development. *By* KIMBERLY HOAGWOOD 140

Part VI. Mood Regulation: Impulsivity

Impulsivity, Emotion Regulation, and Developmental Psychopathology: Specificity Versus Generality of Linkages. *By* STEPHEN P. HINSHAW . . . 149

Neural Substrates Underlying Impulsivity. *By* JEAN A. KING, JEFFREY TENNEY, VICTORIA ROSSI, LAURALEA COLAMUSSI, AND STACY BURDICK. 160

Response Inhibition and Disruptive Behaviors: Toward a Multiprocess Conception of Etiological Heterogeneity for ADHD Combined Type and Conduct Disorder Early-Onset Type. *By* JOEL T. NIGG 170

Part VII. Mood Regulation: Individual Differences

The Development of Affect Regulation: Bringing Together Basic and Clinical Perspectives. *By* RONALD E. DAHL 183

Nonhuman Primate Models to Study Anxiety Emotion Regulation, and Psychopathology. *By* NED H. KALIN AND STEVEN E. SHELTON 189

Irritability in Pediatric Mania and Other Childhood Psychopathology. *By* ELLEN LEIBENLUFT, R. JAMES R. BLAIR, DENNIS S. CHARNEY, AND DANIEL S. PINE 201

**Part VIII. Mental Illness in Children and Adolescents:
Challenges for Progress**

Brain Imaging Studies of the Anatomical and Functional Consequences of
   Preterm Birth for Human Brain Development. *By* BRADLEY S. PETERSON   219

Integrating Neuroscience and Psychological Approaches in the Study of Early
   Experiences. *By* MEGAN R. GUNNAR   238

The Serotonin Transporter Gene in Aggressive Children with and without
   ADHD and Nonaggressive Matched Controls. *By* JOSEPH H. BEITCHMAN,
   KRISTEN M. DAVIDGE, JAMES L. KENNEDY, LESLIE ATKINSON, VIVIEN
   LEE, SOLOMON SHAPIRO, AND LORI DOUGLAS   248

Part IX: Poster Papers

Effortful Control, Attention, and Aggressive Behavior in Preschoolers at Risk
   for Conduct Problems. *By* TRACY A. DENNIS AND
   LAURIE MILLER BROTMAN   252

Functional Neuroimaging of Social Cognition in Pervasive Developmental
   Disorders: A Brief Review. *By* ADRIANA DI MARTINO AND
   F. XAVIER CASTELLANOS   256

Hallucinations in Nonpsychotic Children: Findings from a Psychiatric
   Emergency Service. *By* GAIL A. EDELSOHN, HARRIS RABINOVICH, AND
   RUBEN PORTNOY   261

Subanalysis of the Location of White Matter Hyperintensities and Their Asso-
   ciation with Suicidality in Children and Youth. *By* STEFAN EHRLICH, GIL
   G. NOAM, IN KYOON LYOO, BAE J. KWON, MEGAN A. CLARK, AND
   PERRY F. RENSHAW   265

Obstetric Complications Correlate with Neurobehavioral and Brain Structural
   Alterations in Young Relatives at Risk for Schizophrenia. *By* ANDREW
   R. GILBERT, DEBRA M. MONTROSE, SARAH D. SAHNI, VAIBHAV A.
   DIWADKAR, AND MATCHERI S. KESHAVAN   269

Longitudinal Assessment of Callous/Impulsive Traits, Substance Abuse, and
   Symptoms of Depression in Adolescents: A Latent Variable Approach.
   By CRAIG S. NEUMANN, MICHAEL VITACCO, ANGELA ROBERTSON,
   AND KENNETH SEWELL   276

Sex Differences and Hormonal Effects in a Model of Preterm Infant Brain
   Injury. *By* JOSEPH L. NUÑEZ AND MARGARET M. MCCARTHY   281

Coping Strategies Moderate the Relation of Hypothalamus–Pituitary–Adrenal
   Axis Reactivity to Self-Injurious Behavior. *By* SALLY I. POWERS AND
   ELIZA T. MCARDLE   285

Prenatal Nicotine Exposure and Behavior. *By* V. ROSSI, T. MESSENGER,
   D. PETERS, C.F. FERRIS, AND J. KING   289

Familial Psychiatric Disorders in Child DSM-IV ADHD: Moderation by Child
   Gender. *By* JULIEANN STAWICKI AND JOEL T. NIGG   293

Reorganization of Unresolved Childhood Traumatic Memories Following
   Exposure Therapy. *By* K. CHASE STOVALL-MCCLOUGH AND
   MARYLENE CLOITRE   297

Ineffective Parenting: A Precursor to Psychopathic Traits and Delinquency in Hispanic Females. *By* MICHAEL J. VITACCO, CRAIG S. NEUMANN, VINCENT RAMOS, AND MARY K. ROBERTS 300

Mother Lowers Glucocorticoid Levels of Preweaning Rats After Acute Threat. *By* CHRISTOPH P. WIEDENMAYER, ANA M. MAGARINOS, BRUCE S. MCEWEN, AND GORDON A. BARR 304

Early Deprivation Alters the Vocalization Behavior of Neonates Directing Maternal Attention in a Rat Model of Child Neglect. *By* BETTY ZIMMERBERG, JU H. KIM, ABIGAIL N. DAVIDSON, AND ABIGAIL J. ROSENTHAL 308

Index of Contributors 315

Financial assistance was received from:

Major Funders

• JANSSEN PHARMACEUTICA INC.
• NATIONAL INSTITUTE OF MENTAL HEALTH—NATIONAL INSTITUTES OF HEALTH
  • DIVISION OF MENTAL DISORDERS, BEHAVIORAL RESEARCH AND AIDS
  • DIVISION OF NEUROSCIENCE AND BASIC BEHAVIORAL SCIENCE

Contributors

• NATIONAL INSTITUTE OF NEUROLOGICAL DISORDERS AND STROKE—NATIONAL INSTITUTES OF HEALTH

Preface

JEAN A. KING

University of Massachusetts Medical Center, Department of Psychiatry, Worcester, Massachusetts 01655, USA

This volume of the Annals contains the proceedings of the conference entitled "Roots of Mental Illness in Children." The conference was held at Rockefeller University on March 15–17, 2003. The conference brought together an esteemed group of preclinical and clinical researchers to address the devastating disorders and challenges faced by many youngsters.

The main objective of this conference was to distill information from a multiplicity of researchers using distinctly different approaches, to converge on the issue of mental health disorders in children. The working premise of the conference was that the common symptoms, or dimensions, observed in several childhood disorders may reflect special features of behavioral or neural development that may act synergistically with environmental challenges to confer either susceptibility or resilience to childhood mental health disorders.

We hope that this volume of the *Annals* will contribute to advancing our understanding of the etiology and pathophysiology of childhood mental health disorders by establishing an alternate framework of reference supported by the cross-fertilization of preclinical and clinical perspectives.

The conference could not have taken place without the support of the main sponsors: the New York Academy of Sciences and The National Institute of Mental Health. In addition, special thanks to the planning committee members—Dr. Israel Izja Lederhendler, Ph.D.; Jean A. King, Ph.D.; Craig Ferris, Ph.D.; Bradley S. Peterson, M.D.; Thomas R. Insel, M.D., Ph.D.; Ned H. Kalin, M.D. ; Susan Swedo, M.D., and Ronald E. Dahl, M.D.— who made invaluable contributions to the conceptualization and scope of this conference.

Ann. N.Y. Acad. Sci. 1008: ix (2003). © 2003 New York Academy of Sciences.
doi: 10.1196/annals.1301.040

Introduction

Behavioral Neuroscience and Childhood Mental Illness

ISRAEL I. LEDERHENDLER

National Institute of Mental Health, Bethesda, Maryland 20892, USA

ABSTRACT: Advances in the treatment of mental illness depend, in part, on the elimination of barriers to the use of new basic research findings. Some of the barriers originate in the different research perspectives adopted by clinical and basic researchers. Clinical research is driven by the need to recruit and examine classes of individuals, and so the conceptual framework focuses largely on categories of disorders. Basic researchers, including psychologists and behavioral neuroscientists, investigate fundamental features of behavior such as emotion regulation, attention, or arousal; therefore, disorders are commonly approached from a "dimensional" framework. In the broadest sense dimensions are those features that are common to multiple disorders. Categories are an effort to draw distinctions among disorders. The differences between these frameworks, and the perspectives held among clinicians and basic scientists, are not dichotomous. Many clinicians investigate fundamental aspects of pathophysiology and behavior that apply to multiple disorders, and many basic researchers are developing animal "models" of categorical disorders. It is timely and important to examine these approaches critically, and to work toward formulating perspectives that capture the strengths of each group of researchers so that their common goal of translating research findings into treatments for childhood mental health disorders is strengthened.

KEYWORDS: childhood mental illness; behavioral neuroscience; imaging; genetics; development

Sir Michael Rutter[1] has challenged views that distinguish dimensional from categorical approaches dichotomously. Ultimately, both views are critical to translation. Dimensions of mental disorders offer the advantage of quantitative continuities, but qualitative distinctions must also be recognized. Sir Michael notes a particular danger with the assumption that searching for causality can only be approached dimensionally through questions that relate to individual differences. Even within narrowly defined risk categories, psychosocial outcomes are continuously malleable in individuals. At the same time individuals are always associated with categorical features such as gender, and ethnic and national characteristics. Such features are not

Address for correspondence: Israel I. Lederhendler, Ph.D., National Institute of Mental Health, 6001 Executive Blvd., MSC 9637, Bethesda, MD 20892. Voice: 301-443-1576; fax: 301-443-4822.

ilu@helix.nih.gov

Ann. N.Y. Acad. Sci. 1008: 1–10 (2003). © 2003 New York Academy of Sciences. doi: 10.1196/annals.1301.001

mere passive descriptors. Many of them confer significant associated risk or proba-
bilities of psychopathology through a variety of causal routes. It is clear that a variety
of research strategies will be necessary to understand individual differences in vulnerability to risk. To take advantage of new knowledge that can be drawn from ge-
nomics and brain imaging, the interdependence of categories and dimensions needs
to be appreciated.

WHY THE FOCUS ON CHILDHOOD DISORDERS?

Mental and behavioral disorders in childhood generate a disproportionate societal
burden because the impairments may last throughout the lifespan. Attention deficit
hyperactive disorder (ADHD), for example, may be expressed in terms of academic
failure, greater chances of accidental injury, or inadequate independence as an adult.
Aggression and antisocial behavior in children can be associated with significant
suffering in others, impulsive behavior, or even loss of life, and is often perpetuated
across generations.

Even as we see significant advances and opportunities in the treatments of some
children with impaired emotional, cognitive, and behavioral functioning, there are
concerns that many may be inaccurately diagnosed and inappropriately treated. It is
not entirely clear why there are differences among groups of children receiving psychotropic medication. Wide variation in treatment patterns may indicate a need for
more research on diagnostic criteria, their underlying pathophysiology, and appropriate treatment protocols. Diagnosis, of course, is based largely on categories, and
one underlying concern is that a category can too easily become a label, and a label,
particularly for children, can stick and become a major factor in the child's subsequent development.

Much of today's knowledge about brain and behavioral development is based on
animal studies. There are many opportunities for such studies to have a substantial
impact on the treatment of children with mental and behavioral disorders. But the
pace of translation seems slow. So, can animal studies actually be useful? Almost
certainly animal studies cannot fully "model" any category of mental illness. No single gene, brain area, or behavioral measure can fully represent a disorder. At the
same time it is rare to find a mental disorder that reflects a unitary construct, so examination of its various features is always in order. It is these putative "features" of
a disorder, rather than the disease category itself, that enables contributions from behavioral neuroscience.

Without denying the value of disease categories, a dimensional approach can in
some cases provide a more pragmatic framework for exploiting the findings of animal research. For example, autism or childhood bipolar research might be better
served by behavioral neuroscience if the comparisons between the animals and human data were framed in terms of constructs like attachment, social cognition, or
emotion regulation, than as "autism" *per se*. Another example may be "irritability,"
a proposed feature of childhood bipolar disorder.[2,3] Constructs like these provide a
more heuristic basis for basic research applications to psychopathology than animal
models that attempt to mimic the disorder by behavioral analogy. The genetics and
neurobiology of irritability may also be applicable to ADHD, anxiety, or conduct
disorder. If so, then the basic research can also provide a physiological basis for re-

thinking nosology. It is clear, however, that continued interactions between those who use animals and those who use humans in their research can only enhance the possibilities that emerge from important linkages that have yet to be explored.[4]

Significant opportunities to exploit the advances in genetics and neuroscience for understanding child psychopathology have emerged in the past ten years.[5] For some disorders, genetic factors play a role in risk for mental illness by generating differential vulnerability to subsequent adverse experiences.[6,7] Functional imaging studies have also shown exceptional promise.[8,9] Such tools can find disrupted brain function at the very earliest stages of infant development, and they can help to identify neural circuits and their functional status in children and adolescents who may be at risk.[10] The use of functional imaging in awake responding animals is a pioneering effort that is becoming a critical bridge between the molecular and neural systems data that is needed to fill the gaps exposed by brain imaging in children.[11]

ATTACHMENT AND THE EFFECTS OF SEPARATION

A categorical approach is essential to understanding the role of secure or insecure attachment in populations. Critical knowledge about groups that are at risk depend on establishing operational categories using features such as youth, low-income, "inner-city," and African-American. This is necessary for complex determinations where, among children who reside in family contexts, characterized by maternal psychological distress and low levels of family cohesion, there is particular vulnerablity to developing both internalizing and externalizing behavior problems.[12] The mechanisms by which such complex routes to disorders come about will be more readily discovered when more refined categories and dimensions of biological and psychological processes are brought into play.

Attachments between infants and their caregivers are distinguished by varying degrees of security. Secure attachments help develop individual resilience even in high-risk environments. Insecure attachments, such as those associated with multiple caregivers for institutionalized children, can produce both emotional withdrawal and indiscriminate social extraversion.[13] The successful use of basic animal research depends heavily on comparable behaviors or states associated with secure attachments. Comparable behaviors don't have to model the human case, but they do need to provide heuristic insight into aspects of the pathophysiology.

Social attachments are based on processes of bond formation and use some of the same neural substrates that assign reward and hedonic value to certain signals.[14] For some developmental stages timing plays a critical role in associating parents with security.[15] Adverse early experiences, including maternal separation, can alter later individual reactivity to stressful events and social stimuli.[16,17] The ability to extinguish behavioral responses that were acquired following aversive events may involve somewhat different circuits than rewards leading to formation of a social bond.[18] We know that the effects of maternal separation may be possible to reverse[19] yet the role of extinction circuitry for these developmental changes is not well understood.

The reward and extinction systems may interact in development to create a balance between social approach and withdrawal. It is not clear, however, if the approach and withdrawal systems make up a single continuous dimension or if additional factors such as stress play a role in modulating the balance. Rodents and nonhuman primates have developmental periods that are protective against stressful psychosocial interactions. However, the timing of this period of social buffering, and the anatomical and neurochemical organization of the hypothalamic–pituitary–adrenal (HPA) system that is activated by stress, differ in important ways between species. In humans, as in animals, parent–infant interactions clearly lead to the modulation of maladaptive responses in the stress system. In children these responses lead to increased vulnerability for affective disorders.[20]

RISK ASSESSMENT AND THE SENSE OF SAFETY

The behavior of another person is rarely entirely predictable, particularly when a relationship is not fully established. Social engagement involves considerable uncertainty and the regulation of that uncertainty. The regulation of social interactions may involve uncertainty, stress, fearfulness, and anxiety, at the same time as attachment and affiliation.[21,22] One aspect of the regulation of social uncertainty is the emergence of cognitive skills that help the child understand the safety and risk associated with a particular social context.

The ability to assess risk does not become fully developed until fundamental imperatives for growth, maturation, and feeding have been met. The abuse or neglect of children sets in motion developmental changes that interfere with these requirements. The behavior of neonatal rats in the context of attachment to the dam is a compelling illustration of the interplay among developmental requirements. During the first nine postnatal days, pups learn to approach and prefer the dam's odor regardless of the quality of maternal care. The need for suckling and huddling is so powerful that even when paired with shock the odor preference is acquired. On postnatal day 10 when walking begins, the same pairing produces an odor aversion.[16] The abrupt reversal of this learning involves associative inputs in the olfactory bulbs of odor and norepinephrine from locus coruleus cells in the brain stem. These studies have an eerie resemblance to some attachment patterns in abused or neglected children. It begs the question whether some aspects of developmental psychopathology may be driven by an atypical appetitive system established in the brains of children who are wired to form attachments whether or not the parent is kind.

A complementary approach for tracking the effects of childhood abuse on the development of psychopathology is based on fundamental mechanisms of perceptual learning, particularly processes that involve learning about emotions. The pathological outcomes of physical abuse have been extensively described and documented, but basic research is necessary to effectively target treatments. Unfortunately the emergence of systems for processing and organizing emotions in children has not received adequate experimental attention. This is crucial for understanding how children are influenced by the experience of physical abuse. Pollak[23] has shown that in a context of interpersonal threat, physically abused children process social information about anger very differently while other social emotions are processed in the same manner as nonabused children. At the same time the perceptual preferences and discriminative abilities of physically abused children allow them to categorize angry facial expressions very accurately and using less information than nonphysically abused children. Basic experimental psychology research on perceptual generalization of social information could provide fundamental contributions to medical advances for abused children.

In developing systems, salient experiences such as physical abuse become part of the ontogenetic substrate itself and form a basis of the child's general expectations of others.[24] Such expectations are then reinforced by poor verbal skills and higher aggressiveness than peers who have not experienced abuse.[25] Given that the developmental data are spare, some important insights are available from the application of learning theory to posttraumatic stress disorder (PTSD) in adults.[26] One important similarity between adults that suffered trauma and maltreated children is the presence of overgeneralization to the original fear stimulus and the failure to respond to safety signals. This contributes to resistance to extinction because fear is not inhibited in the presence of safety cues. For adults, the assessment of the experience seems to be actively filtered and rendered more specific, reducing its impact on other systems. The animal and human work are consistent in emphasizing that the circumstances of both extinction training and the initial acquisition must be considered so that the memory of the precipitating experience is minimized when therapy is attempted.[27,28]

Is There a Social Brain?

The evolving science of social cognition is an important effort to link social behavior with perceptions and other assessments related to decisions and communications. This field draws together a set of brain areas and systems that have special significance for social interactions. Although many other brain structures are involved, the amygdala and related brain areas have been a focus for the neurobiology of social behavior as well as emotional behavior.[29,30] The amygdala system is also a central candidate for many of the mechanisms involved with the assessment of social threat and safety. David Amaral and coworkers[31,32] report that bilateral damage of the amygdala in mature macaque monkeys produces socially uninhibited individuals lacking appropriate fear responses to certain inanimate objects. The amygdala may also play a role in the distribution of social and inanimate information to different brain regions. But the amygdala may not be the location where social decisions are processed. The amygdala functions instead as a "brake" on interactions with unfamiliar objects or organisms, while an evaluation of a possible social threat is carried out elsewhere in the brain.[32,33] Such filtering by the amygdala may be significant for the distinct development of social fears and fear of inanimate objects.

A phylogenetically identifiable "social engagement system" has been proposed[34] that supports behaviors that emerged as critical properties of internal bodily reactions and have become integral aspects of brain systems for social behavior. These behaviors provide inputs to the social information stream, as well as a framework for reacting to social situations by individuals at various phyletic levels. Social experiences make their way to the brain and can significantly alter its function throughout much of development.[35] However meaningful comparisons between animal and human systems will require much greater specificity in the behaviors and brain circuits that produce this plasticity.[36,37] Social behaviors cannot be fully appreciated without knowing how social stimuli become part of the information stream in the forebrain. In other words, social behavior is not easily separable from cognition, and cognition must become part of the way we understand social interactions.

ACTIVATION AND INHIBITION OF BEHAVIOR
AND EMOTION REGULATION

The constructs of response inhibition and impulsivity are key to understanding how emotions and behavior are regulated. These constructs are features of a broad spectrum of child and adolescent disorders ranging from problems in motivation and attention, to serious disruptive antisocial behaviors that may include the deliberate injury of others. Neither of these concepts can be considered a unitary process. Fear, anxiety, and stress, for example, also engage systems that energize action, and their impact on this spectrum of disorders is critical and difficult to tease apart. Another state, irritability, in which negative stimuli lead to heightened feelings of anger, has been understudied as a feature of several childhood disorders including depression, oppositional defiant disorder, ADHD, and conduct disorder. When the irritability is episodic it seems to be a significant feature of pediatric bipolar disorder.[3] This degree of overlap among features within diagnostic categories leads to special difficulties in drawing distinctions among disorders in children. There is a clear need for a broader systems level approach in the research, coordinated with more careful consideration of the nosology of these disorders.

Regulation occurs at many levels within the nervous system: Neural activity and behavior commonly adjust in response to sensory inputs when they either exceed or fail to reach expected levels of stimulation. Failures to make such adjustments can indicate possible impairments in attentional and motivational systems that are critical for assessing the context and other conditions that predict reward or punishment. Finally, levels of arousal/activation appropriate to the context, together with the effective processing of multiple streams of information, are necessary for controlling emotional responses and motor outputs.

The role of stress in the regulation of impulsive behaviors has become possible because of the ability to manipulate context, genetics, and gender in development using systems like the spontaneously hypertensive rat.[38] Such studies can expand the scope of inquiry in human systems, such as the role stress plays in producing vulnerability during early development. Research using the powerful resident–intruder paradigm in hamsters highlights some of the same neurochemical systems associated with impulsive behavior in rats. However, uninhibited responding and responding to threat with aggression are not directly comparable to children with conduct disorders.[39] The work does provide an important emphasis on periods of puberty and adolescence that invoke unique processes in neurobehavioral regulation, and on individual differences for the selective inhibition of action.[40]

ADHD and conduct problems, including aggression and antisocial behavior, have numerous variants. These are very significant for deciding on appropriate treatments.[41] At the same time, the subcategories reflecting these major childhood disorders may form a continuous spectrum.[42,43] This spectrum can be very helpful for translating basic research on the development of affect regulation into more verifiable groups. Fundamental psychological and neurobiological processes such as response inhibition and impulse control apply broadly across both ADHD and conduct disorders. Response inhibition systems modulate behavior through interactions with activating and motivational systems as well as with decision making and other processes intrinsic to the child. Impairments may arise from problems that involve arousal, vigilance, motor and executive function, on the one hand, and reduced fear of punishment, as well as problems with response modulation, and verbal IQ, on the other.[43] These are, indeed, areas of basic animal and human research (e.g., see Reference 17) that have great potential relevance for childhood disorders in that they can be the basis for the reformulation of categories related to childhood mood disorders, and they may, in addition, lead to new and better treatments.

If basic research is to help advance diagnosis, it faces a challenge to be more precise in the use of concepts that relate to affect regulation. Primate studies suggest that such regulation can be measured effectively by properties like responsiveness to context, duration, intensity, and activation.[44] The more general conceptual features of regulation may include attentional aspects, activation/arousal dynamics, chronometry, awareness of ones own emotional state, and the recognition of threat or safety signals.[45] The quantitative methodologies developed with animals need to merge with the conceptual understanding of human emotions to understand what is actually dysregulated in childhood disorders.[46] The proposal by Leibenluft,[3] for example, to examine reactive aggression in animals[47] for understanding aspects of irritability, is an excellent example of a dialogue between disciplines leading to new and constructive research.

TRANSLATIONAL RESEARCH

How can we, as a community, promote a basic research portfolio that supports advances in the treatment of mental and behavioral disorders in children? Surely understanding the etiology and pathophysiology of the disorders is key. The diagnostic definitions, while valuable for the practitioner, also imply a tangible quality that contributes to their reification. Biological and social science research are also not immune from reifying ideas. Much of the research depends on the use of everyday words to develop various approaches and theories. The term "innate" for example, had a colloquial meaning, which for many years interfered with advancing our understanding of the relationships between genes, development, and environment in the organization of behavior. Similarly, the reification of a term like "conduct disorder," which describes several kinds of idealized and stereotypic behavior patterns interferes with our ability to unpack the underlying processes and study them independently of the theoretical framework from which they arose.

At the same time diagnostic categories are not arbitrary. They are often supported by important observations and descriptive features, many of which overlap across different diagnoses. These descriptive elements in themselves, are suggestive of a rich supporting comparative literature of basic social, cognitive, and affective neuroscience and behavioral science. This literature includes neural and behavioral development, genetics, social communication, response control, perceiving affect, affiliation, maternal separation and stress, trauma and abuse, parental behavior, submission and dominance, aggression, resilience, ideation, and learning and memory. These studies, many of them based on animal work, may be applicable to every level of analysis relevant to troubled children, but they seem much less relevant to a specific diagnostic category, since that is necessarily an exclusive human definition.

Thus behavioral neuroscience research is directly relevant to mental illness, but perhaps less applicable to specific disease categories. Yet no matter how potentially relevant the data may be, they are ineffective if they are not available, accessible, and meaningful to the practitioner. Without the training and experience in understanding mental illness, it may be an overwhelming challenge for basic researchers to communicate the clinical significance and implications of their findings to practitioners. This creates a translational dilemma that can only be addressed through cross-disciplinary exchange, since translation requires translators.

ACKNOWLEDGMENTS

The views expressed here are my own and do not reflect any official policies or programmatic intentions of the National Institute of Mental Health, NIH.

REFERENCES

1. RUTTER, M. 2003. Categories, dimensions, and the mental health of children and adolescents. Ann. N.Y. Acad. Sci. **1008**: this volume.
2. LIEBENLUFT, E., D.S. CHARNEY, K.E.TOWBIN, *et al.* 2003. Defining clinical phenotypes of juvenile mania. Am. J. Psychiatry **160**: 430–437.
3. LIEBENLUFT, E., R.J.R. BLAIR, D.S. CHARNEY & D.S. PINE. 2003. Irritability in pediatric mania and other childhood psychopathology. Ann. N.Y. Acad. Sci. **1008**: this volume.
4. NELSON, C.A., F.E. BLOOM, J.L. CAMERON, *et al.* 2002. An integrative, multidisciplinary approach to the study of brain–behavior relations in the context of typical and atypical development. Dev. Psychopathol. **14**: 499–520.
5. SKUSE, D.H. 2000. Behavioural neuroscience and child psychopathology: insights from model systems. J. Child Psychol. Psychiatry **41**: 3–31.
6. CASPI, A., J. MCCLAY, T.E. MOFFITT, *et al.* 2002. Role of genotype in the cycle of violence in maltreated children. Science **297**: 851–854.
7. CASPI, A., J. MCCLAY, T.E. MOFFITT, *et al.* 2003. Influence of life stress on depression: moderation by a polymorphisms in the 5-HTT gene. Science **301**: 386–389.
8. GOGTAY, N., J. GIEDD & J.L. RAPOPORT. 2002. Brain development in healthy, hyperactive, and psychotic children. Arch Neurol., **8**:1244–1248.
9. SOWELL, E.R., P.M. THOMPSON, S.E. WELCOME, *et al.* 2003. Cortical abnormalities in children and adolescents with attention-deficit hyperactivity disorder. Lancet 362: 1699–1707.
10. JOHNSON, M.H., H. HANIFE, S.J. GRICE & A. KARMILOFF-SMITH. 2002. Neuroimaging of typical and atypical development: a perspective from multiplelevels of analysis. Dev. Psychopathol. **14**: 521–536.
11. FERRIS, C.F., C.T. SNOWDON, J.A. KING, *et al.* 2001. Functional imaging of brain activity in conscious monkeys responding to sexually arousing cues. NeuroReport, **12**: 2231–2236.
12. KASLOW, N.J., S. HERON, D.K. ROBERTS, *et al.* 2003. Family and community factors that predict internalizing and externalizing symptoms in low-income, African-American children: a preliminary report. Ann. N.Y. Acad. Sci. **1008**: this volume.
13. ZEANAH, C.H. 2003. Attachment relationship experiences and childhood psychopathy. Ann. N.Y. Acad. Sci. **1008**: this volume.
14. INSEL, T.R. & R. FERNALD. 2004. Social neuroscience: how the brain processes social information. Ann. Rev. Neurosci. **27**: In press.
15. SULLIVAN, R.M., M. LANDERS, B. YEAMAN & D.A. WILSON. 2000. Good memories of bad events in infancy Nature **407**: 38–39.
16. ROTH, T.L. & R.M. SULLIVAN. 2003. Consolidation and expression of a shock-induced odor preference in rat pups is facilitated by opioids. Physiol. Behav. **78**: 135–142.
17. SANCHEZ, M.M., C.O. LADD & P.M. PLOTSKY. 2001. Early adverse experience as a developmental risk factor for later psychopathology: Evidence from rodent and primate models. Dev. Psychopathol. **13**: 419–450.

18. MILAD, M.R. & G.J. QUIRK. 2002. Neurons in medial prefrontal cortex signal memory for fear extinction. Nature **420:** 70–74.
19. FRANCIS, D.D., J. DIORIO, P.M. PLOTSKY & M.J. MEANEY. 2002. Environmental enrichment reverses the effects of maternal separation on stress reactivity. J. Neurosci. **22:** 7840–7843.
20. GUNNAR, M.R. 2000. Early adversity and the development of stress reactivity and regulation. *In* The Effects of Early Adversity on Neurobehavioral Development: Minnesota Symposia on Child Psychology. C.A. Nelson, Ed.: 245–278. Erlbaum. New York.
21. DEVRIES, A.C. 2002. Interaction among social environment, the hypothalamic–pituitary–adrenal axis, and behavior. Horm. Behav. **41:** 405–413.
22. KAGAN, J. 1994. Galen's Prophecy. Basic Books. New York.
23. POLLAK, S.D. & D. KISTLER. 2002. Early experience alters the development of categorical representations for facial expressions of emotion. Proc. Natl. Acad. Sci. USA 99: 9072–9076.
24. POLLAK, S.D., D.CICCHETTI, K.HORNUNG & A.REED. 2000. Recognizing emotion in faces: developmental effects of child abuse and neglect. Dev. Psychol. **36:** 679–688.
25. CONNOR, D.F. 2002. Aggression and Antisocial Behavior in Children and Adolescents: Research and Treatment. Guilford. New York.
26. ROTHBAUM, B.O., L. HODGES, D. READY, *et al.* 2001. Virtual reality exposure therapy for Vietnam veterans with posttraumatic stress disorder. J. Clin. Psychiatry **62:** 617–622.
27. FOA, E.B., R. ZINBARG & B.O ROTHBAUM, 1992. Uncontrollability and unpredictability in post-traumatic stress disorder: an animal model. Psychol. Bull., **112:** 228–238.
28. MYERS, K.M. & M. DAVIS. 2002. Behavioral and neural analysis of extinction: a review. Neuron **36:** 567–584.
29. WINANS NEWMAN, S. 1999. The medial extended amygdala in male reproductive behavior. *In* Advancing from the Ventral Striatum to the Extended Amygdala. Ann. N.Y. Acad. Sci. **877:** 242–257.
30. ADOLPHS, R. 2003. Is the amygdala specialized for processing social information? Ann. N.Y. Acad. Sci. **985:** 326–340.
31. AMARAL, D.G. 2002. The primate amygdala and the neurobiology of social behavior: implications for understanding social anxiety. Biol. Psychiatry **51:** 11–17.
32. PRATHER, M.D., P. LAVENEX, M.L. MAULDIN-JOURDAIN, *et al.* 2001. Increased social fear and decreased fear of object in monkeys with neonatal amygdala lesions. Neuroscience **106:** 653–658.
33. KALIN, N.H., S.E. SHELTON, R.J. DAVIDSON & A.E. KELLEY. 2001. The primate amygdala mediates acute fear but not the behavioral and physiological components of anxious temperament. J. Neurosci. **21:** 2067–2074.
34. PORGES, S.W. 2001. The Polyvagal Theory: phylogenetic substrates of a social nervous system. Int. J. Psychophysiol. **42:** 123–146.
35. UMÄS-MOBERG, K. 1997. Physiological and endocrine effects of social contact. Ann. N.Y. Acad. Sci. **807:** 146–163.
36. NELSON, C.A. 2003. Can we develop a neurobiological model of human social–emotional development? Integrative thoughts on the effects of separation on parent-child interactions. Ann. N.Y. Acad. Sci. **1008:** this volume.
37. SKUSE, D.H. 2003. The amygdala, and development of the social brain. Ann. N.Y. Acad. Sci. **1008:** this volume.
38. KING, J.A., J. TENNEY, L. COLAMUSSI & S. BURDICK. 2003. Neural networks underlying impulsivity. Ann. N.Y. Acad. Sci. **1008:** this volume.
39. FERRIS, C.F. 2003. Using an animal model to assess the long-term behavioral and biological consequences of adolescent abuse and exposure to alcohol. Ann. N.Y. Acad. Sci. **1008:** this volume.
40. SPEAR, L.P. 2000. The adolescent brain and age-related behavioral manifestations. Neurosci. Biobehav. Rev. **24:** 417–463.
41. HINSHAW, S. 2002. Intervention research, theoretical mechanisms, and causal processes related to externalizing behavior patterns. Dev. Psychopath. **14:** 789–818.
42. NIGG, J.T. 2000. On inhibition/disinhibition in developmental psychopathology: views from cognitive and personality psychology and a working inhibition taxonomy. Psychol. Bull. **126:** 200–246.

43. NIGG, J.T., O.P. JOHN, L.G. BLASKEY, *et al.* 2002. Big five dimensions and ADHD symptoms: links between personality traits and clinical symptoms. J. Pers. Soc. Psychol. **83:** 451–469.
44. KALIN, N.H. & S.E. SHELTON. 1998. Ontogeny and stability of separation and threat-induced defensive behaviors in rhesus monkeys during the first year of life. Am. J. Primatol. **44:**125–135.
45. DAHL, R.E. 2003. The development of affect regulation: bringing together basic and clinical perspectives. Ann. N.Y. Acad. Sci. **1008:** this volume.
46. GUNNAR, M.R. & B. DONZELLA. 2002. Social regulation of the LHPA axis in early human development. Psychoneuroendocrinology **27:** 199–220.
47. SEIGEL, A. 1990. Neural substrates of aggression and rage in the cat. Prog. Psychobiol. Physiol. Psychol. **14:** 135–233.

Categories, Dimensions, and the Mental Health of Children and Adolescents

Keynote Address

MICHAEL RUTTER

Social Genetic and Developmental Psychiatry Research Centre, Institute of Psychiatry, London SE5 8AF, United Kingdom

ABSTRACT: Concepts of mental disorder, and of the causal processes leading to disorder, have undergone radical changes over recent decades. Genetic findings, for example, have shown that (1) many conditions develop on the basis of a dimensional genetic liability; (2) the boundaries of some conditions extend much more broadly than indicated by the traditional diagnostic categories; and (3) there is substantial overlap between conditions previously thought to be distinctively different. On the other hand, genetic findings have also provided support for the validity of some diagnostic distinctions. Early molecular genetic research was conceptualized on the basis of the expectation that there would be disease-specific genes "for" schizophrenia, bipolar disorder, and the like. It has become apparent that, at best, this constitutes a misleading oversimplification. Almost all mental disorders (in childhood and adult life) have a multifactorial origin, and the genes are likely to operate through a range of direct and indirect routes. Gene–environment correlations and interactions are important, and there is a biological substrate for individual differences in responses to psychosocial stress and adversity, as well as for the effects of such stress and adversity on the organism. The empirical basis for these changes in concepts is reviewed, and the implications for clinical science and practice are considered.

KEYWORDS: mental disorder; genetics; gene–environment correlation

DIMENSIONS AND CATEGORIES

Throughout its history, psychiatric classification has been bedeviled by supposed clashes between dimensional and categorical approaches. The dominant psychiatric classifications, such as Diagnostic and Statistical Manual for Mental Disorders (DSM)–IV[1] and International Classification of Diseases (ICD)–10,[2] are exclusively categorical in organization. This is partly for the good practical reason that many clinical decisions have to be categorical. Thus, the decision has to be made as to whether a patient is, or is not, treated with antidepressant medication. It would make no sense to give a lower dose of the drug if a dimensional score was only moderate,

Address for correspondence: Michael Rutter, M.D., F.R.C.P., Box P080, Social Genetic and Developmental Psychiatry Research Centre, Institute of Psychiatry, De Crespigny Park, Denmark Hill, London SE5 8AF, UK. Voice: 44-0-20-7848-0882; fax: 44-0-20-7848-0881.
j.wickham@iop.kcl.ac.uk

Ann. N.Y. Acad. Sci. 1008: 11–21 (2003). © 2003 New York Academy of Sciences.
doi: 10.1196/annals.1301.002

but a higher dose if the dimensional score was much greater. However, it has long been recognized that there are advantages to combining dimensions and categories,[3] and it is noteworthy that the recent volume on a research agenda for DSM-V[4] accepts this as an important possibility.

Dimensions assume continuity between normality and psychopathology, presuppose linear quantification, and use internal empirical data to quantify and to separate dimensions.[5,6] In contrast, categories function as if there is discontinuity between normality and psychopathology, use quantification (either on symptoms or on impairment or both) to decide diagnostic cutoffs, and presuppose the need to validate by criteria that are external to the defining symptoms.[7–9] Such external validation could be provided by biological findings, drug response, genetic findings, epidemiology, and course of disorder, to mention but some possibilities. When the comparison is expressed in this sort of way, it is tempting to suppose that empirical research should be able to decide which approach is correct or valid. However, this is based on the misconception that there can be one universally "right" answer, whereas it is clear that that is not so.[9,10] Thus, for example, IQ works best as a dimension if the interest is in predicting scholastic attainment or even social functioning in adult life. On the other hand, it works better as a category if the interest is in biological causes (because the causes of severe mental retardation are so different from those that concern individual differences within the normal range).

It is necessary to recognize that a variety of meta-theoretical claims lie behind the dispute between dimensional and categorical approaches. For example, it is argued, quite rightly, that there is greater statistical power provided by dimensional analyses provided that there is a valid linear dimension.[11,12] On the other hand, odds ratios often provide a more realistic impression of the size of effects, and they are preferable for the study of interactions that apply only at certain points on the distribution.[13] For example, Borge et al.[14] found no difference between maternal care and group day care on physical aggression in young children except when the children came from families at high psychosocial risk. In that circumstance, the rate of aggression was higher for children reared by their own parents. Of course, this usually will mean that the risk index is serving as a proxy for some other risk variable that actually constitutes the proximal risk mechanism. In the child-care example, presumably this involves adverse patterns of parental care, rather than whether the care is at home or in a day center. Similarly, numerous studies have shown that teenage parenthood constitutes a major risk factor for childhood psychopathology.[15] This works as a dimension at the bottom of the age range, but there is no beneficial effect from being reared by an older mother rather than a mother in the middle of the age range. Again, that is almost certainly because the risk is not directly mediated by the age of the mother; rather, maternal age is associated with a range of other features that provide the proximal risk.

The second meta-theoretical claim is that dimensions are more open to psychosocial explanations, whereas categories lend themselves better to neurobiological explanations,[16] but this is not the case. For example, IQ, blood pressure, degree of atheroma, and height are important within-individual dimensional features, but they all involve a major biological component. Both the risk factors for coronary artery disease (such as cholesterol levels, neonatal nutrition, smoking, and clotting tendencies) and the outcomes for coronary artery disease are dimensional despite the fact that final outcomes (such as death from coronary occlusion) have to be categorical.

In the field of psychopathology, epidemiological findings have been consistent in showing that most forms of common mental disorder show continuous distributions with no discernable point of demarcation between normality and psychopathology. Indeed, it has been further argued, on the basis of empirical analyses, that the underlying liability distributions show very little evidence of nonnormality.[17] The apparently skewed nature of many scales may be largely measurement artefacts. There is no indication that a qualitatively distinct process generates disorder. Most people readily accept this argument for features such as depression or antisocial behavior, but, until relatively recently, severe disorders such as autism or schizophrenia have been thought of as entirely separate from variations within the normal range. However, genetic evidence has forced rethinking this issue. Thus, schizophrenia and schizotypal personality disorder appear to share the same genetic liability.[18,19] Similarly, autism is associated with a broader range of social and communicative abnormalities.[20,21] However, there are also differences. Thus, the broader phenotype of autism, unlike autism "proper," is not associated with either mental retardation or epilepsy, and most individuals with schizotypal personality disorder do not go on to develop schizophrenia. There is a need to determine the factors involved in the transition from the milder variant to the more severe handicapping disorder.

Psychosocial risk factors for psychopathology similarly show dimensional properties. Most people experience some adversities and only a few experience many.[22] The likelihood that teenagers will develop multiple problems was found to increase exponentially with the number of family adversity features in the Christchurch study.[22]

SPECIFICITY AND NONSPECIFICITY OF RISK EFFECTS

A third meta-theoretical claim is that psychosocial risk factors are nonspecific in their effects and tend to have rather transient sequelae, whereas biological risk factors are diagnosis specific and tend to have lasting consequences. Both claims are rather misleading. Although it is true that many psychosocial risk factors have effects that are diagnostically relatively nonspecific, that is not universally the case. For example, the study of children who experienced gross institutional deprivation in Romania, and who were later adopted into UK families, found no effects on either emotional disturbance or disruptive behavior at age 6 years, but strong effects that were systematically associated with the duration of institutional deprivation in the case of cognitive impairment, quasiautistic patterns, inattention/hyperactivity, and attachment disorder features.[23] Moreover, the effects prove to be surprisingly persistent. Thus, the association between duration of deprivation and cognitive impairment was as strong at the age of 11 years, nearly a decade after adoption, as it was at age 4 years and age 6 years.

At one time, it used to be expected that genetic risks would be diagnosis specific. Researchers undertook molecular genetic studies with the hope of finding genes "for" schizophrenia or autism or bipolar disorder. Of course, genes do not cause any behavioral pattern directly. Rather, they have effects on proteins that only indirectly lead on to a psychopathological phenotype. However, not only are the effects not usually direct, but also they are much less specific than used to be thought. Thus, quantitative genetic studies have shown a substantial overlap in genetic liability be-

tween anxiety and depressive disorders[24–26] and for the shared genetic liability between Tourette syndrome, chronic tics, and some cases of obsessive, compulsive
disorder.[27]

MULTICULTURAL CAUSATION AND MULTIPLE CAUSAL PATHWAYS

Much writing on risk factors for mental disorders tends to make the implicit assumption that there is likely to be just one causal pathway for each mental disorder,
with the research challenge being the search for just what that pathway might comprise. This is a wrong-headed assumption, however, in relation to the whole of medicine and not just mental disorders. Not only is multifactorial etiology usual, but
also, in most cases, there are several rather different routes by which such causal factors come to exert their effects.[28] For example, in the field of respiratory disease,
there are several quite different routes by which an individual may develop the seriously handicapping disorder of obstructive airway disease. Thus, smoking or repeated asthma attacks or infections can set in motion a set of changes that ultimately lead
to the same end point of gross disease. Typically, too, each causal pathway involves
multiple causal factors acting either additively or, often, synergistically.

We also need to recognize that the specificity or nonspecificity of effects is much
influenced by the nature of the risk being studied and also by scaling considerations.
For example, smoking involves multiple different risk factors and causal mechanisms. Equally, obesity predisposes to osteoarthritis, diabetes, and hypertension
through rather different mechanisms. Just because we talk about "smoking" or "obesity" as a risk factor, this does not mean that it actually represents a single risk op-
erating through a single mechanism. It does not. In the same sort of way, family
adversity indices in psychiatry incorporate a most heterogeneous mix of risk factors.
For the most part, we do not know precisely how each risk operates but, when we
do, it is probable that in many cases (perhaps most cases) we will find that apparently diverse effects come about because a single label conceals a multiplicity of
risk features.

These considerations certainly do not mean that we should abandon concepts on
the distinctiveness of different psychiatric syndromes, and, equally, it does not mean
that we should move to a concept of global risk. It would be a counsel of despair to
move to a causal model that is, in effect, a conceptual soup in which causation derives from an unanalyzable mix of multiple diverse risk factors. Instead, we need to
take seriously the challenge to delineate specific causal pathways, without the pre-
supposition that there has to be just one.[29]

ENVIRONMENTAL EFFECTS

Over recent years, there have been evangelistic claims that the most important environmental influences are outside the family[30] and that only extreme environments
have effects of any functional importance.[31,32] Both claims are demonstrably
false.[33,34] Interestingly, these claims have been made with an almost total disregard
for the range of research strategies that may be used to test hypotheses about environmental mediations of causal effects (see Rutter et al. 2001[35]). For example,

Duyme *et al.*[36] showed that not only was adoption associated with a substantial within-individual gain in IQ for children who had been removed from their parents because of abuse or neglect, but crucially the degree to which IQs increased between the preschool years and adolescence was systematically related to the socioeducational level of the adoptive homes. That is important because it is showing the effects of variations in rearing quality within the normal range, using a genetically sensitive design. A different strategy is provided by looking at the effects of varying qualities of parent–child interaction on psychopathology, within monozygotic pairs. This powerful research strategy has been used cross-sectionally in several studies, but the real test is provided by examination of the effects on within-individual change over time when the parental feature is measured through data from a different informant from the one providing information on child psychopathology. Caspi *et al.*[37] showed significant effects between negative expressed parental emotion when the children were aged 5 years and disruptive behavior as assessed on a teacher measure at age 7 years. Several other powerful quasiexperimental designs are available[35] and the findings provide convincing evidence of important environmentally mediated causal effects.[33]

PARTITIONING EFFECTS INTO GENES AND ENVIRONMENT

Most of the literature is based on the general assumption that causal inferences can be partitioned neatly into those that are genetically mediated and those that are environmentally mediated, their summation amounting to 100% of effects. That sounds logical, but, in fact, the assumption is wrong because (1) it ignores random developmental perturbations (which have been termed a third force[38,39]); (2) it fails to include epigenetic effects; (3) it presupposes that the origin of a risk factor identifies the mode of risk mediation; (4) it fails to take account of gene–environment interaction; and (5) it does not consider multistep causal pathways. Let us consider each of these in turn.

Development is biologically probabilistic rather than biologically predetermined.[34,40] That is to say, genes, for example, program the general course of development, but they do not specify what each cell does. For example, brain development involves predictable neuronal migration, but this leads only to an approximation to the optimal end product. Accordingly, neuronal overproduction is followed by selective pruning for the organism to get the pattern right.[34,41]

As a consequence of this probabilistic style of development, it is quite common for there to be minor congenital anomalies of nonfunctional significance. The rate of occurrence of such anomalies is influenced by identifiable risk factors such as maternal age or twinning, but the specific anomaly is not caused by any identifiable factor. A high rate of congenital anomalies is significantly associated with various forms of psychopathology, but the association is not caused by the functional effect of any particular anomaly but rather reflects the sign of development going slightly awry.[42] Epigenetic effects concern influences on gene expression. The two best documented examples concern inactivation of one of the two X chromosomes possessed by females and genomic imprinting (which is the process by which genes are affected according to whether or not the intergenerational transmission is through the father or the mother). These are important in various neuropsychiatric disorders.[43] In addition, however, it may well be that there are hormonal influences that effect gene expression.[44] So far, little is know about this possibility, but such influences may be of importance in relation to the well-documented marked male preponderance in most neurodevelopmental disorders.[45,46]

The standard traditional methods of quantitative genetics tend to assume that the origin of a risk factor and the mode of risk mediation are synonymous, but obviously this is not the case.[47] Smoking provides the most obvious illustration of this. Individual differences in whether people smoke, and in how much they smoke, are influenced by the availability of cigarettes, genetic factors, and cultural influences, but the causal mechanisms involved in the diseases that are heavily predisposed to as a result of smoking have got nothing to do with these influences on individual differences in smoking. Rather, the causation of disease stems from tar carcinogens, carbon monoxide in the smoke, sympathomimetic effects of nicotine on blood vessels, and lung irritation from inhaled smoke.

In the psychopathological field, longitudinal studies have been informative in showing the effect of people's own behavior on the selecting and shaping of environments. For example, Champion et al.[48] showed a major effect of children's behavior at age 10 years on their exposure to risk environments 18 years later. Any proper understanding of risk mechanisms must take account of the factors involved in the origins of risk exposure. However, environments brought about by the individuals themselves may, nevertheless, have substantial consequent effects on behavior. For example, this has been shown in two major longitudinal studies in relation to the effects of a harmonious supportive marriage in early adult life.[49,50] Of course, it is crucial to use sophisticated statistical methods that can take account of unmeasured variables, as well as the effects of the person's own prior behavior and experiences. When this has been done, the effects have proved to be robust.

GENE–ENVIRONMENT INTERPLAY

First, these effects tended to be considered within the context of the study, and concepts, of environmentally mediated risks. That is appropriate, but it is equally important to appreciate that the routes by which genetic factors operate involve indirect effects through temperamental variables, gene–environment correlations, and gene–environment interactions. For example, Kendler used the statistical modeling of twin data to examine the causal pathways involved in adult depression.[51] Four main paths from gene to adult depression were identified: a main effect on depression; an emotional pathway route in which the genetic risks influence both neuroticism and early anxiety with each of those predisposing to depression; a disruptive behavior pathway in which the genetic risks influenced conduct disorder and substance misuse with both of these predisposing to adult depression; and an environmental adversity pathway in which genes had an effect on early family disturbance, on childhood sexual abuse, and childhood parental loss, with each of those predisposing to lifetime adversities and these adversities, in turn, predisposing to recent psychosocial stressors which had a substantial precipitating effect on episodes of depressive disorder. Somewhat similarly, Eaves et al.[52] showed that there were three main genetic routes to adolescent depression: via prepubertal anxiety, which led on to adolescent depression; through gene–environment correlations influencing individual differences in environmental risk exposure; and through gene–environment interactions that moderated susceptibility to environmental risks.

For a long time, the "given wisdom" in behavior genetics was that gene–environment interactions were few and far between, but actually this is not the case.[53] There are several examples of gene–environment interaction in the field of internal medicine, and there is growing evidence of their operation in the field of psychopathology. For example, it has been shown, using quantitative genetic methods, for genetic moderation of risk effects associated with life stressors on anxiety and depression[54] and, using molecular genetic strategies, for the genetic moderation of the effects of maltreatment in childhood on the risk of antisocial behavior.[55]

One of the hopes for molecular genetics is that the discovery of susceptible genes will lead to an understanding of the neural basis of mental disorders. It is likely that it will provide valuable leads for biological studies, but identification of the genes will not, in itself, identify the basic pathophysiology. It will be necessary to determine the effects of the genes on proteins and the effects of proteins in leading to disorder. That will require the use of a broad range of scientific strategies including animal models, proteomics, transcriptomics, and integrative physiology, as well as molecular epidemiology to delineate nature–nurture interplay.[21,42]

VARIETIES OF CAUSAL QUESTIONS

So far, causal pathways are being considered here for individual differences in psychopathological outcome. However, this is far from the only causal question that matters. Thus, for example, over the last century there have been huge secular trends for increases in longevity, reductions in infantile mortality and increases in average height.[42] From a public health point of view, these are hugely important even though it is quite likely that they have made rather little difference to individual differences in risk. Note that although the causes of secular trends and the causes of individual differences may be the same, quite often they are different. Thus, for example, major improvements in infantile mortality and life expectancy during the last century were probably mainly caused by improvements in public sanitation and in nutrition rather than anything to do with medical advances as such.[56] In contrast, in the psychopathological arena there have been changes for the worse in psychosocial disorders in young people.[57] Again, these are of major public health importance but they have been investigated surprisingly little. Accordingly, our knowledge of the factors responsible for these trends over time is pretty rudimentary. Group differences are equally striking. For example, it is well-documented that the incidence of early neurodevelopmental disorders is some two or three times as great in males as in females and that emotional disorders with an onset in adolescence or later, such as depression and eating disorders, tend to be substantially more frequent in females.[45] Up to now, there has been very little empirical research to determine the causal factors that underlie these sex differences (although there has been plenty of theoretical speculation).

There are also important national differences. For example, the murder rate in young people is some fifteen times as high in the United States as it is in Europe.[58] This seems to be almost entirely explicable in terms of the availability of firearms, but other national differences are less well understood. Many researchers have been very reluctant to examine ethnic differences in mental disorder because of the political undercurrents, and prejudice, that tend to underlie debates about ethnicity and psychopathology. However, it is important that the rate of schizophrenia, and to a lesser extent of bipolar disorders, is much increased in Afro-Caribbeans living within the United Kingdom and the Netherlands, although it is not increased in the West Indies.[59] Although schizophrenia is strongly influenced by genetic factors, the ethnic difference is clearly caused by environmental influences of some kind. Finally, there is the rather different issue of the causal influences involved in the course and recurrence of mental disorders, rather than their initial onset. Among other things, kindling effects seem to operate on the course of psychopathology—meaning that the experience of a major mental disorder seems to have an effect on the organism that plays a part in persistence or later recurrence.[60,61]

INDIVIDUAL DIFFERENCES IN RESPONSE TO RISK

Although an early review of effects of so-called "maternal deprivation"[62] highlighted individual differences in response to risk as a major phenomenon requiring explanation, it remains investigated surprisingly little. Nevertheless, all studies of environmental risk factors, both physical and psychosocial, have shown major heterogeneity in response. This has caused an interest in resilience (meaning a relative resistance to, or recovery from, the effects of adversity[63]) as well as sensitizing and steeling effects of stress (meaning effects that increase susceptibility, or decrease susceptibility, to later stressors). It might be thought that if environmental adversity is really extreme, it would have such a global and pervasive effect that it would obliterate individual differences. However, that has not proved to be the case. For example, in the study of children adopted from Romanian orphanages, the range of IQ has extended from the mentally retarded range to the superior even among those who had had at least 2 years of extremely depriving institutional care.[64] There has been similar heterogeneity in relation to social sequelae.[23] The reasons for these marked individual differences in response remain ill-understood.

CONCLUSIONS

In summary, it is necessary to ask where we go from here in the study of risk. A baker's dozen of recommendations derive from the evidence reviewed:

1. It is necessary to use both dimensional and categorical measures.
2. We must recognize that our methods of diagnostic classification are in need of considerable modification but also that how we classify may vary according to the purposes that the classification is to be put.
3. Our approach to concepts of causal questions must be broadened.
4. Rigorous tests must be undertaken to examine hypotheses about environmentally mediated risks, and it will be necessary that these include both familywide and child-specific risks, and also include influences outside as well as inside the family.
5. Research must include a focus on the effects of the environment on the organism while recognizing that the possibilities for such effects are diverse including neuronal damage, biological programming, neuroendocrine effects, and cognitive mechanisms, to mention just some possibilities.

6. As well as considering the consequence of environmental risk, there must be systematic study of the causes of individual variations in environmental risk exposure.

7. Investigations must encompass the study of multistep causal pathways.

8. Research must seek to determine the origins of individual differences in susceptibility to environmental risks of various kinds.

9. We must recognize and investigate the range of diverse routes by which genetic influences can have effects on mental disorder.

10. It is necessary to appreciate that genes may influence individual differences in mental disorder through either protective or risk effects.

11. It is necessary to delineate the mechanisms involved in nature–nurture interplay, as well as determining their effects on mental disorder.

12. Research into risk and protective factors must include investigation of the effects of developmental perturbations, epistatic effects and epigenetic mechanisms.

13. Finally, it will be important over the decades ahead to make use of a wide range of research strategies to study the complex pathways involved in the route from experience of risk to the development of psychopathological phenotype.

REFERENCES

1. AMERICAN PSYCHIATRIC ASSOCIATION. 1994. Diagnostic and Statistical Manual of Mental Disorders. 4th ed. DSM-IV. Washington, DC: American Psychiatric Association.
2. WORLD HEALTH ORGANIZATION. 1993. The ICD-10 Classification of Mental and Behavioural Disorders. Diagnostic Criteria for Research. Geneva, Switzerland: WHO.
3. KENDELL, R.E. 1975. The Role of Diagnosis in Psychiatry. Oxford: Blackwell Scientific.
4. KUPFER, D.J., M.B. FIRST & D.A. REGIER. 2002. A Research Agenda for DSM-V. Washington, DC: American Psychiatric Association.
5. ACHENBACH, T.M. 1988. Integrating assessment and taxonomy. In Assessment and Diagnosis in Child Psychopathology. M. Rutter, A.H. Tuma, and I.S. Lann, Eds.: 300–343. Guilford Press. New York.
6. ACHENBACH, T.M. 1985. Assessment and Taxonomy of Child and Adolescent Psychopathology. Sage Publications. Beverly Hill, CA.
7. RUTTER, M. 1965. Classification and categorization in child psychiatry. J. Child Psychol. Psychiatry 6: 71–83.
8. RUTTER, M. 1978. Diagnostic validity in child psychiatry. Adv. Biol. Psychiatry 2: 2–22.
9. TAYLOR, E. & M. RUTTER. 2002. Classification: conceptual issues and substantive findings. In Child and Adolescent Psychiatry. M. Rutter and E. Taylor, Eds.: 3–17. Blackwell Scientific. Oxford, UK.
10. PICKLES, A. & A. ANGOLD. 2003. Natural categories or fundamental dimensions: on carving nature at the joints and the re-articulation of psychopathology. Dev. Psychopathol. 15: 529–551.
11. FERGUSSON, D.M. & L.J. HORWOOD. 1995. Predictive validity of categorically and dimensionally scored measures of disruptive childhood behaviors. J. Am. Acad. Child Adolesc. Psychiatry 34: 477–485.
12. MACCALLUM, R.C., S. ZHANG, K.J. PREACHER & D.D. RUCKER. 2002. On the practice of dichotomization of quantitative variables. Psychol. Methods 7: 19–40.
13. FARRINGTON, D.P. & R. LOEBER. 2000. Some benefits of dichotomization in psychiatric and criminological research. Crim. Behav. Ment. Health 10: 100–122.
14. BORGE, A.I.H., M. RUTTER, S. CÔTÉ & R.E. TREMBLAY. Early childcare and physical aggression: differentiating social selection and social causation. J. Child Psychol. Psychiatry. In Press
15. MOFFITT, T.E. & THE E-RISK STUDY TEAM. 2002. Teen-aged mothers in contemporary Britain. J. Child Psychol. Psychiatry 43: 727–742.

16. SONUGU-BARKE, E.J.S. 1998. Categorical models of childhood disorder: a conceptual and empirical analysis. J. Child Psychol. Psychiatry **39:** 115–133.
17. VAN DEN OORD, E.J.C.G., A. Pickles & I.D. Waldman. 2003. Normal variation and abnormality: an empirical study of the liability distributions underlying depression and delinquency. J. Child Psychol. Psychiatry **44:** 180–192.
18. KENDLER, K.S., M.C. NEALE & D. WALSH. 1995. Evaluating the spectrum concept of schizophrenia in the Roscommon Family Study. Am. J. Psychiatry **152:** 749–754.
19. SIEVER, K.J., O.F. KALUS & R.S. KEEFE. 1993. The boundaries of schizophrenia. Psychiatric Clin. N. Am. **16:** 217–244.
20. BAILEY, A., S. PALFERMAN, L. HEAVEY & A. LE COUTEUR. 1998. Autism: the phenotype in relatives. J. Autism Dev. Disord. **28:** 381–404.
21. RUTTER, M. 2000. Genetic studies of autism: from the 1970s into the millennium. J. Abnorm. Child Psychol. **28:** 3–14.
22. FERGUSSON, D.M. & M.T. LYNSKEY. 1996. Adolescent resiliency to family adversity. J. Child Psychol. Psychiatry **37:** 281–292.
23. RUTTER, M., J. KREPPNER & T.G. O'CONNOR, on behalf of the English and Romanian Adoptees (ERA) Study Team. 2001. Specificity and heterogeneity in children's responses to profound institutional privation. Br. J. Psychiatry **179:** 97–103.
24. KENDLER, K.S., E.E. WALTERS, M.C. NEALE, et al. 1995. The structure of the genetic and environmental risk factors for six major psychiatric disorders in women: phobia, generalized anxiety disorder, panic disorder, bulimia, major depression, and alcoholism. Arch. Gen. Psychiatry **52:** 374–383.
25. KENDLER, K.S. 1996. Major depression and generalised anxiety disorder. Same genes (partly) different environments—revisited. Br. J. Psychiatry **168** (Suppl. 30): 68–75.
26. SILBERG, J.L., M. RUTTER & L. EAVES. 2001. Genetic and environmental influences on the temporal association between earlier anxiety and later depression in girls. Biol. Psychiatry **49:** 1040–1049.
27. LECKMAN, J.F. & D.J. COHEN. 2002. Tic disorders. In Child and Adolescent Psychiatry. M. Rutter and E. Taylor, Eds.: 593–611. Blackwell Science. Oxford, UK.
28. RUTTER, M. 1997. Comorbidity: concepts, claims and choices. Crim. Behav. Ment. Health **7:** 265–285.
29. RUTTER, M. 2003. Crucial paths from risk indicator to causal mechanism. In The Causes of Conduct Disorder and Serious Juvenile Delinquency. B. Lahey, T. Moffitt and A. Caspi, Eds.: 3–24. Guilford Press. New York.
30. HARRIS, J.R. 1998. The Nurture Assumption: Why Children Turn Out the Way They Do. Bloomsbury. London.
31. SCARR, S. 1992. Developmental theories for the 1990s: development and individual differences. Child Dev. **63:** 1–19.
32. ROWE, D.C. 1994. The Limits of Family Influence: Genes, Experience, and Behavior. Guilford Press. New York.
33. RUTTER, M. 2000. Psychosocial influences: critiques, findings, and research needs. Dev. Psychopathol. **12:** 375–405.
34. SHONKOFF, J.P. & D.A. PHILLIPS. 2000. From Neurons to Neighborhoods: The Science of Early Childhood Development. National Academy Press. Washington, DC.
35. RUTTER, M., A. PICKLES, R. MURRAY & L. EAVES. 2001. Testing hypotheses on specific environmental causal effects on behavior. Psychol. Bull. **127:** 291–324.
36. DUYME, M., A.-C. DUMARET & S. TOMKIEWICZ. 1999. How can we boost IQs of "dull children"? A late adoption study. Proc. Natl. Acad. Sci. USA **96:** 8790–8794.
37. CASPI, A., T.E. MOFFITT & J. MORGAN, et al. 2003. Maternal expressed emotion predicts children's externalizing behavior problems: using MZ-twin differences to identify environmental effects on behavioural development. Dev. Psychol. In press.
38. MOLENAAR, P.C.M., D.I. BOOMSMA & C.V. DOLAN. 1993. A third source of developmental differences. Behav. Genet. **23:** 519–524.
39. JENSEN, A.R. 1997. The puzzle of nongenetic variance. In Intelligence, Heredity, and Environment. R.J. Sternberg, E.L. Grigorenko, Eds.: 42–88. Cambridge University Press. Cambridge, UK.
40. RUTTER, M. & M. RUTTER. 1993. Developing Minds: Challenge and Continuity Across the Lifespan. Penguin and Basic Books. Harmondworth Middlesex & New York.

41. GOODMAN, R. Brain disorders. 2002. *In* Child and Adolescent Psychiatry. M. Rutter and E. Taylor, Eds.: 241–260. Blackwell Scientific. Oxford, UK.
42. RUTTER, M. 2002. Nature, nurture, and development: from evangelism through science toward policy and practice. Child Dev. **73:** 1–21.
43. SKUSE, D. & J. KUNTSI. 2002. Molecular genetic and chromosomal anomalies: cognitive and behavioural consequences. *In* Child and Adolescent Psychiatry. M. Rutter and E. Taylor, Eds.: 205–240. Blackwell Scientific. Oxford, UK.
44. PETRONIS, A. 2001. Human morbid genetics revisited: relevance of epigenetics. Trends Genet. **17:** 142–146.
45. RUTTER, M., A. CASPI & T.E. MOFFITT. 2003. Using sex differences in psychopathology to study causal mechanisms: unifying issues and research strategies. J. Child Psychol. Psychiatry **44:** 1092–1115.
46. MOFFITT, T.E., A. CASPI, M. RUTTER & P.A. SILVA. 2001. Sex Differences in Antisocial Behaviour: Conduct Disorder, Delinquency, and Violence in the Dunedin Longitudinal Study. Cambridge University Press. Cambridge, UK.
47. RUTTER, M., J. SILBERG & E. SIMONOFF. 1993. Whither behavioral genetics? A developmental psychopathological perspective. *In* Nature, Nurture, and Psychology. R. Plomin and G.E. McClearn, Eds.: 433–456. APA Books. Washington, DC.
48. CHAMPION, L.A., G.M. GOODALL & M. RUTTER. 1995. Behaviour problems in childhood and stressors in early adult life. I. A 20 year follow-up of London school children. Psychol. Med. **25:** 231–246.
49. ZOCCOLILLO, M., A. PICKLES, D. QUINTON & M. RUTTER. 1992. The outcome of childhood conduct disorder: implications for defining adult personality disorder and conduct disorder. Psychol. Med. **22:** 971–986.
50. LAUB, J.H., D.S. NAGIN & R.J. SAMPSON. 1998. Trajectories of change in criminal offending: good marriages and the desistance process. Am. Sociol. Rev. **63:** 225–238.
51. KENDLER, K.S., C.O. GARDNER & C.A. PRESCOTT. 2002. Toward a comprehensive developmental model for major depression in women. Am. J. Psychiatry **159:** 1133–1145.
52. EAVES, L., J. SILBERG & A. ERKANLI. 2003. Resolving multiple epigenetic pathways to adolescent depression. J. Child Psychol. **44:** 1006–1014.
53. RUTTER, M. & J. SILBERG. 2002. Gene-environment interplay in relation to emotional and behavioral disturbance. Annu. Rev. Psychol. **53:** 463–490.
54. SILBERG, J., M. RUTTER, M. NEALE & L. EAVES. 2001. Genetic moderation of environmental risk for depression and anxiety in adolescent girls. Br. J. Psychiatry **179:** 116–121.
55. CASPI, A., J. MCCLAY, T.E. MOFFITT, *et al.* 2002. Role of genotype in the cycle of violence in maltreated children. Science **297:** 851–854.
56. MCKEOWN, T. 1976. The Role of Medicine: Dream, Mirage or Nemesis? Nuffield Provincial Hospitals Trust. London.
57. RUTTER, M. & D. SMITH. 1995. Psychosocial Disorders in Young People: Time Trends and Their Causes. Wiley. Chichester.
58. RUTTER, M., H. GILLER & A. HAGELL. 1998. Antisocial Behavior by Young People. Cambridge University Press. New York.
59. JONES, P.B. & W.L.A. FUNG. Ethnicity and mental health: the example of schizophrenia in the African Caribbean population in Europe. *In* Ethnicity and Causal Mechanisims. M. Rutter and M. Tienda, Eds.: Cambridge University Press. New York. In press.
60. KENDLER, K.S., L.M. THORNTON & C.O. GARDNER. 2000. Stressful life events and previous episodes in the etiology of major depression in women: an evaluation of the "kindling" hypothesis. Am. J. Psychiatry **157:** 1243–1251.
61. KENDLER, K.S., L.M. THORNTON & C.O. GARDNER. 2001. Genetic risk, number of previous depressive episodes, and stressful life events in predicting onset of major depression. Am. J. Psychiatry **158:** 582–586.
62. RUTTER, M. 1972. Maternal Deprivation Reassessed. Penguin. Harmondsworth, Middlesex.
63. RUTTER, M. 2000. Resilience reconsidered: conceptual considerations, empirical findings, and policy implications. *In* Handbook of Early Childhood Intervention. J.P. Shonkoff and S.J. Meisels, Eds.: 651–682. Cambridge University Press. New York.
64. O'CONNOR, T., M. RUTTER & C. BECKETT, *et al.* 2000. The effects of global severe privation on cognitive competence: extension and longitudinal follow-up. Child Dev. **71:** 376–390.

Attachment Relationship Experiences and Childhood Psychopathology

CHARLES H. ZEANAH,[a] ANGELA KEYES,[b] AND LISA SETTLES[a]

[a]Institute for Infant and Early Childhood Mental Health, Tulane University Health Sciences Center, New Orleans, Louisiana 70112, USA

[b]Department of Psychology, University of New Orleans, New Orleans, Louisiana, 70122 USA

ABSTRACT: Human infants form attachments to their caregivers gradually over the course of the first year of life. Qualitatively different types of attachments, which can be indentified by the end of the first year, are broadly predictive of subsequent adaptive outcomes for young children. "Disorganized" patterns of attachment have the strongest links to concurrent and subsequent psychopathology, and considerable research has demonstrated both within-the-child and environmental correlates of disorganized attachment. Clinical disorders of attachment have been demonstrated to arise under conditions of social deprivation, such as institutionalization and maltreatment. An emotionally withdrawn/inhibited pattern and an indiscriminate/disinhibited pattern both have been described. Although these clinical types arise under similar conditions of environmental adversity, they tend to have different courses over time. We describe recent findings and highlight areas of emerging consensus and areas of continuing controversy regarding both disorganized patterns of attachment and clinical disorders of attachment in younbg children.

KEYWORDS: attachment; development; caregiver; infant

INTRODUCTION

Attachment is a biologically rooted motivational system in the human infant that develops gradually over the first 2 to 3 years of life and describes the organization of behaviors in the young child designed to promote proximity to one or more discriminated attachment figures in times of stress.

Under species-typical circumstances, the human infant exhibits qualitative behavioral changes in the latter half of the first year of life. By about 9 months of age, the infant begins to protest separation from discriminated adult caregivers and to exhibit initial social reticence with unfamiliar adults. Because of the appearance of separation protest and stranger wariness at this time, the infant is described as "attached" to those caregiving adults who spend significant amounts of time interacting

Address for correspondence: Charles H. Zeanah, Jr., M.D., Department of Psychiatry, Tulane University School of Medicine, Tidewater Building TB-52, 1440 Canal Street, New Orleans, LA 70112. Voice: 504-588-5402; fax: 504-587-4264.
czeanah@tulane.edu

Ann. N.Y. Acad. Sci. 1008: 22–30 (2003). © 2003 New York Academy of Sciences.
doi: 10.1196/annals.1301.003

with and caring for the infant. When activated by stressors (e.g., fear, fatigue, distress), attachment motivates the young child to seek comfort, support, and nurturance from one of a small number of discriminated attachment figures. Attachment research has provided important insights into the role of the parent–child relationship as a regulator of the young child's emotional experience.

Furthermore, infant–caregiver attachment appears to be nearly ubiquitous in human infants, except in conditions of extreme social deprivation. Therefore, attachment may be viewed as an example of experience expectant neural development, although the type of attachment of an infant and caregiver may be experience dependent.[1]

In fact, several patterns of attachment have been identified in young children from examining the organization of the child's behaviors in the Strange Situation Procedure.[2] This laboratory paradigm is designed to examine the balance between the child's exploratory behaviors and proximity seeking behaviors during a series of separations from and reunions with a discriminated attachment figure and an unfamiliar adult. These qualitatively different patterns of infant to caregiver attachment describe the child's use of the caregiver to regulate negative emotions under conditions of stress and have been demonstrated in studies conducted throughout the world.[3] These patterns of attachment include *secure* and several forms of insecure attachment, *avoidant*, *resistant*, and *disorganized*. Secure attachment has been demonstrated to be a protective factor and insecure attachment is a risk factor for psychopathology.[4,5] Secure attachment predicts positive parent–child relationships, better peer relationships, positive child–teacher relationships, higher self-esteem, and greater resiliency. Insecure attachment predicts problematic parent–child relationships, poor peer relations, aggression, anxiety, and conflicted relationships with teachers. Importantly, the young child's attachment with one caregiver may be qualitatively different than the child's attachment to another caregiver, indicating that what is classified is a relationship construct rather than a trait.

Nevertheless, more recently, investigators have begun to contrast organized (secure, avoidant, and resistant) with disorganized attachment, in part, because even stronger links have been demonstrated between disorganized attachment and psychopathology, particularly disturbances in interpersonal relatedness.[6–8] Disorganized attachment has been demonstrated to predict both externalizing and internalizing problems concurrently and in later childhood and adolescence.

DISORGANIZED ATTACHMENT

Attachment classifications as described by the Strange Situation Procedure (i.e., insecure-avoidant, insecure-ambivalent, and secure) define an apparent organizational strategy for obtaining comfort and protection from the attachment figure during stressful and dangerous encounters. In contrast, identification of disorganized attachment developed out of a review of cases that were difficult to classify using Ainsworth's existing system.[9]

Disorganized attachment describes a strategy that is not coherently organized, containing elements of confused, contradictory, incomplete, or absent strategies for obtaining comfort and protection. Behaviorally, this manifests as conflict behaviors such as misdirected behaviors, stereotypical behaviors, freezing, apprehension, and fear of a parent.[10]

Prevalence of Disorganized Attachment

According to the meta-analysis on disorganized attachment by van Ijzendoorn et al.,[11] prevalence of disorganized attachment in a low-risk sample from North America was 15% ($n = 2104$). In the same study, high-risk groups had a significantly higher prevalence of disorganized attachment, ranging from 21% to 48%. Other studies have estimated the prevalence of disorganized attachment to be upward of 80% in high-risk groups, such as maltreating or drug-abusing parents.[12]

Extrinsic Risk Factors

Disorganized attachment behaviors in infants have been associated with the presence of multiple environmental risk factors: (1) parental unresolved loss or trauma,[13,14] (2) poverty,[15] (3) maternal mood disorder, mainly severe and/or chronic maternal depression or bipolar disorder,[6,16] (4) maltreatment,[11] (5) witnessing marital discord or partner violence,[11,17,18] (6) maternal alcoholism and other substance abuse problems,[11,19] (7) high parental expressed emotion,[20] and (8) institutional care.[21,22] Each of these risk factors predispose a child to potentially experiencing parental rejection and threats of abandonment.

Associated Parental Behaviors

Repeated instances of parents' frightening or appearing frightened to their young children is believed to cause fear and disorganized behavior patterns.[7,23] Inappropriate responsiveness to infant cues can include antagonism, withdrawal, role confusion, intrusive behavior, confusion, and contradictory cues.[7,14]

Biological Correlates

Infants with disorganized attachment relationships exhibit both elevated heart rate and higher levels of cortisol during the Strange Situation compared to infants who have organized attachments with their caregivers.[24] Whether these neurobiological differences precede or result from disorganized attachment is unclear.

With regard to vulnerability, a recent study by Hungarian investigators suggested that a polymorphism on the DRD4 gene may increase risk for disorganized attachment.[25] Examining the seven-repeat allele of DRD4, they demonstrated that 63% of infants who were classified disorganized also carried one copy of the D4.7 allele, as compared with 28% of infants classified as having organized attachments. In a replication and extension of the original finding, the same group found that the association of the D4.7 allele and disorganized attachment was strengthened in the presence of the −521 T allele,[26] which had been shown previously to down-regulate in vitro transcription of the DRD4 mRNA by 40%.[27] The relative risk of disorganized attachment in the presence of both the D4.7 allele and the −521 T allele increased to 10. The large increase in D4.7 allele frequency in disorganized infants and the strengthening of this association and increased relative risk in the presence of another allele known to have an impact on gene expression, though far from conclusive, support the association of certain DRD4 alleles and disorganized attachment and indicate a possible vulnerability to disorganized attachment in individuals with these alleles.

Risk Factor or Clinical Disturbance

Without question, of the three insecure classifications, disorganized attachment is most likely to approach being a clinical disorder.[28] In fact, van IJzendoorn and Bakersmans-Kranenberg[29] have proposed just that. They point out that lacking an organized attachment to a caregiver represents a failure of the infant to achieve an important stage-salient task of the first 2 years of life and that disorganized attachment is drastically overrepresented in samples associated with severe psychological abnormalities in parents, as noted above. In addition, disorganized attachment has been linked to specific patterns of parental interactive behaviors, such as "frightening/frightened" and other forms of dysregulated affect. Furthermore, the disorganized classification has stability coefficients in high-risk samples that are comparable to secure attachment.[11,30] Nevertheless, there are problems with approaching clinical disorders of attachment from the standpoint of disorganized attachment. Chief among these is that the heterogeneity of the classification. A child classified as disorganized with a particular caregiver may demonstrate clearly aberrant behavior, such as the complete absence of a strategy for obtaining needed comfort from the attachment figure. Conversely, disorganized behavior may be only a subtle, momentary contradiction in strategies, with no apparent functional impairment. It is hard to delineate the boundaries of disorder within a classification that encompasses such a broad range of behavior. The challenge for those wishing to use disorganized attachment as a way to define attachment disorders is to develop a functional severity scale and a "cut point" that is meaningful and useful.

In addition, the links between disorganized attachment and aberrant parental behavior are not strong enough for the sensitivity and specificity required of a diagnostic procedure. Finally, the rating scale used to designate attachment behaviors as disorganized is not designed to make distinctions in functional severity.

CLINICAL DISORDERS OF ATTACHMENT

The tradition of clinical disorders of attachment, in fact, derives from profiles of young children's behavior following extremes of poor care. Social behavior in maltreated toddlers and in young children raised in institutions has been used to describe clinical disorders of attachment.[31] These children are not merely at risk for subsequent disorder but rather already are experiencing a disorder.

According to the DSM-IV-TR,[32] for example, reactive attachment disorder (RAD) is characterized by "markedly disturbed and developmentally inappropriate social relatedness in most contexts that begins before age 5 years and is associated with grossly pathological care" (p. 127). Two types of RAD are defined. In the inhibited type, "the child persistently fails to initiate and to respond to most social interactions in a developmentally appropriate way" (p. 127). Instead, the child shows a pattern of excessively inhibited, hypervigilant, or highly ambivalent responses (e.g., frozen watchfulness, resistance to comfort, or a mixture of approach and avoidance). In contrast, in the disinhibited type, "the child exhibits indiscriminate sociability or a lack of selectivity in the choice of attachment figures" (p. 128).

Areas of Controversy

Despite having been described in psychiatric nosologies for more than 20 years, clinical disorders of attachment only recently are being investigated. Already, there are several controversies that have yet to be resolved. Below, we summarize current controversies and indicate areas in which more research is needed to reconcile discrepancies. Specifically, we consider the independence of the two types of RAD, problems with indiscriminate sociability as an attachment disorder, disorganized attachment as an attachment disorder, and relationship-specific attachment disorders, or the "secure base distortions."

Independence of Emotionally Withdrawn and Indiscriminate Attachment Disorders

Although the clinical pictures of the two putative types of RAD that are described in DSM-IV and ICD-10 are quite different, their independence has not been demonstrated formally. Two recent studies are relevant to the question of the independence of these two types. In one, we assessed 61 children (mean age, 30 months) living in the largest institution for young children in Romania, and another 33 children who had never been institutionalized, for signs of attachment disorder.[33] In this sample, the emotionally withdrawn/inhibited and indiscriminately social/disinhibited scores were substantially intercorrelated ($R = .66$). Nevertheless, a cluster analysis revealed four clusters of children: those with no attachment disorder, those with emotionally withdrawn attachment disorder, those with indiscriminate attachment disorder, and those with a mixed attachment disorder, that is, having features of both types. These results have been replicated recently in a study of signs of attachment disorder in maltreated toddlers in New Orleans.[34] A cluster analysis in this sample also revealed a cluster of children with a mixed picture of emotionally withdrawn and indiscriminately social attachment behaviors.

These results suggest that both the emotionally withdrawn and indiscriminately social patterns of RAD can be identified readily in samples of at risk children. On the other hand, a mixed picture also seems apparent. Whether this represents a distinct type of disorder or comorbid occurrence of two distinct disorders remains to be demonstrated. In part, answering this question depends on how indiscriminate behavior is understood, and we turn next to that question.

Problem of Indiscriminate Behavior

As noted, indiscriminate behavior has been identified in maltreated children and in children raised in institutions. Follow-up studies of young children adopted from institutions, in fact, have demonstrated that indiscriminate behavior is one of the most enduring signs of social abnormalities.[35] The central controversy concerns whether indiscriminate behavior is an attachment disorder, as defined by DSM-IV, or whether it is an associated feature that arises out of many of the same conditions that cause disordered attachment.

The first problem with considering indiscriminate behavior a disorder of attachment is that it persists, even after remarkable improvements in young children's caregiving environment. Thus, parents of children adopted into Canada from Romanian institutions reported high levels of indiscriminate friendliness in the children both at 11 and 39 months (median) after adoption.[36,37] These results are similar to findings reported by O'Connor and Rutter about young children adopted into the United Kingdom from Romanian institutions. Both at 4 and 6 years, they found that a substantial minority of formerly institutionalized children exhibited indiscriminate behavior.[38,39] Taken together with the earlier findings of Tizard's group,[40] these results underscore the persistence of this unusual behavior pattern even after drastic environmental improvements.

Related to this persistence is a second problem, namely, that indiscriminate behavior diverges from measures of disturbed attachment. For example, Chisholm[37] found that indiscriminate behavior was unrelated to concurrently measured attachment security at 39 months after adoption. Furthermore, although attachment security significantly increased from 11 to 39 months after adoption in her sample, there were no differences in the levels of indiscriminate friendliness from 11 to 39 months after adoption in a group of children reared for more than 8 months in Romanian institutions. In contrast, indiscriminate friendliness decreased significantly from 11 to 39 months in the early adopted, never institutionalized Romanian group.[36,37] Also in keeping with the findings of Chisholm,[37] O'Connor and colleagues[41] found that several 6-year-old children who were classified as securely attached in a home-based version of the Strange Situation Procedure also exhibited a pattern of indiscriminate sociability.

In a recent study of disturbances of attachment in young children living in an institution in Romania, we found that 47% of children who had a favorite caregiver also exhibited high levels of indiscriminate behavior.[33] These findings emphasize that even within institutionalized children, indiscriminate behavior and signs of disturbed attachment diverge.

In fact, it is not yet clear exactly which behaviors comprise indiscriminate sociability. Chisholm[37] and Albus and Dozier[42] have referred to indiscriminate "friendliness," but it is not clear that the behaviors engaged in are actually friendly, because they are often socially awkward or inappropriate in some way. Nevertheless, Hodges and Tizard[43] and Chisholm[37] both emphasized that the behaviors seemed normal, and parents were less concerned about them as time passed. It is also unclear how exactly the behaviors are really "indiscriminate," because the same disinhibition may be evident even after the child has a discriminated attachment figure.[37,41] O'Conner and Rutter[39] have emphasized social boundary violations as a core feature of indiscriminate behavior, although this does not account for children who approach nonattachment figures rather than attachment figures for comfort, support, and nurturance. In fact, heterogeneity of the construct seems likely, and greater specification may be helpful in clarifying some of the controversies.

SUMMARY

Attachment between young children and their intimate caregivers is a nearly ubiquitous human phenomena. In extremely adverse environmental contexts, however, such as severe neglect or institutional rearing, some children are unable to follow the species-typical pattern of forming preferred attachments to discriminated caregivers. These children have no demonstrable attachment to anyone, and they exhibit an absence or distortion of attachment behaviors. Recent research has confirmed that children suffering from these disorders may be reliably identified within high risk groups. Nevertheless, questions remain about how best to classify these disorders. Furthermore, some young children have established attachment relationships that are seriously disturbed, and the best means by which to classify them remains to be demonstrated. We have reviewed those areas about which there is some consensus, as well as highlighted some of the current controversies in the field. The increasing attention that these important clinical problems are beginning to receive suggests that substantial progress in better understanding how to identify, treat, and prevent such problems will become increasingly evident in future investigations.

REFERENCES

1. GREENOUGH, W.T., J.E. BLACK & C.S. WALLACE. 1987. Experience and brain development. Child Dev. **58:** 539–559.
2. AINSWORTH, M.D.S., M.S. BLEHAR, E. WATERS & S. WALL. 1985. Patterns of attachment: a psychological study of the strange situation. Lawrence Erlbaum. Hillsdale, NJ.
3. VAN IJZENDOORN, M.H. & A. SAGI. 1999. Cross cultural patterns of attachment. *In* Handbook of Attachment. J. Cassidy and P. Shaver, Eds.: 713–734. Guilford Press. New York.
4. SROUFE, L.A. 1988. The role of infant-caregiver attachment in development. *In* Clinical Implications of Attachment. J. Belsky and T. Nezworski, Eds.: 18–40. Lawrence Erlbaum. Hillsdale, NJ.
5. WEINFIELD, N., L.A. SROUFE, B. EGELAND & E.A. CARLSON. 1999. The nature of individual differences in infant-caregiver attachment. *In* Handbook of Attachment. J. Cassidy and P.R. Shaver, Eds.: 68–88. Guilford Press. New York.
6. GREEN, J. & R. GOLDWYN. 2002. Annotation: attachment disorganization and psychopathology: new findings in attachment research and their potential implications for developmental psychopathology in childhood. J. Child Psychol. Psychiatry **43:** 679–690.
7. LYONS-RUTH, K., E. BRONFMAN & E. PARSONS. 1999. Atypical attachment in infancy and early childhood among children at developmental risk. IV. Maternal disrupted affective communication, maternal frightened or frightening behavior, and disorganized infant attachment strategies. Monogr. Soc. Res. Child Dev. **64:** 172–192.
8. SOLOMON, J. & C. GEORGE. 1999. The place of disorganization in attachment theory: linking classic observations with contemporary findings. *In* Attachment Disorganization. J. Solomon and C. George, Eds.: 3–32. Guilford Press. New York.
9. MAIN, M. & J. SOLOMON. 1986. Discovery of an insecure-disorganized/disoriented attachment pattern. *In* Affective Development in Infancy. T.B. Brazelton and M.W. Yogman, Eds.: 95–124. Ablex. Norwood, NJ.
10. MAIN, M. & J. SOLOMON. 1990. Procedures for identifying infants as disorganized/disoriented during the Ainsworth Strange Situation. *In* Attachment in the Preschool Years: Theory, Research, and Intervention. M.T. Greenberg, D. Cicchetti, and E.M. Cummings, Eds.: 161–218. University of Chicago Press. Chicago.
11. VAN IJZENDOORN, M.H., C. SCHUENGEL & M.J. BAKERMANS-KRANENBURG. 1999. Disorganized attachment in early childhood: meta-analysis of precursors, concomitants, and sequelae. Dev. Psychopathol. **11:** 225–249.
12. CARLSON, V., D. CICCHETTI, D. BARNETT & K. BRAUNWALD. 1989. Finding order in disorganization: lessons from maltreated infant's attachments to their caregivers. *In* Child Maltreatment: Theory and Research on the Causes and Consequences of Child Abuse and Neglect. D. Cicchett, and V. Carlson, Eds.: 494–528. Cambridge University Press. Cambridge, MA.
13. AINSWORTH, M.D.S. & C. EICHBERG. 1992. Effects on infant-mother attachment of unresolved loss of an attachment figure or other traumatic experience. *In* Attachment across the Life-cycle. P. Marris, J. Stevenson-Hinde, and C. Parkes Eds.: 160–183. Routledge. New York.

14. MAIN, M. & E. HESSE. 1990. Parents' unresolved traumatic experiences are related to infant disorganized attachment status: is frightened and/or frightening parental behavior the linking mechanism? *In* Attachment in the Preschool Years: Theory, Research, and Intervention. M.T. Greenberg, D. Cicchetti, and E.M. Cummings, Eds.: 161–218. University of Chicago Press. Chicago.

15. LYONS-RUTH, K., L. ALPERN & B. REPACHOLI. 1993. Disorganized infant attachment classification and maternal psychosocial problems as predictors of hostile-aggressive behavior in the preschool classroom. Child Dev. **64:** 572–585.

16. TETI, D., D. GELFAND, D. MESSINGER & R. ISABELLA. 1995. Maternal depression and the quality of early attachment. Dev. Psychol. **31:** 364–376.

17. OWEN, M.T. & M.J. COX. 1997. Marital conflict and the development of infant parent attachment relationships. J. Fam. Psychol. **11:** 152–164.

18. ZEANAH, C.H., B. DANIS, L. HIRSHBERG, *et al.* 1999. Disorganized attachment associated with partner violence: a research note. Infant Mental Health J. **20:** 77–86.

19. O'CONNOR, M., M. SIGMAN & N. BRILL. 1987. Disorganization of attachment in relation to maternal alcohol consumption. J. Consult. Psychol. **51:** 831–836.

20. JACOBSEN, T., E. HIBBS & U. ZIEGENHEIM. 2000. Maternal expressed emotion related to attachment disorganization in early childhood: a preliminary report. J. Child Psychol. Psychiatry **41:** 899–910.

21. VORRIA, P, Z. PAPALIGOURA, J. DUNN, *et al.* 2003. Early experiences and attachment relationships of Greek infants raised in residential group care. J. Child Psychol. Psychiatry. **44:** 1208–1220.

22. ZEANAH, C.H., A.T. SMYKE, S. KOGA & E. CARLSON. 2003. Attachment in institutionalized children. Paper presented to the Biennial Meeting of the Society for Research in Child Development, Tampa, FL.

23. SCHUENGEL, C., M.J. BAKERMANS-KRANENBURG & M.H. VAN IJZENDOORN. 1999. Attachment and loss: frightening maternal behavior linking unresolved loss and disorganized infant attachment. J. Consult. Clin. Psychol. **67:** 54–63.

24. SPANGLER, G. & K. GROSSMAN. 1999. Individual and physiological correlates of attachment disorganization in infancy. *In* Attachment Disorganization. J. Solomon and C. George, Eds.: 95–124. Guilford Press. New York.

25. LAKATOS, K., I. TOTH, Z. NEMODA, *et al.* 2000. Dopamine D4 receptor DRD4) gene polymorphism is associated with attachment disorganization in infants. Mol. Psychiatry **5:** 633–637.

26. LAKATOS, K., Z. NEMODA, I. TOTH, *et al.* 2002. Further evidence of the role of the dopamine, DRD4 gene in attachment disorganization. Interaction of the exon 111 bp 48b repeat and the –521 C/T promoter polymorphisms. Mol. Psychiatry **7:** 27–31.

27. OKUYAMA, Y., H. ISHIGURO, M. TORU & T. ARINAMI. 1999. A genetic polymorphism in the promoter region of DRD4 associated with expression in schizophrenia. Biochem. Biophysiol. Res. Commun. **258:** 292–295.

28. ZEANAH, C.H. 1996. Beyond insecurity: a reconceptualization of clinical disorders of attachment. J. Consult. Clin. Psychol. **64:** 42–52.

29. VAN IJZENDOORN, M.H. & M.J. BAKERMANS-KRANENBURG. 2002. Disorganized attachment and the dysregulation of negative emotions. *In* Emotional Regulation and Developmental Health: Infancy and Early Childhood. A. Lieberman and N. Fox Eds.: 139–151. Johnson & Johnson Pediatric Institute. Metuchen, NJ.

30. LYONS-RUTH, K. & JACOBVITZ, D. 1999. Attachment disorganization: unresolved loss, relational violence, lapses in behavioral and attentional strategies. *In* Handbook of Attachment: Theory, Research and Clinical Applications. J. Cassidy and P. Shaver, Eds.: 520–554. Guilford Press. New York.

31. ZEANAH, C.H. & R.N. EMDE. 1994. Attachment disorders in infancy. *In* Child and Adolescent Psychiatry: Modern Approaches. M. Rutter, L. Hersov and E. Taylor, Eds.: 490–504. Blackwell. Oxford, UK.

32. AMERICAN PSYCHIATRIC ASSOCIATION. 2000. Diagnostic and Statistical Manual of Mental Disorders, 4th ed. American Psychiatric Association. Washington, DC.

33. SMYKE, A.T., A. DUMITRESCU & C.H. ZEANAH. 2002. Disturbances of attachment in young children. I. The continuum of caretaking casualty. J. Am. Acad. Child Adolesc. Psychiatry **41:** 972–982.

34. ZEANAH, C.H., S.S. HELLER, A.T. SMYKE, *et al.* Disturbances of attachment in mal-treated infants and toddlers. Child Abuse & Neglect. In press
35. ZEANAH, C.H. 2000. Disturbances of attachment in young children adopted from insti-tutions. J. Dev. Behav. Pediatr. **21:** 230–236.
36. CHISHOLM, K., M.C. CARTER, E.W. AMES & S.J. MORISON. 1995. Attachment security and indiscriminantly friendly behavior in children adopted from Romanian orphan-ages. Dev. Psychopathol. **7:** 283–294.
37. CHISHOLM, K. 1998. A three-year follow-up of attachment and indiscriminate friendli-ness in children adopted from Romanian orphanages. Child Dev. **69:** 1092–1106.
38. O'CONNOR, T., D. BREDENKAMP & M. RUTTER. 1999. Attachment disturbances and dis-orders in children exposed to early severe deprivation. Infant Ment. Health J. **20:** 10–29.
39. O'CONNOR, T. & M. RUTTER. 2000. Attachment disorder behavior following early severe deprivation: extension and longitudinal follow-up. J. Am. Acad. Child Ado-lesc. Psychiatry **39:** 703–712.
40. TIZARD, B. & J. REES. 1975. The effect of early institutional rearing on the behavior problems and affectional relationships of four-year-old children. J. Child Psychol. Psychiatry **27:** 61–73.
41. O'CONNOR, T., R. MARVIN, M. RUTTER, *et al.* 2003. Child-parent attachment following early institutional deprivation. Dev. Psychopathol. **15:** 19–38.
42. ALBUS, K.E. & M. DOZIER. 1999. Indiscriminate friendliness and terror of strangers in infancy. Infant Ment. Health J. **20:** 30–41.
43. HODGES, J. & B. TIZARD. 1989. Social and family relationships of ex-institutional ado-lescents. J. Child Psychol. Psychiatry **30:** 77–97.

Social Engagement and Attachment

A Phylogenetic Perspective

STEPHEN W. PORGES

University of Illinois at Chicago, Department of Psychiatry, Chicago, Illinois 60612, USA

ABSTRACT: This article focuses on the importance of social engagement and the behavioral and neurophysiological mechanisms that allow individuals to reduce psychological and physical distance. A model of social engagement derived from the Polyvagal Theory is presented. The model emphasizes phylogeny as an organizing principle and includes the following points: (1) there are well-defined neural circuits to support social engagement behaviors and the defensive strategies of fight, flight, and freeze; (2) these neural circuits form a phylogenetically organized hierarchy; (3) without being dependent on conscious awareness, the nervous system evaluates risk in the environment and regulates the expression of adaptive behavior to match the neuroception of a safe, dangerous, or life-threatening environment; (4) social engagement behaviors and the benefits of the physiological states associated with social support require a neuroception of safety; (5) social behaviors associated with nursing, reproduction, and the formation of strong pair bonds require immobilization without fear; and (6) immobilization without fear is mediated by a co-opting of the neural circuit regulating defensive freezing behaviors through the involvement of oxytocin, a neuropeptide in mammals involved in the formation of social bonds. The model provides a phylogenetic interpretation of the neural mechanisms mediating the behavioral and physiological features associated with stress and several psychiatric disorders.

KEYWORDS: attachment; vagus; autonomic nervous system; oxytocin; evolution; Polyvagal Theory

A PHYLOGENETIC PERSPECTIVE

As the scientific knowledge of neuroanatomy and neurophysiology expands, there is a growing interest in the role neural processes play in the development of normal social behavior and in the expression of the atypical social behaviors that may provide the roots of mental illness in children. Recent advances in neuroscience have enabled researchers to study nervous system function and structure in the intact living individual. Now neuronal function can be studied, and the structural hypotheses derived from animal models and postmortem histology can be challenged and explained. These new methods of assaying neural structure and function, coupled

Address for correspondence: Stephen W. Porges, Ph.D., University of Illinois at Chicago, Brain Body Center, Department of Psychiatry (mc 912), 1601 West Taylor Street, Chicago, IL 60612, USA. Voice: 312-355-1557; fax: 312-996-7658.

sporges@uic.edu

Ann. N.Y. Acad. Sci. 1008: 31–47 (2003). © 2003 New York Academy of Sciences.
doi: 10.1196/annals.1301.004

with the breakthroughs in molecular genetics, are providing new tools and models, which can be integrated with existing strategies that effectively monitor dynamic neural function by time sampling neuroendocrine and autonomic parameters.

DEFINING SOCIAL BEHAVIOR: THE GREAT CONCEPTUAL DIVIDE

An objective of this conference is to build bridges among researchers who study the development of social behavior with both animal models and clinical populations. It was assumed, as a primary premise of organizing this conference, that both cohorts share the same objective of generating knowledge related to the mechanisms of normal and atypical social behavior that could be translated into clinical practice. The contrasts between the research strategies and methods of the two cohorts are forcing a reevaluation of this assumption.

Animal models often emphasize the role of a specific neural system, neurotransmitter, neuropeptide, hormone, or brain structure as a regulator of social behavior. In contrast, clinical research often focuses on studying aberrant psychological processes in clinical populations. When neurophysiological systems are studied with clinical populations, the research designs focus on establishing correlations with the disorders and, in general, preclude the possibility of distinguishing whether the physiological correlates are causes or effects of the disorder.

Although the two research strategies often use similar terms, the terms may reflect different domains of social behavior. Animal models tend to focus on the establishment of pair bonds and generate paradigms to evaluate the strength of these bonds. In contrast, research with children, investigating normal and atypical social behavior, tends to focus on the behaviors that reduce social and physical distance between individuals. For example, the terminology associated with measuring and defining social behavior differs when contrasting the compromised social engagement strategies expressed by an institutionalized child with the ability to establish pair bonds by a vole.

A final perplexing part of the conceptual divide relates to the translation of neuroscience principles and research findings into clinical practice. The clinician is the third limb of this triad. Paradoxically, although the link between social behavior and mental illness in children emerged directly from clinical observations, the features and dimensions of social behavior studied in both animal models and in laboratory studies of normal and atypical children often deviates from the features that clinicians use to define the pathology. Clinical researchers who conduct studies of social behavior are interested in either how outlier behaviors overlap with features of clinical diagnoses or how behavioral, psychological, and physiological parameters differentiate the clinical population from normal subjects. Often the parameters of interest or, at least, those that distinguish the clinical group from normal subjects focus on processes that do not have an obvious relation to the behaviors observed in clinical settings or used to define the pathology (e.g., cortisol).

Most research in psychopathology accepts the validity of clinical assessment and diagnostic systems (e.g., DSM-IV) as inclusion criteria and then attempts to demonstrate that deficits in psychological processes and/or atypical neurophysiological response patterns underlie the disorder. The research on processes and mechanisms, whether obtained from clinical populations or by studying animal models assumed to express behaviors similar to the clinical populations, does not easily enter the clinical realm and inform clinical assessment. Similarly, other than global diagnoses and quantitative information from standardized assessment instruments, little information from clinical observations regarding the specific features of behavior that have triggered the clinician's concern easily enters the research environment. Thus, the construct of social behavior is treated differently by researchers testing animal models, researchers studying normal social behavior, researchers studying the psychological and neurophysiological mechanisms and processes underlying a clinical diagnosis, and clinicians who diagnose and treat social behavior problems in children. Missing in this mix of metaphors, worldviews, paradigms, and diagnostic models, is a shared agenda to translate research findings into practice (i.e., assessment and treatment) and to use clinical information to inform the theoretical models being tested.

SOCIAL BEHAVIOR AND ATTACHMENT

Several researchers who study the development of social behavior in children have focused on the construct of attachment. Several of these researchers conduct studies derived from the observations of Bowlby[1] and the paradigm building research of Ainsworth et al.[2] Much of the current research on human attachment is based on the Ainsworth typology, which applies a paradigm assessing infant responses to separation. Clinicians and researchers in developmental psychopathology assume that the Ainsworth classification system and recent derivatives[3] will provide insights into the psychological mechanisms of specific disorders. In fact, diagnostic categories now include disorders such as "reactive attachment disorder" (RAD).

The traditional attachment schema derived from the Bowlby theory constitutes only a small part of social behavior. Moreover, traditional attachment theory by focusing on mother–infant relations does not include other putative attachment behaviors that are observed in the enduring bonds between peers, siblings, and mates. Missing from the traditional attachment theories is an articulation of the mechanisms mediating engagement between the individuals bonding or forming attachments.

SOCIAL ENGAGEMENT: THE PREAMBLE OF A SOCIAL BOND

To develop a social bond, individuals have to be in close proximity. This is true for the models focusing on both mother–infant attachment and the strong bonds associated with social monogamy. Both models test the strength and features of the relationship through separation paradigms. There are, of course, major differences between the contexts in which mother–infant attachment and the social bonds of reproductive partners are established and tested. One specific difference is the contrast in mobility between the mother–infant and reproductive partner dyads. In the mother–infant dyad there is an imbalance with the infant having limited abilities to move toward or away from the mother. However, in the reproductive partner dyad, there is a balance between the behavioral repertoires of the two adults.

Although proximity is critical to the establishment of social bonds, proximity is totally caused by the ability to navigate across physical distance via voluntary behavior. If social bonds were dependent on voluntary motor behaviors, then the new-born infant would be greatly disadvantaged because the neural regulation of the spinal motor pathways are immature at birth and take several years to fully develop. However, in mammals not all muscles are driven by corticospinal pathways. Unlike the striated muscles of trunk and limbs, corticobulbar pathways regulate the striated muscles of the face and head. The corticobulbar pathways are sufficiently developed at birth to be available to the full-term infant to signal caregiver (e.g., vocalizations, grimace) and to engage the social (e.g., gaze, smile) and nutrient (e.g., sucking) as-pects of the world. These motor pathways originate in the brainstem and regulate muscles through the branches of five cranial nerves (V, VII, IX, X, XI). Thus, the neural regulation of muscles that provide important elements of social cueing are available to facilitate the social interaction with the caregiver and function collec-tively as an integrated social engagement system.[4]

The muscles of the face and head influence both the expression and receptivity of social cues and can effectively reduce or increase social distance. Behaviorally this is observed as facial expressions, eye gaze, vocalizations, and head orientation. Neu-ral regulation of these muscles can reduce social distance by making eye contact, ex-pressing prosody in voice, displaying contingent facial expressions, and modulating the middle ear muscles to improve the extraction of human voice from background sounds. Alternatively, by reducing the muscle tone to these muscles, the eyelids droop, prosody is lost, positive and contingent facial expressions are diminished, the ability to extract human voice from background sounds is compromised, and the awareness of the social engagement behaviors of others may be lost. Thus, the neural regulation of the striated muscles of the face and head function both as an active so-cial engagement system that reduces psychological distance and as a filter that can influence the perception of the engagement behaviors of others.

Special visceral efferent pathways mediate the neural regulation of the striated muscles of the face and head. Special visceral pathways emerge from three nuclei in the brainstem (nucleus of the trigeminal nerve, nucleus of the facial nerve, and nu-cleus ambiguus) and provide motor pathways that are contained within five cranial nerves (i.e., trigeminal, facial, hypoglossal, vagus, accessory). These pathways reg-ulate structures that evolved from the ancient gill arches. From both clinical and re-search perspectives, the striated muscles of the face and head provide potent information regarding the behavioral dimensions used to express as well as to eval-uate the strength of attachment or the stress to the social bond. For example, facial expressivity and prosody of vocalizations have been used as clinical indicators as well as quantifiable responses of separation distress.[5]

THE SOCIAL ENGAGEMENT SYSTEM: PHYLOGENIC ORIGINS OF BEHAVIORAL AND AUTONOMIC COMPONENTS

The phylogenic origin of the behaviors associated with the social engagement system is intertwined with the phylogeny of the autonomic nervous system. As the striated muscles, via special visceral efferent pathways, evolved into a behavioral system that regulated social engagement behaviors, there was a profound shift in neural regulation of the autonomic nervous system. Phylogenetically, these changes in both somatomotor and visceromotor regulation are observed in the transition from reptiles to mammals. As the muscles of the face and head evolved into an ingestion (i.e., nursing) and social engagement system, a new component of the autonomic nervous system (i.e., a myelinated vagus) evolved that was regulated by a brainstem nucleus, which was also involved in the regulation of the striated muscles of the face and head (i.e., nucleus ambiguus). This convergence of neural mechanisms resulted in an integrated social engagement system with a synergism between behavioral and visceral features of social engagement. Thus, activation of the somatomotor component would trigger visceral changes that would support social engagement, while modulation of visceral state would either promote or impede social engagement behaviors. For example, stimulation of visceral states that would promote mobilization (i.e., fight or flight behaviors) would impede the ability to express social engagement behaviors, whereas increased activity through the myelinated vagus would promote the social engagement behaviors associated with a calm visceral state. Thus, we can infer the specific neural mechanisms related to the effectiveness that feeding and rocking have on promoting calm behavioral and visceral states. Specifically, both the ingestive behaviors associated with feeding and the passive rocking of an infant promote calmness by influencing the myelinated vagus. Feeding activates the muscles of mastication via trigeminal efferent pathways, which, in turn, provide afferent feedback input to the nucleus ambiguus (i.e., the source nucleus of the myelinated vagus). Rocking provides an efficient and direct influence on the vagus by stimulating vagal afferent pathways via the baroreceptors. Moreover, activation of the social engagement system dampens the neural circuits including the limbic structures that support fight, flight, or freeze behaviors.

POLYVAGAL THEORY: THREE NEURAL CIRCUITS REGULATING REACTIVITY

Evolutionary forces have molded both human physiology and behavior. Via evolutionary processes, the mammalian nervous system has emerged with specific neural and behavioral features that react to challenge to maintain visceral homeostasis. These reactions change physiological state and, in mammals, limit sensory awareness, motor behaviors, and cognitive activity. To survive, mammals must determine friend from foe, evaluate whether the environment is safe, and communicate with their social unit. These survival-related behaviors are associated with specific neurobehavioral states that limit the extent to which a mammal can be physically approached and whether the mammal can communicate or establish new coalitions.

Through stages of phylogeny, mammals and especially primates have evolved a functional neural organization that regulates visceral state to support social behavior. The Polyvagal Theory[4,6–8] emphasizes the phylogenetic origins of brain structures that regulate social and defensive behaviors, domains compromised in individuals with autism and several psychiatric disorders. The Polyvagal Theory proposes that the evolution of the mammalian autonomic nervous system provides the neurophysiological substrates for the emotional experiences and affective processes that are major components of social behavior. The theory proposes that physiological state limits the range of behavior and psychological experience. In this context, the evolution of the nervous system determines the range of emotional expression, quality of communication, and the ability to regulate bodily and behavioral state. The Polyvagal Theory links the evolution of the autonomic nervous system to affective experience, emotional expression, facial gestures, vocal communication, and contingent social behavior. Thus, the theory provides a plausible explanation of several social, emotional, and communication behaviors and disorders.

The polyvagal construct emphasizes the neurophysiological and neuroanatomical distinction between two branches of the vagus and proposes that each branch supports different adaptive behavioral strategies. The Polyvagal Theory articulates three phylogenetic stages of the development of the mammalian autonomic nervous system. Each state is associated with a distinct autonomic subsystem that is retained in mammals. These autonomic subsystems are phylogenetically ordered and behaviorally linked to social communication (e.g., facial expression, vocalization, listening), mobilization (e.g., fight–flight behaviors), and immobilization (e.g., feigning death, vasovagal syncope, and behavioral shutdown). The social communication system (i.e., Social Engagement System, see below) is dependent on the myelinated vagus, which serves to foster calm behavioral states by inhibiting the sympathetic influences to the heart and dampening the HPA axis.[9] The mobilization system is dependent on the functioning of the sympathetic nervous system. The most phylogenetically primitive component, the immobilization system, is dependent on the unmyelinated or "vegetative" vagus, which is shared with most vertebrates. With increased neural complexity due to phylogenetic development, the organism's behavioral and affective repertoire is enriched. The theory emphasizes the functional aspect of neural control of both the striated muscles of the face and the smooth muscles of the viscera, because their functions rely on common brainstem structures.

The Social Engagement System

The Polyvagal Theory provides an explicit neurobiological model of how difficulties in spontaneous social behavior are linked to both facial expressivity and the regulation of visceral state, and, alternatively, how social behavior may serve as a regulator of physiological activity. The theory proposes a possible mechanism to explain how these difficulties might form a core domain of several psychiatric profiles. Relevant to this focus on psychiatric disorders are the specific deficits associated with several diagnoses in both the somatomotor (e.g., poor gaze, low facial affect, lack of prosody, difficulties in mastication) and visceromotor (difficulties in autonomic regulation resulting in cardiopulmonary and digestive problems) of the social engagement system. For example, clinicians and researchers have documented these deficits in individuals with autistic spectrum disorders. Deficits in the social engagement system would compromise spontaneous social behavior and social awareness and affect expressivity, prosody, and language development. In contrast, interventions that improve the neural regulation of the social engagement system hypothetically would enhance spontaneous social behavior, state and affect regulation, reduce stereotypical behaviors, and improve language skills.

Embryologically, components of several cranial nerves known as special visceral efferent pathways develop together to form the neural substrate of a social engagement system.[8] This system, as illustrated in FIGURE 1, provides the neural structures involved in social and emotional behaviors. The social engagement system has a control component in the cortex (i.e., upper motor neurons) that regulates brainstem nuclei (i.e., lower motor neurons) to control eyelid opening (e.g., looking), facial

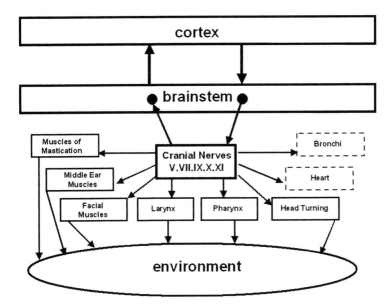

FIGURE 1. The Social Engagement System. Social communication is determined by the cortical regulation of medullary nuclei via corticobulbar pathways. The Social Engagement System consists of a somatomotor component (i.e., special visceral efferent pathways that regulate the muscles of the head and face) and a visceromotor component (i.e., the my-elinated vagus that regulates the heart and bronchi). Solid blocks indicate the somatomotor component. *Dashed blocks* indicate the visceromotor component.

muscles (e.g., emotional expression), middle ear muscles (e.g., extracting human voice from background noise), muscle of mastication (e.g., ingestion), laryngeal and pharyngeal muscles (e.g., vocalization and language), and head-turning muscles (e.g., social gesture and orientation). Collectively, these muscles function as filters that limit social stimuli (e.g., observing facial features and listening to human voice) and determinants of engagement with the social environment. The neural control of these muscles determines social experiences. In addition, the source nuclei (i.e., low-er motor neurons) of these nerves, which are located in the brainstem, communicate directly with an inhibitory neural system that slows heart rate, lowers blood pressure, and actively reduces arousal to promote calm states consistent with the metabolic de-mands of growth and restoration of our neurophysiological systems. Direct corticob-ulbar pathways reflect the influence of frontal areas of the cortex (i.e., upper motor neurons) on the regulation of this system. Moreover, afferent feedback through the vagus to medullary areas (e.g., nucleus of the solitary tract) influences forebrain ar-eas that are assumed to be involved in several psychiatric disorders. In addition, the anatomical structures involved in the social engagement system have neurophysio-logical interactions with the HPA axis, the neuropeptides of oxytocin and vaso-pressin, and the immune system.[4]

The study of comparative anatomy, evolutionary biology, and embryology may provide important hints regarding the functional relation between the neural control of facial muscles and emergent psychological experiences and behavior. The nerves that control the muscles of the face and head share several common features. Pathways from five cranial nerves control the muscles of the face and head. Collectively, these pathways are labeled as special visceral efferent. Special visceral efferent nerves innervate striated muscles, which regulate the structures derived during embryology from the ancient gill arches.[10] The special visceral efferent pathways regulate the muscles of mastication (e.g., ingestion), muscles of the middle ear (e.g., listening to human voice), muscles of the face (e.g., emotional expression), muscles of larynx and pharynx (e.g., prosody and intonation), and muscles controlling head tilt and turning (e.g., gesture). In fact, the neural pathway that raises the eyelids also tenses the stapedius muscle in the middle ear, which facilitates hearing human voice. Thus, the neural mechanisms for making eye contact are shared with those needed to listen to human voice. As a cluster, the difficulties in gaze, extraction of human voice, facial expression, head gesture, and prosody are common features of individuals with autism.

Disorders of the Social Engagement System: Maladaptive or Adaptive Behavioral Strategies?

Individuals with several psychiatric and behavioral disorders have difficulties in establishing and maintaining relations. Several clinical diagnostic categories include features associated with difficulties both in expressing social behavior and in reading social cues (i.e., social awareness). These features are observed in individuals with a variety of primary psychiatric diagnoses including autism, social anxiety, posttraumatic stress disorder, and RAD.

Although a compromised social engagement system results in "maladaptive" social behavior, do these asocial behavioral strategies have "adaptive" features? The phylogeny of the vertebrate autonomic nervous system serves as a guide (i.e., the Polyvagal Theory) to understand these adaptive features. Phylogenetically, the vertebrate autonomic nervous system follows three general stages of development. Each stage supports a different category of behavior with only the phylogenetically most recent innovation (i.e., the myelinated vagus) supporting social engagement behaviors. Because the neural regulation of the myelinated vagus is integrated into the social engagement system, when the social engagement system is compromised the effects are both behavioral and autonomic. The resultant changes in autonomic state support a range of adaptive defensive behaviors. Specifically, the compromised social engagement system is associated, neurophysiologically, with a change in autonomic regulation characterized by a reduction in the influence of the myelinated vagus (i.e., ventral vagal complex including nucleus ambiguus) on the heart. The removal of the regulatory influence of the ventral vagal complex on the heart potentiates the expression of the two phylogenetically older neural systems (i.e., sympathetic nervous system, dorsal vagal complex including dorsal nucleus of the vagus). These two older neural systems foster mobilization behaviors of fight and flight via the sympathetic nervous system or immobilization behaviors of death feigning, freezing, and behavioral shut down via the dorsal vagal complex.

Neuroception: A Nervous System Evaluation of Risk

When individuals meet, what determines the biobehavioral sequence and consequence of their initial interactions? What contextual features and neural mechanisms trigger whether an individual expresses prosocial engagement or the specific defensive behaviors of fight, flight, or freeze? Regardless of the model of attachment or its dependence on cognitive, affective, behavioral, or biological constructs, the critical features that determine the valence of the interaction are related to perceived safety. Thus, the perception of safety is the turning point in the development of relationships for most mammals. The perception of safety determines whether the behavior will be prosocial (i.e., social engagement) or defensive. If the context and the other individual are perceived as safe, then the candidates for the social bond may inhibit the adaptive primitive neurobiological reactions of defense to allow the expression of social engagement. The three stages of the Polyvagal Theory articulate the neural systems that are available for social engagement and the defensive behaviors of fight, flight, and freeze. However, how are the adaptive neurobiological systems for defense functionally subdued to insure that attachment and the formation of social bonds will be the products of appropriate social engagement?

Before a social bond can occur, both individuals have to perceive each other as safe. What mediates the individual's ability to engage? Why would an infant look and coo at a caregiver, but gaze avert and cry as a stranger approached? Why would a gentle embrace be experienced as pleasurable when expressed by a lover and be experienced as assault when expressed by a stranger? Mammals have adaptive neurobehavioral systems for both defensive and social engagement behaviors. However, what enables engagement behaviors to occur, while disenabling the mechanisms of defense? The Polyvagal Theory with its focus on the phylogeny of the vertebrate autonomic nervous system provides a perspective to identify and to understand the plausible mechanisms that enable mammals to functionally switch between positive social engagement and defensive behavioral strategies. To effectively switch from defensive to social engagement strategies, the mammalian nervous system needs to perform two important processes: (1) to assess risk, and (2) if the environment is perceived as safe, to inhibit the more primitive limbic structures that control fight, flight, or freeze behaviors.

The nervous system, through the processing of sensory information from the environment, continuously evaluates risk. Because the neural evaluation of risk does not require conscious awareness, the term *neuroception* is introduced to emphasize the neural circuits that function as a safety-threat detection system capable of distinguishing among situations that are safe, dangerous, or life threatening. Because of the phylogenetic heritage of mammals, neuroception can operate without cognitive awareness via relatively primitive mechanisms that are dependent on subcortical structures (e.g., limbic). As a product of evolution, new neural systems evolved in mammals that involved cortical regulation of subcortical structures and, in many instances, co-opted the defense functions of the primitive structures to support other functions including those related to reproductive behavior and pair bonding.[8]

Based on the relative risk of the environment, both social engagement and defense behaviors may be interpreted as either adaptive or maladaptive. For example, the inhibition of defense systems by the social engagement system would be adaptive and appropriate only in a safe environment. From a clinical perspective, it would be the inability to inhibit defense systems in safe environments (e.g., anxiety disorders, RAD) or the inability to activate defense systems in risk environments (e.g., Williams Syndrome) that might contribute to the defining features of psychopathology. Thus, an invalid neuroception of safety or danger might contribute to maladaptive physiological reactivity and the expression of the defensive behaviors associated with specific psychiatric disorders.

There is a common feature between the invalid neuroception that identifies risk when no risk is there and McEwen's concept of "allostatic load."[11] The physiological reaction to a valid risk, although metabolically costly, is adaptive. Thus, the increased metabolic activity necessary to support the mobilization behaviors of fight and flight are adaptive in the short term, but costly to the organism if maintained. The duration of the response is an important feature that distinguishes between adaptive and maladaptive reactions. The complex mammalian nervous system evolved with a great dependence on oxygen and, unlike the reptile, can survive only for short periods without oxygen. Thus, breath holding for mammals is adaptive only for short periods. In contrast, apnea is adaptive for reptiles, who because of their limited needs for oxygen can inhibit breathing for long periods, whereas apnea is potentially lethal for mammals.[12] Similarly, temporal features, in part, determine the construct of allostatic load. McEwen describes chronic stress or allostatic state as a physiological response that, although having adaptive functions in the short term, can be damaging if used for long periods when it is no longer needed (i.e., invalid neuroception). This cost of adaptation or "maladaptation" McEwen refers to as "allostatic load."

Safety Trumps Fear

In safe environments, autonomic state is adaptively regulated to dampen sympathetic activation and to protect the oxygen-dependent central nervous system from the metabolically conservative reactions of the dorsal vagal complex. However, how does the nervous system know when the environment is safe, dangerous, or life threatening and what neural mechanisms evaluate risk in the environment?

New technologies, such as functional magnetic resonance imaging, have identified specific neural structures that are involved in detecting risk. The temporal lobe is of particular interest in expanding the construct of neuroception and in identifying neural mechanisms that modulate the expression of adaptive defensive behaviors and autonomic states. Functional imaging techniques document that areas of the temporal cortex, fusiform gyrus (FG), and superior temporal sulcus (STS) are involved in detecting features such as movements, vocalizations, and faces, which contribute to an individual being perceived as safe or trustworthy.[13,14] Slight changes in these stimuli can pose threat or signal endearment. Connectivity between these areas of the temporal cortex and the amygdala suggests a top-down control in the processing of facial features that could actively inhibit activity of the structures involved in the expression of defensive strategies.[15]

Neuroanatomical and neurophysiological research with animals provides additional information regarding the modulation and inhibition of defensive behaviors via well-defined connections between the amygdala and the periacqueductal gray (PAG). The PAG is a heterogenous midbrain structure that consists of gray matter surrounding the cerebral aqueduct that connects the third and fourth ventricles. Studies have identified areas of the PAG that are organized to regulate flight, fight, or freeze behaviors and the autonomic states that support these behaviors.[16] Stimulating rostrally within the lateral and dorsolateral PAG produces confrontational defensive behaviors (i.e., fight), while stimulating caudally within the lateral PAG and dorsolateral PAG produces escape behaviors (i.e., flight). Autonomic shifts such as increases in heart rate and blood pressure parallel these behaviors. In contrast, stimulation in the region of the PAG ventrolateral to the aqueduct (vlPAG) evokes a passive reaction of immobility, a decrease in blood pressure, and a slowing of heart rate. Interestingly, excitation of the vlPAG evokes an opioid-mediated analgesia that might adaptively raise pain thresholds. In addition, there is evidence of a functional connection between the central nucleus of the amygdala and the vlPAG that modulates both antinociception and immobilization.[17] Consistent with the Polyvagal Theory, the vlPAG communicates with dorsal vagal complex, whereas the lPAG and dlPAG communicate with the sympathetic nervous system.

In the absence of threat, inhibitory projections from the FG and STS to the amygdala would be available to actively inhibit the limbic defense systems. This inhibition would provide an opportunity for social behavior to occur. Thus, the appearance of a friend or mate would subdue the limbic activation with the biobehavioral consequences of allowing proximity, physical contact, and other social engagement behaviors. In contrast, during situations in which the appraisal of risk is high, the amygdala and various areas of the PAG are activated. The amygdala and PAG only share connections through the central nucleus.[18]

The detection of safety subdues the adaptive defensive systems dependent on limbic structures. Thus, providing a plausible model of how a neural detection of environmental risk (i.e., neuroception) would modulate behavior and physiological state to support adaptive behaviors in response to safe, dangerous, and life-threatening environments. Conceptually, the process of detecting safety is inclusive of the detection of risk. Thus, the neural circuits that mediate the more primitive defense systems have through the processes of evolution been co-opted to support the social behavior necessary for mammalian survival. These behaviors include social engagement and the behaviors associated with social bonding (e.g., reproductive behaviors and nursing).

Co-opting the Immobilization Defense System for Reproductive Behaviors, Nursing, and the Formation of Social Bonds

Immobilization as a defense system is phylogenetically old and is associated with reduced metabolic demands and increased pain threshold. In reptiles, because of their limited need for oxygen, immobilization is a very effective defense strategy. In contrast, because mammals have a great need for oxygen, the inhibition of movement coupled with a shift in autonomic state to support the immobilization behavior (i.e., apnea and bradycardia) can be lethal.[19,20] However, several aspects of mammalian social behavior require immobilization, but immobilization without fear. Immobilization without fear is accomplished by co-opting the structures that regulate immobilization and pain thresholds to serve a broad range of social needs including reproduction, nursing, and pair-bonding. By focusing on the area of the PAG that coordinates freezing behavior, we can see how a primitive immobilization defense system has been modified through evolution to serve the intimate social needs of mammals. In addition, when we study the vlPAG we find that it is rich in receptors for oxytocin, a neuropeptide associated with partuition, nursing, and the establishment of pair bonds.[21,22]

Overlapping with the area of the PAG that organizes immobility (i.e., vlPAG) are areas that when stimulated produce lordosis and kyphosis. The lordosis reflex is a hormone-dependent behavior displayed by female rodents and other mammalian species during mating. In most mammals, lordosis involves the female immobilizing in a crouching posture with her hind end available to the male for copulation. Neural tracing studies have demonstrated that the vlPAG is part of the neural circuit involved in regulating lordosis.[23] Kyphosis is an upright crouching posture that is accompanied by inhibition of limb movements. This posture is stimulated by nipple attachment and provides an opportunity for the dam to feed simultaneously a large litter. When dams initiate a nursing bout, behavioral state shifts immediately from high activity to immobility.[24] When the caudal portion of the vlPAG is lesioned there are important consequences: (1) kyphotic nursing decreases, (2) litter weight gains decrease, and (3) the lesioned rats are more aggressive and more frequently attack strange males.[25]

Test of the Model

The processes of attachment and the formation of social bonds require appropriate social engagement strategies. In the preceding sections, elements of a preliminary model that links social engagement to attachment and the formation of social bonds are presented. The model is expanded from the Polyvagal Theory and emphasizes the following points: (1) there are well-defined neural circuits to support social engagement behaviors and the defensive strategies of fight, flight, and freeze; (2) without being dependent on conscious awareness the nervous system evaluates risk in the environment and regulates the expression of adaptive behavior to match the neuroception of a safe, dangerous, or life-threatening environment; (3) social engagement behaviors and the benefits of the physiological states associated with social support require a neuroception of safety; (4) social behaviors associated with nursing, reproduction, and the formation of strong pair bonds require immobilization without fear; and (5) immobilization without fear is mediated by a co-opting of the neural circuit regulating defensive freezing behaviors through the involvement of oxytocin, a neuropeptide involved in the formation of social bonds.[26,27]

FIGURES 2, 3, and 4 illustrate the role that neuroception plays in determining the neural circuits recruited to regulate social engagement, fight, flight, and freeze behaviors. Each figure illustrates a different environment context (i.e., safe, dangerous, life threat). FIGURE 2 illustrates the assumed neural circuits involved in promoting social engagement behaviors in a safe context. The detection of safe or trustworthy features derived from face, voice, and movement activate a neural circuit that projects from the temporal cortex (i.e., fusiform gyrus, superior temporal sulcus) to the central nucleus of the amygdala to inhibit defensive limbic functions (see FIGS. 3 and 4). This circuit disenables the limbic defense systems that organize and regulate fight, flight, and freeze behaviors and enables the corticobulbar pathways that regulate the social engagement behaviors (see FIG. 1). FIGURE 3 illustrates the neural circuits involved in a response to a neuroception of danger. In response to danger, the limbic defense circuits function to adaptively protect the individual. The specificity of the defense strategy, whether confrontational or avoidant (i.e., fight or

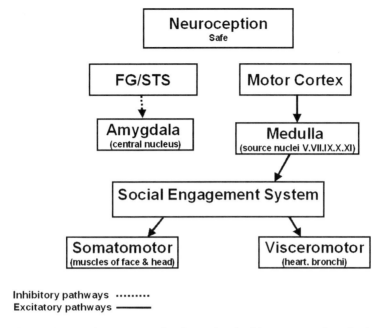

FIGURE 2. Neural structures and pathways involved in a neuroception of safety.

flight), is regulated by the PAG. To support these mobilization behaviors, the sympathetic nervous system is activated and dominates autonomic state. FIGURE 4 illustrates the neural circuits involved in response to life threat. In response to life threat, the mammalian nervous system promotes immobilization or freezing behavior. Freezing, as a defense strategy, is coordinated by the PAG. To inhibit metabolic activity during immobilization, autonomic state is under the control of the dorsal vagal complex. As proposed by the Polyvagal Theory, the autonomic reactions during each adaptive behavioral strategy is hierarchically organized after the phylogeny of both the changes in the vertebrate autonomic nervous system and changes in the behavioral repertoire from immobilization to mobilization to social engagement.

The ability to evaluate whether the environment is safe or if a person is trustworthy is difficult for individuals with a variety of psychiatric diagnoses. Current research suggests that the areas in the temporal cortex (i.e., FG, STS), which are assumed to inhibit limbic defense reactions, are not activated in clinical populations that have difficulties with social engagement behaviors (e.g., autism, schizophrenia). Moreover, individuals with other psychiatric disorders such as anxiety disorders and depression, which have as diagnostic features compromised social behavior, have difficulties in regulating visceral state (e.g., lower vagal regulation of the heart) and supporting social engagement behaviors (e.g., reduced facial expressiveness and motor control of the striated muscles of the face and head). Thus, from a theoretical perspective, a potential root of several psychiatric disorders might be linked to an in-

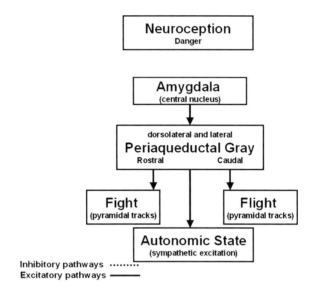

FIGURE 3. Neural structures and pathways involved in a neuroception of danger.

ability to detect safety in the environment and trustworthiness from interactions and, thus, the inability to express appropriate social engagement behaviors.

The study of attachment disorders such as RAD provides an intriguing test of the critical role of neuroception in mediating appropriate attachment and social behavior. RAD is described in both the DSM-IV (American Psychiatric Association, 1994) and the ICD-10 (World Health Organization, 1992) psychiatric diagnostic manuals. RAD comprises two clinical patterns (i.e., inhibited and uninhibited subtypes). The inhibited subtype is characterized by an emotionally withdrawn, unresponsive pattern in which there is an absence of attachment behaviors. The disinhibited subtype is characterized by indiscriminate attachment, which often is directed at strangers. These patterns have been described in institutionalized and maltreated children.[28] From a neuroception perspective, in both subtypes, the evaluation of the risk in the environment is not accurate.

Recent research on the outcomes of children raised in institutions in Romania has stimulated interest in RAD and in developing intervention strategies to remediate these devastating disturbances in social development. If an accurate neuroception of the environment is necessary for normal social behavior, then what features in the environment might potentiate normal social development? A recent study of Romanian toddlers[29] provides insight into the process. In this study, indices of RAD were evaluated in children as a function of the number of different caregivers. Two groups of institutionalized children were evaluated and contrasted with children who were never institutionalized. One group consisted of the standard institution unit in which 20 different caregivers worked rotating shifts with approximately 3 caregivers for 30 children on each shift. A second group consisted of a pilot unit in which the number of children were reduced to approximately 10, and the pool of caregivers was re-

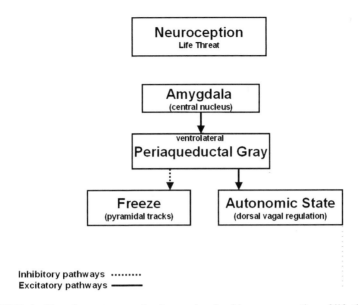

FIGURE 4. Neural structures and pathways involved in a neuroception of life threat.

duced to 4. If neuroception of safety is necessary to promote appropriate social behavior, then familiarity of caregiver would be critical. By having familiar caregivers, the child's detection of the caregiver's face, voice, and movements (the features that define a safe and trustworthy person) should trigger the inhibitory pathways to disenable the limbic defense system and foster the behaviors expressed by the social engagement system. In support of this model, the study demonstrated a monotonic relation between the number of different caregivers that a child had contact with and the indices of RAD. On all measures, the standard unit children were more likely to have higher indices of RAD, and on some measures the pilot group did not differ from the children who were never institutionalized. Thus, once we understand the contextual and social features that inhibit the neural circuits that mediate defensive behavioral strategies, we can optimize the developmental consequences of the neural circuits that promotes social engagement behaviors.

ACKNOWLEDGMENTS

This study was supported in part by a grant from the National Institutes of Health (MH60625). Several of the ideas presented in this article are the product of discussions with C. Sue Carter.

REFERENCES

1. BOWLBY, J. 1982. Attachment and Loss. 2nd ed. Vol. 1. Basic Books. New York.

2. AINSWORTH, M., M. BLEHAR, E. WATERS, *et al.* 1978. Patterns of Attachment: A Psychological Study of the Strange Situation. Erlbaum Publishers. Hillsdale, NJ.
3. CASSIDY, J. & P.R. SHAVER. 1999. Handbook of Attachment: Theory, Research, and Clinical Application. Guilford Press. New York.
4. PORGES, S.W. 2001. The Polyvagal Theory: Phylogenetic Substrates of a Social Nervous System. Int. J. Psychophysiol. **42:** 123–146.
5. NEWMAN, J.D. 1988. The Physiological Control of Mammalian Vocalizations. Plenum Press. New York.
6. PORGES, S.W. 1995. Orienting in a defensive world: mammalian modifications of our evolutionary heritage: a Polyvagal Theory. Psychophysiology **32:** 301–318.
7. PORGES, S.W. 1997. Emotion: an evolutionary by-product of the neural regulation of the autonomic nervous system. Ann. N.Y. Acad. Sci. **807:** 62–77.
8. PORGES, S.W. 1998. Love: an emergent property of the mammalian autonomic nervous system. Psychoneuroendocrinology **23:** 837–861.
9. BUENO, L., M. GUE, M.J. FARGEAS, *et al.* 1989. Vagally mediated inhibition of acoustic stress-induced cortisol release by orally administered kappa-opioid substances in dogs. Endocrinology **124:** 1788–1703.
10. TRUEX, R.C. & M.B. CARPENTER. 1969. Human Neuroanatomy. 6th ed. Williams and Wilkins. Baltimore, MD.
11. MCEWEN, B.S. & J.C. WINGFIELD. 2003. The concept of allostasis in biology and biomedicine. Horm. Behav. **43:** 2–15.
12. PORGES, S.W., T.C. RINIOLO, T. MCBRIDE, et al. 2003. Heart rate and respiration in reptiles: contrasts between a sit-and-wait predator and an intensive forager. Brain Cogn. **52:** 88–96.
13. ADOLPHS, R. 2002. Trust in the brain. Nat. Neurosci. **5:** 192–193.
14. WINSTON, J.S., B.A. STRANGE, J. O'DOHERTY, et al. 2002. Automatic and intentional brain responses during evaluation of trustworthiness of faces. Nat. Neurosci. **5:** 277–283.
15. PESSOA, L., M. MCKENNA, E. GUTIERREZ, et al. 2002. Neuroprocessing of emotional faces requires attention. Proc. Natl. Acad. Sci. USA **99:** 11458–11463.
16. KEAY, K.A. & R. BANDLER. 2001. Parallel circuits mediating distinct emotional coping reactions to different types of stress. Neurosci. Biobehav. Rev. **25:** 669–678.
17. LEITE-PANISSI, C.R., N.C. COIMBRA & L. MENESCAL-DE-OLIVEIRA. 2003. The cholinergic stimulation of the central amygdala modifying the tonic immobility response and antinociception in guinea pigs depends on the ventrolateral periaqueductal gray. Brain Res. Bull. **60:** 167–178.
18. RIZVI, T.A., M. ENNIS, M.M. BEHBEHANI, *et al.* 1991. Connections between the central nucleus of the amygdala and the midbrain periaqueductal gray: topography and reciprocity. J. Comp. Neurol. **303:** 121–131.
19. HOFER, M.A. 1970. Cardiac respiratory function during sudden prolonged immobility in wild rodents. Psychosom. Med. **32:** 633–647.
20. RICHTER, C.P. 1957. On the phenomenon of sudden death in animals and man. Psychosom. Med. **19:** 191–198.
21. CARTER, C.S. 1998. Neuroendocrine perspectives on social attachment and love. Psychoneuroendocrinology **23:** 779–818.
22. INSEL, T.R. & L.J. YOUNG. 2001. The neurobiology of attachment. Nat. Rev. Neurosci. **2:** 129–136.
23. DANIELS, D., R.R. MISELIS & L.M. FLANAGAN-CATO. 1999. Central neuronal circuit innervating the lordosis-producing muscles defined by transneuronal transport of pseudorabies virus. J. Neurosci. **19:** 2823–2833.
24. STERN, J.M. 1997. Offspring-induced nurturance: animal-human parallels. Dev. Psychobiol. **31:** 19–37.
25. LONSTEIN, J.S. & J.M. STERN. 1998. Site and behavioral specificity of periaqueductal gray lesions on postpartum sexual, maternal, and aggressive behaviors in rats. Brain Res. **804:** 21–35.
26. CARTER, C.S. & E.B. KEVERNE. 2002. The neurobiology of social affiliation and pair bonding. In Hormones, Brain, and Behavior. D.W. Pfaff *et al.*, Eds.: 299–337. Academic Press. San Diego.

27. WINSLOW, J.T. & T.R. INSEL. 2002. The social deficits of the oxytocin knockout mouse. Neuropeptides **36:** 221–229.
28. ZEANAH, C.H. 2000. Disturbances of attachment in young children adopted from institutions. J. Dev. Behav. Pediatr. **21:** 230–236.
29. SMYKE, A.T., A. DUMITRESCU & C.H. ZEANAH. 2002. Attachment disturbances in young children. I: The continuum of caretaking casuality. J. Am. Acad. Child Adolesc. Psychiatry **41:** 972–982.

Can We Develop a Neurobiological Model of Human Social–Emotional Development?

Integrative Thoughts on the Effects of Separation on Parent–Child Interactions

CHARLES A. NELSON

Institute of Child Development, Department of Pediatrics, and Center for Neurobehavioral Development, University of Minnesota, Minneapolis, Minnesota 55455, USA

ABSTRACT: After summarizing the main points raised in articles by Kaslow *et al.* and Plotsk, a number of questions that derive from these authors' work are listed. Additional questions are then posed, the answers to which will likely facilitate one's ability to translate animal models of child psychopathology into human terms. After summarizing the various advantages and disadvantages to models using mice, rats, and monkeys, several examples of recent research that have attempted to meld animal models with human studies are described.

KEYWORDS: neuroscience; development; psychobiology; brain; adversity; early experience

INTRODUCTION

The goal of this article is to integrate and synthesize articles by Nadine Kaslow and colleagues and Paul Plotsky, with a specific eye toward addressing the challenges of translating rodent and nonhuman primate models of child psychopathology to the human condition. The article by Kaslow was primarily focused on the various factors that contribute to child maltreatment, notable among them being mothers with a history of intimate partner violence. The article by Plotsky was concerned with the psychobiological and neurobiological sequelae of early adversity in rodents. Although at first glance these articles appear to be addressing quite dissimilar topics, they have in common the theme of the impact of early psychosocial adversity on later development.

Kaslow's article is primarily focused on the antecedent conditions that correlate with child maltreatment. As has been well documented by a number of investigators, African-American children disproportionately experience poverty, violent crime, and racial oppression, all of which, in turn, lead to an elevated risk of emotional problems, behavioral problems, and other psychosocial difficulties. Kaslow describes many of the risk factors that increase the chance of psychosocial sequelae,

Address for correspondence: Charles A. Nelson, Ph.D., Institute of Child Development, University of Minnesota, 51 East River Road, Minneapolis, MN 55455.
canelson@umn.edu

Ann. N.Y. Acad. Sci. 1008: 48–54 (2003). © 2003 New York Academy of Sciences.
doi: 10.1196/annals.1301.005

although she focuses most on mothers with a history of intimate partner violence (IPV). Some of the epidemiological variables that correlate with IPV include family dysfunction, separation from parent, frequent moves, involvement of others in the family's life, and history of maltreatment. The results of a pilot study are reported, in which IPV directly or indirectly contributed a significant portion of the variance in internalizing and externalizing symptoms in children.

Plotsky's article serves as a review of the now-extensive literature on the effects of early stressful experience on brain and behavioral development in rodents. He begins by providing an overview of the hypothalamic–pituitary–adrenal (HPA) axis and then turns his attention to a review of the effects of exposure to stress in the perinatal period. He reported that in the rodent, early adversity (including separation) is associated with (among others): later anxiety-like behaviors, deficits in social behavior, alterations in HPA functioning, down-regulation of hippocampal neurogenesis, and a reduction in dendritic branching and synaptogenesis. He speculates about the mechanisms that may underlie these effects. These included the following. First, the timing of the insult (or the enrichment) interacts with developmental trajectory (i.e., sensitive periods for organization of neural systems). Second, environmental factors interact with existing genetic liabilities. Third, proper organization of the central nervous system requires experience-expectant input. Fourth, experience alters levels of gene expression. Fifth, experience alters dendritic morphology probably via calcium-dependent signaling cascades. Sixth, regionally and temporally specific effects are the result of "conditional" signaling (i.e., GC interacting with other intracellular signaling cascades activated by particular stimulus). Finally, changes in critical central nervous system regions may serve as factors conferring vulnerability or resilience.

Each of these articles adds considerably to our knowledge of the effects of early adverse experiences on later development. They also raise several questions that would prove fruitful areas of future research. For example, in the case of Kaslow's work, one might ask:

1. Do different types of abuse (or different contexts in which abuse occurs) have different functional outcomes?

2. Is there a sensitive period whereby child maltreatment does *not* lead to later intimate partner violence?

3. What are the genotypic and phenotypic profiles of (a) those who abuse children and (b) children who are abused?

4. What are the specific characteristics of "negative environments" and can these be modeled in the animal?

5. How does the experience of being maltreated weave its way into the brain, altering neural circuitry and subsequent behavior, and can this be studied in the human?

6. Finally, is there a sensitive period for intervening so as to alter changes in brain and behavior?

Similarly, some of the questions we need to ponder regarding Plotsky's work include:

1. What is the human analog to "anxious" behavior in the rodent? (And a related question: Can a rat experience anxiety in the conventional human sense, or just display discrete behaviors we associate in the human with the state of being anxious?)

2. What is the human analog to early maternal rodent behavior (e.g., what is the human equivalent to licking and grooming)?

3. What are the functional consequences of reduced neurogenesis, dendritic branching, and synaptogenesis?

4. What would we extrapolate to be the human age-equivalent to the sensitive period for maternal separation in the rodent?

5. Can the maladaptive neurobehavioral sequelae of early separation be (a) ameliorated by rearing in complex environments? (b) avoided by prophylactic pharmacological treatment?

6. Is the rodent the best species for developing a neurobiological model of human social behavior?

7. What are the *functional* consequences of reduced neurogenesis, dendritic branching, and synaptogenesis (i.e., how would this neurobiological imprint manifest itself in behavior)?

There is no doubt that good progress could be made in addressing these questions at the present time. However, a more thorough understanding of these issues would be facilitated by simultaneously improving our knowledge of the following:

1. An understanding of behavioral development in terms of the specific molecules in the specific synapses of specific neurons within specific circuits of the brain … and how these molecules, synapses, neurons and circuits are influenced by experience.

2. Knowledge of the size, complexity, and specific inventories of the mammalian genome and how this information is expressed neurophysiologically, metabolically, and behaviorally.

3. An improvement in our ability to examine the functioning of the brain noninvasively … and to relate such functioning to specific molecules, synapses, etc.

4. An informed comparative perspective, including (a) the ability to distinguish the strengths and weaknesses of a mouse/rat/monkey model of brain and behavior, and (b) the ability to work across species in a seamless fashion, such that the constructs and methods of studying one species easily generalize to another.

Clearly, adopting a comparative perspective concerning the effects of early adversity on later development would go a long way toward addressing these issues; indeed, a comparative perspective is probably *required* to do so. However, here we must consider the various pros and cons to such a perspective. Specifically, which species would be best for modeling which forms of psychopathology in the human? Below I describe some of the advantages and disadvantages of the more commonly used species.

SOME QUALIFIERS TO A COMPARATIVE APPROACH

Mouse Models

The primary advantage of mouse models is what they have to offer regarding behavior genetics; indeed, the mouse genome is now nearly fully worked out, and we have much to gain by incorporating such information into our models. On the other hand, the use of mice in comparative studies is also limited by their limited behavioral repertoire, particularly in context of modeling complex and/or "higher level" human behavior.

Rat Models

There are several advantages to rat models that must be considered. First, they provide an excellent venue for understanding anatomy and circuitry. Second, a fair amount is known about genotype–phenotype interactions. Third, they represent a reasonable approximation for some human social behaviors. In terms of disadvantages, similar to mouse models, they may be limited in modeling complex human behavior (e.g., the limited frontal cortex will likely constrain knowledge of higher cognitive/emotional functions). Second, it is hard to work out the behavior genetics (at least relative to mouse). Third, their short life span may limit generalizability to human behaviors that unfold over long time periods (e.g., higher cognitive functions, illnesses such as schizophrenia).

Monkey Models

Not surprisingly, as one gets closer to the human on the evolutionary scale, the advantages increase exponentially. For example, many nonhuman primates are good for understanding anatomy and circuitry, and for modeling many complex human behaviors (including social–emotional behaviors). They are also not bad for simulating changes over the human life span. Their disadvantages include challenges in working out the genetics, and ethical and political limitations in what kinds of studies can be done (particularly behavioral manipulations).

Over and above the pros and cons of each of the three species listed above, each species also brings with it more general challenges in (1) methods that are species specific; for example, it is unusual to employ patch clamping in human tissue or functional magnetic resonance imaging in the mouse; (2) levels of analysis, thus, the use of gene arrays is much better worked out in the mouse than in the human, whereas linkage studies are fairly common in the human; (3) timetables for brain development; for example, the hippocampus is very immature in the newborn rat, whereas it is much more mature in the human newborn. In addition, there is no substantial prefrontal cortex in the mouse, whereas there is in the human.

FIGURE 1 is an attempt to provide a graphic illustration of the methods available across species.

My remarks thus far may present a rather conservative picture of the challenges of working across species. In the remainder of this article, I draw on some examples of research that I believe represent reasonable solutions to many of the challenges raised above. These examples come from a research network on *Early Experience and Brain Development*, supported by the John D. and Catherine T. MacArthur Foundation.

Some Model Examples of Model Systems

Emotion Recognition (David Amaral, Judy Cameron, Charles Nelson, and Marian Sigman): In our attempt at studying a basic and elementary aspect of social emotional development, we have attempted to examine the recognition of facial emotion across three samples of humans (typically developing 2–3-year-olds, young children

Overall Strategy: Methods and Species

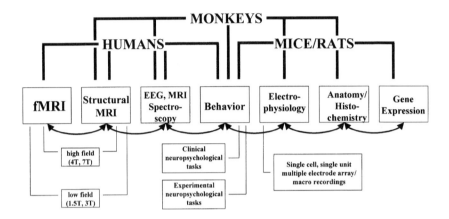

FIGURE 1. Schematic illustration of the various methods available for studying brain and brain function across different species. (Reproduced, with permission, from C.A. Nelson, F.E. Bloom, J. Cameron, D. Amaral, R. Dahl & D. Pine. 2002. An integrative, multidisciplinary approach to the study of brain–behavior relations in the context of typical and atypical development. Dev. Psychopathol. **14:** 499–520.)

with autism, and infants and young children who have experienced institutional rearing in Bucharest, Romania) and two samples of Rhesus monkeys (those with and without lesions to the amygdala and those who have experienced social bond disruption). We began our work by attempting to use an identical experimental protocol across all sites; specifically, the use of a touch-screen monitor to which participants (be they human children or monkeys) would be rewarded for responding to specific stimuli. Thus, we used a simultaneous discrimination task and a match-to-sample task whereby participants would be presented with one facial emotion and then asked to discriminate this from another. Rewards were offered for correct responding. (Indeed, we initially agreed to use the same rewards—M&M's®—because they were equally powerful in motivating both monkeys and children.)

It quickly became apparent that human 2–3-year-olds behaved differently in this paradigm than monkeys, and that monkeys separated from their mothers behaved differently from animals reared with their mothers but who had incurred lesions of the amygdala. For example, some 2-year-old children would not touch the screen because they had been told not to at home (with their family's home computer); others would horde the M&M's in their mouths until their cheeks were close to bursting, at which point they stopped working on the task. Monkeys, in turn, would periodically not work for reward, or would not look at the pictures. In the end, then, it was decided to capitalize on each species' strengths and weaknesses and in so doing, modify the procedures. Thus, whereas David Amaral had great success in using the touch-screen system with his monkeys, Judy Cameron adopted a visual paired comparison procedure, in which no overt response (except an eye movement) was required. Similarly, whereas we were able to use the touch-screen system successfully with 3-year-olds, we could not do so with younger children; in Romania, for example, we adopted the same preferential looking procedure as Judy Cameron.

Overall, we learned from this project that the concept of using identical experimental platforms to test children and monkeys is laudable, but the reality is more complicated.

Social/Cognitive (Jocelyne Bachevalier and Charles Nelson): What is the neural basis for the ability to recognize faces and facial expressions in monkey and human infants? Here, we hope to identify the precise circuitry in the infant monkey that subserves face and emotion recognition. In addition, we seek to identify the neurophysiological "signatures" (vis-à-vis various components of the event-related potential (ERP)) observed in monkey face tasks modeled after those done with human infants. Finally, in the monkey we hoped to ascertain the effects of specific lesions of the "face area" on (1) behavioral performance and (2) specific components of the ERP.

In this project, a clone of Charles Nelson's human ERP laboratory was constructed in Jocelyne Bachevalier's monkey laboratory. Nearly identical experimental procedures as used by Nelson with human infants also was exported to the monkey laboratory, such that (1) electrodes were placed on the head noninvasively using electrode paste and tape, (2) virtually identical ERP recording procedures were being used, and (3) the experimental design of presenting different faces or different facial expressions were being used. Of course, the most obvious difference is that images of human faces are being used in Nelson's human infant laboratory and images of monkey faces are being used in Bachevalier's monkey laboratory. Although in its early stages, thus far the project appears to be succeeding, perhaps because behavioral responses are not being required.

Comparative Studies of EEG Laterality (David Amaral, Nathan Fox, Charles Nelson, and Michael Spezio): Fox and Davidson, among others, have demonstrated that individuals rated as high in positive affect (e.g., high in approach behavior) show greater left versus right frontal EEG activity, whereas those rated as high in negative affect (e.g., wary of novelty) show the reverse pattern (for general overview, see Fox, Henderson & Marshall[1]). What has yet to be definitively determined is the neural source of these EEG asymmetries. For example, although Fox has argued that the source of these frontal EEG asymmetries lie in structures in frontal cortex, it is possible that deeper structures in this circuit, such as the amygdala, are responsible for these asymmetries (e.g., through volume conduction amygdala activity projects to frontal cortex). Thus, EEG activity is being recorded from the amygdala itself, along with surface electrodes attached to the monkey's scalp. To examine the issue of source in more detail, we are also examining how transient deactivation of the amygdala affects EEG asymmetry. Here, recordings are made during the time the amygdala has been "turned off" with muscimol. Finally, in this project we are asking what is the similarity between recordings made from specific structures (e.g., amygdala) versus those we record at the scalp, a question loaded with importance for deriving or estimating sources from scalp-recorded activity.

These are but three examples of projects that attempt to adopt a comparative approach to brain–behavior relations. Clearly, these projects are laden with methodological challenges, some of which already have been identified, and some of which will likely not make themselves known until the projects are further along. Nevertheless, I have used these as examples of how one might translate animal work to human work, and vice versa. The ultimate strength of animal models lies primarily in how closely they can mimic the human condition, and the likelihood of doing so increases as a function of the similarity in methods and constructs across species. As the armamentarium of the cognitive and affective neuroscientist improves, so, too, will the likelihood of successfully translating animal work to human work. Over and above methods, however, one must also be mindful of whether the construct being evaluated is the same across species (and across age, an equally nontrivial issue). I am optimistic that by improving the communication between those studying humans and those developing animal models, both challenges will be overcome.

REFERENCE

1. FOX, N.A., H.A. HENDERSON & P.J. MARSHALL. 2001. The biology of temperament: an integrative approach. *In* Handbook of Developmental Cognitive Neuroscience. C.A. Nelson and M. Luciana, Eds.: 631–645. MIT Press. Cambridge, MA.

Family and Community Factors that Predict Internalizing and Externalizing Symptoms in Low-Income, African-American Children

A Preliminary Report

NADINE J. KASLOW,[a] SHERYL HERON,[b] DEBRA KIM ROBERTS,[a] MARTIE THOMPSON,[c] OMAR GUESSOUS,[d] AND CLAUDIA JONES[a]

[a]Emory University School of Medicine, Department of Psychiatry and Behavioral Sciences, Atlanta, Georgia 30303, USA

[b]Emory University School of Medicine, Department of Emergency Medicine, Atlanta, Georgia 30303, USA

[c]Clemson University, Department of Public Health Sciences, Clemson, South Carolina 29634, USA

[d]Georgia State University, Department of Psychology, Atlanta, Georgia 30303-3082, USA

ABSTRACT: To learn more about the roots of internalizing and externalizing problems in low-income, African-American children, aged 8–12 years, particularly for family and community factors, we aimed to determine which variables (mother's psychological functioning, mother's intimate partner violence status [IPV], family cohesion and adaptability, neighborhood disorder) uniquely predicted a child's internalizing distress and externalizing distress, and the amount of variance explained by the model. Results from the regression model predicting internalizing distress indicates that the five predictor variables accounted for 38% of the variance. Two of the five predictors were significantly related to child's internalizing distress scores: mother's intimate partner violence status and maternal psychological distress. Results from the regression model predicting externalizing distress indicates that the five predictor variables accounted for 8% of the variance. The two predictors significantly related to child's externalizing distress scores were levels of family cohesion and maternal psychological distress. Directions for future research and clinical implications are provided.

KEYWORDS: family factors; community factors; internalizing and externalizing symptoms; African-American children

Address for correspondence: Nadine J. Kaslow, Ph.D., Emory University School of Medicine, Department of Psychiatry and Behavioral Sciences, Atlanta, Georgia 30303. Voice: 404-616-4757; fax: 404-616-2898.
nkaslow@emory.edu

Ann. N.Y. Acad. Sci. 1008: 55–68 (2003). © 2003 New York Academy of Sciences.
doi: 10.1196/annals.1301.007

INTRODUCTION

Historically, African-American children have borne a disproportionate share of the burden of poverty.[1] A greater percentage of these children as compared with their white counterparts are victims of violent crime and racial oppression.[2] Urban, African-American young people exposed to poverty and violence have been found to be at elevated risk of manifesting emotional and behavioral problems and other psychosocial difficulties.[3] Their families frequently encounter stresses associated with young parenthood, a multitude of negative life events, economic hardship, and parental mental health and health problems, all of which may be associated with greater vulnerability to psychological distress in the children.[4–6] Poverty reduces caregivers' capacity to effectively parent and makes them more likely to experience psychological distress in the face of the myriad negative life events commonly associated with residing in economically deprived environments. Furthermore, economic hardship has an adverse impact on children's psychological adjustment in part through its influence on parent's behavior toward their children. Unfortunately, investigations into the role of family and community factors on low-income, African-American children's internalizing and externalizing behavior problems have not captured the sensitivity and complexity of these relationships. To add to our understanding of family and community factors that predict internalizing and externalizing symptoms in low-income, African-American youth, we examined four ecological risk factors: maternal psychological distress, maternal intimate partner violence (IPV) status, family adaptability and cohesion, and neighborhood risks and resources.

Internalizing and Externalizing Behavior Problems in Low-Income and African-American Youth

Data from the standardization sample for the Child Behavior Checklist and the Teacher Rating Form revealed social class findings on many internalizing and externalizing symptoms scales; children from lower income groups have higher problem scores.[7] Also, African-American children received higher scores on 6/21 Teacher Rating Form problem scales.[7]

By the time low-income, African-American children reach first grade, many are already behind nationally standardized norms in their cognitive performance and behavior.[8] There is some evidence to suggest a high correlation among internalizing and externalizing symptoms among low-income, urban, African-American children.[9] In addition, African-American children are more likely to manifest both internalizing behavior problems, such as depression[10] and externalizing behavior problems[11] than are youth from other ethnic backgrounds. This has been attributed to the fact that families confronted by economic struggles associated with poverty often lack the resources to tend to their children's needs and development.[12]

There are multiple risk factors associated with the emergence of behavior problems in low-income African-American children, including attachment insecurity, maladaptive coping strategies, maternal depression, inadequate parenting and discipline, family discord, low levels of extrafamilial social support, and community risks.[13–16] As risk factors pile up, children's behavior problems increase.[8] Several factors that protect against the development of internalizing and externalizing behavior problems also have been reported. For example, greater parental religiosity leads to more cohesive family relationships and low levels of interparental conflict, which in turn are associated with fewer behavior problems in young people.[17]

Maternal Psychological Distress

Over the past two decades, there has been a proliferation of research on the links between maternal psychopathology and distress and internalizing and externalizing behavior problems in children. However, there is a paucity of research focusing on this link within the African-American community. Consistent with the large body of research supporting the link between maternal depression and psychopathology in children,[18] both internalizing and externalizing symptoms in African-American children are linked to depressive symptoms in their mothers.[8,15,19] As another example, early-onset maternal antisocial behavior is predictive of externalizing behavior problems in at-risk youth.[20] Finally, children's subjective experiences of the parents' psychological distress are associated with their own psychological adjustment and symptom presentation.[21]

Intimate Partner Violence

In the United States, between 3.3 and 10 million children between the ages of 3 and 17 years are exposed to IPV annually.[22] The numbers are probably much higher because of the underreporting of IPV. Children who witness IPV often witness mild to severe forms of physical and nonphysical IPV, including serious verbal altercations, choking, and threats with and use of weapons.[23] This type of witnessing can interfere with the child's developing a sense of security and belief in a safe world. Quantitative and qualitative research on child witnesses suggest that the experience of violence and the surrounding stress inducing family circumstances creates a multidimensional impact upon the child and effects the child's adjustment.[24,25]

Children of battered women are two to four times more likely than children from nonviolent homes to exhibit clinically significant emotional and behavioral problems, anxiety, posttraumatic stress disorder, depression, aggression, hostility, social withdrawal, and low self-esteem.[26–30] Whereas some studies have found higher levels of both internalizing and externalizing problems in children from violent homes, other studies report differences only on internalizing problems or externalizing problems. A recent, methodologically sophisticated study found that 30% of youth developed both internalizing and externalizing problems, others demonstrated only internalizing or externalizing problems (39%), and 31% had no symptoms indicative of emotional or behavioral problems.[28] Similar findings were found for boys and girls. The factors that predicted which type of adjustment would occur included the amount and type of aggression children had experienced and their perceptions and appraisals of parental conflict.

Note that a study of the influence of adult IPV on children's internalizing and externalizing behavior problems in a sample of monozygotic and dizygotic twins revealed that adult IPV accounted for 2% and 5% of the variation in children's internalizing and externalizing behavior problems, respectively, independent of genetic effects, suggesting that IPV influences children's behavior problems beyond genetic influences.[31]

Family Environment

Consistent with literature among diverse ethnic groups, there is mounting evidence that the quality of the home environment predicts the emergence of internalizing and externalizing behavior problems in low-income, African-American children.[8] Youth from struggling families evidence markedly poorer psychological adjustment than do youth from well-functioning families.[32] Within the African-American community, low levels of family cohesion are particularly associated with psychological distress,[33] including in extreme forms (e.g., suicidal behavior).[34] The more negative aspects of family functioning that children experience, the more impaired their psychological functioning appears to be.[35]

Conversely, several family factors have been shown to serve as buffers against the emergence of psychological symptoms in children. Specifically, a warm and supportive mother–child relationship and maternal monitoring of child behavior have been associated with fewer internalizing and externalizing behaviors in African-American youngsters in urban communities.[35,36] In a related vein, consistent family routines and harmony in the mother–child dyad have been predictive of lower levels of both internalizing and externalizing behavior problems among rural, African-American children living in the South.[37] Furthermore, when children have available support from extended family members, family stress and maladaptive interaction patterns do not appear to be associated with the manifestation of internalizing and externalizing problems.[38] Finally, among children from single-parent African-American families, adaptive classroom processes (high levels of organization, rule clarity, student involvement) can serve a protective and stabilizing function when parenting processes are dysfunctional.[39]

Neighborhood Factors

Although family factors contribute to child psychosocial adjustment, systems-oriented psychologists, including developmental and community psychologists, as well as sociologists, have underscored the central role of community-level variables.[12,40] Historically, research on the quality of neighborhood settings has focused on structural variables (e.g., family income, number of single-parent households, public services, and number of public assistance recipients). However, these characteristics do not capture what families view as their immediate neighborhoods. Thus, there have been recent efforts to focus on families' subjective perceptions about the neighborhood.[41]

The few studies that have examined neighborhood factors and behavior problems in African-American children indicate that perceptions of risks and resources are more strongly related to child psychological symptoms than are structural indicators.[42] In a sample of 8–12-year-old, predominately African-American urban children, youth living in very poor neighborhoods with moderate crime levels had more externalizing behavior problems than children living in relatively low-crime, low-poverty areas [43]. The link between neighborhood factors and externalizing behavior problems has been found to be mediated by family stress and maternal distress and moderated by family cohesion.[8,43,44] Others also have found that community risk and poverty are linked to both internalizing and externalizing difficulties through proximal family variables.[15] Research also reveals that neighborhood factors may be more influential for African-American children living in urban as compared with rural environments in terms of the manifestation of externalizing problems.[45] Taken together, the relevant research indicates that African-American children, particularly those from low-income urban environments and those living in single-parent households, are at risk for psychosocial adjustment difficulties, including internalizing and externalizing problems. Neighborhood factors play a role in socioemotional outcomes even when family factors are controlled.[46]

PURPOSE

To learn more about the roots of internalizing and externalizing problems in low-income, African-American children, particularly for family and community factors, we had two main objectives. The first aim was to determine which variables (mother's psychological functioning, mother's IPV status, family cohesion and adaptability, neighborhood disorder) uniquely predicted a child's internalizing distress and the amount of variance explained by the model. The second goal of the study was to ascertain which variables (mother's psychological functioning, mother's IPV status, family cohesion and adaptability, neighborhood disorder) uniquely predicted child's externalizing distress and the amount of variance explained by the model. The data presented below are based on findings from a larger study funded by the Centers for Disease Control and Prevention examining the links between IPV and child adjustment and child maltreatment within low-income, urban, African-American mother–child dyads. The findings are based on a relatively small sample, as data collection is not yet complete, and thus should be considered preliminary. The research is being conducted at Grady Health System (GHS), an Emory University School of Medicine affiliated, and large, public, comprehensive hospital system located in downtown Atlanta.

METHOD

Participants

Participants consisted of two groups of African-American women aged 18–64 years who sought treatment at GHS and for one of the 8–12-year-old children for whom they were a legal guardian: (1) 39 who had experienced IPV within the past year (IPV+) and (2) 17 who had never experienced IPV (IPV−). To meet inclusion criteria, the female caregiver (e.g., biological mother, stepmother, grandmother, aunt, and neighbor) must have lived with the child at least 50% of the time during the past year. For the IPV+ group, the primary female caregiver must have reported on the Universal Violence Prevention Screening Protocol (UVPSP)[47] at least one incident of IPV. For the IPV− group, the primary female caregiver must have reported on the UVPSP no prior experiences of being the victim of IPV.

Procedure

Recruitment: IPV Cases

The Principal Investigator (PI) was available by pager 24 h/day, 7 days/week to hospital personnel in one of the four emergency care clinics in the hospital regarding all African-American women, aged 18–64, who indicated on the UVPSP that they had experienced IPV in the prior year, had a child aged 8–12, and had agreed to having the project team contacted. A team member approached eligible and potentially interested women once they had been medically stabilized, explained the study, and answered questions. If the woman was interested in participating, an interview was scheduled for her and one of her randomly selected 8–12-year-old children. These interviews were scheduled at a mutually convenient time within 1 week of the initial encounter and were rescheduled for a maximum of three no-shows or cancellations. Each woman received a reminder call and card to increase the likelihood of participation.

Recruitment: Controls

Team members recruited control participants by approaching another woman in the same setting who denied any IPV experiences on the UVPSP and who had an 8–12-year-old child. They explained the study and answered questions. If the woman was willing to participate, an interview was scheduled for her and a randomly selected 8–12-year-old child using the strategy described above.

Screening

Once consent/assent was obtained, a brief screening occurred to assess the eligibility of each participant. Different team members interviewed the caregiver and the child concurrently in separate rooms. Caregivers were asked about their medical history and completed the Mini-Mental State Examination[48] and the Rapid Estimate of Adult Literacy in Medicine[49] to exclude those with life-threatening medical conditions or those with significant cognitive limitations. A Psychotic Screening Questionnaire ruled out people who were acutely psychotic. Medical history data were gathered for each child to exclude youths with life-threatening conditions. Each child was administered the Peabody Picture Vocabulary Test–III (PPVT-III)[50] to exclude children with IQs less than 70. If a caregiver or child did not meet inclusion criterion, the dyad was excluded after this phase and paid $5 plus transportation costs. The child also received a toy.

Assessment

Because of the overall low rates of functional literacy in the patients who receive services at GHS,[49] we administered the assessment battery verbally to caregiver–child dyads meeting inclusion criteria. Female caregivers completed measures in the following order: background data, and measures of service utilization, psychological functioning, substance abuse, coping strategies, family functioning, family violence, social support, spiritual well-being, life events, and community context. They also completed mothers' rating of their children's psychological functioning. Child participants completed self-report forms as follows: background data, and measures of psychological and adaptive behavior functioning, coping strategies, family functioning, family violence, social support, religious involvement and spiritual, life events, and community context. For this report only, background data; caregiver measures of psychological distress, family functioning, and neighborhood disorder; and caregiver reports of their children's psychological distress were included. Caregiver–child dyads were paid $50 for completing the 2.5–3-h protocol. Transportation costs also were covered. The child also received a toy. Data were collected by research team members who were graduate students, postdoctoral fellows, and residents trained and supervised weekly.

Measures

Demographic Data Questionnaires—Caregiver and Child Forms

The Demographic Data Questionnaire–Caregiver obtained information on the mother's age, sex, education, social class, relationship status, living situation, and medical and medication status. The Demographic Data Questionnaire–Child provided information on the child's age and grade, sex, religion, family and household constellation, educational status, and medical and medication status.

Symptom Checklist 90—Revised

The 90-item Symptom Checklist 90—Revised (SCL-90R)[51] assesses on a five-point Likert scale nine symptom subscales and three overall scales. Only the global severity index summary scale was used. The scale has good reliability and validity.

Family Adaptability and Cohesion Evaluation Scales

The 30-item Family Adaptability and Cohesion Evaluation Scales (FACES II)[52] assesses family adaptability (extent to which the family system is flexible and able to change) and cohesion emotional bonding that family members have toward one another. Responses are on a five-point Likert scale. The adaptability subscale includes four levels: very flexible, flexible, structured, and rigid. The cohesion subscale also consists of four levels: very connected, connected, separated, and disengaged. This scale has good reliability and validity.

Perceived Neighborhood Disorder Scale

The 15-items Perceived Neighborhood Disorder Scale (PNDS)[53] was used to assess perceptions of neighborhood conditions and activities that are indicative of the breakdown of social and physical disorder and order. The scale has good internal consistency reliability.

Child Behavior Checklist

The Child Behavior Checklist (CBCL),[7,54] a 113-item questionnaire, covers the behavior problems of children aged 4–16 years according to caregiver report. Each item is scored on a 0–2 scale. The instrument includes three competence scales and eight syndrome scales (anxious/depressed, withdrawn/depressed, somatic complaints, social problems, thought problems, attention problems, rule-breaking behavior, and aggressive behavior). Based on responses to the syndrome scales, an internalizing, externalizing, and total problem score is obtained. For this study, only the internalizing and externalizing scores were used.

Data Analysis

We first examined the sample composition and the frequencies of the main variables. Because these preliminary data analyses are based on a small sample, we limited our inclusion of predictors to five (at least one predictor per 10 subjects). We next conducted correlational analyses to examine the bivariate associations among the study variables. Last, we conducted two parallel multiple regression models, one predicting child's internalizing distress symptoms (CBCL–internalizing total scale) and one predicting child's externalizing distress symptoms (CBCL–externalizing total scale) to examine the unique contributions of each predictor variable in accounting for variance in distress scores while holding the other predictors constant.

RESULTS

The mothers ranged in age from 22 to 52 years, with the average age being 31.27 years (SD = 6.52). The mothers ranged in number of years of education from 9 to 18, with the mean years of education being 11.97 (SD = 1.97). Approximately one-third (34%) of the women were employed. Almost 18% considered themselves homeless. Over half of the sample (52%) received food stamps and almost one-third (32%) received TANF (temporary asssistance for needy families). Forty-two percent of the sample was single, 20% were married, 14% were separated or divorced, and 23% had a partner to whom they were not married. The children ranged in age from 8 to 12 years, with the mean age being 9.46 (SD = 1.36). Forty-five percent of the children were male and 55% were female.

In our sample of 39 IPV+ women and 17 IPV– women, almost one-third (32%) were above the clinical cut-point based on nonpatient norms for the general severity index of the SCL-90-R. The children also showed high levels of distress. Seven percent were in the borderline clinical range and 20% were in the clinical range on the CBCL–internalizing symptoms scale. Eleven percent were in the borderline clinical range and 32% were in the clinical range on the CBCL–externalizing symptoms scale. In terms of family cohesion, approximately one-third of the sample were classified as "disengaged," 25% were classified as "separated," 39% were classified as "connected," and 2% were classified as "very connected." In terms of family adaptability, one-quarter of the sample were classified as "rigid," 25% were classified as "structured," 28% were classified as "flexible," and 21% were classified as "very flexible." There are no normative data on neighborhood disorder by which to compare our sample.

As seen in TABLE 1, results from the bivariate correlational analyses indicated that children's internalizing and externalizing symptoms were highly related; higher scores on internalizing symptoms co-occurred with higher levels of externalizing symptoms ($R = .67$). Children's internalizing and externalizing distress levels were related to their mothers' level of global psychological distress ($R = .59$ and .29, respectively), such that as mothers' levels of distress increased, so too did their children's distress increase. Family cohesion and family adaptability were strongly correlated; higher levels of adaptability were associated with higher levels of cohesion ($R = .73$). Both family cohesion and family adaptability were negatively related to mothers' global distress levels; as family cohesion and adaptability increased, mothers' levels of global distress decreased ($R = -.55$ and -43, respectively). Family adaptability scores were also significantly related to neighborhood disorder scores; as mothers' ratings of their family's level of adaptability increased, their reports of neighborhood disorder levels decreased ($R = -.41$).

TABLE 1. Correlation coefficients for analysis variables

	1. CBCL–internalizing	2. CBCL–externalizing	3. IPV status	4. SCL-90-GSI	5. Family cohesion	6. Family adaptability	7. Neighborhood disorder
1. CBCL–internalizing	—						
2. CBCL–externalizing	0.67***	—					
3. IPV status	0.24	0.18	—				
4. SCL-90-GSI	0.59***	0.29*	0.67***	—			
5. Family cohesion	−0.22	−0.01	−0.25	−0.55***	—		
6. Family adaptability	−0.24	−0.16	−0.21	−0.43***	0.73***	—	
7. Neighborhood disorder	−0.08	0.09	0.05	0.06	−0.20	−0.41**	—

*$P \leq .05$; **$P \leq .01$; ***$P \leq .001$.

TABLE 2. Results of multiple regressions to predict CBCL–internalizing and CBCL–externalizing symptom score

	Internalizing		Externalizing	
	Beta	t	Beta	t
IPV status	-0.30^*	-2.04^*	-0.08	-0.45
Cohesion	0.31	1.80	0.43^*	2.06^*
Adaptability	-0.21	-1.24	-0.28	-1.32
Neighborhood disorder	-0.14	-1.18	0.04	0.27
SCL-90-GSI	0.87^{***}	5.15^{***}	0.46^*	2.25^*

$^*P < .05$; $^{***}P < .001$.

As seen in TABLE 2, results from the regression model predicting CBCL–internalizing distress indicated that the five predictor variables accounted for 38% of the variance (adjusted $R^2 = -.377$). In this multivariate model, two of the five predictors were significantly related to the child's internalizing distress scores. Specifically, children whose mothers were recent victims of IPV had higher scores on the CBCL–internalizing distress total scale than their counterparts whose mothers had not been victims of IPV. Children whose mothers had higher scores on global psychological distress were also more likely than children whose mothers reported less global distress symptoms to have higher scores on the CBCL–internalizing distress total scale.

Results from the regression model predicting CBCL–externalizing distress indicated that the five predictor variables accounted for 8% of the variance in externalizing distress symptoms (adjusted $R^2 = .078$). In this multivariate model, two of the five predictors were significantly related to child's externalizing distress scores. Specifically, children whose mothers had higher global levels of psychological distress were more likely than children whose mothers reported fewer global distress symptoms to have higher scores on the CBCL–externalizing distress total scale. Contrary to predictions, children whose mothers reported higher levels of family cohesion had higher scores on the CBCL–externalizing distress total scale than their counterparts whose mothers reported lower family cohesion.

DISCUSSION

The participants had relatively low incomes, with high rates of unemployment, homelessness, and dependence on public assistance. Both the caregivers and youth manifested relatively high levels of psychological distress. The majority of the families were relatively low on cohesion and flexibility. Consistent with the literature, there were significant correlations between children's levels of internalizing and externalizing symptoms, as well as between mothers' reports of their children's behavior and maternal psychological distress. In keeping with prior findings, families that were more cohesive were also more adaptable, and healthier family functioning was associated with lower levels of maternal distress and neighborhood disorder.

Family and community factors contributed significantly to the prediction of both internalizing and externalizing distress in 8–12-year-old, urban, African-American children. Children's internalizing symptoms were best predicted by recent experiences of IPV by their female caregivers and by their caregivers' levels of psychological distress. Children's externalizing symptoms were primarily accounted for by caregiver distress and counterintuitively, by higher levels of family cohesion.

The following are directions for future research. This study has focused primarily on determining family and community risk factors for the development of psychological symptoms in low-income, urban, African-American youth. However, most African-American children living in poor, urban communities are resilient and develop in a healthy manner.[55,56] Therefore, future investigations must examine family and community factors that protect children from developing behavior problems. This examination must include variables relevant to the African-American community, including kinship networks and the role of religion and spirituality. In addition, given the findings that IPV and child maltreatment often co-occur, it will be important to ascertain the role child maltreatment plays in enhancing the prediction of childhood psychological distress. Furthermore, given the central role of attachment relationships in the development of internalizing and externalizing problems in children, these relationships need to be assessed. Finally, it is crucial to gather children's view on their own symptoms, family patterns, and neighborhood contexts. These data will be available upon the completion of our study.

Our findings have several clinical implications. Low-income African-American children living in urban environments who manifest either internalizing or externalizing problems are likely to benefit from culturally competent family interventions that target reducing the child's and mother's psychological distress, enhancing family cohesion, and helping the families develop strategies for addressing neighborhood difficulties. It is imperative that these interventions target creating safety in the home environment or enabling families in which the mother is abused to find safety in the community. For those children and women whose psychological distress is clinically significant, psychopharmacological and/or evidenced-based individually oriented psychosocial interventions may be indicated. All of these interventions must build upon the strengths and resiliencies of each individual family member.

ACKNOWLEDGMENTS

This work is funded by a grant from the Centers for Disease Control and Prevention entitled "Domestic Violence and Child Maltreatment in Black Families."

REFERENCES

1. McLoyd, V. 1990. The impact of economic hardship on Black families and children: psychological distress, parenting, and socioemotional development. Child Dev. **61:** 311–346.
2. Coll, C.G. *et al.* 1996. An integrative model for the study of developmental competencies in minority children. Child Dev. **67:** 1891–1914.
3. McLoyd, V. 1998. Socioeconomic disadvantage and child development. Am. Psychol. **53:** 185–204.

4. FOREHAND, R. *et al.* 1998. The Family Health Project: psychosocial adjustment of children whose mothers are HIV-infected. J. Consult. Clin. Psychol. **66:** 513–520.
5. KLEBANOV, P., J. BROOKS-GUNN & G.J. DUNCAN. 1994. Does neighborhood and family poverty affect mothers' parenting, mental health, and social support? J. Marriage Fam. **56:** 441–455.
6. LUSTER, T. & H. MCADOO. 1994. Factors related to the achievement and adjustment of young African American children. Child Dev. **65:** 1080–1094.
7. ACHENBACH, T.M. & L.A. RESCORLA. 2001. Manual for the ASEBA School-Age Forms and Profiles: an integrated system of multi-informant assessment. ASEBA. Burlington, VT.
8. KRISHNAKUMAR, A. & M.M. BLACK. 2002. Longitudinal predictors of competence among African American children: the role of distal and proximal risk factors. J. Appl. Dev. Psychol. **23:** 237–266.
9. STEELE, R.G., L. ARMISTEAD & R. FOREHAND. 2000. Concurrent and longitudinal correlates of depressive symptoms among low-income, urban, African American children. J. Clin. Child Psychol. **29:** 76–85.
10. ROBERTS, R. & M. SOBHAN. 1992. Symptoms of depression in adolescence: a comparison of Anglo, African, and Hispanic Americans. J. Youth Adolesc. **21:** 639–651.
11. RANDOLPH, S.M. *et al.* 2000. Behavior problems of African American boys attending Head Start programs in violent neighborhoods. Early Educ. Dev. **11:** 339–356.
12. BROOKS-GUNN, J., G.J. DUNCAN & J.L. ABER, Eds. 1997. Neighborhood Poverty: Context and Consequences for Children. Russell Sage Foundation. New York.
13. ANAN, R.M. & D. BARNETT. 1999. Perceived social support mediates between prior attachment and subsequent adjustment: a study of urban, African American children. Dev. Psychol. **35:** 1210–1222.
14. DEATER-DECKARD, K. *et al.* 1996. Physical discipline among African American and European American mothers: links to children's externalizing behaviors. Dev. Psychol. **32:** 1065–1072.
15. JONES, D.J. *et al.* 2002. Psychosocial adjustment of African American children in single-mother families: a test of three risk models. J. Marriage Fam. **64:** 105–115.
16. STEELE, R.G. *et al.* 1999. Coping strategies and behavior problems of urban African-American children: concurrent and longitudinal relationships. Am. J. Orthopsychiatry **69:** 182–193.
17. BRODY, G.H., Z. STONEMAN & D. FLOR. 1996. Parental religiosity, family processes, and youth competence in rural, two-parent African American families. Dev. Psychol. **32:** 696–706.
18. GOODMAN, S.H. & I.H. GOTLIB, Eds. 2001. Children of Depressed Parents: Mechanisms of Risk and Implications for Treatment. American Psychological Association. Washington, DC.
19. LEADBEATER, B.J. & S.J. BISHOP. 1994. Predictors of behavior problems in preschool children of inner-city Afro-American and Puerto Rican adolescent mothers. Child Dev. **65:** 638–648.
20. EHRENSAFT, M.K. *et al.* 2003. Maternal antisocial behavior, parenting practices, and behavior problems in boys at risk for antisocial behavior. J. Child Family Stud. **12:** 27–40.
21. SCHERER, D.G. *et al.* 1996. Relation between children's perceptions of maternal mental illness and children's psychological adjustment. J. Clin. Child Psychol. **25:** 156–169.
22. CARTER, L.S., L.A. WEITHORN & R.E. BEHRMAN. 1999. Domestic violence and children: analysis and recommendations. Future Child. **9:** 4–20.
23. MCCLOSKY, L.A., A.J. FIGUEREDO & M.P. KOSS. 1995. The effects of systemic violence on children's mental health. Child Dev. **66:** 1239–1261.
24. CAMPBELL, J.C. & L.A. LEWANDOWSKI. 1997. Mental and physical health effects of intimate partner violence on women and children. Psychiatric Clin. N. Am. **20:** 353–374.
25. PELED, E. 1997. The battered women's movement response to children of battered women: a critical analysis. Violence Against Women **3:** 424–446.
26. BUEHLER, C. *et al.* 1997. Interparental conflict and youth problem behaviors: a meta-analysis. J. Child Fam. Stud. **6:** 233–247.

27. CUMMINGS, E.M. & T. DAVIES. 1994. Children and marital conflict. Guilford. New York.
28. GRYCH, J.H. *et al.* 2000. Patterns of adjustment among children of battered women. J. Consult. Clin. Psychol. **68:** 84–94.
29. HOLDEN, G., R. GEFFNER & E. JOURILES, Eds. 1998. Children exposed to marital violence: theory, research, and applied issues. American Psychological Association. Washington, DC.
30. MCDONALD, R. & E. JOURILES. 1991. Marital aggression and child behavior problems: research findings, mechanisms, and intervention strategies. Behav. Ther. **14:** 189–192.
31. JAFFEE, S.R. *et al.* 2002. Influence of adult domestic violence on children's internalizing and externalizing problems: an environmentally informative twin study. J. Am. Acad. Child Adolesc. Psychiatry **41:** 1095–1103.
32. GORMAN-SMITH, D. *et al.* 2000. Patterns of family functioning and adolescent outcomes among urban African American and Mexican American families. J. Fam. Psychol. **14:** 436–457.
33. SMITH, E.P. *et al.* 2001. Latent models of family processes in African American families: relationships to child competence, achievement, and problem behavior. J. Marriage Fam. **63:** 967–980.
34. SUMMERVILLE, M.B. *et al.* 1994. Psychopathology, family functioning, and cognitive style in urban adolescents with suicide attempts. J. Abnorm. Child Psychol. **22:** 221–235.
35. KLEIN, K. & R. FOREHAND. 2000. Family processes as resources for African American children exposed to a constellation of sociodemographic risk factors. J. Clin. Child Psychol. **29:** 53–65.
36. ARMISTEAD, L. *et al.* 2002. Parenting and child psychosocial adjustment in single-parent African American families: is community context important? Behav. Ther. **33:** 361–375.
37. BRODY, G.H. & D. FLOR. 1997. Maternal psychological functioning, family processes, and child adjustment in rural, single-parent, African American families. Dev. Psychol. **33:** 1000–1011.
38. MCCABE, K.M., R. CLARK & D. BARNETT. 1999. Family protective factors among urban African American youth. J. Clin. Child Psychol. **28:** 137–150.
39. BRODY, G.H. *et al.* 2002. Unique and protective contributions of parenting and classroom processes to the adjustment of African American children living in single-parent families. Child Dev. **73:** 274–286.
40. BROOKS-GUNN, J. *et al.* 1993. Do neighborhoods influence child and adolescent development. Am. J. Sociol. **99:** 353–395.
41. GONZALES, N.A. *et al.* 1996. Family, peer, and neighborhood influences on academic achievement among African American adolescents: one year prospective effects. Am. J. Commun. Psychol. **24:** 365–387.
42. SEIDMAN, E. *et al.* 1998. Structural and experiential neighborhood contexts, developmental stage, and anti-social behavior among urban adolescents in poverty. Dev. Psychopathol. **10:** 259–281.
43. PLYBON, L.E. & W. KLIEWER. 2001. Neighborhood types and externalizing behavior in urban school-age children: tests of direct, mediated, and moderated effects. J. Child Fam. Stud. **10:** 419–437.
44. LINARES, L.O. *et al.* 2001. A mediational model for the impact of exposure to community violence on early child behavior problems. Child Dev. **72:** 639–652.
45. FOREHAND, R. *et al.* 2000. The role of community risks and resources in the psychosocial adjustment of at risk children: an examination across two community contexts and two informants. Behav. Ther. **31:** 395–414.
46. CHASE-LANSDALE, L. & R.A. GORDON. 1997. Economic hardship and the development of five- and six-year-olds: neighborhood and regional perspectives. Child Dev. **67:** 3338–3367.
47. DUTTON, M.A., B. MITCHELL & Y. HAYWOOD. 1996. The emergency department as a violence prevention center. J. Am. Med. Women's Assoc. **51:** 92–96.
48. FOLSTEIN, M.F. *et al.* 2001. Mini-Mental State Examination. Psychological Assessment Resources. Odessa, FL.

49. WILLIAMS, M. *et al.* 1995. Inadequate functional health literacy among patients at two public hospitals. J. Am. Med. Assoc. **274:** 1677–1682.
50. DUNN, L.M., L.M. DUNN & D.M. DUNN. 1997. Peabody Picture Vocabulary Test— Third Edition Manual. American Guidance Service. Circle Pines, MN.
51. DEROGATIS, L. 1992. SCL-90-R: Administration, Scoring, and Procedures Manual: II. Clinical Psychometric Research. Townson, MD.
52. OLSON, D.H. *et al.*, Eds. 1992. Family Inventories: Inventories Used in a National Survey of Families Across the Family Life Cycle. Family Social Science. St. Paul, MN.
53. ROSS, C.E. & J. MIROWSKY. 1999. Disorder and decay: the concept and measurement of perceived neighborhood disorder. Urban Affairs Rev. **34:** 412–432.
54. ACHENBACH, T.M. & C.S. EDELBROCK. 1991. Manual for the Child Behavior Checklists/4-18 and 1991 profile. University of Vermont. Burlington, VT.
55. CICCHETTI, D. & N. GARMEZY. 1993. Prospects and promises in the study of resilience. Dev. Psychopathol. **5:** 741–762.
56. JESSOR, R. *et al.* 1995. Protective factors in adolescent problem behavior: moderator effects and developmental change. Dev. Psychol. **31:** 923–933.

Using an Animal Model to Assess the Long-Term Behavioral and Biological Consequences of Adolescent Abuse and Exposure to Alcohol

CRAIG F. FERRIS

Center for Comparative Neuroimaging, University of Massachusetts Medical School, Worcester, Massachusetts 01655, USA

ABSTRACT: During adolescence or adulthood, male hamster siblings were divided into control and experimental groups and exposed to periods of either mild or traumatic stress outside their individual nests. Mild stress is the simple exposure to a novel environment while the traumatic stressor is repeated daily subjugation by a dominant hamster. Over adolescence and adulthood, animals had free access to alcohol. The behavior and neuroendocrinology were assessed over these developmental periods in response to these environmental conditions. As adults, animals with a history of traumatic stress in adolescence showed inappropriate and excessive aggressive behavior. Their aggression was context dependent. In the presence of equal size hamsters, they showed little aggression; however, they were excessively aggressive toward smaller, younger animals. Testosterone levels and reproductive behavior were normal after adolescent subjugation; however, release of cortisol during agonistic encounters was suppressed. In comparison, hamsters exposed to chronic social subjugation as adults had low plasma testosterone, reduced reproductive behavior, and exaggerated cortisol release during agonistic encounters. Self-ingestion of alcohol during adolescence enhanced testosterone release around the peripubertal period but reduced plasma testosterone levels in adulthood. Exposure to alcohol as adolescents enhanced aggression in adulthood. These data demonstrate a pronounced difference in behavior and neuroendocrinology between adolescent and adult hamsters in their response to traumatic stress.

KEYWORDS: golden hamster; social subjugation; cortisol; testosterone; self-administration of ethanol

INTRODUCTION

It is clear that traumatic events in early life make children more vulnerable to future stressors and enhance the probability of antisocial behaviors.[1] Children exposed to early stressful environments and maltreatment before kindergarten are more aggressive and have more social problems than other children.[2,3] Children exposed to early physical and emotional neglect may develop learning patterns that affect the

Address for correspondence: Craig F. Ferris, Ph.D., Center for Comparative Neuroimaging, University of Massachusetts Medical School, 55 Lake Avenue North, Worcester, MA 01655. Voice: 508-856-5530; fax: 508-856-6426.

craig.ferris@umassmed.edu

Ann. N.Y. Acad. Sci. 1008: 69–78 (2003). © 2003 New York Academy of Sciences.
doi: 10.1196/annals.1301.008

interpretation of hostile social information resulting in inappropriate aggressive responding and general conduct disorder.[4] Furthermore, children with conduct problems are at risk for alcohol and drug abuse, a predisposition exacerbated by the fact that alcoholism and drug taking foster antisocial behaviors and violence.[5]

Unlike the perinatal and early childhood periods, there is little information on the long-term neurobiological and behavioral consequences of abuse during the *peripubertal period* or "adolescence." This is surprising because the incidence rate of physical abuse increases drastically during this developmental period. The 1978 study of national child abuse and neglect by the American Humane Association reported a high incidence rate of abuse toward adolescents between the ages 12 and 17; in fact, data indicate the incidence of adolescent abuse equals or exceeds that of all other age groups.[6]

The work discussed below examines the behavioral and neuroendocrine changes that occur in response to social subjugation and exposure to alcohol in adolescence. The resident/intruder paradigm of offensive aggression was used to socially subjugate adolescent Syrian golden hamsters (*Mesocrecitus auratus*) and later in adulthood to assess their agonistic behavior in the context of social conflict. In addition to this physical abuse, hamsters were allowed to voluntarily consume alcohol during adolescence. Interestingly, the golden hamster is one of only a few mammals that will spontaneously drink alcohol after weaning. At the end of adolescence, exposure to alcohol was stopped and animals were tested for aggression as young adults in the resident/intruder paradigm. These data from adolescent abuse and alcohol exposure were compared with data collected from adult hamsters exposed to similar environmental stressors.

USING HAMSTERS TO STUDY THE EFFECTS OF STRESS AND ALCOHOL EXPOSURE IN ADOLESCENCE

In humans, adolescence is defined as a period of pronounced physical, cognitive, and emotional growth. This period usually begins just before puberty and ends in early adulthood with sexual maturity, social awareness, and independence.[7] In golden hamsters, there is a developmental period analogous to adolescence. In the wild, hamsters wean around postnatal day 25 (P-25), leave the home nest, forage on their own, establish nest sites, and defend their territory.[8,9] Hamsters can begin to establish dominance hierarchies as early as P-35[10] and have a minimal breeding age of 42 days. Androgen levels start to increase between P-28 and P-35.[11,12] Thus, between P-25 and P-42, as hamsters achieve independence from the maternal nest, they increase their weight and size, reach full sexual maturity and reproductive competence, and establish social relationships. This period between P-25 and P-42 is designated as adolescence in golden hamsters. Because hamsters in the wild are solitary and live in their own isolated burrows,[8,9] animals studied in the laboratory setting can be housed individually after weaning, an experimental feature that eliminates the confounding variable of group interactions. Another added benefit to study hamsters is their taste for alcohol. Unlike most other mammals, hamsters will readily drink alcohol in a free-choice paradigm.[13] Immediately after weaning and after isolation in their own nest site on P-25 adolescent hamsters will drink alcohol in addition to water and food *ad libitum*.[14]

The resident/intruder model of aggression relies on the motivation of a resident animal to chase and fight intruders coming into their territory.[15] Residents will show highly specific attack patterns characteristic of offensive aggression, that is, the initiation of attacks and bites, toward intruders. Golden hamsters are particularly amenable to the study of agonistic behavior because they show a high level of spontaneous aggression toward conspecifics.[16] The isolation of hamsters into individual cages as noted above only enhances their aggression toward an intruder.[17,18] Hamsters are nocturnal and their aggression is greatest during the dark phase of the circadian cycle.[16,19] For this reason they were maintained on a reverse light:dark cycle and their behavior was scored and filmed under the illumination of a red light.

SOCIAL SUBJUGATION IN ADULT ANIMALS

Social subjugation is a very significant and natural stressor in the animal kingdom Animals defeated and subjugated during establishment of dominance hierarchies or territorial encounters can be highly submissive in future agonistic interactions. For example, defeated mice display less aggression and more submissive behavior.[20,21] Rats consistently defeated by more aggressive conspecifics show a behavioral inhibition characterized by less social initiative and offensive aggression, as well as an increase in defensive behavior.[22] Repeatedly defeated male hamsters respond in a submissive manner when confronted by aggressive and nonaggressive intruder.[23–25] The generalization of submissive behavior toward nonthreatening, novel stimulus animals is an example of "conditioned defeat."[25] Adult male rhesus monkeys will fight for dominance status when forming a social group with breeding females. When two such established groups are brought together to form one, the dominant or alpha male from each will fight for dominance. The loser is relegated to the lowest social rank in the male hierarchy displaying highly submissive behavior.[26] Chronic social subjugation in male talapoin monkeys reduces social activity and sexual behavior even in the absence of dominant conspecifics.[27]

Many of the behavioral changes observed in adult male animals after social subjugation, like decreased aggression and reproductive behavior, heightened fear, and anxiety are caused, in part, by changes in testosterone and glucocorticoid levels. For example, there is a strong correlation between testosterone levels and aggressive behavior in animals. Castration reduces attacks and bites in intermale aggression in mice, rats, and hamsters, whereas testosterone replacement restores aggressiveness.[18,28–32] Testosterone levels correlate with social dominance and aggressive behavior in rhesus monkeys.[26] Elevated levels of testosterone are observed in victorious animals.[26,33–35] Animals that are socially subjugated have reduced testosterone levels[26,34,36,37] including hamsters (FIG. 1).[24]

Although testosterone levels are reduced in response to social subjugation, glucocorticoid levels are elevated. An initial agonist encounter between two animals is routinely accompanied by an increase in stress hormones levels in both combatants.[38] After the encounter, glucocorticoids levels return to basal values. The release of glucocorticoids is adaptive, helping to mobilize energy reserves. However, during subsequent aggressive encounters, higher levels of glucocorticoids are observed in the defeated, submissive animal, and these levels remain elevated for a longer period of time (FIG. 2).[24,36,37,39–41] Defeat in mice results in elevated corticosterone levels

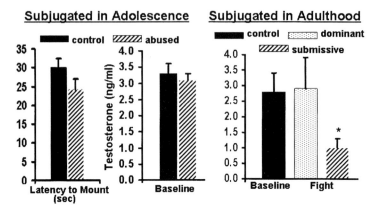

FIGURE 1. Testosterone levels and sexual behavior are normal after abuse in adolescence. The *bar graphs on the left* show a measure of reproductive behavior (latency to mount a receptive female) and plasma levels of testosterone. Two groups (12 in each) of adult male hamsters with a history of social subjugation (abused) or mild stress (control) were sampled. The *bar graph on the right* shows testosterone data from hamsters socially subjugated as adults. Note the stability of testosterone levels of animals chronically subjugated in adolescence as compared with those subjugated in adulthood. *P < .05. (Adapted from Huhman et al.[24])

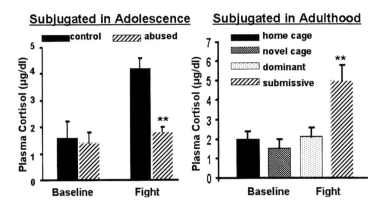

FIGURE 2. Abuse in adolescence alters the adult stress response. The *bar graph on the left* shows cortisol data collected under baseline conditions or after a fight. Two groups (12 in each) of adult male hamsters with a history of adolescence social subjugation (abused) or mild stress (control) were sampled. The *bar graph on the right* shows cortisol levels under different conditions in adult animals. Note the absence of an increase in cortisol during an agonist encounter in animals subjugated in adolescence as compared with those subjugated (submissive) as adults. **P < .01. (Adapted from Huhman et al.[24])

that appear to promote submissive behavior.[39] High basal levels of glucocorticoids are associated with a depressed immune system, diminished reproductive function, bone loss, and increased fear, anxiety, and depression.[42]

ALCOHOL CONSUMPTION IN ADULT ANIMALS

Chronic and acute exposure to alcohol in *adult* animals consistently lowers plasma testosterone.[43–48] In fact, a single intraperitoneal injection of 30% ethanol resulting in blood ethanol concentration (BEC) over 250 mg% suppresses plasma testosterone for up to 4 days.[46] Adult hamsters self-ingesting 10% ethanol show reduced levels of plasma testosterone (see FIG. 4). Testosterone production also is suppressed with acute alcohol intake in humans.[49,50] Alcohol lowers testosterone by directly inhibiting steroidogenesis[51,52] and by interfering with the release of GnRH into the hypophyseal-portal circulation.[53]

SOCIAL SUBJUGATION IN ADOLESCENCE

Recent studies on social subjugation in adolescent hamsters revealed unique neurobiological and behavioral outcomes as compared with adult animals.[54] Male golden hamsters weaned at P-25 were exposed daily to aggressive adults from P-28 to P-42 and tested for offensive aggression as young adults several days later after the cessation of stress. Animals with a history of social subjugation show a context-dependent alteration in their aggressive behavior. They show typical conditioned de-

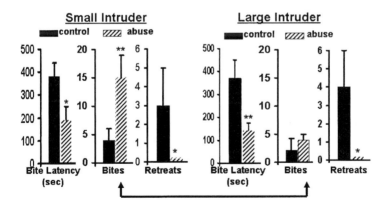

FIGURE 3. Abuse in adolescence alters aggressive behavior. The *bar graphs on the left* show data on aggressive behavior of adult hamsters in their home cage confronting a smaller intruder. The adult residents had a history of adolescent subjugation (abused, $n = 12$) or mild stress (control, $n = 12$). The *bar graphs on the right* show data on aggressive behavior from the same two groups of adult hamsters but confronting a equal-sized intruder. Note the absence of biting attacks from the animals with a history of adolescent abuse toward large intruder as compared with smaller intruders.

feat, fleeing from nonaggressive intruders of comparable age and size. In this respect, they are similar to socially subjugated adult male hamsters. However, when confronted by a smaller, weaker intruder they are exceedingly aggressive, displaying short attack latencies and high number of bites as compared with sibling controls that are not subjugated during adolescence. Data corroborating these findings are shown in FIGURE 3. However, although abused animals show little aggression toward equal-sized nonaggressive intruders, they are not submissive and display no retreats as compared with their sibling controls. They would appear to be impulsive as they show a short bite latency toward a large intruder; however, they do not sustain the attack.

This exaggerated aggressive response toward smaller animals and atypical agonistic behavior toward larger animals was unexpected. Equally surprising, the basal testosterone levels in young adult hamsters exposed to the daily stress of threat and attack throughout adolescence are comparable to control siblings (FIG. 1). Moreover, after an agonistic encounter with an aggressive, larger conspecific, animals stressed in adolescence show much lower cortisol levels than their sibling controls (FIG. 2). Hence, the anticipated decrease in circulating levels of testosterone and increase in glucocorticoids with repeated defeat reported in many studies on adult animals including hamsters[24] do not replicate in adolescent hamsters.

VOLUNATRY ALCOHOL CONSUMPTION IN ADOLESCENCE

The pattern of voluntary alcohol consumption in adolescent hamsters is most interesting.[14] Animals will readily drink from a 10% alcohol solution on P-25, their first day of isolation from the maternal nest site. The daily intake of alcohol increases steadily over the adolescent period with a mean blood ethanol concentration of approximately 53 mg%. There are no physical signs of intoxication. The growth and body weight are not significantly different from sibling controls "yolked" to a regimen of voluntary sucrose consumption. Alcohol consumption peaks around P-35 to P-36 the time of puberty and activation of the hypothalamic-pituitary-gonadal axis. Indeed, the peak in adolescent alcohol consumption of almost 19 g/kg/day is correlated with the first increase in blood levels of testosterone. After this critical pubertal period, the daily consumption of alcohol levels off to approximately 11 g/kg/day and persists into young adulthood.

What is most striking about the relationship between puberty and drinking is the early and enhanced release of testosterone in hamsters exposed to alcohol (FIG. 4). On P-35 and P-36 hamsters exposed to alcohol had twice the blood levels of testosterone of their sibling controls. However, the difference in circulating testosterone levels between alcohol and sucrose exposed hamsters is short lived as the levels of steroid hormone increase in the control animals to equal those of the alcohol animals by young adulthood. One interpretation of these date are that the consumption of alcohol in adolescence "jump starts" the hypothalamic-pituitary-gonadal axis exposing the hamsters to elevated levels of testosterone during puberty. This alcohol-induced change in adolescent neuroendocrinology also appears to have long-term behavioral consequences. Several days after the cessation of alcohol exposure hamsters show exaggerated attack behavior toward smaller intruders as compared with their sibling controls.[14]

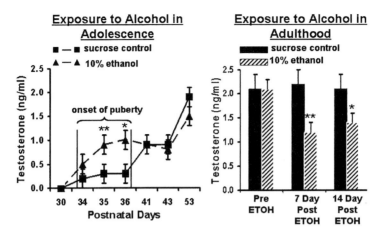

FIGURE 4. Alcohol and testosterone release. The *graph on the left* shows developmental changes in plasma testosterone in adolescent hamsters self-ingesting 10% ethanol as compared with sibling controls "yolked" to sucrose The *bar graph on the right* shows plasma testosterone levels in adult hamsters self-ingesting ethanol ($n = 6$) as compared with sucrose-yolked controls ($n = 6$). Note that ethanol exposure increases testosterone levels in adolescence but decreases steroid hormone levels in adulthood. (Adapted from Ferris et al.[14])

SUMMARY

As young adults, animals with a history of adolescent stress show inappropriate and excessive aggressive behavior. In the presence of adult hamsters, they are very submissive; however, smaller, younger hamsters elicit intense biting attacks. These findings underscore the context-dependent nature of aggressive behavior and the neurobiological and behavioral consequences of stress in adolescence. It is interesting that testosterone is spared in adolescents exposed to chronic social subjugation because adults have a very predictable loss of gonadal hormone after defeat. Similarly, adult animals and humans exposed to alcohol show a very predictable diminution in testosterone levels, but again adolescent hamsters show no such suppression of gonadal hormone. Indeed, they actually show an enhanced activation of the hypothalamic gonadal axis with alcohol exposure. It would seem that nature has set up mechanisms for protecting the reproductive neuroendocrine status of adolescent hamsters and perhaps humans. There would seem to be adaptive value in this protective mechanism because adolescence is a period of heightened social conflict both in animals and humans. Smaller, peripubertal, immature males are not fully able to defend territories and compete for mates. Although they have to wait their turn, they are imbued with a resistance to risk factors that can be devastating to their adult counterparts. Learning and a sustained, if not augmented, gonadal neuroendocrine system may be contributing factors to the inappropriate, excessive offensive aggression displayed by adult hamsters with a history of adolescent social subjugation and alcohol exposure. Whether this particular interaction between brain and environment during rodent adolescence translates to human adolescence is purely speculation.

However, these data in rodent studies clearly demonstrate that the developmental period analogous to human adolescence is unique in its response to stress and exposure to alcohol.

ACKNOWLEDGMENTS

These experiments were supported by grants MH 52280 from the NIMH. The contents of this review are solely the responsibility of the authors and do not necessarily represent the official views of the NIMH.

REFERENCES

1. LUNTZ, B.K. & C.S. WIDOM. 1994. Antisocial personality disorder in abused and neglected children grown up. Am. J. Psychiatry **151:** 670–674.
2. SANSON, A., D. SMART, M. PRIOR & F. OBERKLAID. 1993. Precursors of hyperactivity and aggression. J. Am. Acad. Child Adolesc. Psychiatry **32:** 1207–1216.
3. LANSFORD, J.E., K.A. DODGE, G.S. PETTIT, et al. 2002. A 12-year prospective study of the long-term effects of early child physical maltreatment on psychological, behavioral, and academic problems in adolescence. Arch. Pediatr. Adolesc. Med. **156:** 824–830.
4. DODGE, K.A., J.E. BATES & G.S. PETTIT. 1990. Mechanisms in the cycle of violence. Science **250:** 1678–1683.
5. ITO, T.A., N. MILLER & V.E. POLLOCK. 1996. Alcohol and aggression: a meta-analysis on the moderating effects of inhibitory cues, triggering events, and self-focused attention. Psychol. Bull. **120:** 60–82.
6. SCHELLENBACH, C.J. & L.F. GUERNEY. 1987. Identification of adolescent abuse and future intervention prospects. J. Adolec. Abuse **10:** 1–2.
7. INGERSOLL, G. 1992. Psychological and social development. *In* Textbook of Adolescent Medicine. E.R. McAnarney, R.E. Kreipe, D.P. Orr, and G.D. Comerci, Eds.: 91–98. Saunders. Philadelphia.
8. DIETERLEN, F. 1959. Das Verhalten des Syrischen Goldhamsters (*Mesocricetus auratus* Waterhouse). Z. Tierpsychol. **16:** 47–103.
9. SCHOENFELD, T.A. & C.M. LEONARD. 1985. Behavioral development in the Syrian golden hamster. *In* The Hamster: Reproduction and Behavior, H.I. Siegel, Ed.: 289–318. Plenum Press. New York.
10. WHITSETT, J.M. 1975. The development of aggressive and marking behavior in intact and castrated male hamsters. Horm. Behav. **6:** 47–57.
11. MILLER, L.L., J.M. WHITSETT, J.G. VANDENBERGH & D.R. COLBY. 1977. Physical and behavioral aspects of sexual maturation in male golden hamsters. J. Comp. Physiol. Psychol. **91:** 245–259.
12. VOMACHKA, A.J. & G.S. GREENWALD. 1979. The development of gonadotropin and steroid hormone patterns in male and female hamsters from birth to puberty. Endocrinology **105:** 960–966.
13. ARVOLA, A. & O. FORSANDER. 1961. Comparison between water and ethanol consumption in six animal species in free-choice experiments. Nature **4790:** 819–820.
14. FERRIS, C.F., K. SHTIEGMAN & J.A. KING. 1998. Voluntary ethanol consumption in male adolescent hamsters increases testosterone and aggression. Physiol. Behav. **63:** 739–744.
15. MICZEK, K.A. 1974. Intraspecies aggression in rats: effects of D-amphetamine and chlordiazepoxide. Psychopharmacologia **39:** 275–301.
16. LERWILL, C.J. & P. MAKINGS. 1971. The agonistic behavior of the golden hamster *Mesocricetus auratus* (Waterhouse). Anim. Behav. **19:** 714–721.
17. BRAIN, P.F. 1972. Effects of isolation/grouping on endocrine function and fighting behavior in male and female golden hamsters (*Mesocricetus auratus* Waterhouse). Behav. Biol. **7:** 349–357.

18. PAYNE, A.P. 1973. A comparison of the aggressive behavior of isolated intact and castrated male golden hamsters towards intruders introduced into the home cage. Physiol. Behav. **10:** 629–631.
19. LANDAU, I.T. 1975. Light-dark rhythms in aggressive behavior of the male golden hamster. Physiol. Behav. **14:** 767–774.
20. FRISHKNECHT, H.R., B. SEIGFREID & P.G. WASER. 1982. Learning of submissive behavior in mice: a new model. Behav. Processes **7:** 235–245.
21. WILLIAMS, J. & D.M. LIERLE. 1988. Effects of repeated defeat by a dominant conspecific on subsequent pain sensitivity, open-field activity, and escape learning. Anim. Learn. Behav. **16:** 477–485.
22. VAN DE POLL, N.E., F. DEJONGE, H.G. VAN OYEN & J. VAN PELT. 1982. Aggressive behaviour in rats: effects of winning or losing on subsequent aggressive interactions. Behav. Processes **7:** 143–155.
23. FERRIS, C.F., J.F. AXELSON, A.M. MARTIN & L.R. ROBERGE. 1989. Vasopressin immunoreactivity in the anterior hypothalamus is altered during the establishment of dominant/subordinate relationships between hamsters. Neuroscience **29:** 675–683.
24. HUHMAN, K.L., T.O. MOORE, C.F. FERRIS, et al. 1991. Acute and repeated exposure to social conflict in male golden hamsters: increases in plasma POMC-peptides and cortisol and decreases in plasma testosterone. Horm. Behav. **25:** 206–216.
25. POTEGAL, M., K. HUHMAN, T. MOORE & J. MEYERHOFF. 1993. Conditioned defeat in the Syrian golden hamster (Mesocricetus auratus). Behav. Neural Biol. **60:** 93–102.
26. ROSE, R.M., I.S. BERSTEIN & T.P. GORDON. 1975. Consequences of social conflict on plasmatestosterone levels in rhesus monkeys. Psychosom. Med. **37:** 50–61.
27. EBERHART, J.A., U. YODYINGYUAD & E.B. KEVERNE. 1985. Subordination in male talapoin monkeys lowers sexual behaviour in the absence of dominants. Physiol. Behav. **35:** 673–677.
28. BEEMAN, E.A. 1947. The effect of male hormone on aggressive behavior in mice. Physiol. Zool. **20:** 373–405.
29. VANDENBERGH, J.G. 1971. The effects of gonadal hormones on the aggressive behaviour of adult golden hamsters. Anim. Behav. **19:** 589–594.
30. BARFIELD, R.J., D.E. BUSCH & K. WALLEN. 1972. Gonadal influence on agonistic behavior in the male domestic rat. Horm. Behav. **3:** 247–259.
31. BRAIN, P.F. & A.B. KAMIS. 1985. How do hormones change aggression? The example of testosterone. In Aggression: Functions and Causes. J.M. Ramirez and P.F. Brain, Eds.: 84–115. Publicaciones de la Universidad de Sevilla. Seville.
32. VAN OORTMESSEN, G.A., D.J. DIJK & T. SCHUURMAN. 1987. Studies in wild house mice. II. Testosterone and aggression. Horm. Behav. **21:** 139–152.
33. COE, C.L., S.P. MENDOZA & S. LEVINE. 1979. Social status constrains the stress response in the squirrel monkey. Physiol. Behav. **23:** 633–638.
34. EBERHART, J.A., E.B. KEVERNE & R.E. MELLER. 1980. Social influences on plasma testosterone levels in male talapoin monkeys. Horm. Behav. **14:** 247–266.
35. SAPOLSKY, R.M. 1985. Stress-induced suppression of testicular function in the wild baboon: role of glucocorticoids. Endocrinology **116:** 2273–2278.
36. BRONSON, F.H. & B.F. ELEFTHERIOU. 1964. Chronic physiological effects of fighting in mice. Gen. Comp. Endocrinol. **4:** 9–14.
37. EBERHART, J.A., E.B. KEVERNE & R.E. MELLER. 1983. Social influences on circulating levels of cortisol and prolactin in male talapoin monkeys. Physiol. Behav. **30:** 361–369.
38. SCHUURMAN, T. 1980. Hormonal correlates of agonistic behavior in adult male rats. Prog. Brain Res. **53:** 415–420.
39. LOUCH, C.D. & M. HIGGINBOTHAM. 1967. The relation between social rank and plasma corticosterone levels in mice. Gen, Comp, Endocrinol, **8:** 441–444.
40. ELY, D.L. & J.P. HENRY. 1978. Neuroendocrine response patterns in dominant and subordinate mice. Horm. Behav. **10:** 156–169.
41. RAAB, A., R. DANTZER, B. MICHAUD, et al. 1986. Behavioral, physiological and immunological consequences of social status and aggression in chronically coexisting resident-intruder dyads of male rats. Physiol. Behav. **36:** 223–228.
42. MCEWEN, B.A. 1998. Protective and damaging effects of stress mediators. N. Engl. J. Med. **338:**171–179.

43. BADR, F.M. & A. BARTKE. 1974. Effect of ethyl alcohol on plasma testosterone level in mice. Steroids **23:** 921–927.
44. CICERO, T.J. & T.M. BADGER. 1977. Effects of alcohol on the hypothalamic-pituitary-gonadal axis in the male rat. J. Pharmacol. Exp. Ther. **201:** 427–433.
45. MELLO, N.K., J.H. MENDELSON, M.P. BREE, *et al.* 1985. The effects of ethanol on luteinizing hormone and testosterone in male macaque monkeys. Pharmacol. Exp. Ther. **233:** 588–596.
46. STEINER, J.C., M.M. HALLORAN, K. JABAMONI, *et al.* 1996. Sustained effects of a single injection of ethanol on the hypothalamic-pituitary-gonadal axis in the male rat. Alcoholism: Clin. Exp. Res. **20:** 1368–1374.
47. VAN THIEL, D.H., J.S. GAVALER, R. LESTER & M.D. GOODMAN. 1975. Alcohol-induced testicular atrophy: an experimental model for hypogonadism occurring in chronic alcoholic men. Gastroenterology **69:** 326–332.
48. FRIAS, J., J.M. TORRES, M.T. MIRANDA, *et al.* 2002. Effects of acute alcoholic intoxication on pituitary-gonadal axis hormones, pituitary-adrenal axis hormones, beta-endorphin and prolactin in human adults of both sexes. Alcohol Alcohol **37:** 169–173.
49. MENDELSON, J.H., N.K. MELLO & J. ELLINGBOE. 1977. Effects of acute alcohol intake on pituitary-gonadal hormones in normal human males. J. Pharmacol. Exp. Ther. **202:** 676–682.
50. YLIKAHRI, R., M. HUTTUNEN, M. HARKONEN, *et al.* 1974. Low plasma testosterone values in men during hangover. J. Steroid Biochem. **5:** 655–658.
51. BADR, F.M., A. BARTKE, S. DALTERIO & W. BULGER. 1977. Suppression of testosterone production by ethyl alcohol. Possible mode of action. Steroids **30:** 647–655.
52. CICERO, T.J., E.R. MEYER & R.D. BELL. 1979. Effects of ethanol on the hypothalamic-pituitary-luteinizing hormone axis and testicular steroidogenesis. J. Pharmacol. Exp. Ther. **208:** 210–215.
53. CHING, M., M. VALENCA & A. NEGRO-VILAR. 1988. Acute ethanol treatment lowers hypophyseal portal plasma luteinizing hormone-releasing hormone (LH-RH) and systemic plasma LH levels in orchidectomized rats. Brain Res. **443:** 325–328.
54. DELVILLE, Y., R.H. MELLONI, JR. & C.F. FERRIS. 1998. Behavioral and neurobiological consequences of social subjugation during puberty in golden hamsters. J. Neurosci. **18:** 2667–2672.

Aggressive Behavior in Abused Children

DANIEL F. CONNOR,[a] LEONARD A. DOERFLER,[a,b] ADAM M. VOLUNGIS,[b]
RONALD J. STEINGARD,[a] AND RICHARD H. MELLONI, JR.[c]

[a]Department of Psychiatry, University of Massachusetts Medical School, Worcester,
Massachusetts 01655, USA

[b]Department of Psychology, Assumption College, Worcester, Massachusetts, USA

[c]Department of Psychology, Northeastern University, Boston, Massachusetts, USA

ABSTRACT: Our objective was to investigate the relationship between a lifetime
history of traumatic stress, defined as physical and/or sexual abuse and aggression and psychosocial functioning in a sample of clinically referred and nonclinically referred children and adolescents. This is a retrospective case
comparison study. Three groups of children were identified, assessed, matched
for age, and partially matched for gender. Children clinically referred to residential treatment with a history of abuse ($N = 29$) were compared with children
clinically referred to residential treatment without a history of abuse ($N = 29$),
and a nonclinical group of children residing in the community ($N = 29$). Variables investigating specific types of aggression, IQ, and psychopathology were
assessed across the three groups. Clinically referred children scored worse on
all measures compared with nonclinical community children. Clinically referred abused children scored higher on measures of aggression and significantly higher on measures of reactive aggression and verbal aggression than
clinically referred nonabused children. Clinically referred abused children had
significantly lower verbal IQ scores than clinically referred nonabused children, but no difference in psychopathology. Results support the importance of
assessing specific types of aggression in samples of traumatized youths. Verbal
information processing may be especially vulnerable in abused children and
adolescents and enhance vulnerability to aggressive responding.

KEYWORDS: abuse; child; proactive aggression; reactive aggression

INTRODUCTION

Children who suffer abuse in the developing years are known to have increased
rates of aggressive behavior and conduct problems compared with children who have
not been abused.[1–3] However, studies that investigate relationships between abuse
and aggressive behaviors often define aggressive behaviors nonspecifically, such as
assessing general conduct problems, delinquency, or externalizing behaviors. Stud-

Address for correspondence: Daniel F. Connor, M.D., Department of Psychiatry, 7th Floor,
Room S7-850, University of Massachusetts Medical School, 55 Lake Avenue, North, Worcester,
MA 01655. Voice: 508-856-4094; fax: 508-856-6426.

daniel.connor@umassmed.edu

Ann. N.Y. Acad. Sci. 1008: 79–90 (2003). © 2003 New York Academy of Sciences.
doi: 10.1196/annals.1301.009

ies have not examined more specific types of aggression, such as overt categorical aggression,[4] proactive aggression,[5] and/or reactive aggression.[5] Investigating specific types of aggression may yield associations that are more clinically meaningful than assessing only general categories of conduct problems.

In this report, we explore the relationship between a developmental history of traumatic stress, defined as a lifetime history of physical and/or sexual abuse, and psychosocial adjustment in two groups of seriously emotionally disturbed (SED) children and adolescents (referred to as children) residing in residential treatment (RT), and a community comparison group. Evidence suggests that aggressive and abused children do not respond as well to treatment as nonaggressive and nonabused children in residential treatment.[6] Identifying more specific types of aggression in abused children may be helpful to further understand why some aggressive and abused children have diminished treatment response rates.

Furthermore, we examined psychopathology in our sample to ascertain whether rates or types of psychopathology differed between abused and nonabused children. It is known that abused children suffer more psychopathology than comparison children, including increased rates of depression, anxiety, and conduct problems.[7,8] Abused children in RT may be more aggressive because of differing rates or types of psychopathology.

Given that abused children are known to have lower IQ scores on standardized testing,[9,10] we examined IQ differences between abused and nonabused children clinically referred to residential treatment. Diminished information processing, especially verbal information processing, has been associated with aggressive behavior. For example, aggressive and antisocial youth manifest a verbal IQ deficit of approximately eight points (approximately half a standard deviation) relative to nonantisocial youngsters.[11]

In a sample of SED children, we wanted to know if youths who had been physically or sexually abused were more aggressive than children who had not been abused. In particular, we were interested in understanding whether abused children differed on specific types of aggression. We also investigated differences in IQ and psychopathology to assess the contribution of these factors.

METHODS

Subjects

Subjects included one group of children clinically referred to residential treatment with a history of abuse, one group of children clinically referred to residential treatment with no history of abuse, and a group of nonclinically referred comparison children residing in the community. Clinically referred children (6–17 years old) were recruited from a residential treatment center (RTC). The RTC serves SED children generally referred from their respective school systems, juvenile justice, or state protective services agencies. Community comparison children were recruited by advertisement and word-of-mouth.

All subjects and legal guardians gave consent. The institutional review boards of both the RTC and the University of Massachusetts Medical School approved this study.

Procedures

Children with a history of physical and/or sexual abuse were compared on several dependent variables with children without an abuse history. Subjects were divided into three groups for the purposes of comparison. Group 1 ($N = 29$) consisted of clinically referred children residing in residential treatment with a documented history of sexual and/or physical abuse. Group 2 ($N = 29$) consisted of clinically referred children residing in residential treatment with no documented history of physical and/or sexual abuse. Group 3 ($N = 29$) consisted of comparison community children with no current history of psychiatric disorder or treatment.

Subjects were individually matched on age (within 1 year) and partially matched for gender. Group 1 was composed of 19 males and 10 females with an average age of 12.76 ± 3.19 years. Group 2 was composed of 21 males and 8 females with an average age of 12.76 ± 3.19 years. Group 3 was composed of 13 males and 16 females with an average age of 12.76 ± 3.29 years. At the lower age ranges, complete matching for gender was not possible for all subjects. However, a chi-square analysis did not reveal any significant differences for gender among the three groups [$\chi^2(2) = 5.02$; $P = .08$]. The majority of the subjects (95%) were white, whereas the remaining 5% were of Hispanic, African, or mixed ethnicity.

Clinically referred subjects residing in residential treatment were part of a larger database of children in residential treatment that has been used in previously published research.[4,12] Clinically referred children were selected to participate in this project if they had histories as above and were matched with a community comparison subject.

Assessments

Children were systematically assessed when admitted to the RTC. A board-certified or board-eligible child psychiatrist clinically evaluated all children. Parents, legal guardians, and/or staff workers (who worked closely with children in residential treatment) were interviewed about the child. Low verbal IQ, frequent presence of language-based learning disabilities, and frequent absence of parent/guardians familiar with inpatient children precluded using structured psychiatric diagnostic interviewing. Rating scales were completed by parents at the time of evaluation for control children and completed by clinical staff within 4 months of admission to RTC for clinically referred children. All raters were blind to study aims and hypotheses. Historical variables were obtained by interviewing patients and parent/guardians and by reviewing the child's medical record. This method of assessment has been used in previously published research.[2,12]

Physical and Sexual Abuse

Physical or sexual abuse history was coded as present only if the written medical record supported a documented change of caregiver because of suspected abuse, court appearance because of abuse charges, or a supported protective services evaluation of abuse as mandated by state child protective service law. This represents a more conservative coding strategy than studies that use only self-report data to ascertain abuse history. Interrater reliability on abuse items was assessed between two child psychiatrists using the Kappa statistic.[13] Interrater reliability corrected for chance agreement was excellent on the items history of physical abuse ($K = 0.85$) and history of sexual abuse ($K = 0.93$).

Intelligence

For youths 16 years and older, IQ was assessed by the Wechsler Adult Intelligence Scale.[14] For younger clients, IQ was determined by the Wechsler Intelligence Scale for Children.[15] All IQ tests were administered by consulting clinical child psychologists. Aggression and conflict were measured in several different ways in this study.

Overt Categorical Aggression

To assess categories of aggression in the sample the Overt Aggression Scale modified to assess the frequency and severity of aggression over the month previous to rating, we used the Modified Overt Aggression Scale (MOAS). The MOAS assesses four categories of aggression including verbal aggression (i.e., threats of harm to others), impulsive property destruction (object aggression), self-injurious behaviors (self-aggression), and physical assault (other aggression). This scale has adequate reliability, validity, and is a standard aggression rating scale used in clinical aggression research with children.[16,17] For example, the average Intraclass Correlation Coefficient (ICC) of reliability for physically aggressive behaviors (as scored by the scale for each individual incident) in samples of child and adult psychiatric patients is 0.88, supporting the scale's reliability.[17] For the Modified Overt Aggression Scale assessing behaviors over the previous month, the internal consistency of the scale α = 0.75, and the median interrater reliability coefficient is 0.96.[16] Parents completed scales for outpatients and staff for inpatients.

Proactive and Reactive Aggression

Proactive and reactive aggression were assessed using the proactive/reactive rating scale.[5,18] This rating scale consists of three questions assessing reactive aggression and three questions assessing proactive aggression. Reactive aggression is an aggressive response to a perceived threat. An example of a reactive aggression question is "When this child has been teased or threatened, he or she gets angry easily and strikes back." Proactive aggression is aggression reinforced by instrumental conditioning and the promise of reward achievement. An example of a proactive aggression statement is "This child uses physical force in order to dominate other kids." The statements are written so that the respondent can use a one- to five-point scale, ranging from never to almost always, to indicate how frequently the statement applied to an individual child. Children scoring an average of three or more on either set of proactive/reactive statements were considered to demonstrate that type of aggression. The proactive/reactive aggression scale demonstrates adequate reliability and validity in children.[5,19]

Hostility

We assessed child self-report hostile attributions with the child version of the Buss Durkee Hostility Inventory.[20] This self-report true/false scale yields an expressed hostility factor (score 0–7), and an experienced hostility factor (score 0–6). Expressed hostility is defined as how hostile toward the environment children rate themselves. Experienced hostility is defined as how hostile children rate the environment toward them. For children with a reading level of lower than the third grade, the questions were read aloud by the parent/staff worker completing the scale. The convergent and discriminant validity of this scale has been supported.[20,21] In child samples, the scale test–retest reliability was .57.[22]

Hyperactive/Impulsive Behavior

Classroom teachers assessed child hyperactive/impulsive behaviors by using the 10-item Conners Teacher Questionnaire (CTQ), yielding a total score between 0 and 30. Interrater reliability for the CTQ is $R = .55$. Test–retest factor reliabilities for the CTQ range from .70 to .90.[23,24] Hyperactive/impulsive behavior was included because previous research has shown a significant relationship between hyperactivity/impulsivity and aggression/conduct problems.[25]

Psychopathology

The Devereux Scales of Mental Disorder (DSMD) is a well-validated 110-item behavior rating scale designed to evaluate psychopathology in children and adolescents.[26] Item content and content-related validity adequately reflect DSM-IV criteria. The DSMD assesses psychopathology along continuous dimensions, so that categorical psychiatric diagnoses are not derived from the DSMD. Instead, DSMD T-scores are defined on the basis of DSMD data, including six factor-derived scale scores (conduct, attention/delinquency, anxiety, depression, autism, and acute problems). The conduct scale measures disruptive and hostile acts. The attention/delinquency scale measures problems with attention, impulsivity, hyperactivity, and difficulty complying with societal rules and laws. Fears and worries are measured by the anxiety scale and anhedonia, low mood, and withdrawal by the depression scale. The autism scale measures problems of impaired social interactions and communication. The acute problems scale assesses behaviors that are hallucinatory, primitive, bizarre, self-injurious, or dangerous.

Data Analysis Strategy

One-way ANOVAs were used to examine whether there were significant differences among the three groups on the measures of aggression, psychopathology, and intelligence. When ANOVAs identified significant differences among the three groups, the Student-Newman-Keuls test was used to determine which groups differed significantly. Significance was set at $P \leq .05$ (two-tailed) for this preliminary study.

RESULTS

Aggression Measures

The following measures assessed various facets of aggression including aggressive behaviors, hostile attributions, or types of aggression: Reactive Aggression,

TABLE 1. ANOVA results for aggression measures

Aggression measures	F	Df	P
Reactive aggression	18.02	2, 84	.001
Proactive aggression	9.89	2, 84	.001
Verbal aggression	17.53	2, 84	.001
Object aggression	4.23	2, 84	.02
Self-aggression	4.71	2, 84	.01
Other aggression	4.86	2, 84	.01
Expressed hostility	1.85	2, 80	NS
Perceived hostility	12.77	2, 80	.001
Conner's Teacher Questionnaire	18.39	2, 84	.001

TABLE 2. Means and standard deviations for aggressive measures

Aggression measures	Clinical–Abused	Clinical–Not Abused	Nonclinical Comparison
Reactive aggression	3.37 (1.24)	2.64 (0.92)	1.85 (0.63)
Proactive aggression	2.09 (1.00)	1.84 (0.96)	1.16 (0.30)
Verbal aggression	17.28 (12.13)	11.62 (11.00)	2.84 (2.90)
Object aggression	7.62 (8.98)	7.17 (11.23)	1.86 (2.05)
Self-aggression	4.90 (7.69)	4.14 (7.82)	0.14 (0.74)
Other aggression	8.62 (11.28)	5.97 (13.04)	0.59 (1.62)
Expressed hostility	4.50 (1.71)	4.18 (1.76)	3.67 (1.33)
Perceived hostility	4.04 (1.04)	3.43 (1.10)	2.41 (1.45)
Conner's Teacher Questionnaire	14.03 (8.09)	12.03 (9.34)	2.97 (3.45)

NOTE: Standard deviations in parentheses: $N = 29$ for all measures, except Exprssed Hostility and Perceived Hostility, which have $N = 28$ for Clinical–Abused and Clinical–Not Abused groups, and $N = 27$ for Nonclinical Comparison groups.

Proactive Aggression, Verbal Aggression (threats to others), Object Aggression (impulsive property destruction), Self-aggression (self-injurious behaviors), Other Aggression (physical assault), Expressed Hostility, Perceived Hostility, and the Conner's Teacher Questionnaire (hyperactive/impulsive behavior). TABLE 1 presents the ANOVA results for the aggression measures. With the exception of expressed hostility, the results indicate that there were significant differences among the groups for the aggression measures.

Means and standard deviations for the clinical–abused, clinical–not abused, and nonclinical comparison groups are presented in TABLE 2. With the exception of expressed hostility, the Student-Newman-Keuls tests indicated that both clinical

TABLE 3. ANOVA results for psychopathology measures

Psychopathology measure	F	Df
Conduct	16.15*	2, 75
Delinquency/attention	4.56**	2, 75
Anxiety	14.40*	2, 75
Depression	16.13*	2, 75
Autism	5.27**	2, 75
Acute problems	4.81**	2, 75

NOTE: *$P < .001$; **$P < .02$.

TABLE 4. Means and standard deviations for psychopathology measures

Psychopathology measures	Clinical–Abused	Clinical–Not Abused	Nonclinical Comparison
Conduct	60.00 (10.43)	57.31 (12.54)	43.85 (4.39)
Delinquency/attention	54.34 (8.55)	52.41 (11.59)	46.05 (7.96)
Anxiety	61.86 (11.77)	58.79 (14.01)	44.80 (4.11)
Depression	58.55 (10.15)	57.52 (13.09)	42.95 (3.39)
Autism	55.28 (10.07)	57.03 (16.76)	46.05 (4.65)
Acute problems	56.52 (12.58)	57.14 (16.41)	46.65 (2.01)

NOTE: Standard deviations in parentheses: $N = 29$ for Clinical–Abused group; $N = 29$ for Clinical–Not Abused group; $N = 20$ for Nonclinical Comparison group.

groups had significantly higher levels of aggression than the nonclinical comparison group. In addition, the clinical–abused group had nonsignificantly higher scores on all measures and statistically significant higher scores than the clinical–not abused group on reactive aggression and verbal aggression (see FIGS. 1 and 2).

Psychopathology Measures

The DSMD scale measured several facets of internalizing and externalizing psychopathology: conduct disorders, delinquency/attention, anxiety, depression, autism (i.e., social and language problems), and acute problems. TABLE 3 presents the ANOVA results for the psychopathology measures. Overall, these results indicated that there were significant differences among the three groups on all measures of psychopathology.

Means and standard deviations for the clinical–abused, clinical–not abused, and nonclinical comparison groups are presented in TABLE 4. For all measures, Student-Newman-Keuls tests indicated that both clinical groups had significantly higher levels of psychopathology than the nonclinical comparison group. There were no significant differences between the clinical–abused and clinical–not abused groups on any psychopathology measure.

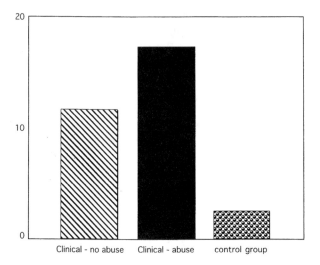

FIGURE 1. Mean verbal aggression scores across the 3 groups. All groups differ significantly from each other.

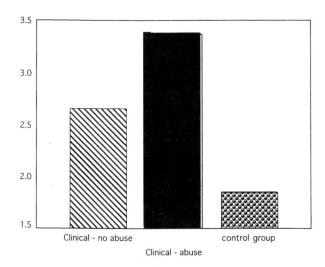

FIGURE 2. Mean reactive aggression scores across the 3 groups. All groups differ significantly from each other.

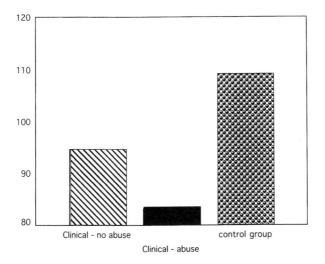

FIGURE 3. Mean verbal IQ scores across the 3 groups. All groups differ significantly from each other.

Intelligence Measures

There were significant differences among the three groups on verbal IQ, $F(2, 83)$ = 16.40, $P < .001$ and performance IQ, $F(2, 83)$ = 6.32, $P < .005$. The Student-Newman-Keuls test indicated that the nonclinical comparison group had higher verbal IQ scores (M = 108.66, SD = 17.16) than the clinical abused group (M = 94.46, SD = 17.10). Both the nonclinical comparison and clinical–not abused groups had significantly higher verbal IQ scores than the clinical–abused group (M = 83.17, SD = 16.68) (see FIG. 3). For performance IQ, the Student-Newman-Keuls test indicated that the nonclinical comparison group (M = 101.97, SD = 18.74) had significantly higher IQ scores than the clinical–not abused (M = 90.82, SD = 19.52) and clinical–abused groups (M = 84.52, SD = 18.50). For performance IQ, the difference between the clinical–abused and clinical–not abused groups was not statistically significant.

DISCUSSION

We completed a study on a small sample of seriously emotionally disturbed children who were clinically referred to residential treatment and a group of nonclinical community comparison children to investigate relationships between a lifetime developmental history of abuse and aggression and psychosocial impairment. This is a preliminary study of these relationships; more conclusive answers will require a larger sample. When evaluating these results both Type I statistical error (probability pyramiding from multiple statistical tests) and Type II error (because of small sample size) should be considered.

Although our results replicate the well-known finding that SED children who are admitted to residential treatment are more impaired on a variety of psychosocial measures than community comparison children, our findings also suggest that clinical children with a history of developmental traumatic stress, such as physical and/or sexual abuse, have greater impairments in several domains of functioning than nonabused clinical youths. One domain that has not received much attention includes aggressive behavior. Clinical children with abuse experiences tended to score higher on all measures of aggression than clinical children without abuse histories. For two measures, reactive aggression and verbal aggression, these differences were statistically significant. These results suggest that early traumatic stress may be associated with aggressive behavior in clinically referred children, even after considering all the other psychosocial factors that cause youths to be referred to residential treatment.

Reactive aggression and verbal aggression were significantly elevated in the group of abused children. Reactive aggression has its theoretical roots in the frustration-aggression model, which states that reactive aggression is an angry, defensive response to threat, frustration, or provocation.[27] Because of their traumatic histories, abused children may have an increased likelihood of misperceiving neutral environmental stimuli as threatening and reacting aggressively to perceived threats, especially with hostile verbal responses.[4,5] Children with abuse histories may have altered stress response thresholds.[28] Early developmental traumatic stress may confer a relatively permanent bias toward self-preservation resulting in heightened aggressive responding and diminished ability to use clinical treatment. In contrast, proactive aggression, defined as a deliberate coercive behavior that is controlled by external reinforcements and is used as a means of obtaining a desired goal, was not elevated in abused children.

Not all aggression measures distinguished the two groups of clinically referred children. This may be caused in part by small sample size and resulting Type II statistical error, but it also highlights the potential importance of categorizing the domain of aggressive behavior more specifically in clinically referred children. Studies that examine specific domains of aggressive behavior may elucidate clinically meaningful relationships between abuse history and particular types of aggressive behavior. For example, our results suggesting a relationship between abuse history and reactive aggression suggest that cognitive behavioral therapies that target a tendency to interpret events as threatening may lead to lessened aggression in clinically referred children. In contrast, children with high proactive aggression scores may benefit from behavioral therapies (e.g., response cost) designed to reduce instrumental aggression.

Children referred to residential treatment have been found to have more psychosocial adjustment problems, including cognitive decrements, increased rates of psychopathology, and poorer long-term adjustment than youths not residing in residential treatment.[7,8] In our sample, psychopathology did not differ between the two groups of clinically referred children (although it did differ in comparison with nonreferred children residing in the community). Thus, differing rates of psychiatric symptoms could not explain the differences in types of aggression found in our sample.

Our results suggest that clinically referred children with histories of abuse show diminished verbal IQ scores relative to clinical children without a traumatic history. In our sample, the relationship between abuse and cognition was specific to verbal IQ. Performance IQ did not differ between the two clinical groups (although PIQ did differ when compared with community comparison children). Our findings are consistent with previous investigations reporting cognitive deficits in abused children.[9,29] Diminished verbal information processing capability may be associated with aggressive behavior in several ways. Diminished linguistic processing may contribute to inefficient use of internal language to modulate behavior. Reduced verbal skills may result in a present oriented cognitive style, which, in turn, may foster more impulsive and irresponsible behaviors. Finally, reduced verbal skills may interfere with children's ability to label their perceptions of the emotions expressed by others and thus may contribute to risk for aggressive responding.[11,30]

SUMMARY

In a sample of seriously emotionally disturbed children referred to residential treatment and nonclinically referred children, developmental traumatic stress, defined as a lifetime history of physical and/or sexual abuse, is related to increased aggression and diminished verbal IQ. Results suggest the importance of categorizing aggression more specifically than the broad domains of externalizing behavioral disorders or conduct problems in traumatized youths. Diminished verbal IQ may contribute to aggressive responding in abused youths. Future directions in abuse research should consider including more specific definitions of aggressive behavior.

REFERENCES

1. BRAXTON, E.T. 1995. Angry children, frightened staff: implications for training and staff development. Res. Treat. Child.Youth **13:** 13–28.
2. CONNOR, D.F. *et al.* 1997. Combined pharmacotherapy in children and adolescents in a residential treatment center. J. Am. Acad. Child Adolesc. Psychiatry **36:** 248–254.
3. JOSHI, P.K. & L.A. ROSENBERG. 1997. Children's behavioral response to residential treatment. J. Clin. Psychol. **53:** 567–573.
4. CONNOR, D.F., R.H. MELLONI, JR. & R.J. HARRISON. 1998. Overt categorical aggression in referred children and adolescents. J. Am. Acad. Child Adolesc. Psychiatry **37:** 66–73.
5. DODGE, K.A. & J.D. COIE. 1987. Social-information processing factors in reactive and proactive aggression in children's peer groups. J. Per. Soc. Psychol. **53:** 1146–1158.
6. CONNOR, D.F. *et al.* 2002. What does getting better mean? Variables associated with child improvement and measurement of outcome in residential treatment. Am. J. Orthopsychiatr. **72:** 110–117.
7. CURRY, J.F. 1991. Outcome research on residential treatment: implications and suggested directions. Am. J. Orthopsychiatr. **61:** 348–357.
8. HOAGWOOD, K. & M. CUNNINGHAM. 1992. Outcomes of children with emotional disturbance in residential treatment for educational purposes. J. Child Fam. Stud. **1:** 129–140.
9. BEERS, S.R. & M.D. DEBELLIS. 2002. Neuropsychological function in children with maltreatment-related posttraumatic stress disorder. Am. J. Psychiatry **159:** 483–486.
10. OATES, R.K. & A. PEACOCK. 1984. Intellectual development of battered children. Austr. N. Z. J. Dev. Disabil. **10:** 27–29.
11. MOFFITT, T.E. & D. LYNAM. 1994. The neuropsychology of conduct disorder and delinquency: implications for understanding antisocial behavior. *In* Progress in Experimental Personality and Psychopathology Research. D.C. Fowles, P. Sutker, & S.H. Goodman, Eds.: 233–262. Springer. New York.
12. CONNOR, D.F. *et al.* 1998. Prevalence and patterns of psychotropic and anticonvulsant medication use in children and adolescents referred to residential treatment. J. Child Adolesc. Psychopharmacol. **8:** 27–38.

13. COHEN, J. 1960. A coefficient of agreement for nominal scales. Educ. Psychol. Measure. **20:** 37–46.
14. WECHSLER, D. 1981. Manual for the Wechsler Adult Intelligence Scale–Revised. The Psychological Corporation. San Antonio, TX.
15. WECHSLER, D. 1991. Wechsler Intelligence Scale for Children. The Psychological Corporation. San Antonio, TX.
16. SORGI, P. *et al.* 1991. Rating aggression in the clinical setting: a retrospective adaptation of the overt aggression scale. J. Neuropsychiatr. Clin. Neurosci. **3:** S52–S56.
17. YUDOFSKY, S.C. *et al.* 1986. The overt aggression scale for the objective rating of verbal and physical aggression. Am. J. Psychiatry **143:** 35–39.
18. DODGE, K.A. *et al.* 1997. Reactive and proactive aggression in school children and psychiatrically impaired chronically assaultive youth. J. Abnorm. Child Psychol. **106:** 37–51.
19. COIE, J.D. *et al.* 1991. The role of aggression in peer relations: an analysis of aggression episodes in boys' play groups. Child Dev. **62:** 812–826.
20. BUSS, A.H., A. DURKEE & M.B. BAER. 1956. The measurement of hostility in clinical situations. J. Abnorm. Soc. Psychol. **52:** 84–86.
21. RILEY, W.T. & F.A. TREIBER. 1989. The validity of multidimensional self-report anger and hostility. J. Clin. Psychol. **45:** 397–404.
22. TREIBER, F.A. *et al.* 1989. The relationship between hostility and blood pressure in children. Behav. Med. **15:** 173–178.
23. CONNERS, C.K. & R.A. BARKLEY. 1985. Rating scales and checklists for child psychopharmacology. Psychopharmacol. Bull. **21:** 809–843.
24. GOYETTE, C.H., C.K. CONNERS & R.F. ULRICH. 1978. Normative data on revised Conners parent and teacher rating scales. J. Abnorm. Child Psychol. **6:** 221–236.
25. HINSHAW, S.P. 1987. On the distinction between attentional deficits/hyperactivity and conduct problems/aggression in child psychopathology. Psychol. Bull. **101:** 443–463.
26. NAGLIERI, J.A., P.A. LEBUFFE & S.I. PFEIFFER. 1994. Devereux scales of mental disorders. The Psychological Corporation. San Antonio, TX.
27. BERKOWITZ, L. 1989. Frustration-aggression hypothesis: examination and reformulation. Psychol. Bull. **106:** 59–73.
28. GLASER, D. 2000. Child abuse and neglect and the brain-a review. J. Child Psychol. Psychiatry. **41:** 97–116.
29. CAHILL, L.T., R.K. KAMINER & P.G. JOHNSON. 1999. Developmental, cognitive, and behavioral sequelae of child abuse. Child Adolesc. Psychiatr. Clin. N. Am. **8:** 827–843.
30. CONNOR, D.F. 2002. Aggression and Antisocial Behavior in Children and Adolescents: Research and Treatment. Guilford Publications. New York.

The Amygdala and Development of the Social Brain

DAVID SKUSE, JOHN MORRIS, AND KATE LAWRENCE

Behavioural and Brain Sciences Unit, Institute of Child Health, London, United Kingdom

ABSTRACT: The amygdala comprises part of an extended network of neural circuits that are critically involved in the processing of socially salient stimuli. Such stimuli may be explicitly social, such as facial expressions, or they may be only tangentially social, such as abstract shapes moving with apparent intention relative to one another. The coordinated interplay between neural activity in the amygdala and other brain regions, especially the medial prefrontal cortex, the occipitofrontal cortex, the fusiform gyrus, and the superior temporal sulcus, allows us to develop social responses and to engage in social behaviors appropriate to our species. The harmonious functioning of this integrated social cognitive network may be disrupted by congenital or acquired lesions, by genetic anomalies, and by exceptional early experiences. Each form of disruption is associated with a slightly different outcome, dependent on the timing of the experience, the location of the lesion, or the nature of the genetic anomaly. Studies in both humans and primates concur; the dysregulation of basic emotions, especially the processing of fear and anger, is an almost invariable consequence of such disruption. These, in turn, have direct or indirect consequences for social behavior.

KEYWORDS: social brain; amygdala; behavior; facial expression

FACE PROCESSING AND THE "SOCIAL BRAIN"

We gain critically important information about how to respond appropriately in social encounters by monitoring the expression on another's face. This observation provides us with information about that person's emotional state. In certain circumstances, another's emotional expressions can evoke that emotion in oneself—viewing an expression of great happiness is one obvious example. Haxby *et al.*[1] proposed that there are dedicated systems for processing emotional expressions in another's face, in which the amygdala and insula play a crucial role.

When we use our social cognitive capacity to interpret the emotional content of a face and its meaning to us, we take into account a wide range of visual cues. These include, whether we know the individual or not (face recognition memory), the facial configuration (e.g., whether the mouth is wide open or shut, whether the eyes are

Address for correspondence: David Skuse, M.D., FRCP, Institute of Child Health, Behavioural and Brain Sciences Unit, 30 Guilford St., London, UK WC1N 1EH. Voice: +44 20 7831 0975; fax: +44 20 7831 7050.

dskuse@ich.ucl.ac.uk

Ann. N.Y. Acad. Sci. 1008: 91–101 (2003). © 2003 New York Academy of Sciences.
doi: 10.1196/annals.1301.010

wide open or narrowed), and, in particular, eye gaze (is this person looking at me, or at something/someone else?) Accurate perception of emotional expression involves the coordinated participation of regions for the visual analysis of expression and regions for representing and producing emotions, in which the amygdala plays a significant role.[2] Studies both from humans with congenital or acquired damage to their amygdalae[3] and from primates in which lesions have been induced[4] show that this subcortical structure influences our ability to gain and to maintain socially appropriate behavior by affecting domains of face-processing ability including face recognition memory, facial expression interpretation and eye-gaze monitoring. Whether its functional integrity is critical for normal social cognitive development in humans has not yet been determined.[5]

AMYGDALA RESPONSIVENESS IN FACE PROCESSING

We observe, from functional magnetic resonance imaging, that there is greater activation in the amygdala (in terms of a blood oxygen level depletion (BOLD) response) when we perceive *fear* compared with other emotional faces.[6] When the amygdala is bilaterally ablated the perception of fear is selectively impaired.[7] We do not fully understand why this is so, but recent evidence suggests that the amygdala responds specifically to eye contact in adults.[8] Behavioral studies in monkeys have shown that eye contact is a critical component of threatening and fear-related displays.[9] A simple stare is often the most effective stimulus in evoking a fight or flight response in nonhuman primates.[10] Consequently, direct eye contact elicits an instinctive "fear-response" in humans and primates that is detectable in terms of autonomic arousal (e.g., skin conductance response[11] (SCR)). The amygdala is an essential and central component of a threat-detection system, with extensive neocortical and subcortical connections that are crucial for the automatic nonconscious responses to a threatening stimulus (e.g., fight and flight).

Our social interactions require complex cortical processing of face stimuli and our reaction to direct eye contact is critically dependent on the social context in which it occurs. Our response to a stimulus that *could* be a threat is normally determined by a full evaluation of that stimulus, by means of complex neocortical connections.

Accordingly, the outcome of interactions between the activated amygdala and social cognition processing centers in the neocortex[12] permits appropriate responses in a social encounter. When patients have suffered amygdala damage, there is impairment in interpreting subtleties of mood from the eye region of others.[13] When eye contact is made, activity is elicited in both conscious (explicit) and nonconscious (implicit) neural pathways, in parallel, and it is the synthesis of perceptions carried by these separate pathways that allows the development of social cognition, based on visual information from faces. We propose that their normal functioning, and their mutual interaction, is essential for the development and maintenance of social cognitive skills.

Implicit Processing of Threat Cues by the Amygdala

Implicit processing of visual stimuli that could constitute a threat, including fearful expressions and other fear-related stimuli (such as snakes or spiders), engages *subcortical* visual pathways that are routed directly to the amygdala, without passing through the visual cortex first.[6,14] Consequently, these stimuli can evoke a very rapid physiological response, before the neocortex has had time to process the information and initiate an appropriate course of action.[14]

The visual pathway from the larger cell bodies (magnocellular retinal ganglion cells) of the retina is differentially sensitive to movement and contrast rather than to detail.[15] They project to both the ventral and dorsal streams of visual processing. The superior colliculus receives its visual input primarily from these magnocellular retinal ganglion cells—which have large and rapidly conducting axons.[16] The principal projection of the magnocellular pathway from the superior colliculus is to the pulvinar and other nuclei in the posterior thalamus.[17] In turn, there are direct projections from the pulvinar nucleus to the amygdala in primates.[18] Activation of pulvinar and superior colliculus by fearful expressions has been shown to occur specifically with low-spatial frequency faces, suggesting that these subcortical pathways may provide coarse fear-related inputs to the amygdala.[19] It is notable the contrast of sclera to iris, and the width of the palpebral fissure, are far greater in humans than in any other primate,[20] thus exaggerating the contrast and impact of direct eye to eye contact.

Morris *et al.*[21] propose that this low-spatial resolution subcortical pathway provides a potential route by which neural responses to the threat posed by "fearful eyes" (and by implication, eye contact in general) can reach the amygdala independently of the geniculostriate neocortical system. They found, using chimerical faces as stimuli in an functional magnetic resonance imaging study, that fearful eyes alone are sufficient to evoke increased neural responses in this nonconscious circuit.[22] This circuit because of its importance for survival has been highly conserved in the evolution of different species, including humans, where its influence interacts with neocortical processes underlying complex social interactions.[10]

The ability to interpret emotions on other's faces is one aspect of our development that underpins our reactivity in social situations, particularly complex situations that demand rapid processing of facial expressions from several individuals simultaneously. Remarkably, our ability to process certain negative emotions—especially the accurate interpretation of the expression of "fear"—is closely correlated in women with face recognition memory, implying the same neural circuits may be used for both purposes in them.[23] Such a correlation is not found in men. Infants are able to discriminate their mother's face from that of a stranger as early as the newborn period,[24] although the ease with which they do so is dependent on the dissimilarity of their faces.[25] They are also especially interested in facial expressions that emphasize wide-open eyes, such as fearful expressions.[26]

Experiential Impact on the Maldevelopment of Face-Processing Systems

Seth Pollak has investigated the role that experience plays in the development of affective strategies, patterns of expressed emotion, and the ability to interpret the emotions of others. For many years, we have known that patterns of emotional expression and recognition are different in maltreated children from those who have not been maltreated.[27] He postulated a role for socioemotional experiences in the onset of brain organization, operationalizing the latter in terms of evoked response potentials (ERPs). In a remarkable series of studies, he found that traumatic experiences during childhood could influence the attention paid by cortical circuits to the sorts of facial expressions associated with abusive experiences, in particular, the expression of anger.[27,28]

Pollak reports that the right frontal ERP component P3b has greater amplitude in maltreated children when they are asked to attend to an angry, as opposed to a fearful or happy face, compared with the equivalent P3b potential in nonmaltreated children. Angry faces may have different implications for maltreated children, for they would be more ambiguous in terms of possible outcomes. It is possible that they therefore command greater processing resources in formerly maltreated children. In a further set of studies Pollak and Kistler[29] found that the threshold for categorical discrimination of anger from other facial expressions (fear and sad) is lower among children who had been maltreated. Formerly maltreated children "over-interpret signals as threatening."

Amygdala-Cortical Connectivity and the Integrity of the Social Brain

Normally, the ability to make an accurate distinction between the facial expression of fear, and that of surprise, entails the interpretation of context. It is possible to distinguish these expressions accurately in an unfamiliar face, but studies of the mistakes made by adults rating the Ekman face series[30] show that fear is most frequently confused with surprise. We hypothesize that inhibitory circuits (probably originating in the ventromedial prefrontal cortex, possibly the anterior cingulate cortex[31,32]) enable us to respond appropriately to the facial expression of (pleasant) surprise—which would normally be encountered within a context that assists the distinction from fear. Obviously, a surprise that is unpleasant or threatening would lead to a fearful response, so the distinction from surprise would be irrelevant to the observer.

The distinction between surprise and fear would not presumably be relevant to any other primate. It is arguable that even our closest primate cousins would not be capable of inhibiting a fear-related social response, as has been suggested by some recent observations of David Amaral. He found, when selective lesions were made in the amygdalae of 2-week-old macaques, that, at 6 months or so of age, the lesioned animals were in adulthood less fearful of novel objects such as rubber snakes than controls, but they were substantially more fearful during dyadic social interactions.[33] Interestingly, this fear was expressed maximally when the animals were face to face with one another. When the animal with the lesion encountered another animal moving away (hence not making face to face contact), it was inclined to follow. That observation suggests the social anxiety was not generalized but was specifically engendered by face to face (or eye to eye) encounters. The finding of social fear in adulthood following lesions to the amygdala that were made in infancy is in striking contrast to his earlier work, which reported social disinhibition as the outcome for macaques whose amygdala lesions were induced in adulthood.[34] On the face of it, there is a paradox needing to be explained here.

We suggest that paradox may be resolved as follows. If a primitive response to social threat can be induced merely by eye contact, then direct contact with the eyes of a conspecific would produce an initial pattern of brain activation that responds as if they were the eyes of a predator. To use eye contact for social purposes, primates have developed all sorts of cortical control mechanisms during evolution to modulate such arousal and harness it to other ends (e.g., social bonding). As discussed, our response to direct eye contact initially is processed by subcortical visual structures—superior colliculus and thalamic pulvinar nucleus. These subcortical responses are normally relayed to the amygdala, which also receives extensive neocortical inputs from sensory regions in temporal lobe and "executive" regions in the prefrontal lobe. Amygdala-mediated fear behavior depends on an integration of all these influences. It is possible that the 6–8-month-old macaques, whose amygdalae had been removed, showed less fear of novel objects, because this behavior depends on neocortical inputs to amygdala—it was a fear that had at least in part to be learned. The reason why they showed more fear of face to face social interactions was because the innate fear signals from collicular and pulvinar processing of eye contact could no longer be subject to prefrontal inhibitory modulation in amygdala, because it had been removed. The pulvinar projects directly to many subcortical and neocortical areas and the amygdala is bypassed. There is presumably sufficient plasticity in brain development at this age for the links between pulvinar and subcortical circuits that mediate stress responses to be enhanced, in the absence of the amygdala. Amaral comments (personal communication) that when the amygdala is removed in adult monkeys, the treated animals do not show the usual physiological response to a social stressor either. A normal monkey interacting for the first time with an unfamiliar animal would exhibit an increased cortisol secretion in the animals without an amygdala. Such a physiological response is not seen in animals whose amygdalae were removed in adulthood. In contrast to the consequences of neonatal lesions, the pulvinar–subcortical circuits that potentially mediate a social stress response are presumably incapable of enhancement, in the absence of the amygdala.

SEXUAL DIMORPHISM IN THE DEVELOPMENT OF "SOCIAL BRAIN"

There is increasing evidence that deficits in social cognitive competence are substantially more common in males than females.[35] The evolution of the sex chromosomes has caused unique mechanisms of regulation, so as to equalize gene expression between the sexes.[36] We hypothesize that imbalance in the expression of certain classes of X-linked genes could account for sexually dimorphic traits independent of the influence of sex steroids, although it is likely such systems would be interacting with hormonal regulators of gene expression. Specifically, we hypothesize that male vulnerability to the symptoms of autistic spectrum disorders, in those of normal intelligence, is influenced by relative haploinsufficiency for one or more X-linked genes that serve to protect females. The ratio of males to females identified with high-functioning (high IQ) autism is at least 10:1, a little-remarked upon yet intriguing observation which must have relevance for our understanding of the neural basis of that condition.[37]

In normal females, one of the two X-chromosomes is inactivated at random, to ensure equal expression of X-linked genes in male and female mammals.[58] Genes that escape X inactivation are found at the tips of the X and Y chromosome arms in the so-called pseudoautosomal regions, where the equivalent nucleotide sequence is identical in both sex chromosomes, thus allowing meiotic recombination to take place. Surprisingly, many genes are now known to escape inactivation elsewhere on the X chromosome. These are nonrandomly distributed, they lie mostly on the short arm, and they do not necessarily have expressed Y homologues.[38] Persistence of a dosage imbalance in such genes, between males (46,XY) and females (46,XX), may be important for sex-specific functions.[36]

X Monosomy as a Developmental Model of Social-Cognitive Impairment

Turner syndrome females have a single X chromosome (45,X or X monosomy) and therefore are haploinsufficient for noninactivated X-linked genes, relative to normal females.[39] Turner syndrome (TS) is a chromosomal disorder, with a prevalence of 1 per 2,500 live female births, in which typically all or a substantial part of one X chromosome is missing because of nondisjunction or chromosome loss during early cleavage of the zygote. In 70% of monosomic (45,X) TS, the single X chromosome is maternally inherited,[40] the remainder being paternally inherited. In monosomy X, this single chromosome is never inactivated, although in normal 46,XX females one of the two X chromosomes is inactivated at random during the blastocyst stage of development. Dosage-sensitive genes that escape X inactivation may contribute to some features of TS if haploinsufficient in X monosomy. For example, SHOX[41] is now known to contribute to the short stature of the syndrome and is normally expressed from the pseudoautosomal region (PAR1) of both the X and Y chromosomes. Most cases of TS show normal verbal intelligence, but almost all have poor visuospatial abilities.[42] Recently, we have discovered the condition is associated with a substantially increased risk of autism (at least 200 times).[43]

We have studied the neural basis of the social-cognitive deficit in TS, which we suspected would be similar in quality to that found in autistic individuals with idiopathic disorders. We discovered reliable deficits in the recognition of faces, and in the identification of a "fearful" facial expression, among X-monosomic women of normal verbal intelligence.[44] Because these deficits were reminiscent of those reported in people with autism,[45] we hypothesized that TS women would possess other anomalies in socioperceptual skills. The processing of gaze was one such feature that interested us, because children with autism and those at risk for developing autism show less eye contact and a reduced ability to follow the gaze of another, especially when the attention of the other is directed to an event of social interest.[46] We confirmed that women with TS had difficulty ascertaining gaze direction from face photographs showing small lateral angular gaze deviations.[47] They also showed selective impairments in "reading the mind from the eyes" and face recognition memory.[44,47] These findings are indicative of an anomaly in the processing of facial information, in particular, that involving the eyes, and implicated functional anomalies in the amygdala and related circuitry of the "social brain."

In view of the parallels with deficits that have been reported in association with autism, we also assessed our 45,X subjects with a cartoon-based task that measures Theory of Mind skills.[48] Our hypothesis, that many 45,X women would score in the autistic range on aspects of this task, was supported. More than 50% scored at least 1 SD below the mean for normal female controls, with no significant association between performance and IQ in the X-monosomic sample.

We subsequently conducted a range of structural and functional imaging studies of the amygdala in TS, the results of which confirm the hypothesis that both the amygdala and its functional connections are abnormal in X-monosomic women. The structural studies show that the size of the amygdala is larger in this condition than in matched comparison 46,XX females.[49] Our functional imaging analyses are still undergoing analysis. In other (unpublished) findings of behavioral studies in TS, which focused on the amygdala's role in fear conditioning, we found most 45,X women had impaired habituation and excessive SCR responses in a well-studied conditioning paradigm.[6] The fact that a deficit in the perception of fear in another's face can be associated with excessive reactivity (rather than hyporeactivity) of the amygdala in fear conditioning is a remarkable dissociation that demands further analysis. The strong implication is that in this condition there is anomalous modulation by the amygdala of cortical circuits concerned with face processing and other aspects of social cognition, and of the amygdala itself by frontal cortical regions. We also have shown recently that the ability to classify fear in facial expressions is correlated with face recognition skill in women, but not in men.[23] This intriguing dissociation between the sexes may reflect sexual dimorphism in the mnemonic functions of the amygdala[50] and could, in turn, have relevance to the observation that males are more vulnerable to disorders of social cognition than females.[37]

Intriguingly, not all 45,X females shared these deficits in fear perception, gaze monitoring, and fear conditioning. About one-third were severely affected, and the remainder had a range of impairments distributed around a median that was low-normal. Examination of the data plotted graphically suggested a bimodal distribution. It is not at this stage clear just what mechanism or mechanisms relating to X monosomy are responsible for our findings. However, the implication is that, directly or indirectly, haploinsufficiency of X-linked genes that normally escape X inactivation (and are not imprinted) causes maldevelopment and dysfunction of the amygdala and related circuits that are essential for processes relating to social cognition.

There is now substantial replicated evidence that the amygdala is sexually dimorphic in structure, and there appears to be an inverse relationship between amygdala volume and the number of X chromosomes in broad terms. Several studies[51,52] have reported larger volumes among 46,XY males than 46,XX females. 47,XXY males have amygdalae of similar volume to 46,XX females, whereas the amygdalae of 47,XXX females are significantly smaller than either group.[53]

In X monosomy the deficit in specific social cognitive abilities is associated with abnormal structure of the amygdala and orbitofrontal cortex.[49] In a separate investigation of adult females who lack part of the short arm (Xp) of the X chromosome,[54] we have deletion-mapped the critical locus to a 5-Mb region at Xp11.3 (Ensembl v 15.33.1). In females who have deleted this region, deficits in performance in tasks of social cognition are similar to those seen in X monosomy (despite the fact that the remainder of the X chromosome is intact). In females who have deleted a more distal region of Xp, performance is similar to that of normal 46,XX females. Details of these experiments and their associated findings are reported in Good *et al.*[49]

Accordingly, close to the centromere on the short arm of the X chromosome lies a region that appears to contain one or more dosage-sensitive genes, which are critical for the normal development and function of the amygdala and its cortical connections. Within the critical region at Xp11.3 the monoamine oxidase (MAO) genes are clearly contenders for a potential influence upon amygdala development. Borowsky et al.[55] showed that three of four members of a family of G protein–coupled receptors that are activated by trace amines, such as beta-phenylethylamine, are expressed exclusively in the human amygdala. Trace amines are exquisitely sensitive to the deaminergic actions of MAO genes (in the case of phenylethylamine it is especially MAOB). Accordingly, relatively low levels of MAOB activity consequent upon haploinsufficiency in males and 45,X females may lead to male-typical patterns of amygdala responsiveness, for example, in the context of emotional learning.[56] Unfortunately, proving that specific genes could contribute to the social-cognitive deficits of X monosomy is far from easy. There is heterogeneous expression from inactivated X-chromosome for some X-linked genes that escape inactivation outside the pseudoautosomal region, indicating there could be variability in X inactivation between tissues for the same genes, and even differences of inactivation patterns between individual females.[38]

Testing of somatic cell hybrids suggest some 5–15% of X-linked genes could escape X inactivation in females, despite the fact they lie outside the pseudoautosomal region. We are particularly interested in the possibility that MAOB and conceivably MAOA could escape X inactivation in some tissues (discussed in Good et al.[49]). If so, activity would be relatively lower in 45,X than 46,XX females (consistent with our observations), as well as being potentially sexually dimorphic with lower activity in males (also consistent with our findings). Such a mechanism could exacerbate sex differences in vulnerability to disorders affecting predominantly males that result from MAOA functional polymorphisms.[57]

CONCLUSIONS

The normal development of social-cognitive skills depends fundamentally on our genotype, but disorders of social cognition are substantially more common among males than females. This observation implies that sex-related biological factors increase male susceptibility, or reduce female vulnerability, or both. We have yet to identify the mechanisms involved, but when we do so we will be substantially closer to understanding the neural basis of disorders such as autism, in which social-cognitive deficits predominate. Increasingly, structural and functional anomalies of the amygdala are reported in autistic conditions. There is substantial evidence that this complex multinuclear structure plays a critical role in the modulation of social behavior in primate species, although it may not be essential for the emergence of species-typical social behaviors. The role played by the amygdala in determining primate reactions to potentially fear-inducing stimuli has been investigated by Skuse (in X-monosomic human females) and Amaral (in macaque monkeys). Both have found evidence for an abnormal response to potential threats, associated with congenital and acquired lesions, respectively. Both studies have found evidence that face to face contact induces abnormal responses in those whose amygdalae are dysfunctional. However, an abnormal physiological response to certain classes of face stimulus can be induced by environmental influences too. Pollak has demonstrated that the early experience of abuse can significantly alter children's perception of angry facial expressions, which may represent a threat to the child, long after the abuse has ceased. The complementary findings from these strands of research emphasize the importance and subtlety of interactions that can occur between biological diathesis and environmental contingencies. When considering the roots of mental illness in children, here we have a fascinating example of how complementary strands from clinical and animal research come together to illuminate one aspect of the social brain and its disorders.

REFERENCES

1. HAXBY, J.V., E.A. HOFFMAN & M.I. GOBBINI. 2002. Human neural systems for face recognition and social communication. Biol. Psychiatry **51:** 59–67.
2. ADOLPHS, R. 2001. The neurobiology of social cognition. Curr. Opin. Neurobiol. **11:** 231–239.
3. CALDER, A.J., A.D. LAWRENCE & A.W. YOUNG. 2001. Neuropsychology of fear and loathing. Nat. Rev. Neurosci. **2:** 352–363.
4. AMARAL, D.G. 2002. The primate amygdala and the neurobiology of social behavior: implications for understanding social anxiety. Biol. Psychiatry **51:** 11–17.
5. AMARAL, D.G. *et al.* 2003. The amygdala: Is it an essential component of the neural network for social cognition? Neuropsychologia **41:** 235–240.
6. BUCHEL, C., J. MORRIS, R.J. DOLAN & K.J. FRISTON. 1998. Brain systems mediating aversive conditioning: an event-related fMRI study. Neuron **20:** 947–957.
7. ADOLPHS, R. *et al.* 1999. Recognition of facial emotion in nine individuals with bilateral amygdala damage. Neuropsychologia **37:** 1111–1117.
8. KAWASHIMA, R. *et al.* 1999. The human amygdala plays an important role in gaze monitoring: a PET study. Brain **122:** 779–783.
9. NAHM, F.K. 1997. Heinrich Kluver and the temporal lobe syndrome. J. Hist. Neurosci. **6:** 193–208.
10. EMERY, N.J. 2000. The eyes have it: the neuroethology, function and evolution of social gaze. Neurosci. Behav. Rev. **24:** 581–604.
11. DONOVAN, W.L. & L.A. LEAVITT. 1980. Physiologic correlates of direct and averted gaze. Biol. Psychol. **10:** 189–199.
12. BROTHERS, L. 1990. The social brain: a project for integrating primate behaviour and neurophysiology in a new domain. Concepts Neurosci. **1:** 27–51.
13. ADOLPHS, R., S. BARON-COHEN & D. TRANEL. 2002. Impaired recognition of social emotions following amygdala damage. J. Cogn. Neurosci. **14:** 1264–1274.
14. MORRIS, J.S., C. BUCHEL & R.J. Dolan. 2001. Parallel neural responses in amygdala subregions and sensory cortex during implicit fear conditioning. Neuroimage **13:** 1044–1052.
15. ELGAR, K. & R. CAMPBELL. 2001. Annotation: the cognitive neuroscience of face recognition: implications for developmental disorders. J. Child Psychol. Psychiatry **42:** 705–717.
16. KAPLAN, E. & E. BENARDETE. 2001. The dynamics of primate retinal ganglion cells. Prog. Brain Res. **134:** 17–34.
17. BENEVENTO, L.A. & J.H. FALLON. 1975. The ascending projections of the superior colliculus in the rhesus monkey (*Macaca mulatta*). J. Comp. Neurol. **160:** 339–361.
18. JONES, E.G. & H. BURTON. 1976. A projection from the medial pulvinar to the amygdala in primates. Brain Res. **104:** 142–147.
19. VUILLEUMIER, P., J.L. ARMONY, J. DRIVER & R.J. DOLAN. 2003. Distinct spatial frequency sensitivities for processing faces and emotional expressions. Nat. Neurosci. **6:** 624–631.
20. KOBAYASHI, H. & S. KOHSHIMA. 1997. Unique morphology of the human eye. Nature **387:** 767–768.
21. MORRIS, J.S., A. OHMAN & R.J. DOLAN. 1999. A subcortical pathway to the right amygdala mediating "unseen" fear. Proc. Natl. Acad. Sci USA **96:** 1680–1685.
22. MORRIS, J.S., M. DEBONIS & R.J. DOLAN. 2002. Human amygdala responses to fearful eyes. Neuroimage **17:** 214–222.

23. CAMPBELL, R. *et al.* 2002.The classification of "fear" from faces is associated with face recognition skill in women. Neuropsychologia **40:** 575–584.
24. PASCALIS, O. *et al.* 1995. Mother's face recognition in neonates: a replication and an extension. Infant Behav. Dev. **18:** 79–86.
25. DE HAAN, M. & C.A. NELSON. 1997. Recognition of the mother's face by six-month-old infants: a neurobehavioral study. Child Dev. **68:** 187–210.
26. NELSON, C.A. & K.G. DOLGIN. 1985. The generalized discrimination of facial expressions by seven-month-old infants. Child Dev. **56:** 58–61.
27. POLLAK, S.D., D. CICCHETTI, K. HORNUNG & A. REED. 2000. Recognizing emotion in faces: developmental effects of child abuse and neglect. Dev. Psychol. **36:** 679–688.
28. POLLAK, S.D., R. KLORMAN, J.E. THATCHER & D. CICCHETTI. 2001. P3b reflects maltreated children's reactions to facial displays of emotion. Psychophysiology **38:** 267–274.
29. POLLAK, S.D. & D.J. KISTLER. 2002. Early experience is associated with the development of categorical representations for facial expressions of emotion. Proc. Natl. Acad. Sci. USA **99:** 9072–9076.
30. EKMAN, P. & W.V. FRIESEN. 1976. Pictures of Facial Affect. Consulting Psychologists. Palo Alto, CA.
31. ALLMAN, J.M. *et al.* 2001. The anterior cingulate cortex. the evolution of an interface between emotion and cognition. Ann. N.Y. Acad. Sci. **935:** 107–117.
32. POSNER, M.I. & M.K. ROTHBART. 1998. Attention, self-regulation and consciousness. Philos. Trans. R. Soc. Lond. B Biol. Sci. **353:** 1915–1927.
33. PRATHER, M.D. *et al.* 2001. Increased social fear and decreased fear of objects in monkeys with neonatal amygdala lesions. Neuroscience **106:** 653–658.
34. EMERY, N.J. *et al.* 2001. The effects of bilateral lesions of the amygdala on dyadic social interactions in rhesus monkeys (*Macaca mulatta*). Behav. Neurosci. **115:** 515–544.
35. BARON-COHEN, S. 2003. The Essential Difference: Men, Women and the Extreme Male Brain. Allen Lane Science. London.
36. DISTECHE, C.M. 1999. Escapees on the X chromosome. Proc. Natl. Acad. Sci. USA **96:** 14180–14182.
37. SKUSE, D.H. 2000. Imprinting, the X-chromosome, and the male brain: explaining sex differences in the liability to autism. Pediatr. Res. **47:** 9–16.
38. CARREL, L., A.A. COTTLE, K.C. GOGLIN & H.F. WILLARD. 1999. A first-generation X-inactivation profile of the human X chromosome. Proc. Natl. Acad. Sci. USA **96:** 14440–14444.
39. ZINN, A.R. & J.L. ROSS. 1998. Turner syndrome and Haploinsufficiency. Curr. Opin. Genet. Dev. **8:** 322–327.
40. JACOBS, P. *et al.* 1997. Turner syndrome: a cytogenetic and molecular study. Ann. Hum. Genet. **61:** 471–483.
41. RAO, E. *et al.* 1997. Pseudoautosomal deletions encompassing a novel homeobox gene cause growth failure in idiopathic short stature and Turner syndrome. Nat. Genet. **16:** 54–63.
42. TEMPLE, C.M. & R.A. CARNEY. 1995. Patterns of spatial functioning in Turner's syndrome. Cortex **31:** 109–118.
43. CRESWELL, C. & D. SKUSE. 2000. Autism in association with Turner syndrome: implications for male vulnerability. Neurocase **5:** 511–518.
44. LAWRENCE, K. *et al.* 2003. Face and emotion recognition deficits in Turner syndrome: a possible role for X-linked genes in amygdala development. Neuropsychology **17:** 39–49.
45. HOWARD, M.A. *et al.* 2000. Convergent neuroanatomical and behavioural evidence of an amygdala hypothesis of autism. Neuroreport **11:** 2931–2935.
46. RUFFMAN, T., W. GARNHAM & P. RIDEOUT. 2001. Social understanding in autism: eye gaze as a measure of core insights. J. Child Psychol. Psychiatry **42:** 1083–1094.
47. LAWRENCE, K. *et al.* 2003. Interpreting gaze in Turner syndrome: impaired sensitivity to intention and emotion, but preservation of social cueing. Neuropsychologia **1571:** 1–12.

48. CASTELLI, F., C. FRITH, F. HAPPE & U. FRITH. 2002. Autism, Asperger syndrome and brain mechanisms for the attribution of mental states to animated shapes. Brain **125:** 1839–1849.
49. GOOD, C.D. *et al.* 2003. Dosage sensitive X-linked locus influences the development of amygdala and orbito-frontal cortex, and fear recognition in humans. Brain **126:** 2431–2446.
50. CAHILL, L. *et al.* 2001. Sex-related difference in amygdala activity during emotionally influenced memory storage. Neurobiol. Learn. Memory **75:** 1–9.
51. GOLDSTEIN, J.M. *et al.* 2001. Normal sexual dimorphism of the adult human brain assessed by in vivo magnetic resonance imaging. Cereb. Cortex **11:** 490–497.
52. GOOD, C.D. *et al.* 2001. Cerebral asymmetry and the effects of sex and handedness on brain structure: a voxel-based morphometric analysis of 465 normal adult human brains. Neuroimage **14:** 685–700.
53. PATWARDHAN, A.J. *et al.* 2002. Reduced size of the amygdala in individuals with 47, XXY and 47, XXX karyotypes. Am. J. Med. Genet. **114:** 93–98.
54. JAMES, R.S. *et al.* 1998. A study of females with deletions of the short arm of the X chromosome. Hum. Genet. **102:** 507–516.
55. BOROWSKY, B. *et al.* 2001. Trace amines: identification of a family of mammalian G protein-coupled receptors. Proc. Natl. Acad. Sci. USA **98:** 8966–8971.
56. CANLI, T. *et al.* 2000. Event-related activation in the human amygdala associates with later memory for individual emotional experience. J. Neurosci. **20:** 99.
57. CASPI, A. *et al.* 2002. Role of genotype in the cycle of violence in maltreated children. Science **297:** 851–854.
58. Lyon, M.F. 1961. Gene action in the X-chromosome of the mouse (Mus musculus L). Nature **190:** 372–373.

Experience-Dependent Affective Learning and Risk for Psychopathology in Children

SETH D. POLLAK

Department of Psychology, University of Wisconsin, Madison, Wisconsin 53706-8190, USA

ABSTRACT: The influence of childhood affective experiences across development may be understood in terms of preparedness to learn about emotion, combined with general immaturity and neuro-plasticity of perceptual systems. Early in development, processing resources are relatively immature and limited in capacity, thereby constraining how much information the young child can absorb. But it is clear that learning about emotions proceeds swiftly in nearly all children, suggesting biological preparedness to track associations between certain stimuli and outcomes. It is proposed here that limited processing capacity, in tandem with dispositions to filter or select key privileged stimuli in the environment, facilitates adaptive, rapid, affective learning. The developmental organization of affective systems is contingent upon those features of input that are most learnable, such as signals that are particularly salient, frequent, or predictable. Therefore, plasticity confers risk for maladaptation in that children's learning will be based upon these prominent features of the environment, however aberrant.

KEYWORDS: child abuse; genes; psychopathology; affective learning; maltreatment; experience; plasticity

INTRODUCTION

The recent publication of several scientific papers[1,2] and popular press books, such as *The Nurture Assumption*,[3] *The Blank Slate*,[4] and *Enough*,[5] suggest that the age-old nature–nurture debate is over. One might gather from the theses advanced in these expositions that there is little question about the degree to which parents and early rearing environments influence rudimentary aspects of children's development beyond providing children's genetic make-up. Rather than being resolved, however, the issue about biology and experience is undergoing a reformulation that suggests the topic is just getting started—again. In the past few months, compelling and sophisticated examples of nature–nurture (or gene–environment) interactions have appeared in the literature.[6–9] These reports highlight the complex, dynamic interplay between biology and experience in shaping children's behavior. As scientists advance our understanding how biological factors (including genetic polymorphisms, variations in neurophysiological processes, and neuroanatomical lesions) are associated with mental health problems, compelling questions emerge about the processes

Address for correspondence: Seth D. Pollak, Ph.D., Department of Psychology, University of Wisconsin at Madison, 1202 West Johnson Street, Madison, WI 53706-8190. Voice: 608-265-8190; fax: 608-262-4029.

spollak@wisc.edu

Ann. N.Y. Acad. Sci. 1008: 102–111 (2003). © 2003 New York Academy of Sciences.
doi: 10.1196/annals.1301.011

through which experience shapes biology, necessitating a more fine-grained approach to explaining mechanisms of change and development.

GENES AS A MECHANISM OF EXPERIENCE

The phenomenon of child maltreatment is at the center of debates about the relative roles of children's early learning environments, parents' genetically influenced characteristics, children's genetically influenced characteristics, and risk for the development of maladaptive behaviors. My students and I examine the effects of child maltreatment from a developmental perspective, viewing child abuse as a manipulation of species-typical experience that may shed light on the role of experience-dependent processes in the emergence of psychopathology. While emphasizing the role of affective learning in the development of psychopathology, we also recognize that even powerful learners are not blank slates. Ultimately, affective learning (like learning in other complex systems) must be explained by a combination of biological predisposition and experiential input. Our hypothesis is that a predisposition for learning about emotions, achieved through general perceptual learning mechanisms, may explain the development of behavior problems in maltreated children.

Genes and anatomical structures, in and of themselves, strike us as very important but not very profound. From a developmental perspective on psychopathology, genes become important when taken together with the context in which they are expressed; anatomy becomes important in terms of how and under what circumstances it is (or is not) used. To fully understand the ontogenesis of mental health problems in children, it is important for psychopathologists to focus not only on what is in children's heads, but on what their heads are in: the give-and-take with the wide welter of signals and sensory input received by the developing brain from the outside world during both fetal and postnatal development. Surprisingly, little research has focused on the *mechanisms* underlying the emergence of emotional processes in children, and the neurodevelopmental processes involved in the organization of affective systems remain largely unknown. This dearth of knowledge is an exigent problem in developmental psychopathology, in which the creation of effective, tailored interventions for children suffering from emotional difficulties requires a clear understanding of the regulatory processes that have gone awry.

Our perspective is not in conflict with, but complementary to, psychiatric molecular genetics. Conceptual problems abound in attempts to disentangle genetic and environmental influences in studies of biologically related parents and children. For example, even if some heritable association between child maltreatment and the development of psychopathology exists, it is not clear what is being genetically transmitted. Might abused children be bound to develop problems even if they were not abused? Have these children inherited characteristics that make them likely to be abused in the first place? Both of these alternatives seem unlikely. Behavioral genetic analyses have ruled out the possibility that heritable characteristics of the child evoke physical maltreatment.[10] To the degree that the sequelae of child abuse are genetically determined, it appears that what are heritable are the characteristics of the parent that are transmitted to children via family environment.[10,11] What children inherit are toxic environments, which highlights the need for better understanding of how children are influenced by such early aversive experiences.

The maltreatment of children is a horrific psychosocial phenomenon in which young infants and children do not receive the protection, care, nurturance, and interactions that are typical of how humans (and many other species) care for the young. More than 2 million children a year are victims of child maltreatment in the United States.[12] Perhaps because it is both obvious and has been demonstrated that children who experience such severe perturbations in care are at very high risk for the emergence of behavioral problems later in life,[13] the precise mechanisms linking the experience of maltreatment with the development of psychopathology are infrequently examined and largely unknown. But this is a critical question: How is it that such adversity early in life can lead to a range of problems including depression, aggression, substance abuse, health problems, and general unhappiness years after abuse has ended? The emotional development of maltreated children provides a compelling clue of where to begin looking. Maltreated children often evince unusual patterns in their abilities to recognize, express, and regulate emotional states.[14–16] Physically abused children often display both withdrawal and aggression,[17–19] readily assimilate and remember cues related to aggression,[20,21] and tend to attribute hostility to others.[22] These processes lead to poorly regulated and situationally inappropriate affect and behavior.[23,24] Our research program has been motivated by the scarcity of investigations targeting specific physiological, perceptual, or cognitive processes that may act as proximal determinants of such affective regulatory problems.

LEARNING FROM AND SENSITIVITY TO EMOTIONAL EXPERIENCE

We propose that exposure to maltreating environments affects children's processing of emotional information, and that these effects may explain children's interpersonal difficulties across situational contexts and developmental epochs. This influence of early experiences may be understood in terms of the general immaturity and neuroplasticity of sensory and perceptual systems.[25,26] On this view, maturational limitations on processing resources aid children's learning about emotion by requiring the child to filter information from the environment. This leaves the development of emotion systems contingent on the most salient aspects of the child's experience, however aberrant. One possible experience-dependent mechanism for these developmental effects is that infants' biological preparedness for emotion includes a general perceptual mechanism that becomes tuned to combinations of signals, which, through experience, combine to form affective neural circuitry and categories. Such a learning mechanism might include the ability to parse sensory inputs into meaningful units and to track the regularity, predictiveness, and temporal synchrony of emotional information. Similar learning mechanisms have been proposed for other cognitive abilities such as cross-modal matching, phonetic discrimination, and word segmentation.[27–29]

Developmental affective learning problems may arise because the emotional signals the maltreated child receives can be disproportionately complicated, inconsistent, poorly conveyed, distressing, limited, threatening, or excessive. Or processing differences may arise simply because abused children learn, first and foremost, to track signs of threat, reflecting an adaptive ability to effectively pair a signal with a meaningful outcome.[30] In abusive environments, displays of anger are likely to be a particularly salient cue with a learned association to threat or harm for abused children, disproportionately recruiting these children's attentional resources. Neurobehavioral plasticity of developing cognitive and perceptual systems figures prominently in this account. Mature, adult computational networks can ignore or effectively filter noise, but, in a developing network, such noise becomes part of the basis of development. For example, a traumatic reaction may occur when an adult is assaulted, because the individual's expectations have been violated. But for a child exposed to chronic maltreatment, violent experiences may form the basis of the child's expectations of others. Irrespective of the initial state of the organism, emotional development is contingent on the nature of the input or experiences which confront the child. Experience matters.

To test and refine our hypothesis, we focus on the problem of emotion recognition: how do signals received from the environment acquire the salience that makes them "emotional" and how do children process such salient cues? We highlight two candidate developmental mechanisms that may be affected by early experience: perceptual sensitivity and attentional control. In one of our earliest studies, we found that physically abused children perceived angry faces as highly salient relative to other emotions.[16] A significant aspect of this study was that we were able to contrast children with different types of maltreatment experience. Physically abused children had experienced abuse by commission—they were directly injured by a parent. In contrast, neglected children experienced abuse by omission— lack of care and responsiveness from parents. Neglected children, who purportedly did not receive adequate scaffolding to master decoding of communicative signals, had difficulty differentiating facial expressions of emotion. Rather than showing global deficits in performance, physically abused children performed well, especially when differentiating angry facial expressions. These data suggest that specific kinds of emotional experiences, rather than simply the presence of stress or maltreatment, differentially affect children's emotional functioning.[16]

Because the ability to allocate attention to emotional cues in the environment is an important feature of adaptive self-regulation,[31] we have used psychophysiological techniques to measure children's selective attentional control for emotional information. Event-related potentials (ERPs) provide an index of central nervous system (CNS) functioning thought to reflect the underlying neural processing of discrete stimuli, especially those involved in attentional resource allocation.[32–34] Our ERP studies reveal that whereas nonmaltreated children and adults responded uniformly when attending to happy, fearful, and angry faces, physically abused children displayed relative increases in brain electrical activity only when actively searching for angry faces. Abused children performed identically to controls when attending to other emotional expressions, suggesting that attentional processes directed toward detecting angry cues distinguish maltreated children's emotion processing.[35,36]

Although it is adaptive for salient stimuli such as emotions to elicit attention, successful behavioral regulation includes some flexibility and control over attention. Such control might include strategic filtering or timely disengagement from stimuli in the environment. Therefore, we began exploring the possibility that early experiences of abuse may affect developing perceptual systems in part by shaping the sensory threshold that anger-related stimuli must pass to recruit attentional focus. Problems with disengagement would also suggest that abused children are less able to utilize strategic attentional control once signals of interpersonal threat have been engaged. Relatedly, problems disengaging from angry faces may also be a function of the depth of processing or strength of engagement of that cue.[37–39] Using a selective attention paradigm, we found that abused children demonstrated an increase in brain electrical activity only when they were required to disengage their attention from angry faces, reflecting increased allocation of cognitive resources.[20] An additional finding from this study was that physically abused children oriented rapidly to spatial locations primed by anger. Importantly, abused and nonmaltreated children did not differ in other types of trials or in response to other emotions, consistent with the hypothesis that physically abused children have a specific problem involving processing of anger, rather than general information processing deficits.

If abused children are overattending to anger, we might expect to observe differences in how these children perceive angry cues from the environment. Therefore, we examined abused children's perception of anger. Categorical perception occurs when perceptual mechanisms enhance differences between categories at the expense of our perception of incremental changes within a category. Perceiving in terms of categories is adaptive in that it allows an observer to efficiently assess changes between categories that are environmentally important (e.g., to see that a traffic light has changed from green to yellow) at the cost of noticing subtle changes in a stimulus that are not important (e.g., such as variations in shades of greens or yellows across individual traffic lights). Children performed a facial discrimination task that required them to distinguish faces that had been morphed to produce a continuum on which each face differed by 20% in signal intensity. To create continua of facial expressions of affect, we used a two-dimensional morphing system to generate stimuli that spanned four emotional categories—happiness, anger, fear, and sadness. We found that the experience of abuse was associated with a change in children's perceptual preferences and also altered the discriminative abilities that influence how children categorize angry facial expressions.[40] Yet, abused children performed identically to controls when discriminating emotions other than anger. These findings suggest that whatever perceptual capacities infants possess when they enter the world, they need to adjust or tune these mechanisms to process specific, salient aspects of their environments. Thus, affective experiences appear to influence perceptual representations of basic emotions.

To further test the hypothesis that children exposed to high levels of threat are especially sensitive to visual cues of anger, we examined whether these children can readily relate visual cues to representations of emotions. The examination of this issue required a technique that could capture the dynamics of emotion recognition, including the sequential and content-based processes of feature detection involved in emotion recognition. To do so, we presented affective stimuli to children incrementally as sequences of emotional expressions that initially were degraded and asked participants to report what emotion they thought they were seeing. As predicted, physically abused children accurately identified facial displays of anger on the basis of less sensory input than did controls.[41]

DEVELOPMENT, BIOLOGY, AND EXPERIENCE

We have proposed that predispositions to attend and learn about emotionally salient events, in tandem with developmental constraints on perceptual systems, leads children in abusive contexts to overprocess environmental signals associated with harm. Over time, such processes may lead to complex information processing atypicalities that compromise healthy, adaptive functioning. Preliminary evidence supporting this position includes findings that physically abused children perceive angry faces as more distinctive than other emotions, develop broad perceptual category boundaries for anger, require less visual information to detect the presence of angry facial expressions, devote more attentional resources to detecting anger, and display increased brain electrical activity when disengaging attention from anger. Our psychophysiological studies also reveal early (precognitive) sensory activation on the part of maltreated children to angry faces based on minimal perceptual input. In short, based on multimethod studies including electrophysiological, cognitive, and perceptual tasks, it appears that early perceptual and attentional processes directed toward angry cues distinguish maltreated children's emotion processing. Abused children seem to have become experts at anger detection. But at what cost? Whereas it is adaptive for salient environmental stimuli to elicit attention, successful self-regulation includes flexibility and control over these processes. We suspect that it is failure of regulatory capacities that lead to abused children's troubles. These studies suggest new ways of understanding the neural mechanisms through which early experience contributes to the development of psychopathology.

Whatever the sequential particulars of the three billion DNA subunits that make up a child's genotype, they are meaningful only in the context of phenotype, of a child's life history and experiences. Critical and unanswered questions concern what experiences turn on and off certain genes, how those genes influence our experiences, what are the mechanisms through which they act in combination with "stressful" experiences to produce psychopathological syndromes. In the latter case, the identification of a gene polymorphism in a clinical population, or even a 100% heritability estimate, cannot address what the gene is doing: how it causes or maintains disorders, how it directs or constrains an organism's interaction with the environment, whether it has the same function early in development as in adulthood, and whether the gene functions similarly across species.

In this regard, nonhuman animal studies, in which experiences can be experimentally manipulated, are essential. Although care must be taken in translating animal studies to humans (see articles by Nelson, Gunnar, and Plotsky, this volume), nonhuman animal maltreatment studies provide important information that can guide future research into the neurodevelopmental processes affected by early experience. For example, the original impetus for isolate rearing in rhesus monkeys was the desire to study learning unfettered by differences in mother–infant interaction.[42] However, these socially deprived animals proved difficult to test in the laboratory because of their heightened emotional reactivity, leading researchers to redirect their studies to emotional processes and behavioral regulation.[42] Early explanations for these emotional effects based on rodents first implicated the hypothalamic–pituitary–adrenocortical (HPA) axis and its limbic-cortical regulatory pathways.[43] Research with monkeys suggested that early experience affects development of the parietal and prefrontal cortices, as well as the limbic-cortical pathways involved in regulating neuroendocrine and behavioral responses to stress.[44,45] Although complementary human evidence is sparse, it is known that both the HPA and sympathetic-adrenomedullary systems in humans undergo reorganization during postnatal life that are associated with the child's social relationships.[46] In addition, EEG activation, a neural correlate of social withdrawal and avoidance, and ERP activation to emotion, a correlate of attention, have been associated with early social experiences.[36,47] As an example, infants of depressed mothers who provided unresponsive and/or intrusive care showed right frontal EEG asymmetries, reflecting increased negative affective states.[48] These data suggest that future research needs to focus on the neural substrates of children's emotional behavior to better understand the effects of experience on development.

The role of context and environment is a central problem in understanding both child mental health problems and the ways to effectively remediate those problems. One issue concerns the difficulty in precisely parametizing the rich, complicated, "booming, buzzing, confusion" of sensory experiences to which humans are exposed within moments of birth. A related problem in the area of child psychopathology is that it is not yet clear which aspects of the environment need to be measured. Moreover, whereas we may be ale to link biological similarities across species, it may be more difficult to link affective experiences between human and nonhuman animals. Maternal care in the rat involves licking and abuse in the monkey is operationalized as biting and dragging. How can we best model in nonhuman animals phenomenon such as being threatened, criticized, and beaten while being blamed, and other experiences encountered by abused children?

CONCLUSIONS

Descriptions of mental health problems observed in different populations of children cannot adequately inform us about the initial state of the organism or the developmental pathways that lead to problem behaviors. The patterns of information processing we have described suggest that children who experienced early abuse are processing certain types of emotional information atypically, while appearing to process other types of emotional information similarly to nonmaltreated children. Tracing the developmental origins of such complex behavior requires a focus on developmental mechanisms, not static lesions or deficits. Maladaptive behavioral outcomes emerge from cascading effects (and interactions) over time. To get at these interactions, we need to consider both developmental biology and context. Such a perspective must take into account anatomical constraints on the developing brain as well as an understanding of what situations the organisms has had to respond to—not only what is in the genome, but what the genome is in. Such a focus on mechanisms of adaptation and maladaptation has important implications for the development of effective prevention and treatment/intervention programs for at-risk children as well. Treatments not directed at underlying mechanisms may address distal symptoms rather than the roots of mental illness in children.

ACKNOWLEDGMENTS

Preparation of this manuscript was supported by a grant from the National Institute of Mental Health (MH61285) to the author. I thank members of the NIMH Early

Experience, Stress Neurobiology & Prevention Science Network (MH 065046), and the NIMH Affect Regulation and Adolescent Brain Maturation Network (MH 67346) for their insights and discussion. I am grateful to my graduate students— Stephanie Tolley-Schell, Alison Wismer Fries, Jessica Friedman, Craig Selinger, Christa Tober, and Elizabeth Shirtcliff—who have challenged and stimulated the ideas presented in this chapter.

REFERENCES

1. DILALLA, L.F. & I.I. GOTTESMAN. 1991. Biological and genetic contributions to violence: Widom's untold tale. Psychol. Bull. **109:** 125-129.
2. TURKHEIMER, E. 2000. Three laws of behavior genetics and what they mean. Curr. Directions Psychol. Sci. **9:** 160–164.
3. HARRIS, J. 1998. The Nurture Assumption: Why Children Turn Out the Way They Do. Free Press. New York.
4. PINKER, S. 2002. The Blank Slate: The Modern Denial of Human Nature. Viking Press. New York.
5. MCKIBBEN, B. 2003. Enough: Staying Human in an Engineered Age. Times Books. New York.
6. BENNETT, A.J., K.P. LESCH, A. HEILS, *et al.* 2002. Early experience and serotonin transporter gene variation interact to influence primate CNS function. Mol. Psychiatry **7:** 118–122.
7. CASPI, A., J. MCCLAY, T.E. MOFFITT, *et al.* 2002. Role of genotype in the cycle of violence in maltreated children. Science **297:** 851–854.
8. CASPI, A., K. SUGDEN, T.E. MOFFITT, *et al.* 2003. Influence of life stress on depression: moderation by a polymorphism in the 5-HTT gene. Science **301:** 386–389.
9. GROSS, C., X.X. ZHUANG, K. STARK, *et al.* 2002. Serotonin(1A) receptor acts during development to establish normal anxiety-like behaviour in the adult. Nature **416:** 396–400.
10. JAFFEE, S.R., C. AVSHALOM, T.E. MOFFITT & A. TAYLOR. 2003. Physical maltreatment victim to antisocial child: evidence of an environmentally-mediated process. J. Abnorm. Psychol. In press.
11. KENDLER, K.S., C.M. BULIK, J. SIBERG, *et al.* 2000. Childhood sexual abuse and adult psychiatric and substance use disorders in women: an epidemiological and cotwin control analysis. Arch. Gen. Psychiatry **57:** 953–959.
12. U.S. DEPARTMENT OF HEALTH AND HUMAN SERVICES. Trends of Well-Being of America's Children and Youth. 2000. U.S. Government Printing Office. Washington, DC.
13. CICCHETTI, D. & J.T.E. MANLY. 2001. Operationalizing child maltreatment: developmental processes and outcomes. Dev. Psychopathol. **13:** 755–757.
14. CAMRAS, L.A., S. RIBORDY, J. HILL, *et al.* 1990. Maternal facial behavior and the recognition and production of emotional expression by maltreated and nonmaltreated children. Dev. Psychol. **26:** 304–312.
15. CAMRAS, L.A., E. SACHS-ALTER & S. RIBORDY. 1996. Emotion understanding in maltreated children: recognition of facial expressions and integration with other emotion cues. *In* Emotional Development in Atypical Children. M. Lewis and M. Sullivan, Eds.: 203–225. Erlbaum. Hillsdale, NJ.
16. POLLAK, S.D., D. CICCHETTI, K. HORNUNG & A. REED. 2000. Recognizing emotion in faces: developmental effects of child abuse and neglect. Dev. Psychol. **36:** 679–688.
17. HOFMAN-POLTKIN, D. & C.T. TWENTYMAN. 1984. A multimodal assessment of behavioral and cognitive deficits in abused and neglected preschoolers. Child Dev. **55:** 794–802.
18. JACOBSON, R.S. & G. STRAKER. 1982. Peer group interaction of physically abused children. Int. J. Child Abuse Neglect **6:** 327.
19. ROGOSCH, F.A., D. CICCHETTI & J. LABER. 1995. The role of child maltreatment in early deviations in cognitive and affective processing abilities and later peer relationship problems. Dev. Psychopathol. **7:** 591–609.

20. POLLAK, S.D. & S. TOLLEY-SCHELL. 2003. Selective attention to facial emotion in physically abused children. J. Abnorm. Psychol. **112:** 323–338.
21. RIEDER, C. & D. CICCHETTI. 1989. Organizational perspective on cognitive control functioning and cognitive affective balance in maltreated children. Dev. Psychol. **25:** 382–393.
22. WEISS, B., K.A. DODGE, J.E. BATES & G.S. PETIT. 1992. Some consequences of early harsh discipline: child aggression and a maladaptive social information processing style. Child Dev. **63:** 1321–1335.
23. KLIMES-DOUGAN, B. & J. KISTNER. 1990. Physically abused preschoolers' responses to peers' distress. Dev. Psychol. **26:** 599–602.
24. MAIN, M. & C. GEORGE. 1985. Responses of abused and disadvantaged toddlers to distress in agemates. Dev. Psychol. **21:** 407–412.
25. BJORKLUND, D.F. 1997. The role of immaturity in human development. Psychol. Bull. **122:** 153–169.
26. POLLAK, S.D., D. CICCHETTI & R. KLORMAN. 1998. Stress, memory, and emotion: developmental considerations from the study of child maltreatment. Dev. Psychopathol. **10:** 811–828.
27. KUHL, P. 1987. The special-mechanisms debate in speech research: categorization tests on animals and infants. *In* Categorical Perception: The Groundwork of Cognition. S. Harnad, Ed.: 355–386. Cambridge University Press. New York.
28. KUHL, P. & A.N. MELTZOFF. 1982. The bimodal perception of speech in infancy. Science **218:** 1138–1141.
29. SAFFRAN, J.R., R.N. ASLIN & E. NEWPORT. 1996. Statistical learning by 8-month-old infants. Science **274:** 1926–1928.
30. RESCORLA, R.A. 1966. Predictability and number of pairings in Pavlovian fear conditioning. Psychometric Sci. **4:** 38–84.
31. POSNER, M.I. & M.K. ROTHBART. 2000. Developing mechanisms of self-regulation. Dev. Psychopathol. **12:** 427–441.
32. COLES, M.G.H. & M.D. RUGG. 1995. Event related brain potentials: an introduction. *In* Electrophysiology of Mind: Event Related Brain Potentials and Cognition. M.G.H. Coles and M.D. Rugg, Eds.: 126. Oxford University Press. Oxford, England.
33. KRAMER, A.F. & J. SPINKS. 1991. Capacity views of human information processing. *In* Handbook of Cognitive Psychophysiology: Central and Autonomic Nervous System Approaches. J.R. Jennings and M.G.H. Coles, Eds.: 179–242. Wiley. New York.
34. POLICH, J. & A. KOK. 1995. Cognitive and biological determinants of P300: an integrative review. Biol. Psychol. **41:** 103–146.
35. POLLAK, S.D., D. CICCHETTI, R. KLORMAN & J. BRUMAGHIM. 1997. Cognitive brain event-related potentials and emotion processing in maltreated children. Child Dev. **68:** 773–787.
36. POLLAK, S.D., R. KLORMAN, J. BRUMAGHIM & D. CICCHETTI. 2001. P3b reflects maltreated children's reactions to facial displays of emotion. Psychophysiology **38:** 267–274.
37. DERRYBERRY, D. & M.A. REED. 2002. Anxiety-related attentional biases and their regulation by attentional control. J. Abnorm. Psychol. **111:** 225–236.
38. FOX, E., R. RUSSO & K. DUTTON. 2002. Attentional bias for threat: evidence for delayed disengagement from emotional faces. Cognition Emotion **16:** 355–379.
39. LABERGE, D. 1995. Attentional Processing: The Brain's Art of Mindfulness. Harvard University Press. Cambridge, MA.
40. POLLAK, S.D. & D. KISTLER. 2002. Early experience alters the development of categorical representations for facial expressions of emotion. Proc. Natl. Acad. Sci. USA **99:** 9072–9076.
41. POLLAK, S.D. & P. SINHA. 2002. Effects of early experience on children's recognition of facial displays of emotion. Dev. Psychol. **38:** 784–791.
42. HARLOW, H.F., M.K. HARLOW & S.J. SUOMI. 1971. From thought to therapy: lessons from a primate laboratory. Am. Sci. **59:** 538–549.
43. LIU, D., J. DIORIO, J.C. DAY, *et al.* 2000. Maternal care, hippocampal synaptogenesis and cognitive development in rats. Nat. Neurosci. **3:** 799–806.

44. SANCHEZ, M.M., C.O. LADD & P.M. PLOTSKY. 2001. Early adverse experience as a developmental risk factor for later psychopathology: evidence from rodent and primate models. Dev. Psychopathol. **13:** 419–450.

45. SIEGEL, S.J., S.D. GINSBERG, P.R. HOF, *et al.* 1993. Effects of social deprivation in prepubescent rhesus monkeys: immunohistochemical analysis of the neurofilament protein triplet in the hippocampal formation. Brain Res. **619:** 299–305.

46. GUNNAR, M.R. 2000. Early adversity and the development of stress reactivity and regulation. *In* The Effects of Adversity on Neurobehavioral Development. Minnesota Symposia on Child Psychology, 31. C.A. Nelson, Ed.: 163–200. Erlbaum. Mahwah, NJ.

47. DAVIDSON, R.J. 1994. Asymmetric brain function, affective style, and psychopathology: the role of early experience and plasticity. Dev. Psychopathol. **6:** 741–758.

48. DAWSON, G. & S. ASHMAN. 2000. On the origins of a vulnerability to depression: the influence of early social environment on the development of psychobiological systems related to risk for affective disorder. *In* The Effects of Adversity on Neurobehavioral Development: Minnesota Symposia on Child Psychology, 31. C.A. Nelson, Ed.: 245–278. Erlbaum. Mahwah, NJ.

Applying Learning Principles to the Treatment of Post-Trauma Reactions

BARBARA OLASOV ROTHBAUM AND MICHAEL DAVIS

Department of Psychiatry and Behavioral Sciences, Emory University School of Medicine, Atlanta, Georgia 30322, USA

ABSTRACT: Posttraumatic stress disorder (PTSD) can be characterized as a failure of recovery caused, in part, by a failure of fear extinction after trauma. By studying the process of extinction, we can be informed regarding the etiology and maintenance of PTSD. The normal response to trauma in humans includes a set of predictable reactions including reexperiencing, avoidance, and hyperarousal that typically extinguish in the days and weeks after the trauma. In the majority of people exposed to trauma, these responses extinguish over time. However, in a substantial minority, extinction fails and these persisting responses become the symptoms of PTSD. Therefore, one of our fundamental hypotheses is that PTSD is a disorder caused in part by the failure of extinction of predictable posttraumatic physiological and psychological reactions. The most empirically validated treatments for PTSD involve exposure of the patient to trauma-related cues in the absence of danger that then lead to the extinction of these reexperiencing, avoidance, and arousal symptoms. There is also mounting evidence that individuals with PTSD are more resistant to extinction. Regarding early interventions with traumatized individuals, there is mounting evidence that some early one-time interventions actually may impede extinction, whereas interventions delivered in more than one session, at least several weeks after the trauma, to individuals continuing to experience above average reactions, generally are effective in preventing the development of PTSD. Thus, there appears to be an interaction between timing of the intervention, number of intervention sessions, and either arousal level and/or risk status in determining whether the intervention will be helpful, harmful, or neutral.

KEYWORDS: posttraumatic stress disorder; trauma; avoidance, arousal

The normal response to trauma in humans includes a set of predictable reactions including reexperiencing, avoidance, and hyperarousal. In the majority of people exposed to trauma, these responses extinguish over time. However, in a substantial minority, extinction fails and these persisting responses become the symptoms of posttraumatic stress disorder (PTSD). Therefore, one of our fundamental hypotheses is that PTSD is a disorder caused in part by the failure of extinction of predictable posttraumatic physiological and psychological reactions. Studying the process of extinction can inform us regarding the etiology and maintenance of PTSD. The most

Address for correspondence: Barbara O. Rothbaum, Ph.D., Psychiatry, The Emory Clinic, 1365 Clifton Road, Atlanta, GA 30322. Voice: 404-778-3875; fax: 404-778-4655.
brothba@emory.edu

Ann. N.Y. Acad. Sci. 1008: 112–121 (2003). © 2003 New York Academy of Sciences.
doi: 10.1196/annals.1301.012

empirically validated treatments for PTSD involve exposure of the patient to trauma-related cues in the absence of danger that then lead to the extinction of these reexperiencing, avoidance, and arousal symptoms.

Exposure to traumatic events is unfortunately a common experience, with estimates ranging between 37% and 92% of individuals.[1] Although the majority of trauma exposed individuals recover from these experiences without substantial long-term impairment, a significant minority of trauma survivors experience debilitating psychological symptoms, with estimates of PTSD ranging between 9%[1,2] and 12.3% of the general population,[3] clearly indicating that it is a major public health concern. Once PTSD has become chronic, it is a debilitating and costly illness.

In differentiating phobias and PTSD, patients with specific phobias show relatively steep generalization gradients, and the fear behavior is displayed only in the presence of the feared stimulus. Hence, the sight of a snake might trigger a strong fear response, whereas a spider will not. In contrast, patients with PTSD have much flatter generalization gradients. Hence, PTSD can be distinguished from specific phobia by fearful reactions to many stimuli related to the original fear stimulus (overgeneralization) and failure to respond to safety cues.[4,5] In PTSD, fear is displayed even in the presence of safety signals, day or night, while awake or asleep.[6] Phobias seem to develop to specific classes of stimuli (reptiles, insects, blood) perhaps from an innate preparedness to fear certain but not all stimuli.[7] The range of conditioned stimuli to which PTSD sufferers respond appears to be much broader than for specific phobias. PTSD sufferers can have conditioned fear reactions to bald men, persons with red hair, or the smell of autumn in the air, indicating that very neutral stimuli can become conditioned in PTSD. As a result, PTSD patients have a very low threshold for fear elicitation to a broad network of stimuli reminiscent of the original trauma. Specific phobias are fairly easily treated, whereas PTSD can be much more intractable. The original conditioning event or events are always identified, by definition, in PTSD, whereas it is often assumed but not identified in specific phobia. Moreover, the human consequences of PTSD are more devastating than those resulting from simple phobias. PTSD is estimated to account for $3 billion in lost work productivity yearly,[8] as well as problems with attempted suicide,[9] physical health and less employment,[10] medical illnesses,[11] increased healthcare utilization,[12] impaired quality of life,[10,13] and a negative impact on personal relationships, daily activities, and work performance.[14] Note, however, that the complexity of PTSD cannot be reduced to or completely explained by learning theory alone.

Prospective studies indicate that PTSD symptoms are almost universal in the immediate aftermath of trauma. Most individuals will experience reexperiencing, avoidance, and hyperarousal initially following the trauma, and then these reactions will extinguish over time. In a prospective study of rape victims, 94% met symptomatic criteria for PTSD in the first week after the assault.[15] Therefore, the symptoms of PTSD should be considered part of the *normal reaction* to trauma, because they occur almost universally after severe enough traumas. Those who respond normally show steadily decreasing PTSD symptoms over time beginning soon after the trauma (see FIG. 1, bottom line), but, for those who do not show a slightly different pattern: PTSD symptoms decrease in the first month after trauma, then remain fairly steady across time (FIG. 1, top line). They do not worsen; they just do not extinguish their original fear reactions. Therefore, PTSD can be viewed as a failure of recovery caused in part by a failure of fear extinction after trauma.

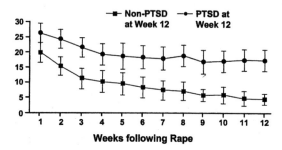

FIGURE 1. PTSD symptoms in rape victims in the first 12 weeks after rape.

ANALYSIS OF PTSD IN TERMS OF FEAR CONDITIONING

PTSD first appeared in the DSM as a psychiatric diagnosis in 1980. In response to this, many theorists and clinicians in the 1980s described the development of the PTSD response following traumatic exposure in terms of conditioning theory.[5,15–17] This view holds that the traumatic event itself is an unconditioned stimulus (UCS) that naturally leads to unconditioned responses (UCRs). Many of the cues present at the time of the original traumatic event become associated with "the intense fear, helplessness, or horror"[18] experienced, by definition, at the time of the event, by the individual who develops PTSD. These conditioned stimuli (CS) then are able to elicit responses similar to the UCRs on subsequent exposure known as conditioned responses (CRs). Through generalization and second-order conditioning, stimuli associated with both the feared and neutral stimuli that were present during the trauma also come to evoke fear. In this way, words, thoughts, and images acquire the capacity to cause anxiety.

Using contemporary learning theory, attempts have been made to account for much of the development and maintenance of the PTSD symptoms.[19,20] Reexperiencing and arousal symptoms are viewed as conditioned emotional responses resulting from classic conditioning that are elicited by environmental stimuli. Exposure to conditioned stimuli in the absence of the negative consequences is hypothesized to extinguish conditioned emotional reactions. Emotional processing theory[21] holds that PTSD emerges because of the development of a fear network in memory that elicits escape and avoidance behavior.[5] Mental fear structures include stimuli, responses, and meaning elements. The fear structure in people with PTSD is thought to include a particularly large number of stimuli elements and therefore is easily accessed. Two conditions have been proposed to be required for fear reduction. First, the fear structure must be activated. Second, new information must be provided that includes elements incompatible with the existing pathological elements so they can be corrected. Exposure therapies have received more empirical support for PTSD than any other intervention, thereby supporting these views that exposure to trauma-related cues in the absence of painful consequences, that is, extinction training, is effective for the conditioned reactions in PTSD.[22]

These conditioned responses of many PTSD sufferers have been well documented. Physiological reactivity to sensory stimuli resembling the original traumatic event even years after the event's occurrence is a prominent characteristic of PTSD and has been reliably replicated in the laboratory.[17,23–26] Evidence exists that individuals with PTSD are more conditionable and more resistant to extinction than trauma-exposed individuals without PTSD.[27,28] This "conditioned emotional response"[16] bears an analogy to the conditioned fear responses in rodents mediated through subcortical and cortical connections to the amygdala.[29] Enhancement of conditioning by stress hormones is mediated at the amygdala.[30] The amygdala is also involved[31] in the modulation of unconditioned responses relevant to PTSD, for example, auditory startle.[32] More generally, successful recovery from trauma involves adequate discrimination of threat versus safe cues. Thus, the original threat stimuli remain fear inducing while similar, but safe stimuli lose their fear-inducing abilities through the process of extinction and safety signal learning (conditioned inhibition). In conditioning terms, then, PTSD can be characterized as a failure of extinction and discrimination.

PTSD, SAFETY SIGNALS, AND EXTINCTION

There is ample evidence, in addition to clinical experience, that individuals with PTSD do not respond to safety signals. Grillon et al.[33] found an increase in startle response in subjects with PTSD compared with controls throughout a fear potentiated session, even during the safe conditions. In a complementary study using classic fear conditioning comparable to that of animal paradigms, Grillon and Morgan[34] found that the PTSD subjects were unable to reduce their fear in response to safety signals within the initial test session. These results provide evidence that PTSD patients have difficulty inhibiting fear in the presence of safety cues.

Extinction is defined as a reduction in the strength or probability of a CR as a consequence of repeated presentation of the CS in the absence of the US. In the case of fear conditioning, the US is the traumatic event. Extinction is distinguished from forgetting because the CR does not diminish appreciably simply with the passage of time but only with repeated presentation of the CS in the absence of the US. Although it might appear in extinction as if the original fear memory is lost, this is not the case. Extinction shows *spontaneous recovery*, defined as a return of the CR after extinction;[35] *context specificity (renewal)*, defined as a return of the CR when testing takes place in a context different from the one where extinction occurred;[36] and *reinstatement*, defined as a return of the CR after some stressful event.[35,37,38] Each of these examples shows that extinction is an active learning process in which newly acquired memories compete with or suppress expression of the original fear memory. The examples also indicate that extinction is relatively fragile and can be disrupted by the passage of time, a shift in context, or stress.[39]

Partly because of the evidence against extinction as an unlearning process, several theorists have suggested that extinction is a special case of conditioned inhibition.[40] In conditioned inhibition, one cue (A) is paired with an aversive event (designated as A+), and another cue, B, is presented in compound with A and not followed by the aversive event (designated AB–). After such training, A becomes the fear-eliciting CS, and B becomes the conditioned inhibitor or safety signal because it signals the absence of the aversive event. Contextual control of extinction can be viewed similarly: the subject learns that the CS is not followed by the US in this context, such that the context effectively serves as a safety signal, at least for that CS.[40]

The strength of conditioned inhibition is directly proportionate to the strength of the excitatory CS-US association.[41] In other words, the stronger the fear that the CS elicits, the stronger the safety signal has to become to overcome this level of fear to produce extinction. It is for this reason that artificial reduction of fear to a CS, as with administration of a benzodiazepine, under some circumstances may preclude conditioned inhibition from developing and interfere with the process of extinction.[42]

On any given extinction trial, reactivation of the traumatic event associated with CS presentation (recall) actually may produce two opposing effects.[43,44] Recall may initiate the process of extinction and thereby lead to a lessening of the fear response to the CS. Recall may also, however, serve as the basis of further fear learning if the memory is sufficiently vivid and elicits enough aspects of the original trauma that the association between the CS and US is further instantiated.[45,46] Thus, the behavioral outcome of nonreinforced CS exposure may depend importantly on the balance between these two opposing effects, a balance that presumably varies with the circumstances of extinction training as well as those of initial acquisition.[39] It is possible, for example, that the memory for the traumatic event may be so vivid in the immediate aftermath of the event that recall serves more to reinforce the memory than to reduce it through extinction,[43] whereas later, when the memory is less vivid, extinction may predominate.

BENEFITS AND LIABILITIES OF PSYCHOLOGICAL DEBRIEFING

Contrary to conventional wisdom, psychological debriefing and other interventions in the immediate aftermath of trauma are not always helpful. In a recent review of early interventions,[47] of 13 one-time intervention studies reviewed, 8 were neutral, 3 produced improvement, and 2 were associated with worsening of symptoms. As an example, in a well-controlled study of motor vehicle accident survivors, it was demonstrated that of patients with initially high PTSD symptoms, if they received psychological debriefing, they did not recover, but if they did not receive the intervention, they were more likely to recover.[48] When interventions offer cognitive behavior therapy over several sessions, and especially target those at risk several weeks after trauma exposure, when the conditioned fear reactions had not decreased, most of the studies indicated benefits.

In trauma-exposed humans, there appears to be an interaction between timing of the intervention, number of intervention sessions, and either arousal level and/or risk status in determining whether the intervention will be helpful, harmful, or neutral. For example, a study explored the effect of timing of critical incident stress debriefing[49] (CISD) with 77 civilian victims of robbery. It was found that those who received CISD within 10 h of the robbery displayed significantly fewer PTSD symptoms over time than a group who received the CISD intervention more than 48 h after the robbery.[50] Moreover, the earlier intervention was effective in reducing PTSD symptoms, whereas the later intervention did not. In another study, only those motor vehicle accident victims considered at risk (defined here as heart rate >94 BPM as found predictive of PTSD in Shalev *et al.*[51]) were randomly assigned to receive either a brief intervention within 24 h and then again within 48 h after the accident[52] or no intervention. The experimental group improved significantly more than the control condition on PTSD symptoms 3–4 months later.

If it is true that the arousal level of the subject influences the degree to which recall leads to strengthening or weakening of the CR, then it is possible that artificial modulation of arousal (e.g., through the use of medications that either exacerbate or inhibit fear) during nonreinforced CS exposure might similarly modulate the efficacy of extinction training. Thus, for example, if extinction training is ineffective at reducing fear when given immediately after training (presumably because of the predominance of fear reconsolidation over fear extinction at this point in time), then extinction might be improved by medications such as propranolol or diazepam that reduce physiological arousal and thereby lessen the degree to which fear associated with recall would serve to strengthen the memory. Conversely, extinction initiated at a more favorable point in time (i.e., one in which the CS no longer elicits as intense a fear response) might be thwarted by pharmacological agents such as yohimbine, which increase peripheral and/or central arousal associated with memory recall and hence might be expected to selectively facilitate the process of fear strengthening.

EXPOSURE-BASED EXTINCTION PROCEDURES FOR PTSD

Exposure therapy for anxiety disorders comprises a set of techniques designed to help patients confront their feared objects, situations, memories, and images in a therapeutic manner. With PTSD, commonly the core components of exposure programs are imaginal exposure, that is, repeated recounting of the traumatic memory, and *in vivo* exposure, that is, repeated confrontation with trauma-related situations and objects that evoke excessive anxiety. Exposure therapy is the most well-supported intervention for PTSD across trauma populations,[22] improving symptoms on average 60% to 80%.[53] The effectiveness of exposure therapy for PTSD lends support to the views that exposure to trauma-related cues in the absence of painful consequences (extinction training) is effective for the conditioned reactions in PTSD. Exposure therapy is based on the same mechanisms of action as extinction.[21] Prolonged imaginal exposure typically involves the patient repeatedly recounting the traumatic memories in a therapist's office, with the therapist providing safety cues and emotional support during the exposure.

Prolonged exposure treatment typically consists of 9 to 12 individual sessions. Typically, the first two sessions are devoted to information gathering, explaining the treatment rationale, and treatment planning, including the construction of a hierarchy of feared situations for *in vivo* exposure. *In vivo* exposure involves actually confronting realistically safe situations, places, or objects repeatedly that are reminders of the trauma until they no longer elicit such strong emotions. During the remaining sessions, survivors are instructed to relive, in their imagination, the traumatic experiences, describing it aloud "as if it were happening now." Exposure continues for about 60 min and is tape-recorded so that survivors can practice imaginal exposure as homework by listening to the tape. After the imaginal exposure in each session, the material that comes up in the exposure is discussed or "processed." Typically, these include themes of guilt, shame, fear, and responsibility. Patients are given homework assignments, instructing them to practice imaginal exposure with the tapes made in the session and to approach feared situations or objects that are realistically safe but that evoke anxiety because of their association with the trauma, called *in vivo* (or "in real life") exposure.[54,55]

A new medium for conducting exposure therapy has been introduced. Virtual reality exposure presents the user with a computer-generated view of a virtual world that changes in a natural way with head motion. For Vietnam veterans with PTSD, patients wear a head-mounted display with stereo earphones that provide visual and audio cues consistent with being in a "Virtual Vietnam." Patients have been exposed to two virtual environments, a virtual Huey helicopter flying over a virtual Vietnam and a clearing surrounded by jungle. In this way, patients are repeatedly exposed to their most traumatic memories but immersed in Vietnam stimuli.[56]

In the treatment guidelines review for the International Society for Traumatic Stress Studies, exposure therapy was the most supported intervention for PTSD, with many methodologically rigorous studies across trauma populations.[57] Exposure therapy has consistently been shown to be more effective than no treatment controls[55,58–62] and has been shown to be superior to supportive counseling for PTSD symptoms.[55] It has been shown to be at least equally effective as cognitive therapy,[63,64] stress inoculation training,[55,58] cognitive processing therapy,[60] and eye movement desensitization and reprocessing[62] in many well-controlled investigations. In several studies, advantages of exposure therapy over these other techniques emerged.[15,58,65]

In summary, we have attempted to present a case that (1) PTSD is caused, in part, by a failure of extinction; (2) PTSD patients have difficulty inhibiting fear in the presence of safety cues; (3) successful therapy may be viewed in terms of facilitating extinction and discrimination; and (4) exposure therapy has been the most successful treatment for PTSD, thereby supporting these views.

REFERENCES

1. BRESLAU, N., R.C. KESSLER, H.D. CHILCOAT, *et al.* 1998. Traumatic and posttraumatic stress disorder in the community: the 1996 Detroit area survey of trauma. Arch. Gen. Psychiatry **55:** 626–631.
2. BRESLAU, N., G.C.D. DAVIS, P. ANDRESKI & E. PETERSON. 1991. Traumatic events and posttraumatic stress disorder in an urban population of young adults. Arch. Gen. Psychiatry **48:** 218–222.
3. RESNICK, H.S., D.G. KILPATRICK, B.S. DANSKY, *et al.* 1993. Prevalence of civilian trauma and post-traumatic stress disorder in a representative national sample of women. J. Consult. Clin. Psychol. **61:** 984–991.
4. FOA, E.B., G. STEKETEE & B. ROTHBAUM. 1989. Behavioral/cognitive conceptualizations of post-traumatic stress disorder. Behav. Ther. **20:** 155–176.
5. FOA, E.B., R. ZINBARG & B.O. ROTHBAUM. 1992. Uncontrollability and unpredictability in post-traumatic stress disorder: an animal model. Psychol. Bull. **112:** 218–238.
6. ROTHBAUM, B.O. & T.A. MELLMAN. 2001. Dreams and exposure therapy in PTSD. J. Trauma Stress **14:** 481–490.
7. KESSLER, R.C. 2000. Posttraumatic stress disorder: the burden to the individual and to society. J. Clin. Psychiatry **61** (Suppl. 5): 4–12.
8. MINEKA, S., M. DAVIDSON, M. COOK & R. KEIR. 1984. Observational conditioning of snake fear in rhesus monkeys. J. Abnorm. Psychol. **93:** 355–372.
9. DAVIDSON, J.R., D. HUGHES, D.G. BLAZER & L.K. GEORGE. 1991. Post-traumatic stress disorder in the community: an epidemiological study. Psychol. Med. **21:** 713–721.

10. ZATZICK, D.F., C.R. MARMAR, D.S. WEISS, *et al.* 1997. Posttraumatic stress disorder and functioning and quality of life outcomes in a nationally representative sample of male Vietnam veterans. Am. J. Psychiatry **154:** 1690–1695.

11. BOSCARINO, J.A. 1997. Diseases among men 20 years after exposure to severe stress: implications for clinical research. Psychosom. Med. **59:** 605–614.

12. AMAYA-JACKSON, L., J.R. DAVIDSON, D.C. HUGHES, *et al.* 1999. Functional impairment and utilization of services associated with posttraumatic stress in the community. J. Trauma Stress **12:** 709–724.

13. MALIK, M.L., K.M. CONNOR, S.M. SUTHERLAND, *et al.* 1999. Quality of life and post-traumatic stress disorder: a pilot study assessing changes in SF-36 scores before and after treatment in a placebo-controlled trial of fluoxetine. J. Trauma Stress **12:** 387–393.

14. NORTH, C.S., S.J. NIXON, S. SHARIAT, *et al.* 1999. Psychiatric disorders among survivors of the Oklahoma City bombing. JAMA **25:** 755–762.

15. ROTHBAUM, B.O., E.B. FOA, D. RIGGS, *et al.* 1992. A prospective examination of post-traumatic stress disorder in rape victims. J. Trauma Stress **5:** 455–475.

16. KOLB, L. 1984. The post traumatic stress disorders of combat: a subgroup with a conditioned emotional response. Mil. Med. **149:** 237–243.

17. PITMAN, R.K., S.P. ORR, D.F. FORGUE, *et al.* 1987. Psychophysiologic assessment of posttraumatic stress disorder imagery in Vietnam combat veterans. Arch. Gen. Psychiatry **44:** 970–975.

18. AMERICAN PSYCHIATRIC ASSOCIATION. 1994. Diagnostic and Statistical Manual of Mental Disorders, 4th ed. American Psychological Association. Washington, DC.

19. HAYES, S.C., W.C. FOLETTE & V.M. FOLLETTE. 1995. Behavior therapy: a contextual approach. *In* Essential Psychotherapies: Theory and Practice. A.S. Gurman and S.B. Messer, Eds.: 128–181. Guilford Press. New York.

20. HAYES, S.C., K.G. WILSON, E. GIFFORD, *et al.* 1996. Emotional avoidance and behavioral disorders: a functional dimensional approach to diagnosis and treatment. J. Consult. Clin. Psychology **64:** 1152–1168.

21. FOA, E.B. & M.J. KOZAK. 1986. Emotional processing of fear: exposure to corrective information. Psychol. Bull. **99:** 20–35.

22. ROTHBAUM, B.O., E.A. MEADOWS, P. RESICK & D.W. FOY. 2000. Cognitive-behavioral therapy. *In* Effective Treatments for Posttraumatic Stress Disorder: Practice Guidelines from the International Society for Traumatic Stress Studies. E.B. Foa, M. Friedman, and T. Keane, Eds.: 60–83. Guilford Press. New York.

23. BLANCHARD, E.B., L.C. KOLB, R.J. GERARDI, *et al.* 1986. Cardiac response to relevant stimuli as an adjunctive tool for diagnosing post-traumatic stress disorder in Vietnam veterans. Behav. Ther. **17:** 592–606.

24. MALLOY, P., J. FAIRBANK & T. KEANE. 1983. Validation of a multimethod assessment of post-traumatic stress disorders in Vietnam veterans. J. Consult. Clin. Psychol. **51:** 488–494.

25. ORR, S.P., N.B. LASKO, L.J. METZGER, *et al.* 1998. Psychophysiological assessment of women with posttraumatic stress disorder resulting from childhood sexual abuse. J. Consult. Clin. Psychol. **66:** 906–913.

26. ORR, S.P., Z. SOLOMON, T. PERI, *et al.* 1997. Physiologic responses to loud tones in Israeli veterans of the 1973 Yom Kippur War. Biol. Psychiatry **41:** 319–326.

27. ORR, S.P., L.J. METZGER, N.B. LASKO, *et al.* 2000. De novo conditioning in trauma-exposed individuals with and without posttraumatic stress disorder. J. Abnorm. Psychol. **109:** 290–298.

28. ROTHBAUM, B.O., M.J. KOZAK, E.B. FOA & D.J. WHITAKER. 2001. Posttraumatic stress disorder in rape victims: autonomic habituation to auditory stimuli. J. Trauma Stress **14:** 283–293.

29. LEDOUX, J.E. 1990. Information flow from sensation to emotion: plasticity in the neural computation of stimulus value. *In* Learning Computational Neuroscience: Foundations of Adaptive Netwroks. G.M. Moore, Ed.: 3–51. MIT Press. Cambridge, MA.

30. MCGAUGH, J.L., I.B. INTROINI-COLLISON, A.H. NAGAHARA, *et al.* 1990. Involvement of the amygdaloid complex in neuromodulatory influences on memory storage. Neurosci. Biobehav. Rev. **14:** 425–431.

31. DAVIS, M., W.A. FALLS & J. GEWIRTZ. 2000. Neural systems involved in fear inhibition: extinction and conditioned inhibition. *In* Contemporary Issues in Modeling

Psychopathology. M. Myslobodsky and I. Weiner, Eds.: 113–142. Kluwer Academic Publishers. Boston.
32. SHALEV, A.Y., Y. RAGEL-FUCHS & R.K. PITMAN. 1992. Conditioned fear and psychological trauma. Biol. Psychiatry. **31:** 863–865.
33. GRILLON, C., C.A. MORGAN, M. DAVIS & S.M. SOUTHWICK. 1998. Effect of darkness on acoustic startle in Vietnam veterans with post-traumatic stress disorder. Am. J. Psychiatry **155:** 812–817.
34. GRILLON, C. & C.A. MORGAN III. 1999. Fear-potentiated startle conditioning to explicit and contextual cues in Gulf War veterans with posttraumatic stress disorder. J. Abnorm. Psychol. **108:** 134–142.
35. PAVLOV, I.P. 1927. Conditioned Reflexes. Oxford University Press. Oxford, UK.
36. BOUTON, M.E. & R.C. BOLLES. 1979. Contextual control of the extinction of conditioned fear. Learn. Motiv. **10:** 455–466.
37. RESCORLA, R.A. & C.D. HETH. 1975. Reinstatement of fear to an extinguished conditioned stimulus. J. Exp. Psychol. Anim. Behav. Process **1:** 88–96.
38. BOUTON, M.E. & R.C. BOLLES. 1979. Role of contextual stimuli in reinstatement of extinguished fear. J. Exp. Psychol. Anim. Behav. Processes **5:** 368–378.
39. MYERS, K.M. & M. DAVIS. 2002. Behavioral and neural analysis of extinction: a review. Neuron **36:** 567–584.
40. BOUTON, M.E. & J.B. NELSON. 1994. Context specificity of target versus feature inhibition in a feature-negative discrimination. J. Exp. Psychol. Anim. Behav. Process **20:** 51–65.
41. WAGNER, A.R. & R.A. RESCORLA. 1972. Inhibition in Pavlovian conditioning: application of a theory. *In* Inhibition and Learning. R.A. Boakes and M.S. Halliday, Eds.: 301–336. Academic Press. London.
42. BOUTON, M.E., F.A. KENNEY & C. ROSENGARD. 1990. State-dependent fear extinction with two benzodiazepine tranquilizers. Behav. Neurosci. **104:** 44–55.
43. EYSENCK, H.J. 1979. The conditioning model of neurosis. Behav. Brain Sci. **2:** 155–199.
44. MYERS, K.M. & M. DAVIS. 2002. Systems reconsolidation: reengagement of the hippocampus with memory reactivation. Neuron **36:** 1–4.
45. NADER, K., G.E. SCHAFE & J.E. LEDOUX. 2000. The labile nature of consolidation theory. Nat. Rev. Neurosci. **1:** 216–219.
46. SARA, S. 2000. Strengthening the shaky trace through retrieval. Nat. Rev. Neurosci. **1:** 212–213.
47. BISSON, J. 2003. Early interventions psychosocial and medication. Following traumatic events. Psychiatric Ann. **33:** 37–44.
48. MAYOU, R.A., A. EHLERS & M. HOBBS. 2000. Psychological debriefing for road traffic accident victims. Br. J. Psychiatry **174:** 589–593.
49. MITCHELL, J. 1983. When disaster strikes: the critical incident stress debriefing process. J. Emerg. Med. Serv. **8:** 36–39.
50. CAMPFIELD, K.M. & A.M. HILLS. 2001. Effect of timing of critical incident stress debriefing CISD on posttraumatic symptoms. J. Trauma. Stress **14:** 327–340.
51. SHALEV, A.Y., T. SAHAR, S. FREEDMAN, *et al.* 1998. A prospective study of heart rate response following trauma and the subsequent development of posttraumatic stress disorder. Arch. Gen. Psychiatry **55:** 553–559.
52. GIDRON, Y., R. GAL, S. FREEDMAN, *et al.* 2001. Translating research findings to PTSD prevention: results of a randomized-controlled pilot study. J. Trauma. Stress **14:** 773–780.
53. FOA, E.B. & B.O. ROTHBAUM. 2003. Is the efficacy of exposure therapy for PTSD augmented with the addition of other CBT procedures? Psychiatric Ann. **33:** 47–53.
54. FOA, E.B. & B.O. ROTHBAUM. 1998. Treating the Trauma of Rape: Cognitive-Behavioral Therapy for PTSD. Guilford Press. New York.
55. FOA, E.B., B.O. ROTHBAUM & D. RIGGS, *et al.* 1991. Treatment of post-traumatic stress disorder in rape victims: a comparison between cognitive behavioral procedures and counseling. J. Consult. Clin. Psychol. **59:** 715–723.
56. ROTHBAUM, B.O., L. HODGES, D. READY, *et al.* 2001. Virtual reality exposure therapy for Vietnam veterans with posttraumatic stress disorder. J. Clin. Psychiatry **62:** 617–622.
57. FOA, E.B., M. FRIEDMAN & T. KEANE. 2000. Effective Treatments for Posttraumatic Stress Disorder: Practice Guidelines from the International Society for Traumatic Stress Studies. Guilford Press. New York.

58. FOA, E.B., C.V. DANCU, E.A. HEMBREE, *et al.* 1999. A comparison of exposure therapy, stress inoculation training, and their combination for reducing posttraumatic stress disorder in female assault victims. J. Consult. Clin. Psychol. **67:** 194–200.

59. MARKS, I., K. LOVELL, H. NOSHIRVANI, *et al.* 1998. Treatment of posttraumatic stress disorder by exposure and/or cognitive restructuring: a controlled study. Arch. Gen. Psychiatry **55:** 317–325.

60. RESICK, P.A., P. NISTHITH & M. ASTIN. A controlled trial comparing cognitive processing therapy and prolonged exposure: preliminary findings. J. Consult. Clin. Psychol. In press.

61. RICHARDS, D.A., K. LOVELL & I.M. MARKS. 1994. Post-traumatic stress disorder: evaluation of a behavioral treatment program. J. Trauma. Stress **7:** 669–680.

62. ROTHBAUM, B.O. & M. ASTIN. Prolonged exposure versus EMDR for PTSD rape victims. *In* Three Clinical Trials for the Treatment of PTSD: Outcome and Dissemination. Symposium presented at the 35th Annual Convention for the Association for Advancement of Behavior Therapy. P.A. Resick, Chair. November 2001. Philadelphia, PA.

63. TARRIER, N., H. PILGRIM, C. SOMMERTIELD, *et al.* 1999. A randomized trial of cognitive therapy and imaginal exposure in the treatment of chronic posttraumatic stress disorder. J. Consult. Clin. Psychol. **67:** 13–18.

64. TARRIER, N., C. SOMMERFIELD, H. PILGRIM & L. HUMPHREYS. 1999. Cognitive therapy or imaginal exposure in the treatment of posttraumatic stress disorder. Br. J. Psychiatry **175:** 571–575.

65. COOPER, N.A. & G.A. CLUM. 1989. Imaginal flooding as a supplementary treatment for PTSD in combat veterans: a controlled study. Behav. Ther. **20:** 381–391.

Developing a Sense of Safety

The Neurobiology of Neonatal Attachment

REGINA M. SULLIVAN

Zoology Department, University of Oklahoma, Norman, Oklahoma, 73019, USA

ABSTRACT: Clinical data suggests a strong negative impact of traumatic attachments on adult mental illness, presumably through organizing brain development. To further explore this clinical issue, a mammalian model of imprinting was developed to characterize the neural basis of attachment in both healthy and traumatic attachments. The altricial neonatal rat must learn the mother's odor for nipple attachment, huddling, and orienting to the mother, all of which are required for pup survival. While it appears maladaptive to depend upon learning for attachment, the unique learning system of neonatal pups greatly enhances odor-preference learning and attachment while pups are confined to the nest. This heightened learning is expressed behaviorally as an enhanced ability to acquire learned odor preferences and a decreased ability to acquire learned odor aversions. Specifically, both odor–milk and odor–shock (0.5 mA) conditioning result in odor-preference acquisition. It appears as though there are at least three brain structures underlying the neonatal rat's sensitive period for heightened odor learning: (1) odor learning is encoded in the olfactory bulb; (2) the hyperfunctioning noradrenergic locus coeruleus (LC) appears to support preference conditioning through release of NE; and (3) the hypofunctioning amygdala appears to underlie pups' difficulty in learning odor aversions. Overall, this suggests that the CNS of altricial infants is specialized for optimizing attachments to their caregiver.

KEYWORDS: mother–infant interactions; olfactory bulb; classical conditioning; norepinephrine; attachment; imprinting; locus coeruleus; amygdala; learning; abuse; stress; corticosterone; fear conditioning

INTRODUCTION

A loving, caring family should be the main source of a child's sense of safety and security. However, according to a 1999 report by the Administration for Children and Families of the U.S. Dept. of Health and Human Services, 11.8 of every 1000 American children are abused or neglected, most often by parents or significant caregiver. Children aged 0–3 years are more likely to be abused than any other age group. Thus, during the critical years for brain development, basic emotional and social learning, and attachment, these children experience mixed messages concerning their safety within the attachment dyad. However, most of these children still form

Address for correspondence: Regina M. Sullivan, Ph.D., University of Oklahoma, Department of Zoology, 730 Van Vleet Oval, Norman, OK 73019. Voice: 405-325-5653; fax: 405-325-2699.
rsullivan@ou.edu

Ann. N.Y. Acad. Sci. 1008: 122–131 (2003). © 2003 New York Academy of Sciences.
doi: 10.1196/annals.1301.013

an attachment to their abuser (Zeanah, Connor, and Dahl chapters in this volume).[1,2] While it is difficult to define safety as it relates to a young child, it is reasonable to say that the abused child develops an attachment within the context of a situation that is not entirely safe.

The infant attachment neural circuitry has been elusive, perhaps because of difficulty in characterizing terms such as love, security, and comfort. In clinical terms, a secure attachment is one in which the child–caregiver relationship provides pleasure, security, and safety for the child, and results in psychological well-being. While these are useful clinical terms, they are difficult terms to place in the developmental neurobehavioral approach required for an animal model. While an animal attachment model ultimately needs to accommodate the clinical literature, we have begun our approach to this issue by simply documenting the unique pathways and structures used by the infant brain while learning about the attachment figure.

HUMAN ATTACHMENT

The study of attachment began in the 1950s, partly in reaction to the distant and nonnurturing approach to child-rearing typical of the day, when mothers were advised to limit contact with their babies to avoid spreading germs and spoiling the child.[3] A notable figure in promoting mother–infant contact was John Bowlby, a psychiatrist treating disturbed adolescents, all of whom had suffered from poor maternal care. The poor mental health of his patient population led Bowlby to conclude that a strong mother–infant attachment was necessary for adult mental health and the quality of all adult relationships. In an attempt to better understand the attachment process, Bowlby characterized four components of attachment: (1) the infant rapidly forms an attachment to the caregiver, (2) the infant seeks caregiver proximity, (3) the caregiver provides a safe haven, and (4) the infant undergoes considerable abuse while remaining in contact with the caregiver. Bowlby's framework for human infant attachment continues to permit the assessment of attachment in an experimentally refined protocol and has provided the foundation for much of the current attachment literature.

The child's attachment to the mother appears to begin before birth, when the baby learns about the mother's voice and odors. Attachment continues after birth when the infant learns the mother's face, and additional qualities of her odors and voice appear to bridge the pre- and postnatal environments.[4–7] The maternal odor produces orienting responses and mouthing and soothes a crying infant,[6,8] and novel odors quickly acquire at least some of these properties through classical conditioning.[9] These odors may have qualities of "safety" or comfort (attenuates crying, orienting) as described in Bowlby's characterization of attachment. It is quite possible that this neonatal learning about the caregiver is the first postnatal expression of learning within the attachment system and perhaps one of the first ways in which our sense of safety is constructed.

ATTACHMENT IN OTHER SPECIES

Remarkably, Bowlby's characterization of human attachment is relevant throughout the animal kingdom. Imprinting in chicks illustrates rapidity of attachment formation, proximity seeking, and willingness to undergo considerable abuse while remaining in contact with the caregiver. Specifically, during imprinting, chicks will continue to follow their mother even while being shocked, although just hours later, in postsensitive period naïve chicks, this treatment results in avoidance.[10] Similar work in young dogs showed that puppies quickly learn a strong attachment to a handler providing either petting, electric shock, or rough treatment. This phenomenon extends to nonhuman primates and abused children, who also exhibit a strong attachment to their abusive caregiver (Dahl, Zeanah, and Settles, and Connor chapters in this volume).[11–14] We hypothesized that this attachment system evolved to ensure altricial animals easily form a repertoire of proximity-seeking behaviors to the caregiver, regardless of the quality of care-giving received.[15]

ANIMAL ATTACHMENT MODEL

To assess the neurobiology of infant attachment, we have developed an infant rat model that conforms to the characteristics of attachment initially described by Bowlby. Rats are an altricial species that must learn about their mother's odor for attachment. Until walking emerges at 10 days of age, pups remain in the nest and spend most of their time nursing.[16] With sensory functioning limited to the somatosensory and chemical senses of taste and smell, pups rely on their olfactory system to orient and seek proximity to the mother. Neonatal rats very rapidly and easily learn this proximity-seeking behavior both within the nest with natural odors and in more controlled learning experiments.[17–20] Pups will also undergo considerable abuse while forming the odor preference that underlies the proximity-seeking behavior: pairing a novel odor with pain (tailpinch or 0.5-mA shock) results in pups learning an *odor preference*.[21–23] Specifically, although neonatal rats show clear pain responses to stimuli such as shock and tail pinch during acquisition, the odor paired with these stimuli is approached during testing. This learning is limited to the neonatal period when pups are confined to the nest. While this attenuated aversive conditioning appears paradoxical, it is possible that this attachment system developed to prevent pups from learning an aversion to the mother during the occasional rough handling typical in the nest.[15] Indeed, considering the importance of proximity-seeking behaviors in procuring mother's milk, warmth, and protection, pups' survival may depend upon pups only learning approach responses to the mother.

As the sensitive period ends, walking develops and the probability of leaving the nest greatly increases.[16] Pups then express the more complex "adult" learning system to deal with the increasingly complex extranest environment. However, with maturation, attachments continue to be formed, especially in behaviors important to survival, such as reproduction (Insel's chapter in this volume).[24–27]

INFANT ATTACHMENT NEURAL CIRCUITRY

Neonatal rats can be easily classically conditioned, yet brain areas important in adult learning are not yet functional (e.g., amygdala, hippocampus, frontal cortex).[23,28–32] Therefore, the neonatal rat must use a different neural pathway to support learning, presumably one designed through evolution to ensure caregiver

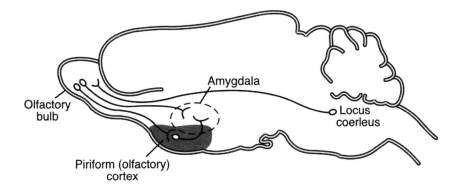

FIGURE 1. Schematic representation of circuitry important for neonatal learning during the sensitive period. To learn an odor preference, an odor must be paired with NE from the locus coeruleus. Odor aversion learning from odor-shock conditioning appears to be prevented due to lack of amygdala participation in this learning.

attachment, and hence survival.[15] Currently, three brain areas appear critical for attachment in the neonatal rat: the olfactory bulb, locus coeruleus, and amygdala (FIG. 1).

Encoding Attachment Odors in the Olfactory Bulb

The first relay station for olfactory information within the brain is the olfactory bulb. During the sensitive period, odor learning produces changes in the olfactory bulb that are odor-specific and retained into adulthood (c-fos, 2-DG, mitral cellmitral cell single-cell recordings, glomerular anatomical changes; see review).[19] The olfactory bulb learning-induced changes appear to be due to the unique responses of the neonatal olfactory bulb to odors paired with reward. Specifically, while the primary-output mitral cells quickly habituate to repeated odor-only presentation, mitral cells fail to habituate if that odor is presented along with a reward,[33] due to the reward activating the release of norepinephrine (NE) from the locus coeruleus (LC, discussed below). Continued activation of mitral cells results in a cascade of metabolic changes within mitral cells that is characteristic of those previously identified following learning in adults.[34,35] Since the information leaving the olfactory bulb is modified following neonatal learning, additional brain areas may also encode information about the attachment odor. Following the sensitive period, odor-learning fails to produce any of the olfactory bulb neural changes,[36] presumably because of the greatly reduced levels of NE released by the mature LC.[37]

The Locus Coeruleus (LC) and Rapid Odor Preference Learning

Olfactory bulb and behavioral changes associated with sensitive-period learning require NE, with the LC as the bulb's sole source.[38] Depleting the olfactory bulb of NE by chemically lesioning the LC or blocking NE receptors in the olfactory bulb prevents sensitive-period learning.[39,40] Moreover, during the sensitive period, presenting an odor while increasing olfactory bulb NE (by chemically stimulating the LC or infusing NE into the bulb) is sufficient to produce an odor preference.[34,39–42] Thus, the NE system appears necessary and sufficient to control pups' odor preference learning during the sensitive period.

The role of NE during the sensitive period is in sharp contrast to the role of NE in post-sensitive-period or adult learning. NE is not necessary for post-sensitive-period learning, although it enhances or attenuates consolidation of memories.[43] We believe this developmental change in NE-dependent learning is due to the dramatic reduction in LC NE release around the end of the sensitive period. Specifically, a 1-s stimulation with either shock or a puff of air results in a 20- to 30-s response in the sensitive-period LC, but only a ms response in the post-sensitive-period LC.[44] According to Rangel and Leon,[37] learning during the post-sensitive period yields a dramatic reduction of olfactory bulb NE as compared to sensitive-period release. The specific mechanisms for enhancing the sensitive-period LC's responsiveness appear to be due to greatly reduced LC $\alpha2$ autoinhibition, enhanced LC $\alpha1$ autoexcitation, and increased LC electrotonic coupling.[44,45] Based on these data, we suggest that the large release of NE from the sensitive-period LC is responsible for enhanced odor-preference learning, and that maturation of the LC signals the termination of rapid NE-dependent preference learning. In support of this, we have successfully reinstated the sensitive-period NE-dependent learning in post-sensitive-period pups by functionally reinstating the neonatal distribution of LC autoreceptors.[46] Specifically, while stimulating the LC, we also reinstated the reduced $\alpha2$ autoinhibition by blocking LC $\alpha2$ receptors and reinstated the enhanced $\alpha1$ autoexcitation through activation of LC $\alpha1$ receptor agonists.

Amygdala Attenuated Odor-Avoidance Learning

The amygdala is a brain area important for both natural fear and fear conditioning (Amaral, Davis chapters in this volume).[29] Our data suggest that failure of the amygdala to participate in odor–shock conditioning during the sensitive period prevents odor-avoidance learning. Specifically, in sensitive-period pups, when odor–shock conditioning produces an odor preference, the amygdala does not participate in learning.[23] Neonatal lesion of the amygdala supports the nonfunctional role of the amygdala in neonatal learning,[47] a procedure that greatly attenuates an adult animal's ability to learn.[48] However, in post-sensitive-period pups, when odor–shock conditioning easily produces odor avoidance, the amygdala participates in fear conditioning. It should be noted that neonatal pups can learn an odor avoidance if that odor is paired with malaise. According to Haroutunian and Campbell,[49] only interoceptive cues (illness), but not exteroceptive cues (shock), support aversive conditioning and are thought not to require the amygdala. This suggests that the developmental emergence of amygdala participation in odor–shock conditioning may underlie the developmental delay in post-sensitive-period emergence of odor–shock-induced fear conditioning.

It is possible that immaturity of the amygdala or lack of functional amygdala connections underlies its lack of participation in odor–shock learning.[32,50–54] Behavioral data are consistent with this interpretation, since other amygdala-based olfactory behaviors also emerge around 10 days of age: fear to predator odor,[55,56] inhibitory conditioning,[57] and passive avoidance.[58,59] However, work from our lab by

Stephanie Moriceau, as well as from other labs, has shown that some amygdala-based behaviors can be induced to emerge at a developmentally earlier age through manipulation of corticosterone (CORT).[60] Normally, at this early stage of development, pups have a hyporesponsive stress period (HRSP) that defines an age range in which stress-induced CORT release is greatly attenuated (Plotsky chapter in this volume).[61,62] Thus, increasing normally low levels of CORT with exogenous CORT injected minutes earlier permits 8-day-old (sensitive period) pups to express fear to predator odor,[55] learn inhibitory conditioning,[63] and fear conditioning.[60] The sites of CORT action need to be determined, since receptors are abundant in many neonatal brain areas, most notably the limbic system and the two stress systems: the LC-amygdala and hypothalamus–pituitary–adrenal (HPA) (Plotsky chapter in this volume).

While NE and CORT appear critically important in neonatal learning, other neurotransmitters are also important. For example, dopamine, NE, and opioids modulate acquisition,[64–67] and Tania Roth in my lab has shown that opioids are critical for neonatal consolidation of the odor–shock-induced odor preference.[68] Other neurotransmitters work directly in the olfactory bulb, with serotonin potentiating the excitatory role of NE on mitral cells[41,69] and GABA modulating the inhibitory control of mitral cells by the granule cells.[35] These neurotransmitter systems have been implicated in other adult attachment behaviors such as mating and infant care (Insel chapter in this volume).[24–27]

ADULT CONSEQUENCES

Clinically, development of a disordered attachment to the caregiver results in a variety of maladaptive behaviors and an increased incidence of many mental illnesses (Kaslow, Ferris, Pollak chapters in this volume).[12,71–73] In our animal model, odors learned during the sensitive period continue to be preferred by pups into adulthood (see review).[19] However, similar to visual stimuli in chick imprinting,[74] the odor's role changes with maturation into enhancement of sexual and maternal behaviors.[26,75,76] The learning-induced changes in the neonatal olfactory bulb still present in the adult bulb are believed to underlie these adult behavioral effects.

Do Human Children Use This Attachment Neural Circuitry?

While the human attachment literature fits well with our animal abuse model, there is insufficient information on human brain development to discuss the neural circuitry of human attachment (Peterson, Skuse chapters in this volume).[77] There has been speculation that the human infant's large NE surge at birth and continued high NE level during early childhood is important for attachment in the newborn, although no causal relationship has been established. Evidence for CORT's role in human attachment is also vague, although considerable data have been gathered on fluctuating CORT levels during childhood (Gunner chapter in this volume). However, regardless of the existence of a homologous neural circuitry for attachment, this work suggests that the brain of newborns is uniquely designed to optimize attachment to their caregivers and suggests a new conceptual framework in which to explore human attachments.

ACKNOWLEDGMENT

This work was supported by grants NICHD-HD33402 and NSF-IBN0117234.

REFERENCES

1. PERRY, B.D. & R. POLLARD. 1998. Homeostasis, stress, trauma, and adaptation. A neurodevelopmental view of childhood trauma. Child Adolesc. Psychiatry Clin. N. Am. **7:** 33–51.
2. SIEGEL, D.J. 2001. Toward an interpersonal neurobiology of the developing mind: attachment relationships, "mindsight," and neural integration. Infant Mental Health J. **22:** 67–94.
3. BOWLBY, J. 1965. Attachment. Basic Books. New York.
4. HEPPER, P.G. 1995. Human fetal olfactory learning. Int. J. Prenatal Perinatol. Psychol. Med. **7:** 147–151.
5. MENNELLA, J.A, A. JOHNSON & G.K. BEAUCHAMP. 1995. Garlic ingestion by pregnant women alters the odor of amniotic fluid. Chem. Senses **20:** 207–209.
6. SCHAAL, B., L. MARLIER & R. SOUSSIGNAN. 2000. Human foetuses learn odours from their pregnant mother's diet. Chem. Senses **25:** 729–737.
7. MOON, C.M. & W.P. FIFER. 2000. Evidence of transnatal auditory learning. J. Perinatol. **20:** 37–44.
8. SULLIVAN, R.M. & P. TOUBAS. 1998. Clinical usefulness of maternal odor in newborns: soothing and feeding preparatory responses. Biol. Neonate **74:** 402–408.
9. SULLIVAN, R.M. *et al.* 1991. Olfactory classical conditioning in neonates. Pediatrics **87:** 511–518.
10. HESS, E.H. 1962. Ethology: an approach to the complete analysis of behavior. *In* New Directions in Psychology. R. Brown, E. Galanter, E.H. Hess, and G. Mendler, Eds. Holt, Rinehart and Winston. New York.
11. HARLOW, H.F. & M.K. HARLOW. 1965. The affectional systems. *In* Behavior of Nonhuman Primates, Vol. 2. A. Schrier, H.F. Harlow, and F. Stollnitz, Eds. Academic Press. New York.
12. SÁNCHEZ, M.M., C.O. LADD & P.M. PLOTSKY. 2001. Early adverse experience as a developmental risk factor for later psychopathology: evidence from rodent and primate models. Dev. Psychopath. **13:** 419–449.
13. HELFER, M.E., R.S. KEMPE & R.D. KRUGMAN. 1997. The Battered Child. University of Chicago Press. Chicago.
14. RAJECKI, D.W., M.E. LAMB & P. OBMASCHER. 1978. Towards a general theory of infantile attachment; a comparative review of aspects of the social bond. Behav. Brain Sci. **3:** 417–464.
15. HOFER, M.A. & R.M. SULLIVAN. 2001. Toward a neurobiology of attachment. *In* Handbook of Developmental Cognitive Neuroscience. C.A. Nelson and M. Luciana, Eds.: 599–616. MIT Press. Cambridge, MA.
16. BOLLES, R.C. & P.J. WOODS. 1965. The ontogeny of behavior in the albino rat. Anim. Behav. **12:** 427–441.
17. CAMPBELL, B.A. 1984. Reflections on the ontogeny of learning and memory. *In* Comparative Perspectives on the Development of Memory. R. Kail and N.E. Spear, Eds.: 23–35. Lawrence Erlbaum Associates. Hillsdale, NJ.
18. SPEAR, N.E. & J.W. RUDY. 1991. Tests of the ontogeny of learning and memory: issues, methods, and results. *In* Developmental Psychobiology: New Methods and Changing Concepts. H.N. Shair, G.A. Barr, and M.A. Hofer, Eds.: 84–113. Oxford University Press. New York.
19. SULLIVAN, R.M. 2001. Unique characteristics of neonatal classical conditioning: the role of the amygdala and locus coeruleus. Integ. Physiol. Behav. Sci. **36:** 293–307.
20. SULLIVAN, R.M. *et al.* 1990. Modified behavioral olfactory bulb responses to maternal odors in preweanling rats. Dev. Brain Res. **53:** 243–247.
21. CAMP, L.L. & J. W. RUDY. 1988. Changes in the categorization of appetitive and aversive events during postnatal development of the rat. Dev. Psychobiol. **21:** 25–42.

22. SULLIVAN, R.M., M.A. HOFER & S.C. BRAKE. 1986. Olfactory-guided orientation in neonatal rats is enhanced by conditioned change in behavioral state. Dev. Psychobiol. **19:** 615–623.
23. SULLIVAN, R.M. *et al.* 2000. Good memories of bad events in infancy: ontogeny of conditioned fear and the amygdala. Nature **407:** 38–39.
24. BRENNEN, P.A. & E.B. KEVERNE. 1997. Neural mechanisms of mammalian olfactory learning. Prog. Neurobiol. **51:** 451–457.
25. INSEL, T.R. & L.J. YOUNG. 2001. The neurobiology of attachment. Nature Rev. Neurosci. **2:** 129–136.
26. FLEMING, A.S. *et al.* 2002. Mothering begets mothering: the transmission of behavior and its neurobiology across generations. Pharmacol. Biochem. Behav. **73:** 61–75.
27. TERRAZAS, A. *et al.* 2002. Twenty-four-hour-old lambs rely more on maternal behavior than on the learning of individual characteristics to discriminate between their own and an alien mother. Dev. Psychobiol. **40:** 408–418.
28. CRAIN, B. *et al.* 1973. A quantitative electron microscopic study of synaptogenesis in the dentate gyrus of the rat. Brain. Res. **63:** 195–204.
29. FANSELOW, M.S. & J.W. RUDY. 1998. Convergence of experimental and developmental approaches to animal learning and memory processes. *In* Mechanistic Relationships Between Development and Learning. T.J. Carew, R. Menzel, and C.J. Shatz, Eds.: 15–28. Wiley. New York.
30. SANANES, C.B. & B.A. CAMPBELL. 1989. Role of the central nucleus of the amygdala in olfactory heart rate conditioning. Behav. Neurosci. **103:** 519–525.
31. STANTON, M.E. 2000. Multiple memory systems, development and conditioning. Behav. Brain Res. **110:** 25–37.
32. VERWER, R.W. *et al.* 1996. Prefrontal development of amygdaloid projections to the prefrontal cortex in the rat studied with retrograde and anterograde tracers. J. Comp. Neurol. **376:** 75–96.
33. WILSON, D.A. & R.M. SULLIVAN. 1991. Olfactory associative conditioning in infant rats with brain stimulation as reward. II. Norepinephrine mediates a specific component of the bulb response to reward. Behav. Neurosci. **105:** 843–849.
34. YUAN, Q. *et al.* 2003. Mitral cell β_1 and 5-HT$_{2A}$ receptor co-localization and cAMP co-regulation: a new model of norepinephrine-induced learning in the olfactory bulb. Learn. Mem. **10:** 5–15.
35. OKUTANI, F. *et al.* 2002. Non-specific olfactory aversion induced by intrabulbar infusion of the GABA(A) receptor antagonist bicuculline in young rats. Neuroscience **112:** 901–906.
36. SULLIVAN, R.M. & D.A. WILSON. 1991. Neural correlates of conditioned odor avoidance in preweanling rats. Behav. Neurosci. **105:** 307–312.
37. RANGEL, S. & M. LEON. 1995. Early odor preference training increases olfactory bulb norepinephrine. Dev. Brain Res. **85:** 187–191.
38. SHIPLEY, M.T., F.J. HALLORAN & J. DE LA TORRE. 1985. Surprisingly rich projection from locus coeruleus to the olfactory bulb in the rat. Brain Res. **239:** 294–299.
39. SULLIVAN, R.M. *et al.* 1994. Bilateral 6-OHDA lesions of the locus coeruleus impair associative olfactory learning in newborn rats. Brain Res. **643:** 306–309.
40. SULLIVAN, R.M. *et al.* 1992. The role of olfactory bulb norepinephrine in early olfactory learning. Dev. Brain Res. **70:** 279–282.
41. MCLEAN, J.H. *et al.* 1993. Serotonergic influences on olfactory learning in the neonatal rat. Behav. Neural Biol. **60:** 152–162.
42. SULLIVAN, R.M. *et al.* 2000. Association of an odor with activation of olfactory bulb noradrenergic β-receptors or locus coeruleus stimulation is sufficient to produce learned approach response to that odor in neonatal rats. Behav. Neurosci. **114:** 957–962.
43. MCGAUGH, J.L. & B. ROOZENDAAL. 2002. The role of adrenal stress hormone in forming lasting memories in the brain. Curr. Opin. Neurobiol. **12:** 205–210.
44. NAKAMURA, S.T. & T. SAKAGUCHI. 1990. Development and plasticity of the locus coeruleus. A review of recent physiological and pharmacological experimentation. Prog. Neurobiol. **34:** 505–526.
45. MARSHALL, K.C. *et al.* 1991. Developmental aspects of the locus coeruleus-noradrenaline system. Prog. Brain Res. **88:** 173–185.

46. MORICEAU, S. & R.M. SULLIVAN. 2003. Reinstating the neonatal sensitive period for olfactory learning. J. Neurosci. Accepted pending revisions.
47. SULLIVAN, R.M. & D.A. WILSON. 1993. Role of the amygdala complex in early olfactory associative learning. Behav. Neurosci. 107: 254–263.
48. MAREN, S. 1999. Neurotoxic basolateral amygdala lesions impair learning and memory but not performance of conditioned fear in rats. J. Neurosci. 19: 8696–8703.
49. HAROUTUNIAN, V. & B.A. CAMPBELL. 1979. Emergence of interoceptive and exteroceptive control of behavior in rats. Science 205: 927–929.
50. BAYER, S.A. 1980. Quantitative 3H-thymidine radiographic analysis of neurogenesis in the rat amygdala. J. Comp. Neurol. 194: 845–875.
51. BERDEL, B., J. MORYS & B. MACIEJEWSKA. 1997. Neuronal changes in the basolateral complex during development of the amygdala of the rat. Int. J. Dev. Neurosci. 15: 755–765.
52. MIZUKAWA, K., I-MING TSENG & N. OTSUKA. 1989. Quantitative electron microscopic analysis of postnatal development of zinc-positive nerve endings in the rat amygdala using Timm's sulphide silver technique. Dev. Brain Res. 50: 197–203.
53. HUNT, P. & B.A. CAMPBELL. 1999. Developmental dissociation of the components of conditioned fear. In Learning, Motivation, and Cognition: The Functional Behaviorism of Robert C. Bolles. M.E. Bouton and M.S. Fanselow, Eds. American Psychological Association. Washington, DC.
54. NAIR, H.P. & F. GONZALEZ-LIMA. 1999. Extinction of behavior in infant rats: development of functional coupling between septal, hippocampal, and ventral tegmental regions. J. Neurosci. 19: 8646–8655.
55. TAKAHASHI, L.K. 1994. Organizing action of corticosterone on the development of behavioral inhibition in the preweanling rat. Dev. Brain Res. 81: 121–127.
56. WIEDENMAYER, C.P. & G.A. BARR. 2001. Developmental changes in c-fos expression to an age-specific social stressor in infant rats. Behav. Brain Res. 126: 147–157.
57. MYSLIVECEK, J. 1997. Inhibitory learning and memory in newborn rats. Prog. Neurobiol. 53: 399–430.
58. BLOZOVSKI, D. & A. CUDENNEC. 1980. Passive avoidance learning in the young rat. Dev. Psychobiol. 13: 513–518.
59. COLLIER, A.C. et al. 1979. Approach-avoidance conflict in preweanling rats: a developmental study. Anim. Learn. Behav. 7: 514–520.
60. MORICEAU, S. & R.M. SULLIVAN. Corticosterone influences on mammalian imprinting. Behav. Neurosci. In press.
61. LEVINE, S. 1962. Plasma-free corticosterone response to electric shock in rats stimulated in infancy. Science 135: 795–796.
62. LEVINE, S. 2001. Primary social relationships influence the development of the hypothalamic—pituitary—adrenal axis in the rat. Physiol. Behav. 73: 255–260.
63. BIALIK, R.J., B.A. PAPPAS & D.C. ROBERTS. 1984. Neonatal 6-hydroxydopamine prevents adaptation to chemical disruption of the pituitary-adrenal system in the rat. Horm. Behav. 18: 12–21.
64. BARR, G.A. & G. ROSSI. 1992. Conditioned place preference from ventral tegmental injections of morphine in neonatal rats. Dev. Brain Res. 66: 133–136.
65. KEHOE, P. & E. BLASS. 1986. Central nervous system mediation of positive and negative reinforcement in neonatal albino rats. Dev. Brain Res. 27: 69–75.
66. ROTH, T. & R.M. SULLIVAN. 2001. Endogenous opioids and their role in odor preference acquisition and consolidation following odor-shock conditioning in infant rats. Dev. Psychobiol. 39: 188–198.
67. WELDON, D.A., M.L. TRAVIS & D.A. KENNEDY. 1991. Posttraining D1 receptor blockade impairs odor conditioning in neonatal rats. Behav. Neurosci. 105: 450–458.
68. ROTH, T. & R.M. SULLIVAN. 2003. Consolidation and expression of a shock-induced odor preference in rat pups is facilitated by opioids. Physiol. Behav. 78: 135–142.
69. MCLEAN, J.H. et al. 1999. pCREB in the neonate rat olfactory bulb is selectively and transiently increased by odor preference-conditioned training. Learn. Mem. 6: 608–618.
70. OKERE, C.O. & H. KABA. 2000. Increased expression of neuronal nitric oxide synthase mRNA in the accessory olfactory bulb during the formation of olfactory recognition memory in mice. Eur. J. Neurosci. 12: 4552–4556.

71. BERNET, C.Z. & M.B. STEIN. 1999. Relationship of childhood maltreatment to the onset and course of major depression in adulthood. Depress. Anxiety 9: 169–174.
72. READ, J. et al. 2001. The contribution of early traumatic events to schizophrenia in some patients: a traumagenic neurodevelopmental model. Psychiatry 64: 319–345.
73. TEICHER, M.H. et al. 1997. Preliminary evidence for abnormal cortical development in physically and sexually abused children using EEG coherence and MRI. Ann. N.Y. Acad. Sci. 821: 160–175.
74. BOLHUIS, J.J. 1999. The development of animal behavior: from Lorenz to neural nets. Naturwissenschaften 86: 101–111.
75. MOORE, C.L., L. JORDAN & L. WONG. 1996. Early olfactory experience, novelty and choice of sexual partner by male rats. Physiol. Behav. 60: 1361–1367.
76. FILLION, T.J. & E.M. BLASS. 1986. Infantile experience with suckling odors determined adult sexual behavior in male rats. Science 231: 729–731.
77. SHORE, A.N. 2001. Effect of secure attachment relationship on right brain development, affect regulation and infant mental health. Infant Ment. Health J. 22: 7–66.

Gene–Environment Interactions and the Neurobiology of Social Conflict

STEPHEN J. SUOMI

Laboratory of Comparative Ethology, National Institute of Child Health & Human Development, National Institutes of Health, DHHS, Bethesda, Maryland 20892-7971, USA

ABSTRACT: Recent research has disclosed marked individual differences in biobehavioral responses to social conflicts exhibited by rhesus monkeys across the life span. For example, approximately 5–10% of rhesus monkeys growing up in the wild consistently exhibit impulsive and/or inappropriately aggressive responses to mildly stressful situations throughout development; those same individuals also show chronic deficits in their central serotonin metabolism. These characteristic patterns of biobehavioral response emerge early in life and remain remarkably stable from infancy to adulthood. Laboratory studies have demonstrated that although these characteristics are highly heritable, they are also subject to major modification by specific early experiences, particularly those involving early social attachment relationships. Moreover, genetic and early experience factors can interact, often in dramatic fashion. For example, a specific polymorphism in the serotonin transporter gene is associated with deficits in early neurobehavioral functioning and serotonin metabolism, extreme aggression, and excessive alcohol consumption among monkeys who experienced insecure early attachment relationships, but not in monkeys who developed secure attachment relationships with their mothers during infancy. Because daughters tend to develop the same type of attachment relationships with their own offspring that they experienced with their mothers early in life, such early experiences provide a possible nongenetic mechanism for transmitting these patterns to subsequent generations.

KEYWORDS: rhesus monkeys; impulsive aggression; 5-HAA; gene-environment interactions

INTRODUCTION

This report summarizes a program of research that has focused on the development of excessive physical aggression in a subgroup of young male rhesus monkeys, with an emphasis on findings linking such patterns of behavior to an apparent deficit in central serotonin metabolism. Ethologists have long argued that the expression of aggression can clearly serve important adaptive functions, having been largely conserved over mammalian evolutionary history.[1] Indeed, the capability to engage in ag-

Address for correspondence: Dr. Stephen J. Suomi, Ph.D., Laboratory of Comparative Ethology, NICHD, NIH, DHHS, 6705 Rockledge Drive, Suite 8030, Bethesda, MD 20892-7971. Voice: 301-496-9550; fax: 301-496-0630.
ss148k@nih.gov

Ann. N.Y. Acad. Sci. 1008: 132–139 (2003). © 2003 New York Academy of Sciences.
doi: 10.1196/annals.1301.014

gressive attack and defense in the service of protecting self, family, and friends from predators and competitors is seemingly crucial for the survival of the individual and the maintenance of any social group across successive generations.

However, excessive and/or inappropriate aggression by any individual has the potential of destroying the very social fabric that binds the group together. The expression of aggression must therefore be regulated, that is, individual group members must come to know which social stimuli merit an aggressive response and which do not, and for those that do, to what degree, and for how long, if the group is to maintain its social cohesion over time. Accordingly, learning how and when to avoid an aggressive encounter and when and how to end it once begun may be at least as important as learning how and when to start or respond to an aggressive act.[2] The development of proficiency in the regulation of aggression appears to be especially important for those advanced primate species whose members live in large social groups that are well-defined in terms of both kinship relationships and social dominance hierarchies. Among the most complex are those of rhesus monkeys (*Macaca mulatta*).

BIOBEHAVIORAL CORRELATES AND CONSEQUENCES OF IMPULSIVE AGGRESSION

Numerous studies carried out in both laboratory and field settings have documented dramatic individual differences among rhesus monkeys and other nonhuman primate species in their biobehavioral responses to social conflicts and other environmental stressors. For example, some rhesus monkeys consistently respond to such challenges with excessive displays of fearful and anxious-like behavior and profound and prolonged activation of the hypothalamic–pituitary–adrenal (HPA) axis.[3] Other monkeys appear to be excessively impulsive and aggressive instead, often initiating severe and inappropriate attacks on others in their social group or unnecessarily provoking aggressive responses from them. Most of these impulsively aggressive individuals, making up perhaps 5–10% of both captive and field populations of rhesus monkeys studied to date, also exhibit apparent deficits in serotonergic function, as reflected by unusually low chronic cerebrospinal fluid (CSF) concentrations of the central serotonin metabolite 5-hydroxy-indoleacetic acid (5-HIAA).[4]

Many of the behavioral patterns and tendencies that distinguish impulsively aggressive monkeys from others in their social group appear as early as late infancy and remain remarkably consistent throughout the whole of development. Young males growing up in field settings who exhibit such patterns initially do so in the context of rough-and-tumble play with peers—their play tends to be excessively aggressive, often escalating inappropriately to actual aggressive exchanges. They also are more likely to engage in other forms of risky behavior, such as taking dangerous leaps from treetop to treetop, than are their peers.[5] At later ages these same males are disproportionately likely to physically confront high-ranking adult males in their social group, often with physically damaging consequences for themselves.[6] Individual differences in CSF 5-HIAA concentrations in rhesus monkeys have been found to be at least as stable throughout development as are the behavioral tendencies previously described. Indeed, CSF 5-HIAA concentrations measured at 14 days of age are significantly correlated with those obtained from the same subjects at 4 years of age, as well as at intermediate ages.[7,8]

Laboratory studies have demonstrated that individuals with the lowest CSF 5-HIAA concentrations are disproportionately likely to have poor state control and visual orienting capabilities during early infancy[9] and perform poorly on delay-of-gratification tasks during childhood.[10] In addition, they exhibit altered sleep patterns,[11] as well as unusually high cerebral glucose metabolism under mild isoflurine anesthesia as adults.[12] These monkeys also tend to consume excessive amounts of alcohol when placed in a "happy hour" setting as adolescents and young adults;[13] in this setting there is also a significant negative relationship between degree of alcohol intoxication and serotonin transporter availability.[14]

In free-ranging settings, rhesus monkey males with the lowest CSF 5-HIAA are far more likely to be expelled from their natal troop prior to puberty[15] and less likely to survive to adulthood than other males in their birth cohort.[16] Young females who have chronically low CSF levels of 5-HIAA also tend to be impulsive, aggressive, and generally rather incompetent socially. However, unlike their male counterparts, they are not expelled from their natal troop, but instead remain with their families throughout their lifetime, although studies of captive rhesus monkey groups suggest that these females usually remain at the bottom of their respective dominance hierarchies.[17] While most of these females eventually become mothers, recent research indicates that their maternal behavior is often inadequate or even abusive, such that the attachment relationships their offspring develop tend to be avoidant, if not disorganized.[2] In sum, wild rhesus monkeys who exhibit poor regulation of impulsive and aggressive behavior and deficits in central serotonin metabolism early in life tend to follow developmental trajectories that often result in premature death for males and chronically low social dominance and poor parenting for females.

GENETIC AND ENVIRONMENTAL INFLUENCES AND GENE–ENVIRONMENT INTERACTIONS

Both laboratory and field studies have reported that individual differences in 5-HIAA concentrations are highly heritable among monkeys of similar age and comparable rearing background.[18] On the other hand, both CSF 5-HIAA concentrations and their just-described behavioral correlates are also clearly subject to major modification by early social experiences, particularly those involving attachment relationships. For example, rhesus monkeys raised from birth away from their biological mothers but in the continuous company of similarly reared age mates for their first 6 months of life typically develop behavioral and physiological patterns that seem to mimic those biobehavioral features characteristic of excessively aggressive monkeys observed in both laboratory settings and naturalistic habitats. Peer-reared monkeys consistently exhibit lower CSF 5-HIAA concentrations than their mother-reared counterparts throughout development, as well as higher rates of impulsive aggression and excessive alcohol consumption in adolescence and early adulthood.[13,20] In short, *both* genetic and early experiential factors can affect a monkey's characteristic pattern of biobehavioral reactivity.

Do these factors operate independently, or do they interact in some fashion in shaping individual developmental trajectories? Recent research has demonstrated several significant interactions between specific genetic and experiential factors in

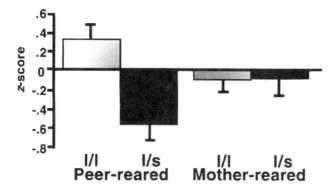

Bennett, Lesch, Heils, Long, Lorenz, Shoaf, Champoux, Suomi, Linnoila, & Higley

FIGURE 1. Effect of 5-HTT Gene and Early Rearing Environment on CSF 5-HIAA. Z-Score means (and standard errors) of CSF concentrations of 5-HIAA in peer-reared LL, peer-reared LS, mother-reared LL, and mother-reared LS subjects. The gene X rearing environment interaction is the result of significantly lower CSF 5-HIAA concentrations in the peer-reared LS monkeys than the other three subject groups. (From Bennett et al.[22])

shaping developmental trajectories for rhesus monkeys. For example, the serotonin transporter gene (5-HTT), a candidate gene for impaired serotonergic function,[20] has length variation in its promoter region that results in allelic variation in 5-HTT expression. A heterozygous "short" allele (LS) confers low transcriptional efficiency to the 5-HTT promoter relative to the homozygous "long" allele (LL), raising the possibility that low 5-HTT expression may result in decreased serotonergic function.[21]

Several studies have now demonstrated that the consequences of having the LS allele differ dramatically for peer-reared monkeys and their mother-reared counterparts. For example, Bennett et al.[22] found that CSF 5-HIAA concentrations did not differ as a function of 5-HTT status for mother-reared subjects, whereas among peer-reared monkeys individuals with the LS allele had significantly lower CSF 5-HIAA concentrations than those with the LL allele (FIG. 1).

One interpretation of this interaction is that mother-rearing appeared to "buffer" any potentially deleterious effects of the LS allele on serotonin metabolism. A similar pattern appeared with respect to aggression: high levels of aggression were shown by peer-reared monkeys with the LS allele, whereas mother-reared LS monkeys exhibited low levels that were comparable to those of both mother-reared and peer-reared LL monkeys, again suggesting a "buffering" effect of maternal rearing.[23] Champoux et al.[24] examined the relationship between early rearing history and serotonin transporter gene polymorphic status on measures of neonatal neurobehavioral development during the first month of life and found further evidence of maternal buffering. Specifically, infants possessing the LS allele who were being reared in the laboratory neonatal nursery showed significant deficits in measures of attention, activity, and motor maturity relative to nursery-reared infants possessing the LL allele, whereas both LS and LL infants who were being reared by competent mothers exhibited normal values for each of these measures (FIG. 2).

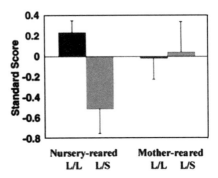

FIGURE 2. Orientation Cluster by Rearing and Genotype. Z-Score means (and standard errors) of composite orienting cluster scores of the standardized neonatal assessment scales for nursery-reared LL, nursery-reared LS, mother-reared LL, and mother-reared LS monkeys obtained during their first month of life. The gene X environment interaction is the result of significantly lower scores for nursery-reared LS infants than for the other three subject groups. (Adapted from Champoux *et al.*[24])

A more dramatic pattern of gene–environment interaction was revealed by an analysis of alcohol consumption data: whereas peer-reared monkeys with the LS allele consumed more alcohol than peer-reared monkeys with the LL allele, the reverse was true for mother-reared subjects, with individuals possessing the LS allele actually consuming *less* alcohol than their LL counterparts.[25] The same pattern was found for relative levels of alcohol intoxication.[26] In other words, the LS allele appeared to represent a risk factor for excessive alcohol consumption among peer-reared monkeys, but a protective factor for mother-reared subjects.

In sum, peer-reared monkeys with the LS allele displayed deficits in measures of neurobehavioral development during their initial weeks of life and reduced serotonin metabolism and excessive alcohol consumption as adolescents compared with those possessing the LL allele. In contrast, mother-reared subjects with the LS allele were characterized by normal early neurobehavioral development and serotonin metabolism, as well as reduced risk for excessive alcohol consumption later in life compared with their mother-reared counterparts with the LL allele. It could be argued on the basis of these findings that having the LS allele of the 5-HTT gene may well lead to psychopathology among monkeys with poor early rearing histories, but might actually be adaptive for monkeys who develop secure early attachment relationship with their mothers.

The implications of these recent findings may be considerable with respect to the cross-generational transmission of these biobehavioral characteristics, in that the attachment style of a monkey mother is typically "copied" by her daughters when they grow up and become mothers themselves.[27] If similar buffering is indeed experienced by the next generation of infants carrying the LS 5-HTT polymorphism, then having had their mothers develop a secure attachment relationship with their own mothers may well provide the basis for a nongenetic means of transmitting its apparently adaptive consequences to that new generation. On the other hand, if contextual factors, such as changes in dominance rank, instability within the troop, or changes in the availability of food, were to alter a young mother's care of her infants in ways that compromised such buffering, then one might expect any offspring carrying the LS polymorphism to develop some if not all of the problems described earlier.

SUMMARY

This report summarized research focusing on a subgroup of rhesus monkeys who spontaneously exhibit excessive and socially inappropriate aggression and other patterns of impulsive behavior, as well as chronic deficits in serotonin metabolism, throughout ontogeny. Clearly, both genetic and environmental factors can influence the development of these behavioral and biological propensities, and indeed they may actually interact in shaping such development. A case in point involves interactions between different polymorphisms of the 5-HTT gene and early rearing experiences. Rhesus monkeys possessing the LS allele exhibit deficits in early neurobiological functioning and serotonin metabolism, extreme aggressiveness and impulsivity, and excessive alcohol consumption relative to monkeys possessing the LL allele, but only if they were peer-reared; no such behavioral or biological deficits are shown by LS monkeys who were reared by competent mothers. Furthermore, because daughters tend to develop the same type of attachment relationship with their own offspring that they experienced with their mothers early in life, such experiences may provide a nongenetic mechanism for transmitting these patterns to subsequent generations of monkeys.

ACKNOWLEDGMENTS

The research summarized in this report was supported by funds from the Division of Intramural Research, National Institute of Child Health and Human Development, National Institutes of Health, DHHS. Additional funding was provided by the DIR, NIAAA, NIH, DHHS.

REFERENCES

1. LORENZ, K. 1966. On Aggression. Harcourt, Brace, & World. New York.
2. SUOMI, S.J. 2000. A biobehavioral perspective on developmental psychopathology: excessive aggression and serotonergic dysfunction in monkeys. *In* Handbook of Developmental Psychopathology. A. J. Sameroff, M. Lewis, and S. Miller, Eds.: 237–256. Plenum Press. New York.
3. SUOMI, S.J. 1991. Up-tight and laid-back monkeys: individual differences in the response to social challenges. *In* Plasticity of Development. S. Brauth, W. Hall, and R. Dooling, Eds.: 27–56. MIT Press. Cambridge, MA.
4. HIGLEY, J.D. & S.J. SUOMI. 1996. Reactivity and social competence affect individual differences in reaction to severe stress in children: investigations using nonhuman primates. *In* Intense Stress and Dental Disturbance in Children. C. R. Pfeffer, Ed.: 3–58. American Psychiatric Press. Washington, DC.
5. MEHLMAN, P.T., J.D. HIGLEY, I. FAUCHER, *et al.* 1994. Low cerebrospinal fluid 5-hydroxyindoleacetic acid concentrations are correlated with severe aggression and reduced impulse control in free-ranging primates. Am. J. Psychiatry **151:** 1485–1491.

6. HIGLEY, J.D., P.T. MEHLMAN, D.M. TAUB, *et al.* 1992. Cerebrospinal fluid monoamine metabolite and adrenal correlates of aggression in free-ranging rhesus monkeys. Arch. Gen. Psychiatry **49:** 436–444.

7. HIGLEY, J.D., S.J. SUOMI & M. LINNOILA. 1992. A longitudinal assessment of CSF monoamine metabolite and plasma cortisol concentrations in young rhesus monkeys. Biol. Psychiatry **32:** 127–145.

8. SUOMI, S.J. 2003. How gene-environment interactions can shape the development of socioemotional regulation in rhesus monkeys. *In* Socioemotional Regulation: Dimensions, Developmental Trends, and InFluences. B.S. Zuckerman and A.F. Lieberman, Eds.: in press. Johnson & Johnson. Skillman, NJ.

9. CHAMPOUX, M., S.J. SUOMI & M.L. SCHNEIDER. 1994. Temperamental differences between captive Indian and Chinese-Indian hybrid rhesus macaque infants. Lab. Anim. Sci. **44:** 351–357.

10. BENNETT, A.J., T. TSAI, W.D. HOPKINS, *et al.* 1999. Early social rearing environment influences acquisition of a computerized joystick task in rhesus monkeys (*Macaca mulatta*). Am. J. Primatol. **49:** 33–34.

11. ZAJICEK, K., J.D. HIGLEY, S.J. SUOMI & M. LINNOILA. 1997. Rhesus macaques with high CSF 5-HIAA concentrations exhibit early sleep onset. Psychiatr. Res. **77:** 15–25.

12. DOUDET, D., D. HOMMER, J.D. HIGLEY, *et al.* 1995. Cerebral glucose metabolism, CSF 5-HIAA, and aggressive behavior in rhesus monkeys. Am. J. Psychiatry **152:** 1782–1787.

13. HIGLEY, J.D., M.L. HASERT, S.J. SUOMI & M. LINNOILA. 1991. A new nonhuman primate model of alcohol abuse: effects of early experience, personality, and stress on alcohol consumption. Proc. Natl. Acad. Sci. USA **88:** 7261–7265.

14. HEINZ, A., J.D. HIGLEY, J.G. GOREY, *et al.* 1998. *In vivo* association between alcohol intoxication, aggression, and serotonin transporter availability in nonhuman primates. Am. J. Psychiatry **155:** 1023–1028.

15. MEHLMAN, P.T., J.D. HIGLEY, I. FAUCHER, *et al.* 1995. CSF 5-HIAA concentrations are correlated with sociality and the timing of emigration in free-ranging primates. Am. J. Psychiatry **152:** 901–913.

16. HIGLEY, J.D., P.T. MEHLMAN, D.M. TAUB, *et al.* 1996. Excessive mortality in young free-ranging male nonhuman primates with low CSF 5-HIAA concentrations. Arch. Gen. Psychiatry **53:** 537–543.

17. HIGLEY, J.D., S.T. KING, M.F. HASERT, *et al.* 1996. Stability of individual differences in serotonin function and its relationship to severe aggression and competent social behavior in rhesus macaque females. Neuropsychopharmachology **14:** 67–76.

18. HIGLEY, J.D., W.T. THOMPSON, M. CHAMPOUX, *et al.* 1993. Paternal and maternal genetic and environmental contributions to CSF monoamine metabolites in rhesus monkeys (*Macaca mulatta*). Arch. Gen. Psychiatry **50:** 615–623.

19. HIGLEY, J.D., S.J. SUOMI & M. LINNOILA. 1996. A nonhuman primate model of Type II alcoholism? Part 2: Diminished social competence and excessive aggression correlates with low CSF 5-HIAA concentrations. Alcohol. Clin. Exp. Res. **20:** 643–650.

20. LESCH, L.P., J. MEYER, K. GLATZ, *et al.* 1997. The 5-HT gene-linked polymorphic region (5-HTTLPR) in evolutionary perspective: alternative biallelic variation in rhesus monkeys. J. Neural Transm. **104:** 1259–1266.

21. HEILS, A. A. TEUFEL, S. PETRI, *et al.* 1996. Allelic variation of human serotonin transporter gene expression. J. Neurochem. **6:** 2621–2624.

22. BENNETT, A.J., K.P. LESCH, A. HEILS, *et al.* 2002. Early experience and serotonin transporter gene variation interact to influence primate CNS function. Mol. Psychiatry **17:** 118–122.

23. BARR, C.S., T.K. NEWMAN, M.L. BECKER, *et al.* 2003. Early experience and rh5-HTTPLR genotype interact to influence social behavior and aggression in nonhuman primates. Genes, Brain Behav. In press.

24. CHAMPOUX, M., A.J. BENNETT, K.P. LESCH, *et al.* 2002. Serotonin transporter gene polymorphism and neurobehavioral development in rhesus monkey neonates. Mol. Psychiatry **7:** 1058–1063.

25. BENNETT, A.J., K.P. LESCH, A. HEILS & M. LINNOILA. 1998. Serotonin transporter gene variation, CSF 5-HIAA concentrations, and alcohol-related aggression in rhesus monkeys (*Macaca mulatta*). Am. J. Primatol. **45:** 168–169.

26. BARR, C.S., T.K. NEWMAN, M.L. BECKER, *et al.* 2003. Serotonin transporter gene variation is associated with alcohol sensitivity in rhesus macaques exposed to early-life stress. Alcohol. Clin. Exp. Res. **27:** 812–817.

27. SUOMI, S.J. 1999. Attachment in rhesus monkeys. *In* Handbook of Attachment: Theory, Research, and Clinical Applications. J. Cassidy and P.R. Shaver, Eds.: 181–197. Guilford Press. New York.

The Policy Context for Child and Adolescent Mental Health Services: Implications for Systems Reform and Basic Science Development

KIMBERLY HOAGWOOD

New York State Office of Mental Health & Columbia University, New York, New York 10031, USA

ABSTRACT: Significant state and national policy initiatives are focusing on strategies for financing and structuring the delivery of evidence-based services for children. These initiatives reflect, in part, an increased awareness of and respect for scientific standards about effective treatments and services. At the same time, major studies of system reform and organizational behavior are calling into question the effectiveness of current practices and identifying the complexities of taking science-based services to scale. Four major policy initiatives are described and the implications of scientific developments within the basic neurosciences for improving policy, practice, and service in children's mental health is discussed.

KEYWORDS: policy; children's mental health; services; financing

INTRODUCTION

Much of the impetus for the current policy directions in children's mental health occurred during the late 1990s when the Office of the Surgeon General, in conjunction with federal departments, agencies, and foundations, issued a series of reports on the status of children's mental health. These included the Surgeon General's Report on Mental Health, released in December 1999;[1] the Surgeon General's National Action Agenda on Children's Mental Health (2000);[2] the Surgeon General's Report on Youth Violence (2001);[3] and the supplemental report on Race, Culture and Ethnicity (2001).[4] The release of these reports coincided with intensified legislative activities on financing, insurance coverage, and service delivery. These developments were spurred by the release of a number of other major reports on children's mental health, including the Child Mental Health Foundation and Agencies Network (FAN) Monograph "Off to A Good Start" (2000);[5] the Institute of Medicine's "From Neurons to Neighborhoods: The Science of Early Childhood Development" (2001);[6] and

Address for correspondence: Kimberly Hoagwood, Ph.D., New York State Office of Mental Health & Columbia University, 1078 Riverside Drive, #78, New York, NY 10031. Voice: 212-543-2574; fax: 212-543-5966.

hoagwood@childpsych.columbia.edu

Ann. N.Y. Acad. Sci. 1008: 140–148 (2003). © 2003 New York Academy of Sciences.
doi: 10.1196/annals.1301.015

the National Institute of Mental Health's "Blueprint for Change: Research on Child and Adolescent Mental Health Research" (2001),[7] which outlined a comprehensive research plan to accelerate the pace of intervention development and deployment for children with mental health problems. Together these documents voiced an ethical imperative that a public health responsibility existed to *improve and use* the science base as a means of reforming mental health services for children and their families.

This paper briefly summarizes four major mental health policy initiatives for children, youth, and families that have been spurred by these documents. It describes new findings on the implementation and adoption of new technologies, with respect to understanding the organizational context within which services are delivered. Finally, it describes the implications of these research and policy developments for improving the linkage between basic science and clinical care.

MAJOR POLICY DEVELOPMENTS

Recent state and national policy initiatives in youth mental health services are targeting four major areas for reform. These include identification of so-called evidence-based practices, which encompass psychosocial and pharmacological treatments, clinical services, and preventive models; financing of mental health services, including managed care and parity legislation; shifting roles of families as change agents in treatment planning; and increasing support for community-based services.

Evidence-Based Practices: Their Steep Rise in Popularity

Since 1995, the terms "evidence-based treatment," "evidence-based medicine," or "evidence-based practices" has permeated the rhetoric of science and policy on mental health. A Medline search from 1900 to 1990 revealed only 70 uses of the term "evidence-based medicine" in those 90 years, whereas between 1995 and 2002—a mere 7 years—the term was used more than 5300 times.[8] Clearly these phrases have touched a chord that is deeply resonant with public policy and scientific audiences. A review of the Web sites for the four major departments within the federal government that oversee health policy for youth [Department of Health and Human Services (DHHS),[9] Department of Education (DOE), Department of Justice (DOJ), and Department of Defense (DOD)] revealed that 26 different federal agencies were now using this phrase to describe their policies.

In the field of children's mental health services research, the term "evidence-based practice" has tended to refer to a body of scientific knowledge about service practices (e.g., referral, assessment, case management) or about the effectiveness of clinical treatments or services (e.g., cognitive-behavioral psychosocial treatments; stimulant medications) on child or adolescent mental health problems. Entry into the list of evidence-based practices generally requires that the practice, service, or treatment in question be examined in more than one study using rigorous randomized experimental designs.

Operational criteria have been proposed by the Division of Clinical Psychology of the American Psychological Association (1998), and applied to studies of specific psychosocial treatments for childhood disorders. A similar process has been developed for evaluating the evidence for pharmacological treatments;[10] preventive programs;[11] and school-based mental health services.[12]

There are important differences in the ways in which deployment of effective psychosocial, pharmacological, or service programs occurs. For example, in pharmaceutical medicine, evidence-based approaches have been built into the regulatory standards developed by the FDA to review scientific evidence and identify effective medications. The strength of the evidence for pharmacological treatments is regulated by the FDA, and an industry for their distribution has grown up around this. In contrast, psychosocial treatments, services, and preventive interventions do not have regulatory backing, and their distribution depends largely upon the resourcefulness of individuals who developed the treatments or services .[13]

A new initiative from the MacArthur Foundation, entitled the Youth Mental Health Initiative, under the leadership of John Weisz, is further extending the reach of evidence-based practices by thoroughly reviewing the evidence for therapies targeted at the most common childhood disorders, and by testing two alternative methods of delivering evidence-based practices within community-based mental health clinics. A parallel project will investigate the organizational, system, and payment issues that influence the ability of providers and clinics to adopt new practices. The findings from these two projects will be used to plan a later phase of the initiative, which will examine dissemination strategies for deploying evidence-based practices to a broad array of clinics, providers, youths, and families.

Family-Centered Services: The Growth of the Family/Consumer Movement

Among the values that have become intrinsic to the movement toward community-based services has been the premise that parents, guardians, or consumers must be integrally involved in treatment planning and delivery if the quality of care for children is to improve. The federal government through the Substance Abuse and Mental Health Services Administration (SAMHSA) has supported the development of an infrastructure within state mental health agencies to support consumer involvement in service planning, and most states have consumer or recipient offices to strengthen this involvement. Numerous family advocacy organizations now exist to support the needs of families with children who have emotional or behavioral problems more generally, and for those with specific psychiatric disorders (e.g., ADHD, bipolar disorders, depressive disorders). Simultaneously, there have been several major initiatives in primary care (through Institutes for Healthcare Improvement, for example) to reform health care services nationally by positioning consumers centrally in treatment planning so that they are empowered to make decisions about their own health care. These initiatives within both general health care and mental health care are leading to innovations in delivery, such as providing families with vouchers to function as case managers for their child's care. The movement away from office-based practice and toward empowerment of consumers is likely to increase significantly over the next decade.

One reason that family involvement in service delivery has become integral to state and local planning is because the problems of access to services for youth with mental health needs are pervasive in most communities, but even more so among low-income, urban communities of color. The Surgeon General's Mental Health

Supplement Report on Race, Culture and Ethnicity (2001) underscored the importance of attending to issues of race, culture, and ethnicity if access to services is to be improved. Within low-income, urban communities, as many as 40% of youth exhibit significant mental health issues.[14] Yet even when minority youth and families initially access necessary mental health services, high rates of "no shows" and attrition are notable: fewer than 40% of those initially requesting services actually are receiving them by the point of the expected third face-to-face contact.[15]

Financing Policies

Among the most significant of the federal policies that have arisen in the past several years, owing in large measure to the release of the Surgeon General's reports on mental health, have been those targeting the financing of children's mental health services. These have included significant increases in funding from sources outside of traditional mental health block grants, including expanded funding for Medicaid, S-CHIP, certain educational programs (e.g., Head Start, Safe and Drug Free Schools), privately insured pharmacy benefits, among other sources. More particularly, policies focusing on the application of behavioral managed care in the public and private sectors and on expansion of health insurance coverage under S-CHIP for uninsured children are diminishing the traditional role of mental health agencies to single-handedly effect policy reforms. A related set of financing issues has included expansion of the parity for mental health and general health benefits. These policies have shaped the delivery of and reimbursement mechanisms for mental health services for children and their families, and they have simultaneously created significant opportunities for improving delivery of higher quality care.

Medicaid Expansion and S-CHIP

The policies involving expansions of public health insurance, including Medicaid expansions in the late 1980s and the introduction of S-CHIP in the late 1990s, have altered the insurance distribution for children who use mental health services. The share of all children, and of children using services, who are uninsured has fallen,[16] because public insurance now covers children who would otherwise have been uninsured. In addition, public insurance coverage has displaced private insurance. For example, in 1998, nearly one-quarter of children with a diagnosed mental health problem were publicly insured,[16] and this is consistent with past trends in which public insurance has tended to cover a disproportionate share of children with mental health problems.[17] Among poor minority children, those eligible for Medicaid are likely to have higher rates of mental health problems than privately insured children.[16] One implication of these policy shifts in health insurance coverage for states is that State Medicaid directors must now consider both seriously and less-seriously ill children in making decisions about service distribution.

Behavioral Managed Care

Medicaid programs in most states, as well as many private insurers, have shifted much of their mental health coverage into behavioral managed care. By 1999, for example, 42 states operated some form of managed behavioral health care, and this was triple the number in 1996 (SAMHSA, 2000). Behavioral managed care for youth mental health care has generated substantial savings, mainly through marked reductions in the use of inpatient services and a consequent rise in outpatient services. It is not clear whether these reductions have generated negative outcomes for children, because no studies have yet examined the overall effects of behavioral managed care on mental health outcomes. But the significant cost savings suggest that managed behavioral care is here to stay. The movement toward managed care does raise a potential risk for underservice, cost shifting, and disenrollment. In fact, a study of Medicaid managed care in Pennsylvania found a higher rate of disenrollment for children with psychiatric admissions than for those with nonpsychiatric admissions.[18] There is also a potential for this sudden rise of managed care to shift the burden of mental health care to public systems, such as juvenile justice, special education, or child welfare.[19]

Parity

Parity of mental health and general health benefits in the past five years has been partially achieved through legislative efforts. For example, in 1996, the federal government passed the Mental Health Parity Act (which was implemented in 1998). This act required parity in benefits only if mental health coverage was also offered. It applied only to lifetime and annual dollar limits and did not require parity in co-payments, deductibles, or limits on days or visits. So while it represents a major policy advance by offering for the first time mental health coverage, it also represents only a partial solution to the problem of insurance coverage for mental health problems.

Community-Based Services

In the mid-1980s, a series of initiatives focused on strengthening the community-based service system for children and adolescents. Under the auspices of the Child and Adolescent Service System Program (CASSP), a series of state grants were awarded by NIMH to create youth and family bureaus within state systems. This was given principled footing through the creation of a model, called the system of care model, developed by Stroul and Friedman.[20] This model articulated a series of values, centered around maintaining children within their communities, coordinating services, involving families integrally in delivery and planning of treatments and services, and attending to the cultural relevance of services.

The most important federal initiative to support community-based services has been the Comprehensive Community Mental Health Services for Children and Families (CMHSC). Supported by the Center for Mental Health Services (CMHS) of SAMHSA, this program constitutes the single largest federal program supporting mental health services for youth with serious emotional or behavioral problems and is currently financed at close to $100 million per year.

A significant trend since the mid-1980s has been an increase in use of outpatient mental health services and reduced reliance on inpatient care, associated with the existence of community-based services.[16,20,21] The increase in the provision of these services, however, has not kept pace with reductions in inpatient service use, so adequate supplies of community-based services are still unavailable in many parts of the country.[16,23,24] Furthermore, the types of community-based services that are offered often bear little resemblance to the research base on effective practice.

SUMMARY OF POLICY INITIATIVES

These policy initiatives involving evidence-based practices, financing of services, family-centered policies, and community-based care reflect a significant shift in public health emphasis that has focused attention to the potential contributions that research-based findings can make to service delivery. At the same time, research on children's services are focusing increasingly on ways in which organizational behavior of service systems can be changed to better accommodate research-based practices. Some of these new developments in organizational research have direct implications for delivery of services and for incorporation of research-based findings into standard practice.

ORGANIZATIONAL SYSTEMS ISSUES IN THE IMPLEMENTATION OF EVIDENCE-BASED PRACTICES

A significant turning point in youth mental health policy occurred after the publication of the seminal system of care studies by Bickman *et al.*,[25,26] who demonstrated that system coordination improved access to services, satisfaction with services, and costs. However, these studies also demonstrated that clinical outcomes for children were the same whether children were receiving coordinated services through systems of care or not. As a result of these studies, attention was shifted away from general studies of "systemness" to the clinical effectiveness of services within these systems of care, and especially to the types, dosage, and intensity of treatments delivered.[27] Interest in the effectiveness of clinical care has created a zeitgeist in which examination of the integration of evidence-based practices within systems of care has been possible.[28]

At the same time, studies from literatures within business and industrial organizational research are identifying factors that enable organizational systems to accept or reject innovations, such as evidence-based care, and to implement or shun new technologies. These studies have demonstrated that an organization's structure and leadership affect the extent to which work environments allow experimentation with innovations or the adoption of new technologies.[29] These studies have also identified other important dimensions of organizations, notably organizational culture (i.e., norms and values), climate (i.e., psychological impact of work environment), and work attitudes (i.e., commitment), which predict innovation. These studies suggest that flexible structures, strong leadership, constructive cultures, nonrestrictive climates, and positive work attitudes contribute to innovation in organizations and the adoption of cutting-edge technologies.[29]

The bulk of organizational research has not yet been conducted in mental health service organizations, with the exception of the ongoing and important work of Schoenwald *et al.*[30] Studies are now being planned under the new MacArthur Foundation Youth Mental Health Initiative to assess the effects of organizational characteristics on the adoption of evidence-based technologies. Such studies will provide important information for policy planning purposes as to how the organizational context of mental health clinics affects the abilities of administrators, supervisors, and front-line clinicians to provide services to children and families and to improve their practices.

IMPLICATION OF BASIC SCIENCE FOR POLICY AND PRACTICE

Some of the key challenges in linking basic science findings to policy revolve around questions of pace, relevance, and adaptation. Key questions include: How can the pace of basic science work on neurogenesis, neuronal sculpting, and brain imaging lead to the development of new treatments that can be readily deployed within a changing service context? How can the mechanisms underlying and influencing brain development, neuronal signaling, and synaptic plasticity lead to more tailored and individualized treatments? How can the early-life neural antecedents of disorders that are expressed later in life as well as the neural substrates of disorders that appear during childhood, such as ADHD, autism, childhood mood disorders, anxiety disorders, and eating disorders, be used to identify early interventions that can be adapted for a range of service systems?

After nearly four decades of research into the cellular and molecular bases of brain development, it has become apparent that the developing child's environment, both *in utero* and *ex utero*, plays a large role in shaping his or her brain circuitry and subsequent behavioral performance. It also has been demonstrated that early plasticity of brain circuitry can play a positive role in optimizing the brain for the environment in which it develops. This has been most dramatically illustrated in functional imaging studies of individuals born with sensory deficits, who therefore were forced to use other modalities for the basic skills of reading or speaking. Brain regions not normally utilized in such skills are incorporated into new brain circuits. However, this adaptation occurs only if the unusual modalities are utilized for these purposes during early childhood. Such findings suggest that a mechanistic understanding or even a behavioral time-keyed map of functional human brain development could help educators and clinicians to develop more efficient strategies for using brain plasticity to facilitate learning.

In addition, findings from basic developmental neuroscience research have implications for clinical adaptation. The use of well-characterized animal model systems now permits manipulations of key genes and of nurturing environments such that these models can help to illuminate the causal relationships between specific risk factors and pathological outcomes. Lack of precision in detecting causal pathways has led to inefficiencies in service delivery, because services are organized administratively according to bureaucratic structures rather than clinically in terms of particular individualized clinical needs. One potentially significant contribution of basic developmental neuroscience may well be greater precision in specifying these causal pathways that in consequence may lead to more customized and effective care.

Improved understanding of the early-life neural antecedents of disorders may also prove to be helpful in establishing accurate diagnoses and developing early interventions. In addition, the identification of the biological bases of emotional and cognitive dysfunction may well help to alleviate the social stigma that currently permeates much of the public perception of mental health.

CONCLUSIONS

While the scientific knowledge base on brain development and clinical care in children's mental health is rapidly improving, major impediments to delivery and deployment of effective services exist.[13,31] Obstacles to improving services reside at organizational systems levels, and are inherent in the governance, financing, and structures by which services are delivered. However, significant state and national policy initiatives are currently focused on more closely aligning science and practice. These initiatives present unprecedented opportunities for more closely linking scientific developments on basic developmental neuroscience, on effective clinical care, and on organizational systems to policy reform, and improve the chances that children and families will have access to and receive quality care.

REFERENCES

1. U.S. PUBLIC HEALTH SERVICE. 1999. Mental Health: A Report of the Surgeon General. U.S. Department of Health and Human Services. Washington, DC.
2. U.S. PUBLIC HEALTH SERVICE. 2000. Report of the Surgeon General's Conference on Children's Mental Health: A National Action Agenda. Washington, DC.
3. U.S. PUBLIC HEALTH SERVICE. 2001. Youth Violence: A Report of the Surgeon General. Department of Health and Human Services. Washington, DC.
4. U.S. PUBLIC HEALTH SERVICE. 2001. The Surgeon General's Mental Health Supplement on Culture, Race and Ethnicity. Department of Health and Human Services. Washington, DC.
5. FOUNDATIONS AND AGENCIES NETWORK. 2000. Off to a Good Start. Foundations and Agencies Network Monograph. Washington, DC.
6. INSTITUTE OF MEDICINE (IOM). 2000. From Neurons to Neighborhoods: The Science of Early Childhood Development. National Academy Press. Washington, DC.
7. NATIONAL ADVISORY MENTAL HEALTH COUNCIL. 2001. Workgroup on Child and Adolescent Mental Health Intervention Development and Deployment. Blueprint for Change: Research on Child and Adolescent Mental Health. NIH Publication No. 01-4985. National Institute of Mental Health. Rockville, MD.
8. HOAGWOOD, K. & J. JOHNSON. 2003. School psychology: a public health framework I. From evidence-based practices to evidence-based policies. J. School Psychol. 41: 3–21.
9. SUBSTANCE ABUSE AND MENTAL HEALTH SERVICES ADMINISTRATION. 2000. State Profiles, 1999, on Public Sector Managed Behavioral Health Care, DHHS Publication No. (SMA) 00-3432. Department of Health and Human Services. Washington, DC.
10. JENSEN, P.S., V.S. BHATARA, B. VITIELLO, et al. 1999. Psychoactive medication prescribing practices for US children: gaps between research and clinical practice. J. Am. Acad. Child Adolesc. Psychiatry 38: 557–565.
11. GREENBERG, M.T., C. DOMITROVICH & B. BUMBARGER. 2001. The prevention of mental disorders in school-aged children: current state of the field. Prev. Treat. 4: Article 1. Available at http://journals.apa.org/prevention/volume4/pre0040001a.html
12. RONES, M. & K. HOAGWOOD. 2000. School-based mental health services: a research review. Clin. Child Fam. Psychol. Rev. 3: 223–241.
13. HOAGWOOD, K., B.J. BURNS, L. KISER, et al. 2001. Evidence-based practice in child and adolescent mental health services. Psychiatr. Serv. 52: 1179–1189.
14. TOLAN, P.H. & D. HENRY. 1996. Patterns of psychopathology among urban poor children: comorbidity and aggression effects. J. Consult. Clin. Psychol. 64:, 1094–1099.

15. MCKAY, M., J. STOEWE, K. MCCADAM & J. GONZALES. 1998. Increasing access to child mental health services for urban children and their care givers. Health & Soc. Work **23:** 9–15.
16. GLIED, S. & A.E. CUELLAR. 2003. Trends and issues in child and adolescent mental health. Health Affairs **22:** 39–50.
17. COSTELLO, E.J., A. ANGOLD, B.J. BURNS, *et al.* 1996. The Great Smoky Mountain Study of Youth: Goals, designs, methods, and the prevalence of DSM III-R disorders. Arch. Gen. Psychiatry **53:** 1129–1136.
18. SCHOLLE, S.H., K.J. KELLEHER, G. CHILDS, *et al.* 1997. Changes in Medicaid managed care enrollment among children. Health Affairs **16:** 164–170.
19. HUTCHINSON, A.B. & E.M. FOSTER. 2003. The Effect of Medicaid managed care on mental health care for children: a review of the literature. Mental Health Serv. Res. **5:** 39–54.
20. RINGEL, J. & R. STURM. 2001. National estimates of mental health utilization and expenditures for children in 1998. J. Behav. Health Serv. Res. **28:** 319–333.
21. NATIONAL ADVISORY MENTAL HEALTH COUNCIL. 2001. National Advisory Mental Health Council Workgroup on Child and Adolescent Mental Health Intervention Development and Deployment. Blueprint for Change: Research on Child and Adolescent Mental Health. NIMH Blueprint Report. National Institute of Mental Health. Washington, DC.
22. NATIONAL INSTITUTE OF MENTAL HEALTH. 2001. Proceedings of a Conference on Research Ethics in Mental Health Science Involving Minority Populations of Children. Fordham University. New York.
23. BURNS, B.J., E.J. COSTELLO, A. ANGOLD, *et al.* 1995. Children's mental health service use across service sectors. Health Affairs **14:** 147–159.
24. BURNS, B.J., E.J. COSTELLO, A. ERKANLI, *et al.* 1997. Insurance coverage and mental health service use by adolescents with serious emotional disturbance. J. Child Fam. Stud. **6:** 89–111.
25. BICKMAN, L., M. FOSTER & E.W. LAMBERT. 1996. Who gets hospitalized in a continuum of care? J. Am. Acad. Child Adolesc. Psychiatry **35:** 74–80.
26. BICKMAN, L., W.T. SUMMERFELT & K. NOSER. 1997. Comparative outcomes of emotionally disturbed children and adolescents in a system of services and usual care. Psychiatr. Serv. **48:** 1543–1548.
27. HOAGWOOD, K. 1997. Interpreting nullity. The Fort Bragg experiment—a comparative success or failure? Am. Psychol. **52:** 546–550.
28. GLISSON, C. & L.R. JAMES. 2001. The cross-level effects of culture and climate in human service teams. J. Organ. Behav. **23:** 767–794.
29. SCHOENWALD, S.K. & S.W. HENGGELER. 2002. Services research and family based treatment. *In* Family Psychology: Science-Based Interventions. H. A. Liddle, D. A. Santisteban, R. F. Levant, and J. H. Bray, Eds.: 259–282. American Psychological Association. Washington, DC.
30. BURNS, B.J., K. HOAGWOOD & P.J. MRAZEK. 1999. Effective treatment for mental disorders in children and adolescents. Clin. Child Fam. Psychol. Rev. **2:** 199–254.
31. BURNS, B.J. 2003. Children and evidence-based practices. Psychiatr. Clin. North Am. **26:** 955–969.

Impulsivity, Emotion Regulation, and Developmental Psychopathology: Specificity Versus Generality of Linkages

STEPHEN P. HINSHAW

Department of Psychology, University of California, Berkeley, California 94720, USA

ABSTRACT: Impulsivity, closely related to the construct of response (dis)inhibition, is central to conceptions of both attention-deficit/hyperactivity (ADHD) and aggressive-spectrum or disruptive behavior disorders. The multifaceted nature of inhibitory deficits requires careful specification in any explanatory accounts of psychopathology. A host of brain regions and neural interconnections are involved in response inhibition; neural models are likely to be complex at the levels of neurotransmitter systems and white-matter tracts. Despite the substantial heritability of ADHD and the substantial continuity of early-onset forms of aggression, developmental processes (including gene–environment correlations and interactions) and transactional models are crucial to the unfolding of regulated versus dysregulated behavioral outcomes. Thus, stressful prenatal and childhood environments must be investigated with as much precision as genetic loci and neural pathways. Differentiating executive inhibition (believed to be largely dopaminergic and frontal/frontal–striatal in nature) from motivational inhibition (believed to be largely noradrenergic/serotonergic and limbic in nature) is necessary to distinguish subtypes of youth with attentional and aggressive problems, and to differentiate key etiologic processes. Indeed, the executive function deficits in children with ADHD appear to independent of their emotion dysregulation, which is specific to an aggressive subgroup. Sex differences in response inhibition and sex differences in its linkages to psychopathology are relatively unexplored. For progress in subsequent research to occur, the following are required: precision in measurement at both biological and behavioral levels; contrasts with clinical comparison samples and comorbid groups (as well as normal control samples); prospective longitudinal investigations; and attention to both developmental processes and contextual variables, including stressful life events, socialization practices, and cultural parameters.

KEYWORDS: impulsivity; response inhibition; attention-deficit/hyperactivity disorder (ADHD); disruptive behavior disorders; aggression; comorbidity; neuropsychology; emotion regulation

Address for correspondence: Department of Psychology, Tolman Hall #1650, University of California, Berkeley, CA 94720-1650. Voice: 510-642-9035; fax: 510-643-5336.
hinshaw@socrates.berkeley.edu

Ann. N.Y. Acad. Sci. 1008: 149–159 (2003). © 2003 New York Academy of Sciences.
doi: 10.1196/annals.1301.016

INTRODUCTION

The impairments and costs of attentional deficits/hyperactivity and conduct problems/aggression are considerable at multiple levels: personal, family-related, community-wide, and societal. First, attention-deficit/hyperactivity disorder (ADHD) yields significant impairment in terms of academic failure, family disharmony, peer rejection, high risk for accidental injury, and failure to attain adequate independence.[19] Second, aggression and antisocial behavior, which are defined in current diagnostic systems as oppositional defiant disorder or conduct disorder, produce enormous suffering in victims, yield loss of property and even of life, and engender the propensity for recurrent, intergenerational forms of transmission when aggressive youth become abusive partners and parents.[39,48] Both ADHD and conduct problems have been investigated from dimensional as well as categorical perspectives, in epidemiologic as well as clinical investigations, and from behavior genetic paradigms as well as family socialization models.[21,23] A core development of the past two decades has been the realization that both types of behavior patterns may be related, in fundamental ways, to problems of disinhibition as well as behavioral and emotional dysregulation. Analyzing trends in such work is a key focus of this chapter.

At one level, progress with respect to these conditions has been noteworthy, given the field's ability to make accurate and reliable diagnoses of the domains of interest, to observe multiple correlates of each problem domain (including psychobiological variables), and to establish the efficacy of several forms of intervention, both pharmacologic and psychosocial.[39] At another level, however, the picture is far from optimistic.[22,41] For one thing, the *validity* of the diagnostic categories in use can be severely questioned, given that their descriptive nature may well mask relevant subtypes that are indicative of divergent underlying causal processes and neural substrates. For another, there is a real question as to the lasting nature of the treatments that have been promoted in the field, no doubt related to the still-hazy nature of our understanding of specific rather than general risk factors and of core underlying mechanisms and maintaining factors. Thus, comprehending the biological roots of serious externalizing disorders of youth, in conjunction with the complex interactions and transactions of such biological variables with environmental triggers and processes, is a major priority. In the following pages, I define relevant terms and processes, comment on the chapters of Dr. King[27] and Dr. Nigg[36] on animal and human models of impulse control and inhibition, point out the need for developmental perspectives to inform further research, describe "disconnects" between cognitive and emotion-based accounts of the relevant behavior patterns, and highlight key areas for future investigation.

KEY TERMS, CONCEPTS, AND PRINCIPLES

First, the term *externalizing* refers to dimensions of child behavior marked by aggressive, defiant, and antisocial tendencies as well as aspects of overactivity and impulsivity, whereas *internalizing* patterns pertain to anxiety, depression, and social withdrawal. (Note that pure attentional deficits lie close to the midpoint of the externalizing versus internalizing continuum.)[1] It has been conclusively established that, whereas the two externalizing subdomains of interest—ADHD-related behaviors and aggressive behavior patterns—are moderately intercorrelated, they maintain partial independence with respect to family histories, key correlates, and longitudinal course.[16,46] Thus, a key research goal is to discover which psychobiological factors and processes may distinguish these two critical subcomponents of externalizing behavior.

Second, *impulsive tendencies* are explicitly part of the definition of ADHD, constituting a class of behaviors marked by quick action in the absence of adequate reflection.[2] They comprise an implicit component of aggressive disorders, particularly those marked by an early onset of core symptoms and a reactive (rather than planned) style of aggressive responding.[2,21] Indeed, developmental subtyping of aggressive children is crucial for investigation of underlying mechanisms, given that clear differences between child-onset and adolescent-onset subtypes of youth with conduct disorder exist.[33] The early-onset subgroup, in fact, is at far higher risk in terms of a variety of neuropsychological, temperamental, attachment-related, and familial antecedent factors.[21,33]

Third, in terms of scientific accounts of impulsivity and response inhibition, earlier literature began to parse these conceptions, with *cognitive* impulsivity, related to overly quick performance on cognitive tests, found to be empirically separable from *behavioral* impulsivity, usually measured by observations or adult informant ratings of actions ranging from thoughtless to dangerous.[32,47] In a major review of a large body of subsequent research, Joel Nigg[35] integrated personality and cognitive perspectives and proposed a taxonomy of at least eight different forms of inhibitory processes, which narrowed down to three consolidated types: (1) a motivated form related to fear of punishment, believed to emerge within the first six months of life and mediated by septo-hippocampal brain regions; (2) another motivated form linked to fear of novel stimuli, believed to emerge by 7 to 8 months of age and mediated by the amygdala; and (3) an effortful, executive type of inhibition, emerging by the end of the first year of life and continuing to develop rapidly throughout childhood, mediated primarily by fronto-striatal circuitry. His analysis afforded an unprecedented level of specificity with respect to the potential for linking inhibitory control with psychopathology.

Fourth, what other important variables and processes are related to the onset and maintenance of either ADHD or aggressive conduct problems? In brief, there are a large number of such proposed mechanisms. With regard to ADHD, attentional deficits of various types (e.g., problems in selective attention, sustained attention, covert spatial attention), cognitive energetic principles (e.g., arousal and alertness), problems in time perception, faulty reward mechanisms, executive function deficits, verbal as well as nonverbal working memory problems, and emotion dysregulation have all been invoked in explanatory accounts.[4,11] Furthermore, regarding etiology, it is well-established that ADHD-related symptomatology is moderately heritable.[45] Socialization practices, however, may still be crucial for promoting persistence and intensification of symptom display and impairment.[17,24]

As for aggressive conduct problems, a combination of vulnerable early temperament, attachment difficulties between parent and child, verbal learning deficits, ongoing hostility in parent–child relations, and emotionally dysregulated performance are key components of current formulations, particularly for the early-onset variant.[33] The influence of cultural variables (e.g., violence in media; access to weapons) is essential for a full accounting, particularly given large increases in the average levels of violent behavior during the last century.[42] Furthermore, incompetence in parenting is *causally* related to the development and intensification of aggressive behavior patterns, meaning that socialization is particularly salient for this domain, even though biological predispositions make it likely that parents both react to and shape hostile behavior.[18,29]

Thus, both ADHD and conduct disorders are overdetermined. Indeed, it is quite likely that *equifinality* is at play with regard to each condition,[8] whereby apparently similar clinical presentations at the symptom level mask fundamentally different risk and etiologic processes in different individuals and subgroups. The highly descriptive focus of current diagnostic systems means, in fact, that they are highly likely to "lump" differing causal pathways into the same taxon, promoting a lack of replication of core findings in the field. Note that such causal pathways feature reciprocal sets of influences between intraindividual vulnerabilities and socialization practices, which unfold over time in transactional fashion.[44] Although the main effects of genes, biological processes, or environmental influences may be operative in some cases, the usual pattern appears to be one of gene–environment correlations and interactions.[14,21] Thus, despite the temptation to ascribe the "roots of mental disorder in children" to a set of biological processes, it is essential to avoid the temptation to account for ADHD and disruptive behavior disorders in reductionistic, neurobiological terms.

ANIMAL MODELS AND HUMAN MODELS

How might constructs of response inhibition and vulnerability to psychopathology be visualized in both animal and human models? King focuses on neural substrates of attentional deficits and hyperactivity through animal models, which implicate (1) dopaminergic and noradrenergic brain systems, particularly those in the frontal lobes (and those linking frontal with midbrain regions) as pertinent to attentional dysregulation, and (2) serotonergic systems that subserve impulse control functions, with attendant linkages to behavioral and emotional dysfunction.[27] Intriguingly, despite the strong heritability of ADHD-related behavior patterns, King's model implicates stress during early development as an essential causal factor in alteration of dopaminergic, noradrenergic, and serotonergic pathways. Indeed, she hypothesizes that youth with ADHD are more vulnerable to stress than are comparison youth, particularly regarding those stressors that involve hormonal alterations in the developing brain. In this sense, such hypotheses are quite consistent with contemporary models in developmental psychopathology, which hold that one of the key genetically mediated aspects of behavioral disorders may well be particular vulnerability to environmental or biological stress.[9,42]

Nigg deals with human models of the development of response inhibition.[36] Utilizing his own analysis of various types of inhibition, he focuses on (1) executive inhibition, a deliberate suppression of ongoing responses in relation to longer-term goals and plans, sometimes termed effortful control versus (2) motivational inhibition, an unconscious suppression of ongoing responses in relation to novel or fearful stimuli, linked with theories of a temperamental reactivity and behavioral inhibition systems.[38] His essential point is that models of normal development, as well as

ADHD and conduct disturbance, involve a balance and blending of these two inhibition systems, which interact developmentally. Multiprocess models like this are more likely to account for the heterogeneity of symptomatology and impairment across externalizing behavior disorders than are single-process, single-neurotransmitter, or single-system accounts.

DEVELOPMENTAL CONSIDERATIONS, MULTIFACTOR MODELS

With respect to the development of differing *attentional* mechanisms in infants and toddlers, Columbo provides a masterful synthesis.[10] Although its details are beyond the scope of the current chapter, key points are that (1) shifts in infants' gaze duration (reflecting early-developing attentional mechanisms) are apparent as early as 2–3 months and again at 4–5 months of age, reflecting maturation of arousal/alertness and visual disengagement processes, respectively; and (2) after the development of disengagement processes facilitates a decrease in gaze duration from 6–18 months, increases again appear, related to voluntary, sustained attentional processes.[10] Progress in elucidating these areas has been directly enhanced by integrating cognitive science and attention science paradigms with those from neuroscience. Still lacking, however, are parallel developmental accounts of the unfolding of inhibitory and regulatory mechanisms. Nigg's model does posit that differing forms of response inhibition will emerge at different ages in babies and toddlers: Motivated forms of inhibition pertaining to response to novelty or fear-producing stimuli emerge in the first year of life, whereas executive, effortful inhibition of prepotent responses in the service of longer-term goals does not appear until 12 months and beyond, probably reflecting the slower development of frontal-lobe functioning.[35] Yet investigations underlying such age trends are largely cross-sectional; sorely needed are precise longitudinal accounts of the unfolding of such processes and mechanisms that include biological indicators of cognitive and motivational functioning.

I note that in the area of inhibited temperament spearheaded by Kagan, in which feared stimuli are strikingly avoided by a subset of infants, a multidisciplinary, prospective program of research has indeed occurred. Note that infant fearful inhibition is indexed by an amalgam of biological (e.g., cortisol secretion) and behavioral (e.g., "shutting down" in the face of novelty) indicators. Indeed, this work shows significant, albeit far from complete, persistence of fearful inhibition across the time span from infancy to preadolescence.[25] The most striking longitudinal findings, however, relate to the concept of *multifinality,* by which similar initial states in given organisms may lead to decidedly different outcomes, depending on a host of developmental and environmental factors that interact with the initial state.[8] Specifically, whereas almost no inhibited infants emerge as utterly gregarious and outgoing children and preadolescents, a number of inhibited, fearful infants do develop into reasonably socially competent (albeit shy) youth if caregivers push them into social situations rather than overly protect them. Hence, biologically driven, temperamental tendencies related to inhibition shift across development, given optimal kinds of environmental supports and presses.

Furthermore, Eisenberg and colleagues have provided rich longitudinal data on the interplay between "dispositional regulation" (aligned in large part with the construct of executive control or inhibition) and emotion regulation, with respect to the development of prosocial versus antisocial outcomes in children.[12] Their contention is that the development of intentional, executive inhibitory processes is a necessary precondition for the emergence of emotional regulation; in particular, without sufficiently developed attentional processes, emotion-producing stimuli may not be fully attended to, leading to dysregulated response tendencies. Differing constructs and measurement tendencies across different laboratories, however, and differing ethnicities and social classes of participating families, complicate facile interpretations of such trends.

I emphasize once again that the main effects in these regards are highly likely to be supplemented by interactive or transactional processes. For instance, early patterns of insecure attachment between caregivers and children do not appear to yield high risk for aggressive or externalizing outcomes in and of themselves; it is only in the presence of other risk factors (e.g., difficult temperament, continuing patterns of unresponsive parenting) that aggressive outcomes are likely.[15] Indeed, transactional processes are striking throughout the field: Raine and colleagues have shown that neither early neonatal complications alone nor early psychosocial rejection of the infant alone yield high rates of violent criminality, but their combination markedly increases the risk.[40] And, strikingly, in a New Zealand birth cohort, the effects of child maltreatment on subsequent indicators of antisocial behavior were markedly attenuated in the presence of the child's possession of a specific allele of a monoamine oxidase (MAO) gene.[7] With respect to impulsivity and inhibition, urgently required are specific indicators of different types of inhibitory control at very young ages, ideally featuring biological and even genetic moderator variables, that can be followed over time in relation to differing parenting styles, cultural contexts, and schooling environments in terms of risk for externalizing outcomes. Without full consideration of developmental progressions and interactive contextual variables, the study of biological roots of externalizing behavior will feature static accounts with low predictive power.[17]

DISCONNECTIONS BETWEEN COGNITIVE
AND EMOTION-BASED ACCOUNTS

The construct of emotion regulation is a "hot topic" in developmental psychopathology, given the appearance of strongly emotional underpinnings of a number of forms of behavioral disturbance, particularly the mood lability and erratic behavior pertinent to ADHD and the anger and explosiveness often associated with early-onset conduct disorder.[21] As just noted, the work of Eisenberg and colleagues suggests that effortful inhibition may be a prerequisite for the development of prosocial behavior, empathy, and emotion regulation. In all such work, the concept of emotion regulation is a complicated one, as it assumes that there is excess emotion to be regulated. A key question, therefore, is whether children with externalizing problems have an overabundance of emotional reactivity, a deficit in emotional regulation, or possibly both.

Even if such thorny problems of distinguishing reactivity from regulation can be solved, it may be mistaken to assume automatic linkages across domains. From my own team's research investigations, an intriguing pattern has emerged. First, utilizing large samples of children with carefully diagnosed ADHD, along with matched comparison children, we have found that there are clear ADHD-related deficits in terms of executive function (EF), measured via carefully administered neuropsychological tests. Furthermore, such results hold almost identically for the ADHD subgroups with comorbid oppositional defiant disorder or conduct disorder, signifying that EF deficits are independent of externalizing or disruptive comorbidity.[20,37] (Note, however, the comorbid children do appear to have lower scores with respect to verbal performance.)

Second, in a subset of the boys, we administered a parent–child interaction that pulled for emotion regulation processes. Specifically, as the boys and their parents built an engaging model, two of the key pieces were missing from the materials. All boys and families noted the missing pieces, and large individual differences in the initial display of emotional upset and the subsequent regulation of such emotion were observed.[31] Importantly, problems in emotion regulation were found only in the boys with ADHD who were also extremely aggressive, as measured independently of the parent–child interaction via staff ratings and observations in a naturalistic summer program.[31] Thus, we have evidence for a "disconnection" between EF deficits, presumably linked to effortful control and the cognitive type of inhibition from Nigg's taxonomy, and emotion dysregulation. The former are ubiquitous among boys with ADHD, but the latter pertain only to an aggressive subgroup of such boys. It is tempting to speculate that the neural locus of the executive dysfunction pertinent to ADHD lies in the largely dopaminergic pathways of fronto-striatal tracts, whereas the emotion dysregulation patterns of the aggressive subgroup are found in limbic structures and interconnections. The possibility exists, in any event, that different types of inhibitory control underlie ADHD-related symptoms *per se* versus the emotionally explosive and dysregulated problems that accompany only a subset of such youth.

ADDITIONAL ISSUES: COMORBIDITY, SEX DIFFERENCES, AND CULTURE

Comorbidity is defined as the co-occurrence of two (or more) independent disorders in the same individual. It presents a host of diagnostic, methodological, conceptual, and etiologic issues for the field of psychopathology.[3,6] For example, comorbidity may be wrongly inferred if diagnostic criteria overlap at the level of symptoms or developmental continuities, yet "true" comorbidity could indicate separate etiologies for those with co-occurring conditions versus single disorders. I note briefly the crucial importance of this topic for the investigation of inhibition in relation to externalizing disorders. First, unless comorbid conditions are included in research samples of interest, the generalizability of findings will be severely constrained, as comorbidity is the rule, not the exception, in child psychopathology.[3] Second, as noted just previously, unless the potential comorbidity of ADHD-related symptomatology with aggression is taken into account, potential associations of interest will be obscured. Note, in this regard, that research on clinical samples should ideally include each single-disorder condition in addition to the dual-diagnosis condition, in order to tease apart separate, additive, and multiplicative effects. Third, research on single and comorbid disorders should facilitate inference as to which subprocesses of interest pertain to which specific dimensions or categories of psychopathology.

In terms of treatment response, for example, a key finding in recent years was that when ADHD presents with comorbid anxiety disorders, children respond to behavioral/psychosocial interventions as well as they do to pharmacologic treatments.[30,34] The strong suggestion is that an overabundance of fearful inhibition in a subgroup of children with ADHD yields a fundamentally different pattern of response to standard treatments, perhaps indicating a preferential response to contingencies in children who combine the cognitive disinbition of ADHD with the noteworthy fearful, motivational inhibition associated with serious clinical anxiety. Although speculative, such conjectures indicate the richness of theoretical accounts that are possible with research on comorbid psychopathology and their potential relevance to treatment response.

Sex differences in inhibitory processes as potential mediators of sex differences in the clinical display of psychopathology are an underinvestigated, though potentially crucial, topic in the field. It is well known that boys outnumber girls with respect to externalizing psychopathology, even in community samples, suggesting that genetic or temperamental differences along with divergence in rates of cognitive maturity interact with early socialization practices with respect to the preferential display of ADHD-related symptomatology and aggressive tendencies in boys.[26] At the same time, sex differences may have been exaggerated in past research, given that girls appear to show a greater likelihood of showing the inattentive type of ADHD (and even, perhaps, for showing greater persistence in ADHD symptoms across the life span) and of revealing a proclivity for relational (rather than physical) forms of aggression.[21] The is field is ripe, therefore, for sophisticated investigations of girls as well as boys that feature (1) precise biological and behavioral specification of parameters related to inhibitory control, and (2) longitudinal designs that can trace patterns of continuity and discontinuity across time. Note that the goal of such research is not simply to document male versus female differences in symptoms and impairment, but to elucidate developmental processes that yield impairment as well as resilience.

Finally, I note the importance of culture in all such formulations. Symptoms are shaped not only by genes and neurobiological individual differences but also by familial, social, and cultural influences.[5] At the same time, the field must be alert to the possibility that underlying genetic or temperamental differences may differ across cultural and ethnic subgroups of our increasingly diverse population.[22] Again, neurobiological factors unfold in family and cultural contexts; ignoring these in the design of our research will be done at the peril of incomplete specification of etiologic and maintaining processes and mechanism.[13]

FUTURE DIRECTIONS

The field of developmental psychopathology is in a unique position to integrate the explosion of current information regarding neurobiological factors relevant to brain development and plasticity with the contextual factors known to shape neural and psychological development. A crucial set of processes that lie at the interface of these areas of investigation pertain to inhibitory control of cognition, emotion, and behavior. Future progress in the field will require, first, specification as to the nature of particular subtypes of inhibition under investigation in a particular paradigm.[35] Without such specification, different forms of inhibitory control will become confused, differential patterns of developmental unfolding will become lost, and results will be prone to contribute disinformation. Second, multiple measures of such constructs are mandatory, including biological as well as behavioral measures. Indeed, linking of key psychobiological processes with the types of behaviors that are used to infer inhibition and disinhibition remains a key research goal. Third, an integrative account of inhibition must actively incorporate measures of stress and environmental context as well as biological and behavioral parameters. Developmental outcomes, in fact, are likely to be predicted with greater specificity and precision via interactive and transactional models than by univariate conceptions of causal pathways. Fourth, as should be clear from the preceding pages, prospective longitudinal investigations must take place side by side with careful, experimental cross-sectional studies if the continuities and discontinuities in etiologic and maintaining processes are to be uncovered. Careful attention must be paid to the assessment and analysis of moderator and mediator variables and processes in such research.[28] Fifth, intervention and prevention studies, in future years, could consider examining changes in inhibitory mechanisms as potential mediators of clinical change in externalizing symptomatology. The experimental nature of such research provides for important causal tests of the role of inhibitory mediational processes.[18]

What is truly exciting about current developments is the potential for far greater specification of multiple levels of interacting influences, toward the end of uncovering the essential inhibitory mechanisms (and their linkages with mood regulation and behavioral control) that underlie the troublesome group of externalizing disorders.[21,43] Both basic and clinical research serve to benefit from increased focus on specifically defined inhibitory processes in relation to normal development and psychopathology.

ACKNOWLEDGMENT

Work on this chapter was supported by National Institute of Mental Health Grants R01 45064 and N01 12009.

REFERENCES

1. ACHENBACH, T.M. 1991. Manual for the Child Behavior Checklist/4-18 and 1991 profile. University Associates in Psychiatry. Burlington, VT.
2. AMERICAN PSYCHIATRIC ASSOCIATION. 1994. Diagnostic and Statistical Manual of Mental Disorders, 4th ed. American Psychiatric Press. Washington, DC.
3. ANGOLD, A., E.J. COSTELLO & A. ERKANLI. 1999. Comorbidity. J. Child Psychol. Psychiatry 40: 57–87.
4. BARKLEY, R.A. 1997. ADHD and the Nature of Self-Control. Guilford Press. New York.
5. BRONFENBRENNER, U. 1977. Toward an experimental ecology of human development. Am. Psychol. 32: 513–531.
6. CARON, C. & M. RUTTER. 1991. Comorbidity in child psychopathology: concepts, issues, and research strategies. J. Child Psychol. Psychiatry 32: 1063–1080.

7. CASPI, A. *et al.* 2002. Role of genotype in the cycle of violence of maltreated children. Science **297:** 851–854.
8. CICCHETTI, D. & F.A. ROGOSCH. 1996. Equifinality and multifinality in developmental psychopathology. Devel. Psychopathol. **8:** 597–600.
9. CICCHETTI, D. & E.F. WALKER, EDS. 2001. Stress and development: biological and psychological consequences. Dev. Psychopathol. (Special Issue) **13:** 413–753.
10. COLUMBO, J. 2002. Infant attention grows up: the emergence of a developmental cognitive neuroscience perspective. Curr. Dir. Psychol. Sci. **11:** 196–200.
11. DOUGLAS, V.I. 1998. Cognitive control processes in attention-deficit/hyperactivity disorder. *In* Handbook of Disruptive Behavior Disorders. H.C. Quay and A.E. Hogan, Eds.: 105–138. Kluwer Acacemic/Plenum. New York.
12. EISENBERG, N. *et al.* 1998. Contemporaneous and longitudinal prediction of children's sympathy from dispositional regulation and emotionality. Dev. Psychol. **34:** 910–924.
13. GARCIA COLL, C. & M. GARRIDA. 2000. Minorities in the United States: sociocultural context for mental health and developmental psychopathology. *In* Handbook of Developmental Psychopathology, 2nd ed. A.J. Sameroff and M. Lewis, Eds.: 177–195. Kluwer Academic. Dordrecht, The Netherlands.
14. GOTTLIEB, G. 1998. Normally occurring environmental and behavioral influences on gene activity: from central dogma to probabilistic epigenesis. Psychol. Rev. **105:** 792–802.
15. GREENBERG, M.T., M.L. SPELTZ & M. DEKLYEN. 1993. The role of attachment in the early development of disruptive behavior problems. Dev. Psychopathol. **5:** 191–213.
16. HINSHAW, S.P. 1987. On the distinction between attentional deficits/hyperactivity and conduct problems/ aggression in child psychopathology. Psychol. Bull. **101:** 443–463.
17. HINSHAW, S.P. 1999. Psychosocial intervention for childhood ADHD: etiologic and developmental themes, comorbidity, and integration with pharmacotherapy. *In* Rochester Symposium on Developmental Psychopathology, Vol. 9. D. Cicchetti and S.L. Toth, Eds.: 221–270. University of Rochester Press. Rochester, NY.
18. HINSHAW, S.P. 2002. Intervention research, theoretical mechanisms, and causal processes related to externalizing behavior patterns. Dev. Psychopathol. **14:** 789–818.
19. HINSHAW, S.P. 2002. Is ADHD an impairing condition in childhood and adolescence? *In* Attention-Deficit Hyperactivity Disorder: State of the Science, Best Practices. P.S. Jensen and J.R. Cooper, Eds.: 5-1–5-21. Civic Research Institute. Kingston, NJ.
20. HINSHAW, S.P. *et al.* 2002. Preadolescent girls with attention-deficit/hyperactivity disorder: II. Neuropsychological performance in relation to subtypes and individual classification. J. Consult. Clin. Psychol. **70:** 1099–1111.
21. HINSHAW, S.P. & S.S. LEE. 2003. Oppositional defiant and conduct disorder. *In* Child Psychopathology, 2nd ed. E.J. Mash and R.A. Barkley, Eds.: 144–198. Guilford Press. New York.
22. HINSHAW, S.P. & T. PARK. 1999. Research issues and problems: toward a more definitive science of disruptive behavior disorders. *In* Handbook of Disruptive Behavior Disorders. H.C. Quay and A.E. Hogan, Eds.: 593–620. Plenum. New York.
23. JENSEN, P.S. & J.R. COOPER, EDS. 2002. Attention-Deficit Hyperactivity Disorder: State of the Science, Best Practices. Civic Research Institute. Kingston, NJ.
24. JOHNSTON, C. & E.J. MASH. 2001. Families of children with attention-deficit/hyperactivity disorder: review and recommendations for future research. Clin. Child Fam. Psychol. Rev. **4:** 183–207.
25. KAGAN, J. 1997. Temperament and the reactions to the unfamiliar. Child Dev. **68:** 139–143.
26. KEENAN, K. & D. SHAW. 1997. Developmental and social influences on young girls' early problem behavior. Psychol. Bull. **121:** 95–113.
27. KING, J.A. *et al.* 2003. Neural substrates underlying impulsivity. This volume.
28. KRAEMER, H.C. *et al.* 2001. How do risk factors work together? Mediators, moderators, and independent, overlapping, and proxy risk factors. Am. J. Psychiatry **158:** 848–856.
29. LYTTON, H. 1990. Child and parent effects in boys' conduct disorder: a reinterpretation. Dev. Psychol. **26:** 683–697.
30. MARCH, J.S. *et al.* 2000. Anxiety as a predictor and outcome variable in the Multimodal Treatment Study of Children with ADHD (MTA). J. Abnorm. Child Psychol. **28:** 527–541.

31. MELNICK, S.M. & S.P. HINSHAW. 2000. Emotion regulation and parenting in AD/HD and comparison boys: linkages with social behaviors and peer preference. J. Abnorm. Child Psychol. **28:** 73–86.
32. MILICH, R. & J. KRAMER. 1984. Reflections on impulsivity: an empirical investigation of impulsivity as a construct. In Advances in Learning and Behavioral Disabilities. K. Gadow and I. Bialer, Eds.: 57–94. JAI Press. Greenwich, CT.
33. MOFFITT, T.E. 1993. Adolescence-limited and life-course-persistent antisocial behavior: a developmental taxonomy. Psychol. Rev. **100:** 674–701.
34. MTA COOPERATIVE GROUP. 1999. Moderators and mediators of treatment response for children with attention-deficit/hyperactivity disorder. Arch. Gen. Psychiatry **56:** 1088–1096.
35. NIGG, J.T. 2000. On inhibition/disinhibition in developmental psychopathology: views from cognitive and personality psychology and a working inhibition taxonomy. Psychol. Bull. **126:** 220–246.
36. NIGG, J.T. 2003. Response inhibition and disruptive behaviors: toward a multiprocess conception of etiological heterogeneity for ADHD combined type and conduct disorder early-onset type. This volume.
37. NIGG, J.T., S.P. HINSHAW, E.T. CARTE & J. TREUTING. 1998. Neuropsychological correlates of childhood attention deficit hyperactivity disorder: explainable by comorbid disruptive behavior or reading problems? J. Abnorm. Psychol. **107:** 468–480.
38. QUAY, H.C. 1993. The psychobiology of undersocialized conduct disorder: a theoretical perspective. Dev. Psychopathol. **5:** 165–180.
39. QUAY, H.C. & A.E. HOGAN, EDS. 1998. Handbook of Disruptive Behavior Disorders. Kluwer Academic/Plenum. New York.
40. RAINE, A. 2002. Biosocial studies of antisocial and violent behavior in children and adults: a review. J. Abnorm. Child Psychol. **30:** 311–326.
41. RICHTERS, J. 1997. The Hubble hypothesis and the developmentalist's dilemma. Dev. Psychopathol. **9:** 193–229.
42. RUTTER, M., A. PICKLES, R. MURRAY & L. EAVES. 2001. Testing hypotheses on specific environmental causal effects on behavior. Psychol. Bull. **127:** 291–324.
43. RUTTER, M. & L.A. SROUFE. 2000. Developmental psychopathology: concepts and challenges. Dev. Psychopathol. **12:** 265–296.
44. SAMEROFF, A.J. 2000. Developmental systems and psychopathology. Dev. Psychopathol. **12:** 297–312.
45. TANNOCK, R. 1998. Attention deficit hyperactivity disorder: advances in cognitive, neurobiological, and genetic research. J. Child Psychol. Psychiatry **35:** 65–99.
46. WASCHBUSCH, D. 2002. A meta-analytic examination of comorbid hyperactive-impulsive-attention problems and conduct problems. Psychol. Bull. **128:** 118–150.
47. WHITE, J.L. et al. 1994. Measuring impulsivity and examining its relationship to delinquency. J. Abnorm. Psychol. **103:** 192–205.
48. WIDOM, C.S. 1997. Child abuse, neglect, and witnessing violence. In Handbook of Antisocial Behavior. D. Stoff, J. Breiling, and J. Maser, Eds.: 159–170. Wiley. New York.

Neural Substrates Underlying Impulsivity

JEAN A. KING, JEFFREY TENNEY, VICTORIA ROSSI, LAURALEA COLAMUSSI, AND STACY BURDICK

Department of Psychiatry, Center for Comparative NeuroImaging, University of Massachusetts Medical School, Worcester, Massachusetts 01655, USA

ABSTRACT: Attention deficit hyperactivity disorder (ADHD) is a neuropsychiatric disorder whose three main symptoms are impulsiveness, inattention, and hyperactivity. Although ADHD is an early developmental disorder, it may persist into adulthood, resulting in deficits associated with poor academic performance, frequent job changes, poor and unstable marriages, and increases in motor vehicle accidents. Of the three primary symptoms of ADHD, deficits in impulse control are the most challenging to the social network and the judicial system. While the etiology of ADHD remains unknown, recent work suggests that the central deficits in ADHD may be due to poor response inhibition that is linked to monoamine and prefrontal lobe deficiencies. In the past, preclinical studies designed to understand the lack of impulse control have generally been relegated to studies linked to aggression and drug abuse. With the use of innovative noninvasive techniques, like anatomical and functional magnetic resonance imaging, selective neurochemical and behavioral paradigms have converged with preclinical reports and lend support to the premise that monoaminergic neurotransmitter systems and the cortio-striatal circuitry are essential to impulse control. Furthermore, new emerging data on neural substrates underlying impulsivity have incorporated brain regions involved in reinforcement, reward, and decision making such as the nucleus accumbens, cerebellum, and amygdala. As noninvasive brain imaging, neurochemical, and behavioral approaches are combined, our knowledge of the neural networks underlying impulsivity will hopefully give rise to therapeutic approaches aimed at alleviating this disorder.

KEYWORDS: ADHD; impulsivity; animal models; brain regions; MRI

INTRODUCTION

Attention deficit hyperactivity disorder (ADHD) is a neuropsychiatric disorder that affects a large population of children, with prevalence rates ranging from 4% to 12%.[1] ADHD is characterized by a triad of symptoms: hyperactivity, inattention, and

Address for correspondence: Jean A. King, Ph.D., Department of Psychiatry, Center for Comparative NeuroImaging, University of Massachusetts Medical School, 55 Lake Ave. North, Worcester, MA 01655. Voice: 508-856-4979; fax: 508-856-6426.

jean.king@umassmed.edu

Ann. N.Y. Acad. Sci. 1008: 160–169 (2003). © 2003 New York Academy of Sciences.
doi: 10.1196/annals.1301.017

impulsivity. Of this triad, impulsivity, or the failure to resist a drive or impulse that is oftentimes harmful to the self or others, can be a debilitating challenge to the caretakers and school systems alike. When left untreated, the expression of impulsivity can become a formidable burden to both the social and judicial systems, since a significant portion (approximately 60%) of ADHD children maintain this status into adolescence and even adulthood.[2]

Elucidating the neurophysiological basis of impulsivity has been the focus of several areas of research, because it is a central feature of numerous psychiatric disorders, including aggression, antisocial personality disorder, borderline personality disorder, obsessive compulsive disorder, and psychosis.[3–5] Recent efforts to selectively study impulsivity from other coexisting features have been addressed using preclinical behavioral assessments of paradigms related to rapid decision making, intolerance to the delay of reward, and the tendency to prematurely terminate chains of responses.[6–7] For example, in a preclinical study, the observation that rats exhibiting impulsivity would consistently choose smaller immediate rewards rather than larger delayed rewards[8] provided valuable clues into the behavioral manifestations and neuroanatomical basis of impulsivity.

In the absence of focused studies on individual features of ADHD, the general hypothesis regarding the neural substrates underlying this disorder has been influenced primarily by the effectiveness of pharmacological agents such as methylphenidate and dextroamphetamine. These stimulants have been shown to modulate the activity of the dopaminergic and noradrenergic neurotransmitter systems in cortical and subcortical brain regions.[9] The specific role of these neural substrates in ADHD is being expanded rapidly with the use of noninvasive magnetic resonance imaging (MRI). In fact, early reports utilizing these imaging techniques have confirmed that regions of the frontal lobe were compromised in ADHD boys compared to controls.[10] In addition to frontal lobe deficits, recent reports have alluded to dysfunctions in the cerebellum,[11] cortico-striatal,[12] and cortico-striato–thalamo-cortical circuitries[13] in ADHD individuals.

These observations have also been supported by data from other imaging techniques. In positron emission tomography (PET) studies, a decrease in the rate of glucose metabolism has been seen in many cortical areas, including the prefrontal cortex,[14] while functional MRI (fMRI) studies clearly demonstrate that the brain regions involved in processing a task may be utilized differently in ADHD than controls.[12] Therefore, converging evidence from different methodologies support the hypothesis that dysfunction in cortico-striatal monoaminergic systems can lead to disruption in information transfer between regions critical to executive and motor functions subserving behavioral responses like attention and disinhibition.[12] However, when impulsivity is approached as a distinctive core feature of ADHD, one member of the monoaminergic system, serotonin, appears to play a primary role.[15–16]

The Role of Serotonin in Impulsive Behavior

Serotonin [5-hydroxytryptamine (5-HT)] located within the CNS originates in the raphe nuclei of the brainstem. The CNS 5-HT system consists of two ascending and one descending pathway. According to the current classification of serotonin receptors, seven classes of 5-HT receptor types are known based on their selective

TABLE 1. Effects of serotonin drugs on impulsive behavior

Drug	Serotonin Effect	Impulsivity Effect
8-OH-DPAT	5-HT$_{1A}$ agonist	Significantly decreased impulsivity
WAY 100 635	5-HT$_{1A}$ antagonist	Significantly increased impulsivity
DOI	5-HT$_2$ agonist	Significantly increased impulsivity
Ritanserin	5-HT$_2$ antagonist	Trend of decreased impulsivity
RU 24969	5-HT$_{1A/1B}$ agonist	Significantly increased impulsivity
MDL 72222	5-HT$_3$ antagonist	No significant effect
Metergoline	5-HT antagonist (nonspecific)	No significant effect
p-Chloramphetamine (pCA)	Selective serotonin reuptake inhibitor (SSRI)	Weak biphasic effects Increased at high dose and decerased at low dose
Citalopram	5-HT releaser	No significant effect

SOURCE: Adapted from Evenden.[7]

pharmacological profiles. Serotonin receptors belong to the G protein-coupled receptor (GPCR) superfamily, with the exception of 5-HT$_3$ receptors, which function as ligand-gated ion channels. The GPCR superfamily is comprised of at least 14 distinct members, making it one of the most complex neurotransmitter systems.[17]

Over two decades ago, Linoilla and colleagues[18] demonstrated that low levels of serotonin could lead to impulsive, violent, or self-destructive behavior in humans. The underlying assumption that CNS depletion of 5-HT resulted in increased impulsive responses was further supported by clinical data that used pharmacological challenges as a means of indirectly assessing the 5-HT system,[19–20] along with preclinical studies that assessed behavioral paradigms.[21–23] However, a recent report directly challenges the 5-HT deficit impulsivity model.[24] Utilizing a more direct measure of 5-HT levels in the prefrontal cortex, the data demonstrated that increases in 5-HT efflux in this region may also be responsible for lack of impulsive control.

One possible explanation for inconsistencies in the data may be the complexity of the serotonin system. In a very comprehensive preclinical study design, Evenden[7] investigated the effects of several serotonin drugs on impulsive behavior, and found that these agents differentially affected impulsive behavior (see TABLE 1). Approaching the behavioral trait of impulsivity as a composite of several factors, including the tendency to prematurely terminate a chain of responses, a paced fixed consecutive number (FCN) schedule and pharmacological interventions were used to demonstrate that stimulation of 5-HT$_{1A}$ receptors reduces impulsivity measures, whereas stimulation of 5-HT$_{1B}$ receptors increases impulsivity.[7] With the advent of noninvasive techniques, the latter neuropharmacological studies are being combined with functional brain imaging to simultaneously assess anatomical and functional substrates in an effort to possibly resolve the conflicting data further.

Noninvasive Neuroimaging

Functional magnetic resonance imaging is a noninvasive procedure for studying brain activity. Functional MRI has greater spatial and temporal resolution than positron emission tomography and single-photon emission computerized tomography. It also has the advantage of being much more convenient and safe, because it does not require the production and administration of radioactive molecules to the subject. Functional MRI is a technique that relies on the oxygenation status of hemoglobin, and is therefore indirectly reflective of changes in blood flow and volume. The signal intensity changes related to alterations in blood oxygenation are referred to as blood oxygenation-level-dependent (BOLD) contrast.[25–26] Enhanced neuronal activity is concomitant with increases in metabolism and changes in cerebral blood flow and volume to the area of activation.[27–28] Therefore, the activation maps produced using BOLD imaging correlate with the spatial location of synaptic activity.[29]

Although most fMRI studies utilize methods related to on-off paradigms,[12] pharmacological fMRI techniques using continuous input stimuli are becoming more common.[30] A primary goal of the present study design was to better understand the brain regions, temporal sequence, and maybe even the action mechanism of the chosen drug. With this in mind, the following preliminary study was performed to explore the role of a 5-HT drug known to decrease impulsivity[7] in an animal model exhibiting this behavior.

Animal Model of ADHD

Although several animal models of ADHD have been proposed, including rats with neurotoxic brain lesions,[31] dopamine alteration and hypertension,[32–36] as well as mice with gene deletion,[37] the spontaneous hypertensive rat (SHR) model has been proposed as the most acceptable and frequently used animal model for ADHD.[34–36,38] This animal model was used in studies focused on exploring all features of ADHD, including impulsivity. As expected, researchers demonstrated that SHR rats took longer to master an FCN schedule, and also exhibited increased levels of impulsivity when compared to controls.[4] The successful use of this animal model of ADHD prompted the current study, which attempted to evaluate changes in brain activity accompanying a pharmacological intervention that resulted in a decrease in impulsivity.

METHODS

Experimental Procedures

Male Wistar Kyoto (WKY) and Spontaneously Hypertensive rats (SHR) weighing 200–300 grams were obtained from Charles River Laboratories (Charles River, MA). Animals were housed in pairs in Plexiglas cages (48 cm × 24 cm × 20 cm), maintained on 12:12 light:dark cycle (lights on at 9:00 h) and provided food and water *ad libitum*. All animals were acquired and cared for in accordance with the guidelines published in the Guide for the Care and Use of Laboratory Animals (National Institutes of Health Publications No. 85-23, Revised 1985).

Imaging Studies

Four rats were anesthetized with medetomidine (Domitor, 0.02 mg), and implanted with an intracerebral ventricular line for drug injection. During MRI sessions, rats were first lightly sedated with ketamine HCl (Ketaset, 2.0 mg) plus medetomidine (Domitor, 0.02 mg), and secured in the MRI head and body restrainer (Insight NeuroImaging Systems, Worcester, Massachusetts). Once securely restrained, anesthesia was reversed with atipamezole (Antiseden, 0.1 mg). The animals were fully conscious within 5–10 min. Since disruption in 5-HT is thought to be involved in impulsivity, a 5-HT$_{1A}$ agonist, 8-OH-2(di-*n*-propylamino)tetralin (8-OH-DPAT), shown to be effective in relieving impulsivity (see TABLE 1), was used to assess regions that may be significant in this disorder.

All images were acquired using a 4.7T/40-cm (Oxford Magnet Technology, Oxford, UK) horizontal magnet interfaced to a Paravision console (Bruker Medical Instruments, Massachusetts). High-resolution anatomical data sets were acquired using a fast spin echo (RARE) sequence (TR = 2.5 s; TE = 56 ms; echo train length = 8; field of view = 3 × 3 cm; data matrix = 256 × 256; slice thickness = 1.0 mm; number of slices = 18) at the end of each imaging session. Drug-induced changes in fMRI were monitored in the presence of 8-OH-DPAT (10 μL, i.c.v. injection of 2.0 mg/mL) at a concentration effective in relieving impulsivity. 8-OH DPAT was purchased from Sigma-Aldrich Inc, St. Louis, Missouri. Functional images were acquired for 20 minutes using a spin echo (RARE) sequence (TR = 2000 ms; TE = 8 ms; FOV = 3 × 3 cm; matrix = 64 × 64; slice thickness = 1.0 mm; number of slices = 18). Regions of interest (ROI) were drawn manually on the images according to a rat brain atlas and analyzed for changes in BOLD signal intensity at baseline and after drug administration. STIMULATE software was used to perform statistical comparisons of baseline periods to periods after drug administration with the Student's paired *t*-test to generate an activation map of the ROIs for each dataset.[39] The control and drug-activated imaging periods were defined as the average change in BOLD activity over time.

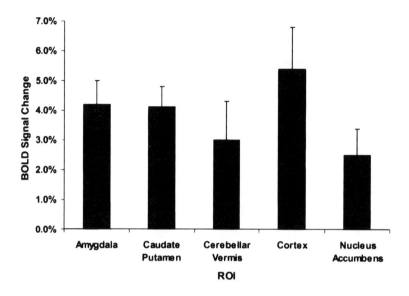

FIGURE 1. Change in BOLD signal intensity for each ROI. The BOLD signal intensity change following DPAT administration is shown for ROIs (mean ± SEM, $N = 3$ rats). BOLD signal was averaged for each rat over the entire acquisition.

RESULTS

The data obtained from these studies are summarized in FIGURE 1. Administration of 8-OH-DPAT resulted in significant changes in BOLD signal intensity in the cortico-striatal circuitry.

FIGURE 1 depicts the average percent change (mean ± S.E.) in positive BOLD signal intensity for the ROIs with the largest recorded signal intensities. These areas are the cortex, caudate putamen, amygdala, cerebellar vermis, and nucleus accumbens. Since all the structures analyzed are bilateral and no significant differences were found between the left and right sides, the results listed in FIGURE 1 are a combination of both hemispheres. It is also important to note that these percent-change values represent an average for the entire time series. The largest increase in BOLD signal was seen in the cortex (5.4%), followed by the amygdala (4.2%) and caudate putamen (4.1%). Finally, the cerebellar vermis and nucleus accumbens showed average BOLD signal increases of 3.0% and 2.5% above baseline, respectively.

DISCUSSION AND CONCLUSIONS

The data from this study using fMRI and 8-OH-DPAT to identify areas of brain activation associated with impulsivity corroborate the findings from clinical and preclinical behavioral and fMRI studies. Since metabolic, structural, functional and behavioral studies have implicated cortical sites in ADHD,[9,13,38,40] and specifically impulsivity,[16,41] the changes in BOLD activity observed in the prefrontal cortex in this study occurred as expected. However, the involvement of other brain regions that are as critical to this disorder as the traditional cortical regions is becoming apparent. For example, the role of the cortico-striatal circuitry in subserving ADHD is supported by both the current observation of increases in activation in the caudate putamen, along with other reports utilizing a myriad of methodological designs.[11,12,16] However, it is becoming clear that rather than a closed loop, the cortico-striatal circuitry is an intricate system involving other brain regions that may also be critical to the expression of impulsivity.

In the current study, three surprising regions, namely, the nucleus accumbens, amygdala, and cerebellum, experienced significant increases in BOLD activity. Although support for the participation of these sites in ADHD and impulsivity are less forthcoming, several studies lend support[8,42–45] to a direct role for each region in the overall circuitry subserving this disorder. For example, Cardinal and colleagues[8] investigated the role of lesions of the nucleus accumbens core on a delayed reinforcement choice task. Their report demonstrated that this lesion was selective for control of impulsive behavior, since lesions in other sites, namely the prefrontal cortex and cingulated cortex, were ineffective in modulating this behavior. The authors suggested that the nucleus accumbens was a principal site for evaluating the impact of reinforcers, a system known to be compromised in individuals with impulse control deficits. In addition, other preclinical studies utilizing the SHR animal as a model for ADHD also support the possible disruption of the nucleus accumbens in this disorder.[44,45] Similarly, other studies in both human and animal subjects point to the involvement of additional anatomical regions, particularly the amygdala[46,47] and cerebellum,[11] in the neural circuitry regulating impulsivity.

Therefore, the present preliminary study, along with data collected from many laboratories concerning the neurochemical,[24] neuropharmacological,[7] and neuroanatomical[16] basis of impulsivity, strongly suggests that the monoamine neurotransmitters system, specifically the serotonin system, with its abundant receptor distribution throughout the cortex, may subserve this disorder. As noted, impulsivity, or the failure to resist an impulse or drive, is a primary symptom of many disorders associated with disinhibition of behavior. Thus, the involvement of brain regions such as the nucleus accumbens and amygdala, which are linked to reward, reinforcement, and decision making, may be critical to the expression of impulsivity as a core symptom of the ADHD personality.

REFERENCES

1. KENT, L., F. MIDDLE, Z. HAWI, *et al.* 2001. Nicotinic acetylcholine receptor α 4 subunit gene polymorphism and attention deficit hyperactivity disorder. Psychiatr. Genet. **11:** 37–40.
2. WENDER, P. 1995. Attention Deficit Hyperactivity Disorder in Adults. Oxford University Press. New York.
3. EVENDEN, J.L. & C.N. RYAN. 1996. The pharmacology of impulsive behavior in rats: the effects of drugs on response choice with varying delays of reinforcement. Psychopharmacology **128:** 161–170.

4. EVENDEN, J.L. & B. MEYERSON. 1999. The behavior of Spontaneously Hypertensive and Wistar Kyoto rats under a paced fixed consecutive number schedule. Psychopharmacology **63:** 71–82.
5. NAKAMURA, K., M. KURASAWA & M. SHIRANE. 2000. Impulsivity and AMPA receptors: aniracetam ameliorates impulsive behavior induced by a blockade of AMPA receptors in rats. Brain Res. **862:** 266–269.
6. EVENDEN, J.L. 1998. The pharmacology of impulsive behavior in rats III: the effects of amphetamine, haloperidol, imipramine, chlordiazapoxide and ethanol on a paced fixed consecutive number schedule. Psychopharmachology **138:** 295–304.
7. EVENDEN, J.L. 1998. The pharmacology of impulsive behavior in rats IV: the effects of selective serotonergic agents on a paced fixed consecutive number schedule. Psychopharmachology **140:** 319–330.
8. CARDINAL, R.N., D.R. PENNICOTT, C.L. SUGATHAPALA, *et al.* 2001. Impulsive choice induced in rats by lesions of the nucleus accumbens core. Science **292:** 2499–2501.
9. BIEDERMAN, J. & S.V. FARAONE. 2002. Current concepts on the neurobiology of attention-deficit/hyperactivity disorder. J. Atten. Disord. **6**(Suppl. 1): S7–S16.
10. GIEDD, J.N., F.X. CASTELLANOS, B.J. CASEY, *et al.* 1994. Quantitative morphology of the corpus callosum in attention deficit hyperactivity disorder. Am. J. Psychiatry **151:** 665–669.
11. SCHWEITZER, J.B., D.O. LEE, R.B. HANFORD, *et al.* 2003. A positron emission tomography study of methylphenidate in adults with ADHD: alterations in resting blood flow and predicting treatment response. Neuropsychopharmacology **28:** 967–973.
12. TEICHER, M.H., C.M. ANDERSON, A. POLCARI, *et al.* 2000. Functional deficits in basal ganglia of children with attention-deficit/hyperactivity disorder shown with functional magnetic resonance imaging relaxometry. Nat. Med. **6:** 470–473.
13. HALE, T.S., A.R. HARIRI & J.T. MCCRACKEN. 2000. Attention-deficit/hyperactivity disorder: perspectives from neuroimaging. Ment. Retard. Dev. Disabil. Res. Rev. **6:** 214–219.
14. DURSTON, S. 2003. A review of the biological bases of ADHD: what have we learned from imaging studies? Ment. Retard Dev. Disabil. Res. Rev. **9:** 184–195.
15. LEYTON, M., H. OKAZAWA, M. DIKSIC, *et al.* 2001. Brain regional alpha-[11C]methyl-L-tryptophan trapping in impulsive subjects with borderline personality disorder. Am. J. Psychiatry **158:** 775–782.
16. DOLAN, M., W.J. DEAKIN, N. ROBERTS & I. ANDERSON. 2002. Serotonergic and cognitive impairment in impulsive aggressive personality disordered offenders: are there implications for treatment? Psychol. Med. **32:** 105–117.
17. HANNON, J. & D. HOYER. 2002. Serotonin receptors and systems: endless diversity? Acta Biol. Szeged. **46:** 1–12.
18. LINNOILA, M., M. VIRKKUNEN, M. SCHEININ, *et al.* 1983. Low cerebrospinal fluid 5-hydroxyindolacetic acid concentration differentiates impulsive from non-impulsive violent behavior. Life Sci. **33:** 2609–2614.
19. COCCARO, E.F., L.J. SIEVER, H.M. KLAR, *et al.* 1989. Serotonergic studies in patients with affective and personality disorders: correlates with suicidal and impulsive aggressive behavior. Arch. Gen. Psychiatry **46:** 587–599.
20. EVANS, J., H. PLATTS, S. LIGHTMAN & D. NUTT. 2000. Impulsiveness and the prolactin response to d-fenfluramine. Psychopharmacology **149:** 147–152.
21. SOUBRIÉ, P. 1986. Serotonergic neurons and behavior. J. Pharmacol. **17:** 107–112.
22. WOGAR, M.A., C.M. BRADSHAW & E. SZABADI. 1993. Effects of lesions of the ascending 5-hydroxytryptaminergic pathways on choice between delayed reinforcers. Psychopharmacology **111:** 239–243.
23. RICHARDS, J.B. & L.S. SEIDEN. 1995. Serotonin depletion increases impulsive behavior in rats. Soc. Neurosci. Abstr. **21:** 1693.
24. DALLEY, J.W., E.A. THEOBALD, D.M. EAGLE, *et al.* 2002. Deficits in impulse control associated with tonically-elevated serotonergic function in rat prefrontal cortex. Neuropsychopharmacology **26:** 716–728.
25. OGAWA, S., T.M. LEE, A.S. NAYAK & P. GLYNN. 1990. Oxygenation-sensitive contrast in magnetic resonance image of rodent brain at high magnetic fields. Magn. Reson. Med. **14:** 68–78.

26. OGAWA, S., R.S. MENON, D.W. TANK, *et al.* 1993. Functional brain mapping by blood oxygenation level-dependent contrast magnetic resonance imaging. Biophys. J. **64:** 803–812.

27. SOKOLLOFF, L., M. REIVICH, C. KENNEDY, *et al.* 1977. The [^{14}C] deoxyglucose method for the measurement of local cerebral glucose utilization: theory, procedure, and normal values in the conscious and anesthetized albino rat. J. Neurochem. **28:** 897–916.

28. RAMSEY, N.F., B.S. KIRKBY, P. VAN GELDEREN, *et al.* 1996. Functional mapping of human sensorimotor cortex with 3-D BOLD fMRI correlates highly with H$_2$^{15}O PET rCBF. J. Cereb. Blood Flow Metab. **16:** 755–764.

29. LOGOTHETIS, N.K., J. PAULS, M. AUGATH, *et al.* 2001. Neurophysiological investigation of the basis of the fMRI signal. Nature **412:** 150–157.

30. STEIN, E.A., R. RISINGER & A.S. BLOOM. 2000 Functional MRI in pharmacology. *In* Functional MRI. C.T.W. Moonen and P.A. Bandettini, Eds.: 525–538. Springer-Verlag. New York.

31. ARCHER, T. 1989. Neurotoxin-induced cognitive and motor activity modifications: a catecholamine connection. *In* Attention Deficit Disorder: Clinical and Basic Research. T. Sagvolden and T. Archer, Jr., Eds.: 287–322. Hillsdale Erlbaum. New York.

32. SHAYWITZ, M.B.A., J.H. KLOPPER, R.D. YAGER & J.W. GORDON. 1976. Paradoxical response to amphetamine in developing rats treated with 6-hydroxydopamine. Nature **261:** 153–155.

33. SAGVOLDEN, T., M.A. METZGER, H.K. SHIORBECK, *et al.* 1992. The spontaneously hypertensive rat (SHR) as an animal model of childhood hyperactivity (ADHD): changed reactivity to reinforcers and to psychomotor stimulants. Behav. Neural Biol. **58:** 13–112.

34. MOOK, D.M. & A. NEURINGER. 1994. Different effects of amphetamine on reinforced variations versus repetitions in spontaneously hypertensive rats (SHR). Physiol. Behav. **56:** 939–944.

35. SAGVOLDEN, T., H. AASE, P. ZEINER & D.F. BERGER. 1998. Altered reinforcement mechanisms in attention-deficit hyperactivity disorder. Behav. Brain Res. **94:** 61–71.

36. BOIX, F., S.W. QIAO, F. KOLPUS & T. SAGVOLDEN. 1998. *L*-deprenyl treatment alters brain monoamine levels and reduces impulsiveness in an animal model of attention-deficit hyperactivity disorder. Behav. Brain Res. **94:** 153–162.

37. GIROS, B., M. JABER, S.R. JONES, *et al.* 1996. Hyperlocomotion and indifference to cocaine amphetamine in mice lacking the dopamine transporter. Nature **379:** 606–612.

38. RUSSELL, V.A. 2002. Hypodopaminergic and hypernoradrenergic activity in prefrontal cortex slices of an animal model for attention-deficit hyperactivity disorder—the spontaneously hypertensive rat. Behav. Brain Res. **130:** 191–196.

39. STRUPP, J.P. 1996. Stimulate: a GUI based fMRI analysis software package. Neuroimage **3:** S607.

40. BARBELIVIEN, A., S. RUOTSALAINEN & J. SIRVIO. 2001. Metabolic alterations in the prefrontal and cingulate cortices are related to behavioral deficits in a rodent model of attention deficit hyperactivity disorder. Cereb. Cortex **11:** 1056–1063.

41. JENTSCH, J.D. & J.R. TAYLOR. 1999. Impulsivity resulting from frontostriatal dysfunction in drug abuse: implications for the control of behavior by reward-related stimuli. Psychopharmacology **146:** 373–390.

42. BERQUIN, P.C., J.N. GIEDD, L.K. JACOBSEN, *et al.* 1998. Cerebellum in attention-deficit hyperactivity disorder: a morphometric MRI study. Neurology **50:** 1087–1093.

43. ANDERSON C.M., A. POLCARI, S.B. LOWEN, *et al.* 2002. Effects of methylphenidate on functional magnetic resonance relaxometry of the cerebellar vermis in boys with ADHD. Am. J. Psychiatry **159:** 1322–1328.

44. RUSSELL, V.A. 2003. In vitro glutamate-stimulated release of dopamine from nucleus accumbens core and shell of spontaneously hypertensive rats. Metab. Brain Dis. **18:** 161–168.

45. RUSSELL, V., A. DE VILLIERS, T. SAGVOLDEN, *et al.* 1995. Altered dopaminergic function in the prefrontal cortex, nucleus accumbens and caudate-putamen of an animal model of attention-deficit hyperactivity disorder–the spontaneously hypertensive rat. Brain Res. **676:** 343–351.

46. FILIPEK, P.A., M. SEMRUD-CLIKEMAN, R.J. STEINGARD, *et al.* 1997. Volumetric MRI analysis comparing subjects having attention-deficit hyperactivity disorder with normal controls. Neurology **48:** 589–601.
47. TRINH, J.V., D.L. NEHRENBERG, J.P. JACOBSEN, *et al.* 2003. Differential psychostimulannt-induced activation of neural circuits in dopamine transporter knockout and wild type mice. Neuroscience **118:** 297–310.

Response Inhibition and Disruptive Behaviors

Toward a Multiprocess Conception of Etiological Heterogeneity for ADHD Combined Type and Conduct Disorder Early-Onset Type

JOEL T. NIGG

Department of Psychology, Michigan State University, East Lansing, Michigan 48824, USA

ABSTRACT: Response disinhibition is one of several processes that may account for disruptive behavior problems. It is associated with both attention deficits/hyperactivity (ADHD-C) and early onset, unsocialized conduct disorder (CD-E). Response inhibition is not a unitary construct. It is best understood via a dual process model of regulatory control. Executive inhibition refers to deliberate suppression of immediate motor behavior in the service of a distal goal in working memory, with relatively low anxiety activation. It is instantiated in the same frontal–striatal–thalamic neural loops as executive function and corresponds in temperament theory to effortful control. Motivational or reactive inhibition refers to anxiety-provoked interruption of behavior in the context of unexpected, novel, or punishment-cue indicators. Along with reward-response and hostile/angry response it corresponds to reactivity in temperament theory, and invokes limbic responsivity. With regard to these types of inhibitory control, ADHD-combined type is predominantly associated with dysfunctional executive inhibition. CD-E is predominantly associated with dysfunctions in the motivational inhibition process, with smaller, secondary effects in executive control. However, in both syndromes etiological heterogeneity is notable. For example, recent evidence indicates that executive inhibitory control is familial, but characterizes only a subset of children with ADHD-C. Recent dual-process models for both ADHD-C and CD-E are therefore important; they are noted and integrated. Examination of the correlates of behavioral inhibition in the subgroups with these inhibitory deficits may prove fruitful in clarifying the diverse routes to disruptive psychopathology in children.

KEYWORDS: ADHD; conduct disorder; psychopathy; hyperactivity; inhibition; executive control; reactivity; heterogeneity; dual-process models

THE TAXONOMIC AND DEVELOPMENTAL LANDSCAPE OF SEVERE DISRUPTIVE BEHAVIOR

The diverse disruptive behavior problem domain includes three broad syndromes in psychiatric taxonomy. Attention deficit/hyperactivity disorder (ADHD) has three

Address for correspondence: Joel T. Nigg, Ph.D., Associate Professor, Department of Psychology, Michigan State University, East Lansing, MI 48824-1117. Voice: 517-353-8690; fax: 517-432-2476.

nigg@msu.edu

Ann. N.Y. Acad. Sci. 1008: 170–182 (2003). © 2003 New York Academy of Sciences.
doi: 10.1196/annals.1301.018

subtypes in the DSM-IV:[1] primarily inattentive (ADHD-I), primarily hyperactive (ADHD-H), and combined (ADHD-C). The ICD-10[63] identifies hyperkinetic disorder, which overlaps with a subset of ADHD-C and possibly ADHD-PI, and hyperkinetic conduct disorder, which receives a conduct disorder (CD), not an ADHD diagnosis. ADHD-C and/or hyperkinetic disorder are the primary focus of "disinhibition" theories of ADHD.

CD, characterized by violation of societal rules and the rights of others, involves at least two distinct problem domains: overt (aggression, stealing with confrontation), and covert (lying, vandalizing) antisocial behaviors. Whereas DSM-IV distinguishes *early*- from *late*-onset CD, the literature specifies an undersocialized/ aggressive/ psychopathic subgroup when invoking inhibitory dysfunction.[16] There is substantial, though not perfect, overlap of this group with CD–early onset type (CD-E). Thus, while we conceptually distinguish psychopathy (difficult to validate in childhood) from CD-E, their overlap enables us to specify the undersocialized subgroup of CD-E as the focus of disinhibition theories of CD.[16]

The overlap of ODD and CD or aggression with ADHD-C is substantial.[23] Most children with CD-E also are impulsive, such that studying a "pure" CD-E group is difficult. ADHD-C without CD is more readily identified, although even the latter may have above-average levels of aggression. Developmentally, oppositional behaviors nearly always precede conduct problems, although not all cases of oppositional-defiant disorder (ODD) go on to develop CD.[30] Neurobiological theories of oppositional-defiant disorder are not distinct from those for ADHD or CD. The developmental relation of oppositional and conduct problems to ADHD-C remains unclear. In some cases, ADHD may be a precursor to CD.[46] Children who exhibit both ADHD and conduct problems/aggression are at highest risk for negative outcomes.[31] Heterogeneity within the disruptive behavior domain is thus notable. Inhibition theories discussed herein pertain almost entirely to a subset, namely, to ADHD-C and to CD-E.

THEORIES OF DYSFUNCTIONAL NEUROPSYCHOLOGICAL MECHANISMS IN ADHD-C AND CD-E

Context: Transactional Models

A basic tenet of current psychopathological theory is that, to be valid, a psychiatric disorder must involve a dysfunction in a core psychological (or biological) process.[62] The extensive dysregulated behavior of children with ADHD-C or CD-E might be related to a variety of such core dysfunctions. Most theorists agree that the development and maintenance of disruptive behavior problems involve transactions between socialization context (family, peers, school, culture) and intrinsic child characteristics. Socialization and/or self-regulation are likely disrupted early in development.[24,31] The aim of neurocognitive models is to clarify the intrinsic (child-side) element of these problematic developmental pathways. Of course, to the extent any such deficits are heritable, one can speculate also about their role in parent vulnerability, thus invoking genotype-environment corrections and interactions in process accounts. Our interest here, however, is the putative dysfunction in the child.

(handwritten margin note: I also disagree here)

Candidate Neurocognitive Contributors

The similarity of the behavioral and social problems of children with ADHD-C or CD-E to cases of observed neural injury have long fueled speculation about neurological abnormality in these children. By the late twentieth century these theories became sophisticated due to advancing knowledge in the neurosciences. Currently, neurocognitive hypotheses still under investigation for CD-E (or psychopathy in adults) include lack of fear of punishment[33,53] (similar to what I call motivational inhibition later), response modulation,[36] executive function problems,[35,58] and low verbal IQ.[16,35] For ADHD-C the list includes arousal,[64] reward response,[55] activation or effort,[59] regulation,[12] attentional alerting,[5] motor, and executive[4,57] deficits. When focusing on inhibition concepts, then, it is important to note that modulatory systems (e.g., arousal, activation, alerting) interact with motivational incentive and with executive control in both (1) ongoing behavior and (2) development. Thus it is problematic to assume a theory involving only one process acting in isolation. All of these interrelated regulatory systems thus remain under investigation, along with their relative role in these disorders.

(handwritten margin notes: I ⟵ disagree Not even close to fit overlap)

BEHAVIORAL INHIBITION

As a commonly cited candidate core dysfunction in ADHD-C and CD-E, inhibitory control has been variously operationalized and too often imprecisely invoked, necessitating some organization of the constructs, and measures involved.[38] Key distinctions can be considered from both a neuroanatomical and a functional perspective. Neurally, these involve components or selected loops within the multiple parallel thalamo–cortical–basal ganglia neural loop structure closely related to motivation, affect and behavioral regulation. Functionally, researchers have considered distinctions between suppression of contents of working memory versus that of a motor response; or suppression of a competing (unintended) response versus an intended response.[22] Several apparent inhibition or interference control processes can thus be identified in attention, memory, and language,[9] and appear to develop at distinct rates in children.[10] Alternately, one can consider suppression of interference or conflict at the stages of stimulus or response selection versus response suppression.[8] Disagreement continues as to whether putative measures of inhibition in cognitive processing (e.g., attention, memory, language) in fact require active inhibition, or simply withdrawal of their activation, to explain resolution of response conflict.[34] Nonetheless, for purposes of sorting out an etiological taxonomy of disruptive behavior disorders, the key functional definition concerns suppression of a prepared *motor* response, rather than cognition *per se*, or response suppression rather than selection. Then, within this behavioral inhibition domain, it is crucial to distinguish between *executive* and *motivational* suppression or interruption of a prepotent behavior.[38,39]

Most of the early *inhibition*-related theories of disruptive behavior were influenced by early work of Lykken[33] and Gray[22] in relation to psychopathy, which then generalized to a septal–hippocampal model of a broad range of undercontrolled behavior, including impulsivity, hyperactivity, and ADHD-C.[19,51] These earlier disinhibition conceptions did not differentiate motivational from executive suppression of behavior. In the past two decades, the revived "frontal metaphor" of ADHD-C has fueled renewed interest in the multicomponential construct of executive functions.[47] In particular, interest has developed in the function of behavioral inhibition (variously defined) as a crucial component of executive dysfunction in ADHD-C. Those developments led to some confusion over what type of behavioral inhibition is at issue. However, progress in child temperament and psychophysiological research have clarified the usefulness of the distinction between (1) "reactive" (motivational) and (2) "executive" control processes.[38,54]

Executive and motivational control processes are closely related during ongoing regulation of real behavior. However, data to support their conceptual distinction arise both from temperament studies in toddlers and from physiological and statistical analyses of cognitive performance measures in middle childhood.[11,29,54] Psychologically, the two processes differ as to the extent of anxiety involved and the temporal quality of the incentive (immediate versus distal). Their relative influence in dynamic behavioral control thus depends on the incentive context. Do they relate differentially to ADHD-C and CD-EO?

Executive Behavioral Inhibition and ADHD-C

Executive inhibition refers to deliberate suppression or cessation of a prepotent, but task-inappropriate, response in order to protect other responses necessary to achieve a later, internally represented goal. Most commonly, a motor response that is cued and prepared is suppressed, canceled,[34] or inhibited, in the service of internal goals held in working memory as new information is received. This process is deliberate, requires cognitive resources, and can occur without substantial fear or anxiety. It is not active at all times, but is activated when task context requires it. Several reviews have concluded that executive dysfunction, particularly behavioral inhibition defined in this way, is an important component in ADHD-C.[4,47,57]

The best evidence for this claim comes from studies of the stop task,[32] which has extensive empirical and theoretical support as a measure of deliberate suppression of a motor response. At least 15 studies have now been reported on ADHD with this task.[39] Although not all are supportive, in aggregate they suggest an abnormal inhibition process in that children with ADHD-C need more warning time to prevent the prepotent response. This function is thought to depend on neural loops linking basal ganglia, frontal cortex, thalamus, and cerebellum. These networks depend heavily on dopaminergic modulation, although other neurotransmitters are also important.[8] Anatomically, recent evidence suggests the particular importance of intact activation of right-lateralized inferior frontal gyrus[2] and of structures in the basal ganglia, especially the caudate.[8] Both regions are generally abnormal in functional and structural neuroimaging studies of groups of children with ADHD-C.[18] Other tasks thought to address executive behavioral inhibition and to depend on inferior or orbital prefrontal cortical regions, such as the Go–No-Go and oculomotor antisaccade tasks, provide more mixed but still generally positive support.[39]

Although relatively clear deficits on these types of tasks are consistent with an executive control theory of ADHD-C, questions remain as to whether this is the "primary" etiological deficit in ADHD for two reasons. First, it may be that modulating or preparatory functions may account for failures on executive inhibition tasks such as the stop task. Efforts to utilize physiological and ERP measures to evaluate whether abnormal alerting to the warning stimulus[7,49] or motivational states[45,60] account for stop-inhibition failures have yielded mixed results; further such investigations are needed.

Second, agreement that the deficit is specific to ADHD-C has been lacking. The ADHD-C stop-inhibition deficit is independent of co-occurring ODD or CD symptoms.[37] However, similar, although smaller ($d = 0.50$ vs. $d = 0.64$), effects are also observed in relation to CD behaviors.[44] Conflicting results across laboratories have left it unclear to what extent the stop task or other executive effects in CD (or CD-E) are explained by co-occurring ADHD-C symptoms,[47,56] or also pertain specifically to CD or aggression.[58] Further complicating the specificity picture, child gender may moderate specificity of stop-signal findings in ADHD-C versus ADHD-I.[40] Whereas these caveats are noteworthy from a causal theory viewpoint, the primary importance of specificity is to univariate (one deficit necessary and sufficient to cause a disorder), rather than multivariate causal models;[17] the latter are most viable here.

Meantime, we find converging evidence in personality and temperament data. The early "effortful control" system in very young children is thought to involve the same neural system as the executive control processes related to ADHD-C. It is related developmentally to the adolescent and adult personality trait of *conscientiousness*, which reflects planfulness.[54] We have shown that in adulthood, conscientiousness is robustly associated with symptoms of inattention/disorganization, even with symptoms of antisocial behavior statistically controlled, whereas the reverse it not true.[42] Those data offer evidence from another level of analysis associating ADHD-C with executive regulation problems.

On balance, executive inhibition remains a viable candidate for one core neurocognitive dysfunction in ADHD-C. Similar deficits are observed in children with CD, but evidence is less consistent for a unique role in CD-E apart from ADHD-C. Even in ADHD-C, it remains unclear to what extent this deficit is causally primary, in part due to questions about the degree of its specificity.

Motivational Behavioral Inhibition and CD-E

Motivated inhibition is well described by Gray[20] and by Kagan[27] in their related but distinct models of a behavioral inhibition system (BIS). Temperament researchers refer to this behavioral inhibition system as a "reactive" process,[54] indicating a relatively reflexive orienting of attention. It is also referred to as a motivational process, to connote its responsivity to emotionally salient incentive cues. This system detects and responds to immediate contextual cues for punishment, unexpected "mismatch,"[20] or social unfamiliarity.[27] The psychological motivation is anxiety.

Notably, behavior does not stop entirely (the "freeze" response to panic or fear is associated with a different neural circuit in Gray's model[21]). Instead, the current behavior is interrupted, autonomic arousal is increased, and attention is redirected to the "threat" stimulus, potentially including motor behavior to inspect it.[21] Suppression is thought to involve "bottom up" limbic activation interrupting motor programs.[20] According to Gray, the relevant "conceptual nervous system" involves the medial septal area and hippocampus, which receive ascending noradrenergic inputs (from the locus coeruleus) and serotinergic inputs (from the median raphe nucleus). They in turn have linkages to orbital frontal cortex.[20] However, more recent evidence suggests that the amygdala may be more important in this type of behavioral inter-ruption than was suggested by Gray. Kagan[27] also emphasizes the subcortical amygdala system as well as the hippocampus and projections to striatum, along with adrenergic innervation.

In animal studies, the BIS is activated by cues for quite severe punishment (e.g., electric shock[20]) or threat (a rat is exposed to strong cat scent[21]). In humans, it is typically probed with a modified Go–No-Go task with monetary reward and pun-ishment cues,[36] but one can question the extent to which these human experiments activate the BIS described by Gray. Nonetheless, several studies of children with ADHD-C using variations on reward-cue tasks have generally failed to support a def-icit in motivational inhibition[25,39] whereas physiological studies of heart rate and skin conductance responses provide mixed results.[26,48] On the other hand, despite these measurement and replication difficulties, deficits consistent with motivational disin-hibition in CD-E are well supported in behavioral[14,43,66] and physiological[15,16,52] data. However, it is important to note that the latter effects are moderated by SES, with extreme adversity rendering psychophysiological effects nonsignificant.[53]

In children, the measurement approach advocated by Kagan and colleagues in-volves exposure to novel social conditions. Because of the distinct measurement par-adigms, it is not clear that Kagan's concept is isomorphic with Gray's. Gray emphasizes response to learned cues for punishment, anchoring his argument in classic conditioning theory. Kagan, on the other hand, emphasizes innate response to unfamiliar social situations, suggesting a link to social anxiety. Preschool children followed longitudinally reveal distinct developmental trajectories for inhibition to learned punishment cues versus inhibition to novel social encounters.[3] Thus, failure to support a deficit in response to cues for punishment may not pertain entirely to response to social anxiety or novelty. The latter is underresearched in relation to *spe-cific* forms of disruptive behavior problems. However, children with low early tem-peramental inhibition, as defined by Kagan, are at risk for later global externalizing problems[6] and delinquency,[28] suggesting a possible link to CD-E. Links to ADHD-C are not well studied. There is also need for more work to clarify the reach of this construct, in particular the neural concomitants of response to ambiguous versus novel versus threatening cues, and their relations to specific disruptive behavior syndromes.

On balance, motivational behavioral inhibition (low arousal to cues for punish-ment or mismatch) appears closely aligned with CD-E, but not clearly aligned with ADHD-C apart from CD. A caveat is that it remains unclear whether the main CD-E deficit is inhibition or response regulation/signal detection.[36]

Summary

Many studies did not carefully identify ADHD-C or CD-E, disagreement contin-ues about putative inhibition measures, and co-occurrence of ADHD-C and CD-E confers greatest risk.[35] Yet it is useful in organizing the literature to view executive suppression of behavior as most aligned with ADHD-C, and motivational suppres-sion with CD-E. Of course, these processes do not operate in isolation; they modu-late one another and interact with arousal, reward response, and affect state. Most crucial to consider at this point, however, are heterogeneity and the developmental implications of this framework.

HETEROGENEITY

A partial etiological dissociation of ADHD-C and CD-E may be based on preferentially linking them, respectively, with executive and motivational inhibitory control. Yet effect sizes and the associated heterogeneity in clinical samples pose an important limitation to the reach of such a heuristic. To take the case of ADHD-C, typical effect sizes for inhibitory problems in relation to control samples are in the range of $d = 0.65$.[37,44,47] Effects for physiological measures of motivational response in CD-E are only slightly larger; the average effect size of low resting heart rate in antisocial behavior is $d = 0.84$.[52] These yield distributions that overlap 50–60% with normal control variation. Thus, any clinical cutoff to establish those with "impaired" inhibition would select only a subset of children with ADHD-C or CD-E.

To take the case of ADHD for illustration, in the Michigan State Child Attention Study, a stop-signal RT = 420 ms classified 8% of control children and 55% of children with ADHD-C as "impaired" on the executive inhibition measure. Similar data are observed in other labs in the United States[13] and in neuroimaging studies.[18] In our data set, children with ADHD with "impaired" inhibition had siblings with slower SSRT than siblings of ADHD with "normal" inhibition (SSRT = 432 vs. 296 ms, $P < .05$); weaker results emerged for parents.[41] The two groups of ADHD children did not differ substantially in severity of behavioral disturbance with regard to ADHD symptoms. Although results were mixed, they suggest that a valid etiological *subgroup* might be related to a deficit in executive control or inhibition.

As a result, even if we believe we have "explained" some of the children's ADHD-C or CD-E, what is the psychological dysfunction in the others, if any? Further, what is the developmental etiology of the inhibitory problem? Several reviewers have suggested recently that ADHD-C may be characterized by some combination of executive inhibition and dysfunctional reward response,[39,55,61] perhaps reflecting two etiological pathways. On the other hand, exogenous as well as endogenous contributors may need further consideration. Unpublished data from the Michigan State Attention Study indicate that child perception of marital conflict and stop-signal RT contribute independently to child ADHD symptoms. Regardless of which specific model proves correct, developmental models likely must specify more than one "core process" or more than one developmental pathway in order to account for the majority of cases of ADHD-C as now defined. Similar caveats likely hold for CD-E, where data again suggest more than one etiological pathway. One recent empirical framework suggests that childhood CD includes (1) a low-anxiety, disinhibited aggressive pathway as suggested here, and (2) a low IQ, or social-adversity pathway.[16] What composite picture of diverse pathways results?

DIVERSE DEVELOPMENTAL PATHWAYS

The clearest account of the interrelated development of executive and motivational control processes in children comes from collaborative temperament and cognitive development reviews.[50] The suggestion is that during infancy, attention and behavior respond to reactive–motivational processes (inhibition to anxiety-provoking stimuli, approach to reward-provoking stimuli). In the toddler years, deliberate or effortful control of attention and behavior begins to emerge. These pro-

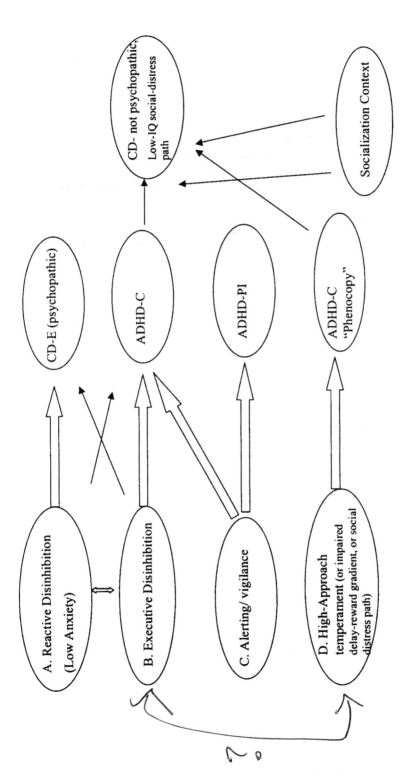

FIGURE 1. *See following page for legend.*

cesses depend on one another during development. Thus, extreme reactivity may disrupt development of effortful control, or weak effortful control may prevent consolidation of affect regulation processes.[54] One thus can imagine multiple pathways in early development related to distinct kinds of temperamental or cognitive vulnerability (based on genotype, perinatal injury, or genotype-family fit), as suggested in FIGURE 1. Two basic pathways logically anchor this conception (pathways A and B in FIG. 1). Those can then be added to by incorporating existing heterogeneity models for CD[16] or ADHD.[61] The resulting multiple-pathway picture reflects what seems to be emerging from collaborative temperament and neuroscientific studies.

In the first (early-onset, primary-CD pathway A), temperament is underreactive (insensitivity to punishment cues), perhaps accompanied by high-hostility (anger) reactivity, interfering not only with socialization (as often suggested in theories of antisocial development[24,31]) but with other self-regulatory capacities. Thus, the ability to effortfully regulate attention is difficult to master in the toddler years, because the control system is facing an impaired reactive system outside of the "expectable" range, or is receiving less than the minimum support needed (in the case of low reactivity to anxiety). If socialization processes fail to compensate adequately, primary reactivity problems should lead to secondary, but milder, executive dysfunction, while CD-E would lead to possible comorbid ADHD. The clinical outcome would be a psychopathic profile with secondary executive weakness.

The second pathway, B, would have a later emergence, beginning in the toddler years with primary weakness of the effortful control (precursor to the executive) system. As that system fails to develop normally, regulation of reactive processes is weak, and those processes are secondarily affected. The longitudinal prediction here would be for primary ADHD-C, with secondary problems in motivational response (a frequent clinical observation), including poor regulation of reward response and anger, depending on socialization supports. CD might develop secondarily, depending on socialization. The clinical presentation features clear executive deficits, but reactive deficits may be smaller.

Other pathways lead to copies of these syndromes. The nonexecutive ADHD path may reflect extreme approach tendencies from a temperament viewpoint, dysfunctional reward response,[61] or severe psychosocial disruption. Alerting dysfunction, suspected in ADHD-C, may also occur in isolation in ADHD-PI. The nonpsychopathic CD pathway is described by Frick in his dual-pathway model of CD.[16]

FIGURE 1. Composite of two dual-pathway models. Pathways for ADHD-C include (**A**) an executive inhibition subtype (also involving alerting pathways), and (**B**) a secondary subtype related either to psychosocial adversity, reward-dysfunction/extreme approach temperament, or other processes. Pathways for Conduct Disorder include (**C**) a CD-E subtype involving motivational disinhibition, low anxiety, and psychopathic characteristics in early-onset/psychopathic subtype, and (**D**) a second subtype developing in the presence of adverse socialization, perhaps often based on one or both of the ADHD types. Pathways A and B are related, because disruption of executive or reactive processes can cause secondary problems in development of the other system. However, pathway A is theorized to begin disrupting socialization earlier than pathway B. This schematic is not exhaustive as to potential etiological subgroups in CD (e.g., there may be another, high-anxiety, psychopathic group) or ADHD.

CONCLUSION

Specifying inhibitory control problems in the disruptive behavior domain is limited by conceptual imprecision, poor clinical specification of samples, and disputes about measurement paradigms. The most salient issue, however, concerns etiological heterogeneity within the two most important disruptive disorders likely to reflect behavioral inhibitory problems, namely ADHD combined type (ADHD-C) and early-onset, unsocialized aggressive conduct disorder (CD-E). These partially distinct syndromes both involve impulsive behaviors, but with somewhat different developmental determinants and contexts for expression of impulsivity. A useful heuristic for future research is to consider that (1) a subset of ADHD-C cases reflects a later (toddler) onset developmental pathway triggered by primary failure of executive control neural systems, with secondary breakdowns in reactive and affective processes, and (2) a subset of CD-E cases reflects an early-onset (infancy) developmental pathway triggered by primary failure of reactive or motivational control processes, with secondary breakdown in executive control. This model explains smaller executive deficits in CD paired with relatively larger executive deficits in ADHD-C. I emphasized that in each syndrome, only a subset of cases that currently meet DSM-IV criteria would be expected to exhibit the putative inhibitory deficit. Further, in those with such deficits, the distinction I propose might be a matter of the relative degree and sequence of emergence of problems in both executive and reactive systems. Nonetheless, it is suggested that this distinction can be observed in the literature and warrants longitudinal investigation.

Finally, I argued that etiological heterogeneity is apparent within ADHD-C or CD-E on measures of inhibitory dysfunction. This state of affairs requires that future theories incorporate more than one pathway or process leading to the syndromes of ADHD-C and CD-E. Consistent with this need, "dual process" theories have recently become more explicit in order to account for etiological heterogeneity in both ADHD[5,39,61] and CD.[16] Future studies should consider individual (etiological) differences within these DSM-IV-defined samples. Future theories that consider multiple regulatory processes, along with better specification of socialization contexts, will better account for heterogeneity and enable a stronger, etiologically based clinical nosology of disruptive behavior disorders.

ACKNOWLEDGMENT

Work on this paper was supported by National Institute of Mental Health Grant MH59105 to Joel Nigg.

REFERENCES

1. AMERICAN PSYCHIATRIC ASSOCIATION. 1994. Diagnostic and Statistical Manual of Mental Disorders, 4th ed. American Psychiatric Association. Washington, DC.
2. ARON, A.R., P.C. FLETCHER, E.T. BULLMORE, et al. 2003. Stop signal inhibition disrupted by damage to right inferior frontal gyrus in humans. Nature Neurosci. **6:** 115–116.
3. ASENDORPF, J.B. 1990. Development of inhibition during childhood: evidence for situational specificity and a two-factor model. Dev. Psychol. **26:** 721–730.

4. BARKLEY, R.A. 1997. Behavioral inhibition, sustained attention, and executive function: constructing a unified theory of ADHD. Psychol. Bull. **121:** 65–94.
5. BERGER, A. & M.I. POSNER. 2000. Pathologies of brain attentional networks. Neurosci. Biobehav. Rev. **24:** 3–5.
6. BIEDERMAN, J., J.F. ROSENBAUM, D.R. HIRSHFELD, et al. 1990. Psychiatric correlates of behavioral inhibition in young children of parents with and without psychiatric disorders. Arch. Gen. Psychiatry **47:** 21–26.
7. BRANDEIS, D., T.H. VAN LEEUWEN, K. RUBIA, et al. 1998. Neuroelectric mapping reveals precursor of stop failures in children with attention deficits. Behav. Brain Res. **94:** 111–125.
8. CASEY, B.J., N. TOTTENHAM & J. FONSSELLA. 2002. Clinical, imaging, lesion, and genetic approaches toward a model of cognitive control. Dev. Psychobiol. **40:** 237–254.
9. DAGENBACH, D. & T.H. CARR. 1994. Inhibitory Processes in Attention, Memory, and Language. Academic Press. San Diego.
10. DEMPSTER, F.N. 1993. Resistence to interference: developmental changes in a basic processing mechanism. In Emerging Themes in Cognitive Development: Vol. 1, Foundations. M.L. Howe and R. Pasnak, Eds.: 3–27. Springer-Verlag. New York.
11. DERRYBERRY, D. & M.K. ROTHBART. 1997. Reactive and effortful processes in the organization of temperament. Dev. Psychopathol. **9:** 633–652.
12. DOUGLAS, V.I. 1988. Cognitive deficits in children with attention deficit disorder with hyperactivity. In Attention Deficit Disorder: Criteria, Cognition, Intervention. L.M. Bloomingdale and J. Sergeant, Eds.: 65–81. Pergamon Press. New York.
13. DOYLE A.E., J. BIEDERMAN, L.J. SEIDMAN, et al. 2000. Diagnostic efficiency of neuropsychological test scores for discriminating boys with and without attention deficit-hyperactivity disorder. J. Consult. Clin. Psychol. **68:** 477–488.
14. FINN, P.R., C.A. MAZAS, A.N. JUSTUS & J. STEINMETZ. 2002. Early-onset alcoholism with conduct disorder: Go/No-Go learning deficits, working memory capacity, and personality. Alcohol. Clin. Exp. Res. **26:** 186–206.
15. FOWLES, D.C. 2000. Electrodermal hyporeactivity and antisocial behavior: does anxiety mediate the relationship? J. Affective Disord. **61:** 177–189.
16. FRICK, P.J. 1998. Callous-unemotional traits and conduct problems: applying the two-factor model of psychopathy to children. In Psychopathy: Theory, Research, and Implications for Society. D.J. Cooke et al., Eds.: 161–187. Kluwer Publishers. Amsterdam.
17. GARBER, J. & S.D. HOLLON. 1991. What can specificity designs say about causality in psycyhopathology research? Psychol. Bull. **110:** 129–136.
18. GIEDD, J.N., J. BLUMENTHALL, E. MOLLOY & X.F. CASTELLANOS. 2001. Brain imaging of attention deficit/hyperactivity disorder. Ann. N.Y. Acad. Sci. **931:** 33–49.
19. GORENSTEIN, E.E. & J.P. NEWMAN. 1980 . Disinhibitory psychopathology: a new perspective and a model for research. Psychol. Rev. **87:** 301–315.
20. GRAY, J.A. 1982. The Neuropsychology of Anxiety: An Enquiry into the Functions of the Septo-Hippocampal System. Oxford University Press. New York.
21. GRAY, J.A. & N. MCNAUGHTON. 1996. The neuropsychology of anxiety: reprise. In The Nebraska Symposium on Motivation, Vol 43: Perspectives on Anxiety, Panic, and Fear. R. Zinbarg, R.J. McNally, D.H. Barlow, B.F. Chorpita, and J. Turovsky, Eds.: 61–134. University of Nebraska Press. Lincoln.
22. HARNISHFEGER, K.K. 1995. The development of cognitive inhibition: Theories, definitions, and research evidence. In Interference and Inhibition in Cognition. F. N. Dempster and C. J. Brainerd, Eds.: 175–204. Academic Press. New York.
23. HINSHAW, S.P. 1987. On the distinction between attentional deficits/hyperactivity and conduct problems/aggression in child psychopathology. Psychol. Bull. **101:** 443–463.
24. HUGHES, C., A. WHITE, J. SHARPEN & J. DUNN. 2000. Antisocial, angry, and unsympathetic: "hard to manage" preschoolers' peer problems and possible cognitive influences. J. Child Psychol. Psychiatry **41:** 169–179.
25. IABONI, F., V.I. DOUGLAS & A.G. BAKER. 1995. Effects of reward and response costs on inhibition in ADHD children. J. Abnorm. Psychol. **104:** 232–240.
26. IABONI, F., V.I. DOUGLAS & B. DITTO. 1997. Psychophysiological response of ADHD children to reward and extinction. Psychophysiology **34:** 116–123.

27. KAGAN, J. 1997. Temperament and the reactions to the unfamiliar. Child Dev. **68:** 139–143.
28. KERR, M., R.E. TREMBLAY, L. PAGANI & F. VITARO. 1997. Boys' behavioral inhibition and the risk of later delinquency. Arch. Gen. Psychiatry **54:** 809–816.
29. KINDLON, D., E. MEZZACAPPA & F. EARLS. 1995. Psychometric properties of impulsivity measures: temporal stability, validity and factor structure. J. Child Psychol. Psychiatry **36:** 645–661.
30. LAHEY, B.B. & R. LOEBER. 1994. Framework for a developmental model of oppositional defiant disorder and conduct disorder. *In* Disruptive Behavior Disorders in Childhood. D.K. Routh, Ed.: 139–180. Plenum Press. New York.
31. LAHEY, B.B., I.D. WALDMAN & K. MCBURNETT. 1999. The development of antisocial behavior: an integrative causal model. J. Child Psychol. Psychiatry **40:** 669–682.
32. LOGAN, G.D. & W.B. COWAN. 1984. On the ability to inhibit thought and action: a theory of an act of control. Psychol. Rev. **91:** 295–327.
33. LYKKEN, D.T. 1957. A study of anxiety in the sociopathic personality. J. Abnorm. Soc. Psychol. **55:** 6–10.
34. MACCLEOD, C.M., M.D. DODD, E.D. SHEARD, *et al.* 2003. In opposition to inhibition. *In* The Psychology of Learning and Motivation, Vol 43. B.H. Ross, Ed.: 163–214. Academic Press. San Diego, CA.
35. MOFFITT, T. 1993. The neuropsychology of conduct disorder. Dev. Psychopathol. **5:** 135–151.
36. NEWMAN, J.P. & J.F. WALLACE. 1993. Diverse pathways to deficient self-regulation: implications for disinhibitory psychopathology in children. Clin. Psychol. Rev. **13:** 690–720.
37. NIGG, J.T. 1999. The ADHD response inhibition deficit as measured by the Stop Task: replication with DSM-IV combined type, extension, and qualification. J. Abnorm. Child Psychol. **27:** 391–400.
38. NIGG, J.T. 2000. On inhibition/disinhibition in developmental psychopathology: views from cognitive and personality psychology and a working inhibition taxonomy. Psychol. Bull. **126:** 200–246.
39. NIGG, J.T. 2001. Is ADHD an inhibitory disorder? Psychol. Bull. **127:** 571–598.
40. NIGG, J.T., L. BLASKEY, C.L. HUANG-POLLOCK & M.D. RAPPLEY. 2002. Neuropsychological executive functions and ADHD DSM-IV subtypes. J. Am. Acad. Child Adolesc. Psychiatry **41:** 59–66.
41. NIGG, J.T., L. BLASKEY, J.A. STAWICKI & J. SACHEK. 2003. Evaluating the endophenotype model of ADHD neuropsychological deficit: executive cognitive functioning in parents and siblings of children with DSM-IV ADHD combined and inattentive subtypes. Manuscript under review.
42. NIGG, J.T., O.J. JOHN, L. BLASKEY, *et al.* 2002. Big five dimensions and ADHD symptoms: links between personality traits and clinical symptoms. J. Pers. Soc Psychol. **83:** 451–469.
43. O'BRIAN, B.S. & P.J. FRICK. 1996. Reward dominance: associations with anxiety, conduct problems, and psychopathology in children. J. Abnorm. Child Psychol. **24:** 223–240.
44. OOSTERLAAN, J., G.D. LOGAN & J.A. SERGEANT. 1998. Response inhibition in AD/HD, CD, comorbid AD/HD+CD, anxious, and control children: a meta-analysis of studies with the stop task. J. Child Psychol. Psychiatry **39:** 411–425.
45. OOSTERLAAN, J. & J.A. SERGEANT. 1998. Response inhibition and the effects of reward and response-cost: a comparison between ADHD, disruptive, anxious, and normal children. J. Abnorm. Child Psychol. **26:** 161–174.
46. PATTERSON, G.R., D.S. DEGARMO & N. KNUTSON. 2000. Hyperactive and antisocial behaviors: comorbid or two points in the same process? Dev. Psychopathol. **12:** 91–106.
47. PENNINGTON, B.F. & S. OZONOFF. 1996. Executive functions and developmental psychopathology. J. Child Psychol. Psychiatry **37:** 51–87.
48. PLISZKA, S.R., J.P. HATCH, S.H. BORCHERDING & G.A. ROGENESS. 1993. Classical conditioning in children with attention deficit hyperactivity disorder (ADHD) and anxiety disorders: a test of Quay's model. J. Abnorm. Child Psychol. **21:** 411–423.
49. PLISZKA, S.R., M. LIOTTI & M.G. WOLDORFF. 2000. Inhibitory control in children with attention-deficit/hyperactivity disorder: event related potentials identify the process-

ing component and timing of an impaired right-frontal response-inhibition mechanism. Biol. Psychiatry **48:** 238–246.

50. POSNER, M.I. & M.K. ROTHBART. 2000. Developing mechanisms of self-regulation. Dev. Psychopathol. **12:** 427–441.

51. QUAY, H.C. 1988. Attention-deficit disorder and the behavioral inhibition system: the relevance of the neuropsychological theory of Jeffrey A. Gray. *In* Attention-Deficit Disorder: Criteria, Cognition, Intervention. L.M. Bloomingdale and J. Sergeant, Eds.: 117–126. Pergamon. New York.

52. RAINE, A. 1996. Autonomic nervous system factors underlying disinhibited, antisocial, and violent behavior. Ann. N.Y. Acad. Sci. **794:** 46–59.

53. RAINE, A. 2002. Biosocial studies of antisocial and violent behavior in children and adults: a review. J. Abnorm. Child Psychol. **30:** 311–326.

54. ROTHBART, M.K. & J.E. BATES. 1998. Temperament. *In* Handbook of Child Psychology. Vol 3. Social, Emotional, and Personality Development. N. Eisenberg, Ed.: 105–176. Wiley. New York.

55. SAGVOLDEN, T., H. AASE, P. ZEINER & D.F. BERGER. 1998. Altered reinforcement mechanisms in attention deficit/hyperactivity disorder. Behav. Brain Res. **94:** 61–71.

56. SCHACHAR, R., V.L. MOTA, G.D. LOGAN, *et al.* 2000. Confirmation of an inhibitory control deficit in attention-deficit/hyperactivity disorder. J. Abnorm. Child Psychol. **28:** 227–235.

57. SCHACHAR, R., R. TANNOCK & G. LOGAN. 1993. Inhibitory control, impulsiveness, and attention deficit hyperactivity disorder. Clin. Psychol. Rev. **13:** 721–739.

58. SEGUIN, J.R., B. BOULERICE, P.W. HARDEN, *et al.* 1999. Executive functions and physical aggression after controlling for attention deficit hyperactivity disorder, general memory, and IQ. J. Child Psychol. Psychiatry **40:** 1197–1208.

59. SERGEANT, J.A., J. OOSTERLAAN & J. VAN DER MEERE. 1999. Information processing and energetic factors in attention-deficit/hyperactivity disorder. *In* Handbook of Disruptive Behavior Disorders. H.C. Quay and A.E. Hogan, Eds.: 75–104. Kluwer/Plenum. New York.

60. SLUSAREK, M., S. VELLING, D. BUNK & C. EGGERS. 2001. Motivational effects on inhibitory control in children with ADHD. J. Am. Acad. Child Adolesc. Psychiatry **40:** 355–363.

61. SONUGA-BARKE, E.J.S. 2002. Psychological heterogeneity in AD/HD—A dual pathway model of behaviour and cognition. Behav. Brain Res. **130:** 29–36.

62. WAKEFIELD, J.C. 1992. Disorder as harmful dysfunction: a conceptual critique of the DSM-III-R definition of mental disorder. Psychol. Rev. **99:** 232–247.

63. WORLD HEALTH ORGANIZATION. 1993. The ICD-10 Classification of Mental and Behavioral Disorders: Diagnostic Criteria for Research. World Health Organization. Geneva, Switzerland.

64. ZENTALL, S. & T. ZENTALL. 1983. Optimal stimulation: a model of disordered activity and performance in normal and deviant children. Psychol. Bull. **94:** 446-471.

The Development of Affect Regulation: Bringing Together Basic and Clinical Perspectives

RONALD E. DAHL

Department of Psychiatry, University of Pittsburgh, Pittsburgh, Pennsylvania 15213, USA

ABSTRACT: Some discussion of the development of affect regulation in relation to two papers by Drs. Kalin and Leibenluft is provided. The goals are to frame the broader issues, including the conceptualization and definitions of affect regulation, to address questions about the development of affect regulation, and to consider ways to bridge between basic and clinical approaches to understanding disorders of affect regulation emerging in childhood and adolescence. The conceptual framework for affect regulation presented here focuses on interactions between cognitive systems and affective systems. It also appears that this area of research is at a very early point in its development—one rich with opportunities to bridge between basic research in affective neuroscience, developmental psychology, and developmental psychopathology, and holds great promise to advance understanding regarding the earliest roots of these disorders.

KEYWORDS: affect regulation; development; developmental psychopathology; mood

INTRODUCTION

The conference session titled "Mood Regulation: Individual Differences," focused on several interesting questions about the development of affect regulation. In addition to the goals of understanding the underlying mechanisms and normal development of affect regulation, the long-term goals of this research is aimed at generating new insights about affect *dys*regulation—questions relevant to understanding the roots of mental disorders in children.

For example, a key aspect of the paper by Dr. Kalin (this volume) examines the development of neurobehavioral systems involved in fear and defensive behaviors in primates as a way to gain insights into the development of anxiety disorders in children. The paper by Dr. Leibenluft (this volume) addresses questions about irritable mood and its relevance to pediatric bipolar disorder and other forms of childhood psychopathology. In trying to integrate these presentations it is important to place

Address for correspondence: Ronald E. Dahl, M.D., Department of Psychiatry, University of Pittsburgh, TDH E-724, Pittsburgh, PA 15213. Voice 412-246-5818; fax: 412-246-5880
dahlre@upmc.edu

Ann. N.Y. Acad. Sci. 1008: 183–188 (2003). © 2003 New York Academy of Sciences.
doi: 10.1196/annals.1301.019

these questions within a larger framework of understanding the normal development of affect regulation.

CONCEPTUALIZING AND DEFINING AFFECT REGULATION

One of the first steps is to begin with a definition of affect regulation. Within a wide spectrum of affective experiences (including the experience, expression, and interpretation of emotions) affect *regulation* represents the subset of processes involved in the control of feelings—particularly the strategic control of feelings in the service of a goal or purpose. The emphasis here is in on the modulation of affective experiences in *adaptive* ways. Typically, this modulation involves inhibition, delay, or altering emotional expression/behavior in ways that incorporate social rules, long-term goals, or avoiding future negative consequences. For example, a child crying in reaction to an immunization is not necessarily demonstrating affect regulation. However, if the same child is partially suppressing the cry with the goal of trying to meet social expectations of acting "big," this would represent affect regulation.

Ross Thompson[1] in a thoughtful discussion of affect regulation from a developmental perspective provided this widely referenced definition: "emotion regulation consists of the extrinsic and intrinsic processes responsible for monitoring, evaluating, and modifying emotional reactions, especially their intensive and temporal features, to accomplish one's goals."

From the perspective of affective neuroscience, it appears that most processes of affect regulation are organized in relation to two different types of goals: appetitive (seeking and obtaining rewards) and aversive (avoiding threats/punishments).

It is also important to acknowledge that these regulatory processes include both conscious as well as many unconscious processes organized around these principles of reward seeking and threat avoidance. That is, crucial aspects of affect regulation involve implicit learning of skills related to the control of affect that are occurring through patterns of learning, but are largely outside of conscious awareness.

Another aspect in defining affect regulation—one that often receives less attention—is to consider *what* is being regulated or controlled. At one level, affect regulation is aimed at the adaptive modulation of emotional *behavior* (e.g., emotional responses such as the control of facial expression, tone of voice, emotional verbalizations, or actions that are linked to strong feelings). However, affect regulation also includes adaptive modulation of an *internal state* that facilitates achieving a goal.

For example, fear evokes an increased state of arousal that can be adaptive in situations where increased physical and cognitive demands may be required to escape, fight, or problem-solve to deal with an urgent threat. However, excessive fear-arousal can be quite maladaptive, such as many people experience in the fear-provoking situation of giving a public speech. Learning to effectively modulate an internal state such as fear arousal in various emotional contexts and situations requires affect regulation skills that can facilitate a goal such as public speaking (or more generally, the ability to think clearly and control behavior in highly emotional situations).

This example has particular relevance in adolescence, when difficulties thinking clearly and/or acting responsibly under conditions of high arousal or strong feelings can contribute to a wide range of reckless behaviors, including many with severe consequences.

This conceptual framework for affect regulation involves interactions between cognitive systems (necessary for learned rules, future consequences, strategy, etc.) and affective systems (involved in the direct experience and expression of states of emotion and arousal).

THE DEVELOPMENT OF AFFECT REGULATION

From a developmental perspective, the establishment of early links between cognitive control and affective systems to serve goals begin early in childhood.[1–5] There are also major developmental changes in affect regulation that continue through adolescence. With the onset of puberty and the increasing independence and social challenges of adolescence, young people are experiencing new powerful emotions and the need to control their feelings in many highly arousing situations with progressively less parental/adult supervision.

The adaptive modulation of emotions underpins the development of a broader range of skills for navigating behavioral choices under conditions of strong affect. Normative adolescent activities—risk-taking, experimenting with rule-breaking, testing parental limits, early romantic relationships—invoke many strong and conflicting feelings. Learning to navigate and control such feelings in service to long-term goals and/or to avoid negative consequences creates enormous challenges in the lives of most adolescents. It is also important to consider that many of these situations involve *competing* emotional states, interactions between fears and desires, as well as the balance of long-term goals and consequences. For example, a young adolescent's first physical romantic encounters may create both terrifying and exciting sensations in the same moment. More importantly, problems in the development of affect-regulation skills or failure to establish adaptive ways to navigate strong feelings can have enormous long-term consequences in the health and well being of adolescents.

AFFECTIVE INFLUENCES ON DECISION MAKING

From a clinical and social policy perspective, there is increasing recognition of the importance of emotion in decision making, relevant to a wide range of risk-taking behaviors.[6–11] In many ways, this perspective is increasingly blurring the older traditional boundaries of cognitive versus emotional processes. This is important because the "decision" to engage in a specific behavior with long-term health consequences—such as smoking a cigarette, drinking alcohol, or engaging in unprotected sex—cannot be completely understood within the framework of "cold" cognitive processes (*cold* cognition refers to thinking processes under conditions of low emotion and/or arousal, while *hot* cognition refers to thinking under conditions of strong feelings or high arousal and may be much more important to understanding risky choices in many real life situations).

One example is illustrated by the differences between adolescents' understanding of the risks of pregnancy or HIV in the context of a health class and decision-making sequences in the heat of passion leading to high rates of unprotected sex. In the context of powerful feelings the "decision" to proceed or refrain from sex, and/or to use condoms may receive little influence from "cold" rational thinking processes. Behavioral choices under conditions of strong affect are difficult to influence by cool rational thoughts alone. Even when knowledge of risks and consequences do impact such behavior, it is often accomplished through indirect ways such as: (1) helping adolescents anticipate and avoid the "hot" situations that tend to "melt" logical decision-making processes; and (2) by strategically evoking strong counterfeelings (e.g., an adolescent on the verge of unprotected sex thinks about the risk of pregnancy or HIV in a way that creates a strong *fear* response). The general point, however, is that decision-making sequences regarding risky behavior in adolescence cannot be fully understood without considering the role of emotions, with key aspects of these "decision" processes involving interactions between thinking and feeling processes.

A second example to illustrate these concepts is to consider a young teen being pressured by friends to try smoking or drinking. His "decision" is unlikely to emerge simply from a logical evaluation of the benefits versus the risks of using these substances. Instead, it is quite likely that a complex set of competing feelings will exert a strong influence on his behavior, including the *fear* of being teased or rejected by his peers, the *anxiety* of being caught and punished by adults, the *excitement* of taking risks, and the *desire* to look tough and independent to impress friends.

It is also important to acknowledge that many of these emotional/motivation influences can influence behavior outside of any conscious awareness.[12,13] The domain of feelings (e.g., impulses, fears, desires, rewarding sensations, etc.) is also critically important to understanding the behavioral transitions from initial experimentation with a substance, to repeated use, to habitual use, to pharmacological dependence, because it appears that some of these "decisions" move even further from the domain of consciously weighed choices and increasingly "automatic" behavior as dependence develops.[14]

AFFECT DYSREGULATION: LINKS TO SPECIFIC CLINICAL DISORDERS

The concept of affect regulation is increasingly popular among many clinicians and investigators interested in developmental psychopathology. There is an inherent assumption, for example, that affective disorders involve dysregulation of affect. Yet, there is a relative lack of specificity in models regarding how affect regulation is altered in these disorders. Moreover, there is limited empirical evidence of specific changes in affect regulation.

This point can be illustrated by bringing an affect regulation model to the consideration of anxiety disorders in children and adolescents. At one level an anxiety disorder involves an increased and/or inappropriate activation of threat and arousal that leads to impairments in functioning. However, there are several competing hypotheses regarding possible changes in affect regulation. Is this due to a lower threshold to activate fear? An increased intensity of fear? Difficulties terminating fear once threat is activated? Normal fear responses that are activated in inappropriate contexts? Greater awareness/monitoring of internal state, leading to increased subjective distress related to the activation of normal fear responses? Each of these possibilities, or combinations of these changes, would lead to different hypotheses about the fundamental level of dysregulation.

The development of more specific models of affect regulation and dysregulation in the development of anxiety disorders in children can also be informed by several areas of basic research. As outlined in the paper by Dr. Kalin (this volume), studies of nonhuman primates are providing new insights into the basic mechanisms of fear processing and responses that can help to inform clinically relevant questions that cannot be addressed in human studies.

Similar types of specific questions can be posed regarding affect dysregulation in relation to major depression in children and adolescents. For example, is depression related to a lower threshold to activate negative affect (sadness)? Is it linked to longer duration or greater intensity of negative affect once this is activated? Does depression have more to do with decreases in the experience of positive affect? Is it related to decreased motivation to engage in rewarding activities? Altered monitoring/ interpretation of affective experiences? Or, is this primarily related to cognitive errors in interpreting emotional cues? Any or all of the preceding examples could apply to the affect dysregulation underpinning depression, yet some would lead to very different predictions in some type of experiments, and most importantly, have different implications regarding treatment and prevention strategies.

As discussed in the paper by Dr. Leibenluft (this volume), these questions about specific aspects of affect dysregulation become even more complex within the framework of early-onset bipolar disorder. It is important to break down these complex questions into simpler components, such as the questions about the conceptualization and measurement of irritability that she outlined. It is only by parsing these complex issues into testable hypotheses about specific aspects of emotion regulation that one can perform the kind of clinical studies needed to inform mechanistic understanding that can provide new approaches to early interventions.

Once these complex issues have been broken down into specific hypotheses about specific aspects of emotion regulation in the development of specific affective disorders, they can be tested within a framework of affective neuroscience. For example, several groups are using tools such as ERP and fMRI to examine specific aspects of fear processing in children with clinical disorders.[15–17]

SUMMARY

In many ways, this is an extremely exciting time in these areas of developmentally oriented clinical research. The field is at a very early point—one rich with opportunities—in the ability to bridge between basic research in affective neuroscience, developmental psychology, and developmental psychopathology, to begin to generate new insights regarding the earliest roots of these disorders. Progress will require a great deal of conceptual as well as methodological advances to help bridge between these different approaches. Conferences and discussions as are occurring under the auspices of this New York Academy of Sciences meeting represent key steps in these advances.

REFERENCES

1. THOMPSON, R.A. 1994. Emotion regulation: a theme in search of definition. *In* Child Development, Vol. 59(2/3). N.A. Fox, Ed.: 25–52. University of Chicago Press. Chicago, IL.

2. GARBER, J. & K.A. DODGE. 1991. The Development of Emotion Regulation and Dys-regulation. Cambridge University Press. Cambridge.
3. COLE, P.M., M.K. MICHEL & L.O. TETI. 1994. The development of emotion regulation and dysregulation: a clinical perspective. *In* Child Development, Vol. 59(2/3). N.A. Fox, Ed.: 73–100. University of Chicago Press. Chicago, IL.
4. KOCHANSKA, G., T.L. TJEBKES & D.R. FORMAN. 1998. Children's emerging regulation of conduct: restraint, compliance, and internalization from infancy to the second year. Child Dev. **69:** 1378–1389.
5. EISENBERG, N. & R.A. FABES. 1999. Emotion, emotion-related regulation, and quality of socioemotional functioning. *In* Child Psychology: A Handbook of Contemporary Issues. L. Balter and C.S. Tamis-LeMonda, Eds.: 318–335. Psychology Press. Philadelphia.
6. DAMASIO, A.R. 1995. Descartes' Error: Emotion, Reason and the Human Brain. Putnam. New York .
7. ZAJONC, R.B. 1980. Feeling and thinking: preferences need no inferences. Am. Psychol. **35:** 151–175.
8. SLOVIC, P. 1987. Perception of risk. Science **236:** 280–285.
9. BENTHIN, A. *et al.* 1995. Adolescent health-threatening and health-enhancing behaviors: a study of word association and imagery. J. Adolesc. Health **17:** 143–152.
10. SLOVIC, P. 2000. What does it mean to know a cumulative risk? Adolescent's perceptions of short-term and long-term consequences of smoking. J. Behav. Decis. Making **13:** 259–266.
11. LOEWENSTEIN, G. & J.S. LERNER. 2003. The role of affect in decision making. *In* Handbook of Affective Science. R. Davidson, K. Scherer, and H. Goldsmith, Eds.: 619–642. Oxford University Press. New York.
12. WHALEN, P.J., S.L. RAUCH & J.L. ETCOFF. 1998. Masked presentation of emotional facial expression modulate amygdala activity without explicit knowledge. J. Neurosci. **18:** 411–418.
13. JOHNSRUDE, I.S. *et al.* 1999. Conditioned preference in humans: a novel experimental approach. Learn. Motiv. **30:** 250–264.
14. LOEWENSTEIN, G.F. 1999. A visceral amount of addiction. *In* Getting Hooked: Rationality and Addiction. J. Elster and O.J. Skog, Eds. Cambridge University Press. Cambridge.
15. POLLAK, S. *et al.* 1997. Cognitive brain event-related potentials and emotion processing in maltreated children. Child Dev. **68:** 773–787.
16. PINE, D.S. *et al.* 2001. Cortical brain regions engaged by masked emotional faces in adolescents and adults: an fMRI study. Emotion **1:** 137–147.
17. THOMAS, K.M. *et al.* 1999. A developmental functional MRI study of spatial working memory. Neuroimage **10**(Pt. 1): 327–338.

Nonhuman Primate Models to Study Anxiety, Emotion Regulation, and Psychopathology

NED H. KALIN[a,b] AND STEVEN E. SHELTON[a]

[a]Department of Psychiatry, University of Wisconsin-Madison, Madison, Wisconsin 53711, USA

[b]Department of Psycholology, University of Wisconsin-Madison, Madison, Wisconsin 53711, USA

ABSTRACT: This paper demonstrates that the rhesus monkey provides an excellent model to study mechanisms underlying human anxiety and fear and emotion regulation. In previous studies with rhesus monkeys, stable, brain, endocrine, and behavioral characteristics related to individual differences in anxiety were found. It was suggested that, when extreme, these features characterize an anxious endophenotype and that these findings in the monkey are particularly relevant to understanding adaptive and maladaptive anxiety responses in humans. The monkey model is also relevant to understanding the development of human psychopathology. For example, children with extremely inhibited temperament are at increased risk to develop anxiety disorders, and these children have behavioral and biological alterations that are similar to those described in the monkey anxious endophenotype. It is likely that different aspects of the anxious endophenotype are mediated by the interactions of limbic, brain stem, and cortical regions. To understand the brain mechanisms underlying adaptive anxiety responses and their physiological concomitants, a series of studies in monkeys lesioning components of the neural circuitry (amygdala, central nucleus of the amygdala and orbitofrontal cortex) hypothesized to play a role are currently being performed. Initial findings suggest that the central nucleus of the amygdala modulates the expression of behavioral inhibition, a key feature of the endophenotype. In preliminary FDG positron emission tomography (PET) studies, functional linkages were established between the amygdala and prefrontal cortical regions that are associated with the activation of anxiety.

KEYWORDS: prefrontal cortex; fear; inhibition; EEG; CRF; amygdala; PET

USING RHESUS MONKEYS TO STUDY ANXIETY, EMOTION REGULATION, AND PSYCHOPATHOLOGY

Studies from our laboratory, and others, have demonstrated that the rhesus monkey is an ideal species to study mechanisms underlying the regulation of emotion as it relates to human psychopathology.[1-6] Rhesus monkeys and humans have similar-

Address for correspondence: Ned Kalin, M.D., University of Wisconsin-Madison Medical School, 6001 Research Park Blvd., Madison, WI 53711. Voice: 608-263-6079; fax: 608-263-9340.

nkalin@facstaff.wisc.edu

Ann. N.Y. Acad. Sci. 1008: 189–200 (2003). © 2003 New York Academy of Sciences.
doi: 10.1196/annals.1301.021

ities in social behavior, stress-related endocrine function, and brain structure, and rhesus monkeys display psychopathology that appears very similar to that of humans.[1] Of particular importance is the well-developed prefrontal cortex in the rhesus monkey and the rich bidirectional connections between the amygdala and orbitofrontal cortex.[7–9] These features distinguish primates and humans from other species and likely underlie key components of emotion regulation.[1,10] Furthermore, like humans, rhesus monkeys have a long period of maternal–infant nurturance, which is necessary for normal emotional, social, and physical development.[3] In addition, relatively subtle differences in primate maternal–infant interactions are associated with differences in the behavioral and biological reactivity of the developing offspring.[11–13] Studies from our laboratory demonstrate the scientific value of working across human and nonhuman primate species and the feasibility of using similar experimental paradigms in these species. For example, using functional imaging studies in humans, we and others identified the amygdala and key regions of prefrontal cortex as being involved in emotion regulation.[10,14] To understand the mechanisms underlying emotion regulation, we used the rhesus monkey to selectively lesion key components of this circuitry. In addition to studying the behavioral and physiological effects of these lesions, we are using positron emission tomography (PET) to understand the functional linkages between the amygdala and prefrontal cortex.

UNDERSTANDING INDIVIDUAL DIFFERENCES IN ADAPTIVE ANXIETY RESPONSES PROVIDES A FOUNDATION FOR A NONHUMAN PRIMATE MODEL OF ANXIOUS TEMPERAMENT

Our studies have used rhesus monkeys to understand mechanisms underlying adaptive anxiety and fear responses with the idea that this understanding will provide insights into mechanisms underlying anxiety-related psychopathology.[1,15] This approach has proved to be very useful, since we have characterized stable individual differences in behavioral inhibition, brain corticotropin-releasing factor (CRF) activity, and prefrontal electrical activity that are associated with a monkeys' degree of anxiety.[16–19] Furthermore, we demonstrated important behavioral and physiological parallels between monkeys and children with extreme behavioral inhibition and anxious temperaments.[16,18,20,21] Importantly, extreme and stable behavioral inhibition in children is associated with acute distress and increased risk of developing anxiety and disorders.[22,23]

Our initial studies established the human intruder paradigm as a reliable method to assess individual differences in monkeys' adaptive anxiety responses.[16] The human intruder paradigm consists of three changing conditions, all of which are stressful but vary in the challenge that is presented to the monkey. The test begins with the the test monkey's separation from mother or a conspecific, the alone condition (A). This elicits separation-induced distress responses—cooing vocalizations and increased locomotion. These defensive behaviors serve to maximize the opportunity of recruiting mother or other close conspecifics for help. During the no eye contact condition (NEC), which occurs next, a human intruder enters the test room and presents the profile of her face to the monkey. During NEC the monkey stops vocalizing, becomes behaviorally inhibited, and engages in freezing behavior. While freezing, the monkey remains still with a tense posture and continuously scans the environment. When the monkey senses threat in the environment and has not yet been detected by the potential predator, it attempts to remain inconspicuous by freezing. Finally, during the stare condition (ST), the monkey stops freezing and displays threatening behaviors as it is directly stared at by the intruder. When the monkey is detected and cannot

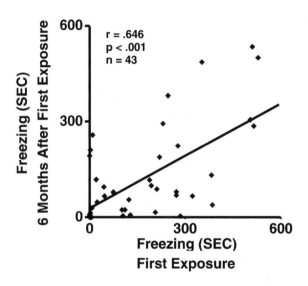

FIGURE 1. Freezing stability in monkeys tested at a 6-month interval.

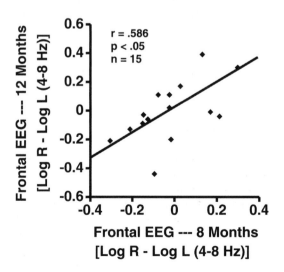

FIGURE 2. Stability of EEG asymmetry in monkeys tested at a 4-month interval.

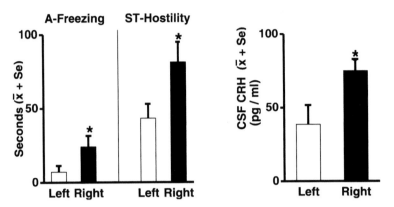

FIGURE 3. Factors associated with extreme left and right frontal activity (*$P < .05$).

flee, an adaptive response is to engage in defensive hostile behavior.[16] We consistently found stability in individual differences in the duration of NEC-induced freezing responses,[1,16] as well as in asymmetric patterns of frontal EEG activity and cerebrospinal fluid (CSF) CRF concentrations (FIGS. 1 and 2).[18,19,21]

To develop a model of human anxiety disorders and anxious temperament, we used an extreme groups approach. From a large group of monkeys, we selected those with extreme patterns of asymmetric right and left prefrontal electrical brain activity to explore the hypothesis that monkeys with extreme right frontal activity would have increased levels of anxiety as well as the physiological concomitants of anxiety. Extensive work in humans demonstrates that individuals with asymmetric right prefrontal brain electrical activity are more likely to have dispositional negative affect.[14] Similar to findings in humans, we found that monkeys with extreme right frontal EEG activity engage in more freezing behavior (FIG. 3) and have higher levels of cortisol.[17,18] In addition, monkeys with extreme right frontal EEG activity have elevated CSF CRF concentrations (FIG. 3).[19] This is important since CRF is a neuropeptide that mediates adaptive and maladaptive anxiety and depressive responses.[2] Based on these data, we proposed that the combination of excessive threat-induced freezing, extreme right frontal brain activity, and elevated cortisol and CRF constitute the anxious endophenotype.[18,19] These findings are analogous to the behavioral and physiological descriptions of extremely inhibited young children[20,24] that are at increased risk to develop anxiety disorders.

ENVIRONMENTAL AND GENETIC FACTORS THAT ARE IMPORTANT IN MEDIATING THE DEVELOPMENT OF INDIVIDUAL DIFFERENCES IN EMOTION REGULATION AND ANXIETY

The Serotonin Transporter Polymorphism

Recent studies suggest that polymorphisms in the serotonin transporter gene may increase the vulnerability to develop psychopathology. While it is likely that numerous genetic alterations are involved, the case for gene environment interactions in relation to this system is compelling. Serotonin (5-HT) has been implicated in the regulation of emotion, behavior, and vegetative functions.[25,26] The 5-HT transporter, located presynaptically, functions to regulate synaptic 5-HT levels by promoting the intracellular transport of 5-HT. It is now known that a functional polymorphism located on the promoter region of the 5-HT transporter gene affects 5-HT transporter expression and serotonin-related behaviors.[27,28] The polymorphism constitutes either a short (S) or long (L) allele, with the S allele being associated with decreased numbers of the 5-HT transporter and an overall reduction in 5-HT activity. Studies demonstrate that the S allele is dominant and when present, is associated with increased levels of anxiety and aggression, as well as with anxiety disorders and depression.[26–29] While the data have been generally consistent, a recent study reported that the L allele was associated with an increased incidence of shyness in children.[30] The factors that account for this discrepant finding remain unknown. The S allele has also been linked to brain reactivity. As was recently demonstrated with functional imaging, individuals with the S allele have heightened amygdala activity when presented with fearful facial expressions.[31] A similar polymorphism has been identified in rhesus monkeys (rh5-5HTTLPR) and is functional.[32–35] In a free-ranging group of rhesus monkeys, male adolescents homozygous for the S allele have been found to leave their natal group earlier than males with an L allele.[34] In a retrospective study of behavioral reactivity in rhesus infants, those infants with the S allele were found to be more behaviorally reactive to stress compared to those homozygous for the L allele, and some rearing x genotype interactions were noted.[35] A very recent finding has emerged from a prospective study of a large cohort of children demonstrating an interaction between the S allele and stress in mediating depression. In this study, a history of stressful life events was more likely to be associated with later depression in individuals with the S allele as compared to individuals homozygous for the L allele.[36]

Effects of Early Rearing Environment

Studies in rodents, nonhuman primates, and humans demonstrate the importance of early stress exposure in increasing the risk of developing accentuated behavioral and physiological reactivity to stressors later in life, as well as in the development of anxiety and depressive disorders.[2,37–41] Now human primate and rodent studies demonstrate that alterations in maternal–infant interactions can produce long-term consequences in offsprings' stress responsive hormonal and monoamine systems, and it appears that the effects of stress on maternal–infant interactions are key in mediating the deleterious consequences of early stress exposure.[2,41–43] In a series of rodent studies, Meaney and Plotsky showed that prolonged maternal separation results in less licking and grooming directed toward the infant. This change in the mother's interaction with her offspring is responsible for the offsprings' propensity to develop heightened behavioral and hormonal reactivity to stress exposure. These offspring also display increased brain CRF gene expression and alterations in hippocampal glucocorticoid receptors.[44,45] It also has been shown that individual differences in offsprings' stress responsivity are correlated with naturally occurring differences in the amount of licking and grooming a mother directs toward her pups.[46]

In primates, Harlow and others established the importance of early maternal–infant interactions in the development of normal social behavior and emotional re-

sponses.[47,48] Studies employing long-term maternal–infant separations or social isolation resulted in offspring that displayed heightened anxiety responses, depressive-
like behaviors, physiological alterations, and changes in brain monoamine systems.[4,5,42,43] A recent study in squirrel monkeys demonstrated that relatively brief in-
termittent separations during infancy resulted in selective increases in right
ventromedial prefrontal cortical volumes as assessed by MRI later in life.[49] This is of
interest since we demonstrated that increased right-sided prefrontal brain electrical
activity is associated with the anxious endophenotype in monkeys and dispositional
negative affect in humans.[14,17,18] Other work has demonstrated the negative consequences of prenatal and early postnatal stress on the development of rhesus monkeys'
pituitary–adrenal[42] and immune responses.[50,51] Recently, it has been reported that
nursery-reared rhesus monkeys have decreased CSF oxytocin concentrations.[52]
    Paradigms that are more subtle have been employed by primate researchers to
study the influences of early stress on an offspring's emotional development. In this
regard, a variable-foraging-demand (VFD) paradigm has been used, in which
through its unpredictability increases maternal frustration, which is hypothesized to
affect maternal–infant interactions.[12] Results in bonnet macaques demonstrate that
compared to offspring reared with their mothers in either high- or low-foraging-
demanding environments, offspring reared in the VFD environment display persistent alterations in social behavior including increases in anxiety and elevated concentrations of CSF CRF, somatostatin, 5-HIAA, and HVA.[53–56] While some
differences have been reported,[53,56] these characteristics are remarkably similar to
those we have characterized as the anxious endophenotype.[16] It is important to note
that the VFD manipulation is only presented for a few months and does not affect
the amount of food eaten by the developing infant. A series of studies in squirrel
monkeys performed by Lyons and coworkers has demonstrated the negative consequences of a high-foraging-demand environment on maternal–infant interactions
and offspring's development. These studies demonstrated that high-foraging-
demand mothers spent less time caring for their infants and the offspring had alterations in pituitary–adrenal and behavioral responsivity to stressors.[57] It is notable
that the old-world macaque are relatively unaffected by high-demand foraging and
are much more sensitive to VFD conditions. This difference between old- and new-
world species is likely due to differences in rearing styles, HPA regulation, and brain
maturation.

Model of Prefrontal Cortical, Amygdala, and Brain Stem
Interactions in Regulating Anxiety

    Data from humans with focal brain damage, imaging studies in normals, and pa-
tients, and preclinical models, implicate a diverse set of brain structures involved in
emotion processing.[14,58–60] In prefrontal cortex, the orbitofrontal and ventromedial
regions have been the most consistently implicated in emotion processing. These regions are important in predicting the rewards and punishments associated with future
behavior and are involved in long-term or habitual responding. Animal studies suggest that the ventromedial prefrontal cortex also plays a role in the extinction of acquired fears and anxiety.[60–62] It is for these reasons that we believe that the
orbitofrontal and ventromedial prefrontal cortex may play a role in maintaining the
expression of the anxious endophenotype. Some functional overlaps between these

prefrontal regions and the amygdala have been demonstrated,[63] and in primates these prefrontal regions are bidirectionally linked to the basolateral regions of the amygdala.[9] These linkages provide an opportunity to mediate the regulatory influences of the orbitofrontal and ventromedial prefrontal cortex on amygdala and vice versa. The amygdala plays an important role in cued fear conditioning.[60] Information enters the amygdala via the basolateral regions and is conveyed to the central nucleus of the amygdala (CeA). The CeA is highly interconnected with other subcortical brain regions, such as the brain stem, and has efferents that facilitate behavioral and physiological responses to acute stressors.[9,64] Other human studies suggest that the amygdala is important in detecting potential threats and ambiguities in the environment and that its activity rapidly habituates.[65,66] Consistent with this, our studies revealed a role for the primate amygdala in mediating behavioral and physiological responses to the acute presentation of fearful stimuli.[15] Our recent CeA lesion studies also suggest that the CeA modulates the expression of individual differences in adaptive anxiety responses that are known to be long term and stable (unpublished data). Furthermore, it was recently demonstrated that children who were extremely behaviorally inhibited early in life demonstrate increased novelty-induced amygdala reactivity as adults.[67] Other studies in rodents suggest that the bed nucleus of the stria terminalis has a role in the expression of anxiety.[68]

The lateral prefrontal cortex (LPFC) has traditionally been associated with cognitive processes such as attention and working memory;[7,8] however, more recent evidence suggests a role for LPFC in emotion regulation.[69–71] The LPFC is bidirectionally linked to the orbitofrontal prefrontal cortex, as well as the hippocampus and brain stem regions containing the monoamine nuclei.[7,72,73] The hippocampus plays a role in contextual fear conditioning[74–76] and the monomine brain stem nuclei are important in modulating diverse functions, including arousal. It is likely that through these connections LPFC activity influences emotion regulation and anxiety. Furthermore, the brain stem to LPFC pathways likely play a role in mediating the effects of stress and anxiety on working memory and attention.

Initial Studies Examining Brain Mechanisms Underlying Adaptive Anxiety and Fear Responses

To further understand the mechanisms mediating primate anxiety and its physiological concomitants, we performed studies lesioning the primate amygdala. Initially, we demonstrated that total ibotenic acid lesions resulted in blunted fear and hormonal responses to the presentation of novel fearful stimuli.[15] In this initial study we did not find a significant effect of the lesions on behavioral inhibition or freezing. In a more recent study, we selectively lesioned monkeys' CeA. The CeA is of interest, since in rodent studies it has been demonstrated to be a critical site integrating behavioral, autonomic, and physiological responses to stressors. In contrast to our earlier study, a preliminary analysis of the results demonstrates that CeA-lesioned animals engaged in significantly less behavioral inhibition or freezing behavior when exposed to the human intruder paradigm. However, the monkeys' ability to adaptively regulate this behavior across changing contexts remained intact. The lesions also resulted in reductions in plasma ACTH and CSF CRF concentrations (unpublished data). These findings suggest a role for the primate CeA in mediating reactivity to stress and fear-related events. Taken together with human functional imaging data, these findings support the possibility that over activity of the amygdala is involved in the pathophysiology of anxiety disorders. To further examine the role of other brain regions that are part of the circuitry underlying anxiety and its adaptive and maladaptive regulation, we currently are in the process of lesioning orbitofrontal frontal cortex.

Another approach that we are using to characterize the neural substrates underlying adaptive fear and anxiety responses has been to perform [18]FDG PET studies in monkeys to assess local cerebral metabolic rates of glucose utilization (lCMRGlc). The ability to combine selective lesion studies with functional brain imaging in our primate model allows us to understand mechanisms underlying the functional relationships among components of the circuitry underlying fear and anxiety. Furthermore, this approach has the potential to clarify findings from human functional imaging studies that cannot elucidate mechanisms. We recently acquired a MicroPET scanner specifically designed to image nonhuman primates. Initial results confirm our ability to achieve a resolution of two cubic millimeters and demonstrate anxiety-related activation of regions of monkey prefrontal cortex and limbic structures, some of which appear to be attenuated in monkeys with CeA lesions (unpublished data).

SUMMARY

Rhesus monkeys are ideally suited to investigate mechanisms underlying emotion expression and regulation. Our studies have emphasized using nonhuman primates to model adaptive and maladaptive anxiety responses in humans, focusing on behavioral and physiological aspects of anxiety and their underlying brain substrates. We have proposed the anxious endophenotype in monkeys, similar to extreme behavioral inhibition in children, as an early risk marker that predicts the development of anxiety disorders. The anxious endophenotype is a constellation of excessive threat-induced freezing behavior, extreme right-side frontal electrical brain activity, increased plasma cortisol, and increased CSF CRF. Studies using MicroPET imaging are underway to more precisely characterize the brain activation patterns that are associated with this temperamental disposition. Using lesioning strategies, we have also begun to investigate the role of the amygdala and orbitofrontal cortex in mediating various aspects of the anxious endophenotype, and initial results suggest involvement of the CeA in modulating the duration of threat-induced freezing and levels of CSF CRF. Future work will focus on the role of other brain regions, such as lateral prefrontal cortex, as well as genetic and environmental factors that alter the risk for the development of the anxious endophenotype.

ACKNOWLEDGMENTS

This work was supported by grants MH 46729 and MH 52354, by the HealthEmotions Research Institute, and Meriter Hospital. We gratefully acknowledge the technical assistance of Kim Lee, Helen Van Valkenberg, Katie Tietz, Meg Grimes, Jehan King, Tina Johnson, Andrew Roberts, Ph.D., Jeffrey Droster, Chris

Nizzi, and Richard Davidson, Ph.D. We also thank the staff at the Harlow Primate laboratory and the National Primate Research Center (this is NIH-NCPP publication number 43-009), UW-Madison for their support.

REFERENCES

1. KALIN, N.H. & S.E. SHELTON. 2000. The regulation of defensive behaviors in rhesus monkeys: implications for understanding anxiety disorders. *In* Anxiety, Depression & Emotion, Vol. 1. R. Davidson, Ed.: 50–68. Oxford University Press. New York.
2. BAKSHI, V.P. & N.H. KALIN. 2002. Animal models and endophenotypes of anxiety and stress disorders. *In* Neuropsychopharmacology: The Fifth Generation of Progress. K.L. Davis, D. Charney, J.T. Coyle, and C. Nemeroff, Eds.: American College of Neuropsychopharmacology. Philadelphia.
3. HARLOW, H.F. 1959. Love in infant monkeys. Sci. Am. **200**: 68–74.
4. MCKINNEY, W.T. & W.E. BUNNEY. 1969. Animal model of depression. I. Review of evidence implications for research. Arch. Gen.Psychiatry **21**: 240–248.
5. REITE, M. 1977. Maternal separation in monkey infants: a model of depression. *In* Animal Models in Psychiatry and Neurology. I. Hanin and E. Usdin, Eds.: 127–140. Pergamon Press. Oxford.
6. SUOMI, S.J. 1983. Models of depression in primates. Psychol. Med. **13**: 465–468.
7. GOLDMAN-RAKIC, P.S. 1987. Circuitry of primate prefrontal cortex and regulation of behavior by representational memory. *In* Handbook of Physiology—The Nervous System. V.F. Plum, Ed.: 373–417. Oxford University Press. New York.
8. FUSTER, J.M. 2002. Physiology of executive functions: the perception-action cycle. *In* Principles of Frontal Lobe Function. D.T. Stuss and R.T. Knight, Eds.: 96–108. Oxford University Press. New York.
9. AMARAL, D.G. *et al.* 1992. Anatomical organization of the primate amygdaloid complex. *In* The Amygdala. J. Aggleton, Ed.: 1–66. Wiley-Liss. New York.
10. DAVIDSON, R.J. *et al.* 2000. Emotion, plasticity, context, and regulation: perspectives from affective neuroscience. Psychol. Bull. **126**: 890–909.
11. ROSENBLUM, L.A. & G.S. PAULLY. 1984. The effects of varying environmental demands on maternal and infant behavior. Child Dev. **55**: 305–14.
12. ANDREWS, M.W. & L.A. ROSENBLUM. 1991. Attachment in monkey infants raised in variable- and low-demand environments. Child Dev. **62**: 686–693.
13. ANDREWS, M.W. & L.A. ROSENBLUM. 1994. The development of affiliative and agonistic social patterns in differentially reared monkeys. Child Dev. **65**: 1398–1404.
14. DAVIDSON, R.J. 2002. Anxiety and affective style: role of prefrontal cortex and amygdala. Biol. Psychiatry **51**: 68–80.
15. KALIN, N.H. *et al.* 2001. The primate amygdala mediates acute fear but not the behavioral and physiological components of anxious temperament. J. Neurosci. **21**: 2067–2074.
16. KALIN, N.H. & S.E. SHELTON. 1989. Defensive behaviors in infant rhesus monkeys: environmental cues and neurochemical regulation. Science **243**: 1718–1721.
17. KALIN, N.H. *et al.* 1998. Individual differences in freezing and cortisol in infant and mother rhesus monkeys. Behav. Neurosci. **112**: 1–4.
18. KALIN, N.H. *et al.* 1998. Asymmetric frontal brain activity, cortisol, and behavior associated with fearful temperaments in rhesus monkeys. Behav. Neurosci. **112**: 286–292.
19. KALIN, N.H., S.E. SHELTON & R.J. DAVIDSON. 2000. Cerebrospinal fluid corticotropin releasing hormone levels are stable in monkeys with patterns of brain activity associated with fearful temperament. Biol. Psychiatry **47**: 579–585.
20. KAGAN, J., J.S. REZNICK & N. SNIDMAN. 1988. Biological bases of childhood shyness. Science **240**: 167–171.
21. DAVIDSON, R.J., N.H. KALIN & S.E. SHELTON. 1992. Lateralized effects of diazepam on frontal brain electrical asymmetries in rhesus monkeys. Biol. Psychiatry **32**: 438–451.
22. BIEDERMAN, J. *et al.* 1990. Psychiatric correlates of behavioral inhibition in young children of parents with and without psychiatric disorders. Arch. Gen. Psychiatry **47**: 21–26.

23. HIRSHFELD, D.R. *et al.* 1993. A 3-year follow-up of children with and without behavioral inhibition. J. Am. Acad. Child Adolesc. Psychiatry **32:** 814–821.
24. BUSS, K.A. *et al.* 2003. Right frontal brain activity, cortisol, and withdrawal behavior in 6-month-old infants. Behav. Neurosci. **117:** 11–20.
25. LUCKI, I. 1998. The spectrum of behaviors influenced by serotonin. Biol. Psychiatry **44:** 151–162.
26. GREENBURG, B.D. *et al.* 2000. Association between the serotonin transporter promotor polymorphism and personality traits in a primarily female population sample. Am. J. Med. Genet. **96:** 202–216.
27. LESCH, K.P. *et al.* 1996. Association of anxiety-related traits with a polymorphism in the serotonin transporter gene regulatory region. Science **274:** 1527–1531.
28. HAHN, M.K. & R.D. BLAKELY. 2002. Monoamine transporter gene structure and polymorphisms in relation to psychiatric and other complex disorders. Pharmacogenom. J. **2:** 217–235.
29. MAZZANTI, C.M. *et al.* 1998. Role of the serotonin transporter polymorchism in anxiety-related traits. Arch. Gen. Psychiatry **55:** 936–940.
30. ARBELLE, S. *et al.* 2003. Relation of shyness in grade school children to the genotype for the long form of the serotonin transporter promoter region polymorphism. Am. J. Psychiatry **160:** 671–676.
31. HARIRI, A.R. *et al.* 2002. Serotonin transporter genetic variation and the response of the human amygdala. Science **297:** 319.
32. LESCH, K.P. *et al.* 1997. The 5-HT transporter gene-linked polymorphic region (5-HTTLPR) in evolutionary perspective: alternative biallelic variation in rhesus monkeys. Rapid communication. Neural Transmit. **104:** 1259–1266.
33. HEINZ, A. *et al.* 1998. Serotonin transporter availability correlates with alcohol intake in non-human primates. Mol. Psychiatry **8:** 231–234.
34. TREFILOV, A. *et al.* 2000. Natal dispersal in rhesus macaques is related to Serotonin transporter gene promotor variation. Behav. Genet. **30:** 295–301.
35. CHAMPOUX, M. *et al.* 2002. Serotonin transporter gene polymorphism, differential early rearing, and behavior in rhesus monkey neonates. Mol. Psychiatry **7:** 1058–1063.
36. CASPI, A. *et al.* 2003. Influence of life stress on depression: moderation by a polymorphism in the 5-HTT gene. Science **301:** 386–389.
37. HEIM, C. *et al.* 1997. Persistent changes in corticotropin-releasing factor systems due to early life stress: relationship to the pathophysiology of major depression and post-traumatic stress disorder. Psychopharmacol. Bull. **33:** 185–192.
38. HEIM, C. *et al.* 2002. Altered pituitary-adrenal axis responses to provocative challenge tests in adult survivors of childhood abuse. Am. J. Psychiatry **158:** 575–581.
39. HEIM, C. *et al.* 2002. The role of early adverse experience and adulthood stress in the prediction of neuroendocrine stress reactivity in women: a multiple regression analysis. Depress. Anxiety **15:** 117–125.
40. KENDLER, K.S., C.O. GARDNER & C.A. PRESCOTT. 2002. Toward a comprehensive developmental model for major depression in women. Am. J. Psychiatry **159:** 1133–1145.
41. ESSEX, M.J. *et al.* 2002. Maternal stress beginning in infancy may sensitize children to later stress exposure: effects on cortisol and behavior. Soc. Biol. Psychiatry **52:** 776–784.
42. CLARKE, A.S. *et al.* 1994. Long-term effects of prenatal stress on HPA axis activity in juvenile rhesus monkeys. Dev. Psychobiol. **27:** 257–269.
43. KRAEMER, G.W. *et al.* 1989. A longitudinal study of the effect of different social rearing conditions on cerebrospinal fluid norepinephrine and biogenic amine metabolites in rhesus monkeys. Neuropsychopharmacology **2:** 175–189.
44. PLOTSKY, P.M. & M.J. MEANEY. 1993. Early, postnatal experience alters hypothalamic corticotropin-releasing factor (CRF) mRNA, median eminence CRF content and stress-induced release in adult rats. Mol. Brain Res. **18:** 195–200.
45. MEANEY, M.J. *et al.* 1996. Early environmental regulation of forebrain glucocorticoid receptor gene expression: implications for adrenocortical responses to stress. Dev. Neurosci. **18:** 49–72.
46. LIU, D. *et al.* 1997. Maternal care, hippocampal glucocorticoid receptors, and hypothalamic-pituitary-adrenal responses to stress. Science **277:** 1659–1662.

47. HARLOW, H.F. & R.R. ZIMMERMAN. 1959. Affectional responses in the infant monkey. Science **130:** 421–432.
48. HARLOW, H.F. & M.K. HARLOW. 1969. Effects of various mother-infant relationships on rhesus monkey behavior. *In* Determinants of Infant Behavior, Vol. IV: 15–36.
49. LYONS, D.M. *et al.* 2002. Experience-dependent asymmetric variation in primate prefrontal morphology. Behav. Brain Res. **136:** 51–59.
50. Coe, C.L. *et al.* 1989. Influence of early rearing on lymphocyte proliferation responses in juvenile rhesus monkeys. Brain Behav. Immun. **3:** 47–60.
51. COE, C.L. *et al.* 2002. Prenatal stress diminishes the cytokine response of leukocvtes to endotoxin stimulation in juvenile rhesus monkeys. J. Clin. Endocrinol. Metab. **87:** 675–681.
52. WINSLOW, J.T. 2003. Rearing effects on cerebrospinal fluid oxytocin concentration and social buffering in rhesus monkeys. Neuropsychopharmacology **28:** 910–918.
53. COPLAN, J.D. *et al.* 1996. Persistent elevations of cerebrospinal fluid concentrations of corticotropin-releasing factor in adult nonhuman primates exposed to early-life stressors: implications for the pathophysiology of mood and anxiety disorders. Proc. Natl. Acad. Sci. USA **93:** 1619–1623.
54. COPLAN, J.D. *et al.* 1998. Cerebrospinal fluid concentrations of somatostatin and biogenic amines in grown primates reared by mothers exposed to manipulated foraging conditions. Arch. Gen. Psychiatry **55:** 473–477.
55. COPLAN, J.D. *et al.* 2001. Variable foraging demand rearing: sustained elevations in cisternal cerebrospinal fluid corticotropin-releasing factor concentrations in adult primates. Biol. Psychiatry **50:** 200–204.
56. ROSENBLUM, L.A. *et al.* 2001. Response of adolescent bonnet macaques to an acute fear stimulus as a function of early rearing conditions. Dev. Psychobiol. **39:** 40–45.
57. LYONS, D.M. *et al.* 1998. Postnatal foraging demands alter adrenocortical activity and psychosocial development. Dev. Psychobiol. **32:** 285–291.
58. DOLAN, R.J. 2002. Emotion, cognition, and behavior. Science **298:** 1191–1194.
59. DREVETS, W.C. 1998. Functional neuroimaging studies of depression: the anatomy of melancholia. Annu. Rev. Med. **49:** 341–361.
60. LEDOUX, J.E. 2000. Emotion circuits in the brain. Annu. Rev. Neurosci. **23:** 155–184.
61. MORGAN, M.A. & J.E. LEDOUX. 1995. Differential contribution of dorsal and ventral medial prefrontal cortex to the acquisition and extinction of conditioned fear in rats. Behav. Neurosci. **109:** 681–688.
62. MILAD, M.R. & G.J. QUIRK. 2002. Neurons in medial prefrontal cortex signal memory for fear extinction. Nature **420:** 70–74.
63. BAXTER, M.G. *et al.* 2000. Control of response selection by reinforcer value requires interaction of amygdala and orbital prefrontal cortex. J. Neurosci. **20:** 431–439.
64. DAVIS, M. 1992. The role of the amygdala in conditioned fear. *In* The Amygdala. J. Aggleton, Ed.: 255–305. Wiley-Liss. New York.
65. FISCHER, H. *et al.* 2003. Brain habituation during repeated exposure to fearful and neutral faces: a functional MRI study. Brain Res. Bull. **59:** 387–392.
66. DAVIS, M. & P.J. WHALEN. 2001. The amygdala: vigilance and emotion. Mol. Psychiatry **6:** 13–34.
67. SCHWARTZ, C.E. *et al.* 2003. Inhibited and uninhibited infants "grown up": adult amygdalar response to novelty. Science **300:** 1952–1953.
68. DAVIS, M. 1998. Are different parts of the extended amygdala involved in fear versus anxiety? Biol. Psychiatry **44:** 1239–1247.
69. WATANABE, M. 2002. Integration across multiple cognitive and motivational domains in monkey prefrontal cortex. *In* Principles of Frontal Lobe Function. D.T. Stuss and R.T. Knight, Eds. Oxford University Press. New York.
70. GRAY, J.R., T.S. BRAVER & M.E. RAICHLE. 2002. Integration of emotions and cognition in the lateral prefrontal cortex. Proc. Natl. Acad. Sciences USA **99:** 4115–4120.
71. OCHSNER, K.N. *et al.* 2002. Rethinking feelings: an fMRI study of the cognitive regulation of emotion. J. Cogn. Neurosci. **14:** 1215–1229.
72. ARNSTEN, A.F.T. & P.S. GOLDMAN-RAKIC. 1984. Selective prefrontal cortical projections to the region of the locus coeruleus and raphe nuclei in the rhesus monkey. Brain Res. **306:** 9–18.

73. BARBAS, H. & D.N. PANDYA. 1991. Patterns of connections of the prefrontal cortex in the rhesus monkey associated with cortical architecture. *In* Frontal Lobe Function and Injury. H.S. Levin, H.M. Eisenberg, and A. Benton, Eds. Oxford University Press. Cambridge.
74. PHILLIPS, R.G. & J.E. LeDoux. 1992. Differential contribution of amygdala and hippocampus to cued and contextual fear conditioning. Behav. Neurosc. **106:** 274–285.
75. ANAGNOSTARAS, S.G., G.D. GALE & M.S. FANSELOW. 2001. Hippocampus and contextual fear conditioning: recent controversies and advances. Hippocampus **11:** 828–831.
76. RUDY, J.W., R.M. BARRIENTOS & R.C. O'REILLY. 2002. Hippocampal formation supports conditioning to memory of a context. Behav. Neurosci. **116:** 530–538.

Irritability in Pediatric Mania and Other Childhood Psychopathology

ELLEN LEIBENLUFT, R. JAMES R. BLAIR, DENNIS S. CHARNEY, AND DANIEL S. PINE

Mood and Anxiety Program, National Institute of Mental Health, National Institutes of Health, Department of Health and Human Services, Bethesda, Maryland 20892, USA

ABSTRACT: Irritability is an important symptom in childhood psychopathology that has received relatively little research attention. Recent controversy concerning the diagnosis of mania in children has focused attention on how little is known about how to assess irritability in a systematic way, and about its diagnostic associations. For example, subtyping irritability according to course (chronic vs. episodic), precipitants, and family history may facilitate the identification of psychopathology and the study of pathophysiology. While normative and pathologic irritability can be differentiated reliably, the validity of the distinction is unclear. In addition, there is a need for scales designed to measure the severity of irritability in children with mood and anxiety disorders. In order to facilitate research, we propose a definition of irritability from the perspective of affective neuroscience. Because reactive aggression may be a helpful animal model for irritability, we review the neural circuitry mediating this behavior. Behavioral paradigms that evoke frustration, as well as those that assess the ability to inhibit a prepotent motor response, maintain attentional focus, execute response reversal, recognize angry faces, and regulate emotional responses, may be useful in the study of irritability. Examples of such paradigms are described, and the pharmacology of irritability is reviewed briefly.

KEYWORDS: irritability; childhood psychopathology; reactive aggression; childhood mania; bipolar disorder (BPD)

INTRODUCTION: CHILDHOOD MANIA AND IRRITABILTY

Irritability is among the most common symptoms in children presenting for psychiatric assessment and care. In the current psychiatric diagnostic system, irritability is a criterion for oppositional defiant disorder (ODD), major depressive disorder (MDD), and mania.[1] As discussed below, the fact that irritability is a core criterion for a manic episode in many standardized psychiatric diagnostic systems[2] has resulted in considerable controversy. The case of MDD is unique in that irritability only qualifies as a criterion for MDD before adulthood. This convention largely derives from clinical observation, as no large-scale epidemiological studies provide strong

Address for correspondence: Ellen Leibenluft, M.D., National Institute of Mental Health, National Institutes of Health, Department of Health and Human Services, Room 4N-208, 10 Center Dr. MSC 1255, Bethesda, MD 20892-1255. Voice: 301-496-9435; fax: 301-402-8497.
LEIBS@MAIL.NIH.GOV

Ann. N.Y. Acad. Sci. 1008: 201–218 (2003). © 2003 New York Academy of Sciences.
doi: 10.1196/annals.1301.022

TABLE 1. DSM-IV criteria for manic episodes

A. A distinct period of abnormally and persistently elevated, expansive, or irritable mood, lasting at least 1 week (or any duration if hospitalization is necessary).

B. During the period of mood disturbance, three or more of the following symptoms have persisted (four if the mood is only irritable) and have been present to a significant degree:

　　1) inflated self-esteem or grandiosity
　　2) decreased need for sleep (e.g., feels rested after only 3 hours of sleep)
　　3) more talkative than usual or pressure to keep talking
　　4) flight of ideas or subjective experience that thoughts are racing
　　5) distractibility (i.e., attention too easily drawn to unimportant or irrelevant external stimuli)
　　6) increase in goal-directed activity (either socially, at work or school, or sexually) or psychomotor agitation
　　7) excessive involvement in pleasurable activities that have a high potential for painful consequences (e.g., engaging in unrestrained buying sprees, sexual indiscretions, or foolish business investments)

C. The symptoms do not meet criteria for a Mixed Episode.

D. The mood disturbance is sufficiently severe to cause marked impairment in occupational functioning or in usual social activities or relationships with others, or to necessitate hospitalization to prevent harm to self or others, or there are psychotic features.

E. The symptoms are not due to the direct physiological effects of a substance (e.g., a drug of abuse, a medication, or other treatment) or a general medical condition (e.g., hypothyroidism).

SOURCE: Reprinted with permission from the American Psychiatric Association.[1]

evidence of a unique developmental relationship between irritability and MDD. In addition to being a criterion for ODD, MDD, and mania, irritability is also a major cause of morbidity and distress among children with pervasive developmental disorder (PDD), anxiety disorders, and attention deficit hyperactivity disorder (ADHD). To further complicate the situation, parents of toddlers and adolescents are quick to note that irritability is often observed in the course of normal development.

Recent research on pediatric mania highlights how little we know about the definition and measurement of irritability or about its association with psychopathology.[3,4] There is widespread agreement that the symptom is almost universal in children with mania. However, there is controversy about the role that irritability should play in the diagnosis of pediatric mania. In DSM-IV, the "A" criterion for a manic episode requires that a patient (child or adult) experience "a distinct period of abnormally and persistently elevated, expansive, or irritable mood" (TABLE 1).[1] However, researchers interested in pediatric mania debate whether irritability alone should warrant the diagnosis of juvenile mania (or, alternatively, whether the patient should also be required to have a history of "elevated or expansive mood"). In addition, there is disagreement as to whether *episodic* irritability should be required for the diagnosis of mania in children, or whether *chronic* irritability should suffice. Thus, some researchers argue that the "A" criterion should be stricter in children than adults (i.e., elation or grandiosity should be required for the diagnosis),[5] while others argue that the "A" criterion should be looser in children than adults (i.e., chronic, as well as episodic, irritability should meet the criterion).[3,6] To guide research in the near term, we have suggested a classification system for pediatric mania in which children are included in the "narrow phenotype" if they have clear episodes of mania meeting full DSM-IV duration criteria (i.e., 7 days for mania, 4 for hypomania) and a lifetime history of at least one episode characterizing by ela-

TABLE 2. Proposed phenotyping system for juvenile mania

I. Narrow phenotype

  The child has a lifetime history of at least one manic or hypomanic episode that met full DSM-IV criteria, including the duration criteria (7 days for mania, 4 days for hypomania) and during which the patient exhibited elevated or expansive mood and/or grandiosity.[5]

II. Intermediate phenotypes

  A. Mania or hypomania not otherwise specified (NOS): The child meets DSM-IV criteria for mania or hypomania, except that his/her episodes are between one and three days in duration.

  B. Irritable mania or hypomania: The child has distinct episodes of mania meeting DSM-IV criteria (including the duration criteria), but has never had an episode characterized by elevated or expansive mood.

III. Broad phenotype: Severe mood and behavior dysregulation

Inclusion criteria:

  i. Aged 7–17, with the onset of symptoms before age 12.

  ii. Abnormal mood (specifically, anger or sadness) present at least half of the day most days, and of sufficient severity to be noticeable by people in the child's environment (e.g., parents, teachers, peers).

  iii. Hyperarousal, as defined by at least three of the following: insomnia, agitation, distractibility, racing thoughts or flight of ideas, pressured speech, intrusiveness.

  iv. Compared to his/her peers, the child exhibits markedly increased reactivity to negative emotional stimuli that is manifest verbally or behaviorally. For example, the child responds to frustration with extended temper tantrums (inappropriate for age and/or precipitating event), verbal rages, and/or aggression toward people or property. Such events occur, on average, at least three times a week.

  v. The symptoms noted in numbers ii, iii, and iv above are currently present and have been present for at least 12 months without any symptom-free periods exceeding two months.

  vi. The symptoms are severe in at least one setting (e.g., violent outbursts, assaultiveness at home, school, or with peers). In addition, there are at least mild symptoms (distractibility, intrusiveness) in a second setting.

Exclusion criteria:

  i. The individual exhibits any of these cardinal bipolar symptoms:

  Elevated or expansive mood;

  Grandiosity or inflated self-esteem;

  Episodically decreased need for sleep.

  ii The symptoms occur in distinct periods lasting more than 4 days.

  iii The patient's illness meets criteria for schizophrenia, schizophreniform disorder, schizoaffective illness, PDD, or PTSD.

  iv. Patient's symptoms would meet criteria for substance use disorder in past 3 months.

  v. IQ < 80.

  vi. The symptoms are due to the direct physiological effects of a drug of abuse, or to a general medical or neurological condition.

SOURCE: Adapted from Leibenluft *et al.*[7]

tion or grandiosity. Alternatively, children are included in the "broad phenotype" if they have chronic irritability and hyperarousal[7] (TABLE 2).

Thus, when clinical researchers interested in pediatric mania meet, the talk quickly turns to irritability. How can normative irritability be distinguished from pathologic irritability, and how can its severity be measured? Is the distinction between episodic and chronic irritability important? Since irritability is among one of the most impairing symptoms of children with bipolar disorder (BPD),[5,6,8] how can it be treated?

Researchers interested in the pathophysiology of pediatric mania and other psychiatric illnesses have an additional set of questions regarding irritability. How can we define it within a coherent theoretical framework? Are there suitable animal models on which to base human research? What do we know about the neural circuitry and neurochemistry mediating irritable behavior, and how can we learn more?

The purpose of this paper is to review our current state of knowledge regarding irritability, with a particular focus on issues germane to pediatric BPD. First, we review current assessment tools and their approach to defining and operationalizing this important psychiatric symptom, and review what is known about the associations of irritability in childhood and adolescence with gender, age, and subsequent psychopathology. Then, we suggest a definition that may facilitate pathophysiological research as well as more precise measurement. Since reactive aggression in animals may be an appropriate model for human irritability, we review the neural circuitry mediating this behavior in mammals, as well as relevant neuroimaging studies in humans. Finally, we suggest behavioral paradigms that might be used to study irritability, and discuss the literature regarding its treatment. Throughout, we highlight the many important questions that remain regarding irritability and its role in childhood psychopathology.

THE EPIDEMIOLOGY AND MEASUREMENT OF IRRITABILITY IN CHILDREN

Because irritability is a diagnostic criterion for a number of psychiatric illnesses, standardized diagnostic interviews and rating scales have operationalized the concept, generally by using synonyms for the word itself or by using examples of behaviors observed in irritable people. For example, standardized semistructured diagnostic interviews define irritability as "anger; crankiness; bad temper; short-tempered; resentment or annoyance, whether overtly expressed or not; easily lose temper; touchy or easily annoyed" (KSADS)[9] or as "cranky; angry toward people you had no reason to; talk back; temper tantrum (DISC)."[10] The Children's Depression Rating Scale defines irritability as "grumpy, crabby, talked back, sassy, wouldn't do something your parents asked you to do."[11]

There is evidence that, in the case of diagnostic instruments, these descriptions are precise enough to allow trained interviewers to differentiate normative from pathologic irritability reliably. While reliability on individual items is not typically reported, research groups using the KSADS or the WAH-U-KSADS (a version of the KSADS designed specifically for the purpose of diagnosing mania in children) report high interrater reliability in the diagnosis of mania, MDD, ODD, and other illnesses characterized by irritability.[8,12] Recently, we analyzed data from a longitudinal, population-based study in which the DISC was administered to the same set of subjects in early adolescence, late adolescence, and early adulthood.[13–15] Using items from the diagnostic sections for ODD, MDD, and mania, we constructed chronic and episodic irritability scales, and found that the correlation of episodic irritability scores between early and late adolescence was 0.79, whereas the correlation of chronic irritability scores between those two time points was 0.56. In contrast, the correlation between episodic and chronic irritability scores measured *at the same time point* was considerably lower (i.e., 0.26–0.34). In addition to demonstrating that the constructs of episodic and chronic irritability are separable and that each has reasonable stability, these data indicate that interrater reliability is sufficiently high to yield consistent results over a period of approximately 2 years.

While trained observers appear to be able to differentiate normative from pathological irritability reliably, the validity of the differentiation remains unknown. Virtually no research attempts to delineate features distinguishing normal irritability from irritability that represents a manifestation of a pediatric mood or behavioral disorder, and few studies chart developmental changes in irritability in normative samples. Studies do examine how the prevalence of DSM-IV disorders characterized by aggression and oppositional behavior, as well as dimensional measures of these symptoms, fluctuate across age groups, genders, and social strata.[16–18] For example, overall acts of unrestrained aggressive behavior tend to decline as children mature, but rates of more serious, potentially dangerous aggression increase during adolescence, although few subjects ever commit such acts. Gender differences in rates of oppositional behavior diminish during adolescence, and this change occurs in the face of relatively marked overall increases in oppositional behavior among adolescents.

Using the CBCL, an empirically derived dimensional measure of developmental psychopathology, Achenbach studied how the item "stubborn, grumpy, irritable" mapped onto DSM-IV diagnoses in nonclinical samples. Originally, the symptom loaded on a factor associated with a syndrome currently conceptualized as ADHD[19] (in DSM-IV, mood lability and temper outbursts appear as associated features of ADHD). In more recent iterations, the symptom loads on a factor associated with aggressive behavior and symptoms of ODD.[18] The consistent loading of irritability on factors related to aggression reinforces the relevance of animal models of aggression to the pathophysiology of the symptom, as discussed below.

In normal development, individuals exhibit an increasing ability to control their behavior in the face of negatively experienced emotions as they mature from toddlers into school-age children and adolescents.[20–22] This maturation in emotion regulation is invoked as an explanation for age-related reductions in such expressions of irritability as temper-tantrum frequency and severity.[20] In order to better understand interindividual differences in emotion regulation, investigators have begun to connect research on the development of emotion regulation with research on personality organization. In personality research, irritability has been conceptualized as a manifestation of "big-five" higher-order personality traits, that is, as a high emotionality or neuroticism-related personality factor observable in children and adolescents as well as adults.[23] Developmental changes in irritability have therefore been seen as a normal aspect of both emotional maturation and personality formation. Nevertheless, as noted earlier, the boundaries between normal and abnormal manifestations of irritability remain poorly specified.

Thus, while pathologic irritability can be identified reliably, the validity of the differentiation remains unknown and depends on future research studying the association of different forms and degrees of irritability with psychopathology. In addition, the measurement (rather than simply the identification) of pathologic irritability poses a considerable problem and is an important area for future research. Indeed, a consensus has emerged among researchers in pediatric mania that the development of a sensitive and specific rating scale designed to measure irritability in children with psychopathology would be an important advance in the field. Rating scales for depression or mania include only one item on irritability, and in the case of the Young Mania Rating Scale, the anchors are not well-defined.[24] A mania scale now under development, the K-SADS Mania Rating Scale, is designed to measure mania in children, and has specific anchors for the irritability item.[25] However, it is unclear whether a single item can capture all of the clinically important dimensions of irritability with the precision needed for treatment trials in which this symptom is the primary outcome variable. These clinical dimensions include the duration of irritable states, the frequency of outbursts, and the severity of the behavior during the outbursts (e.g., verbal irritability, destruction of property, assaultiveness). The Overt Aggression Scale (OAS), which has been used in treatment trials, documents observable verbal and physical aggression, and has excellent reliability and validity.[26] However, the OAS does not document milder, but clinically important, manifestations of irritability (e.g., subjective experience, sarcastic retorts to requests). With the exception of the OAS and a rating scale designed for use in children with PDD,[27] we are unaware of rating scales that measure irritability in children with psychopathology. We are currently piloting such a scale, designed to measure the irritability seen in the children with the "broad phenotype" of BPD (TABLE 2).[7]

DEFINING AND SUBTYPING IRRITABILITY IN CHILDREN

Efforts to develop better instruments to measure irritability, study it in clinical and epidemiological samples, and understand its neurophysiology, would be advanced by a definition of the symptom that is clinically relevant and draws on current theories about emotion. We suggest that irritability can be defined as an emotional state characterized by having a low threshold for experiencing anger in response to negative emotional events. Anger, in turn, can be defined as a dysphoric state associated with aggressive impulses. The manifestations of anger span a continuum from subjective experience to behavior that includes verbal and/or physical aggression. In irritable children, common precipitants of anger include frustration of goal-directed behavior (i.e., interruption of consummatory behavior) and loss or threat of loss (often, separation from caregiving figures). We suggest that irritability can be viewed as one form of lability, where lability refers to the tendency to experience rapid shifts in emotional state. Thus, children with depression or other psychiatric illnesses may manifest, in addition to irritability, labile sadness, with the sudden onset of tearfulness or social withdrawal. Children with mania, on the other hand, experience not only irritability, but also labile sadness and labile euphoria (the latter consisting of sudden shifts into an excessively elated, "silly" state). This model must be substantiated by research demonstrating that irritability is a separate construct from sadness, depression, and elation and that, while these mood states may covary, they are distinguishable.

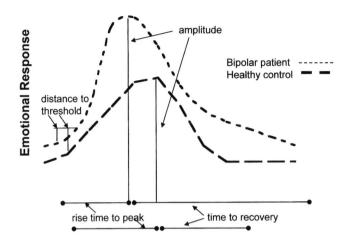

FIGURE 1. Affective chronometry (after Davidson[28]). (Reprinted from Leibenluft *et al.*,[108] with permission from Elsevier.)

Our definition of irritability can be viewed in light of Davidson's[28] suggestion that interindividual differences in emotional reactivity be described in terms of "affective chronometry," a systematic description of the course of an emotional response to an emotional stimulus (FIG. 1). Individuals differ in the threshold that such stimuli must exceed to elicit a response, as well as in the duration and amplitude of their response. Our definition highlights the fact that a stimulus that elicits a manageable, mild emotional response from a nonirritable child elicits a dramatic, intense response from an irritable child. While most 10-year-olds feel disappointed and unhappy when told to stop playing a video game and go do their homework, an irritable 10-year-old might cry, scream, and even become destructive in a similar situation. This example highlights that, while our definition of irritability centers on the magnitude of the stimulus needed to elicit the angry response, the more extreme forms of irritability are associated with responses that are of higher amplitude and longer duration than those of a child's unaffected peers.

It is also instructive to examine our definition of irritability within the framework of a large literature characterizing emotional states in terms of valence and arousal.[29,30] These authors use the term arousal to indicate the intensity of the activation evoked by an emotional stimulus, although the physiological mechanisms mediating arousal remain ill-defined.[30] Valence refers to the extent to which an emotional stimulus is appetitive or aversive, with positive valence stimuli evoking "approach" responses and pleasant subjective experiences, while negative valence stimuli evoke avoidant responses and dysphoria. Within this theoretical framework, irritability is clearly a high arousal state, but its categorization in terms of valence is problematic. That is, while anger and irritability share with negative valence states an association with unpleasant affect, they share with positive valence states an association with approach behaviors (since aggression can be viewed as an approach behavior). Other groups studying the psychology of anger have noted the difficulty of classifying this emotion within current theories of emotion;[31] further explorations of the psychobiology of anger should be helpful in this regard.

An important question for future work is the extent to which pathologic irritability should be divided into subtypes. As previously noted, in the case of pediatric mania an important question is whether episodic, but not chronic, irritability is characteristic of mania. Also as noted earlier, we found that these two types of irritability could be differentiated because, over the three waves of a longitudinal study, correlations within each subtype were higher than between subtypes. In the same study, we found that the irritability subtypes differed in terms of their associations with psychiatric diagnosis. Specifically, episodic irritability in early adolescence was associated with BPD and anxiety disorders in late adolescence and with BPD in early adulthood. In contrast, chronic irritability in early adolescence was associated with ODD and ADHD in late adolescence and with MDD in early adulthood.

These data demonstrate that this one method of subtyping may be important, and that other methods should be explored. For example, irritability subtypes differentiated by precipitant or context (e.g., separation vs. frustration) might be mediated by different neural circuits, and might require different biological and psychosocial interventions. In addition, it may be important to subtype irritable children according to family history of irritability (as well as, of course, familial psychopathology), since studies in adults indicate that the heritability of the symptom may be substantial.[32,33]

NEURAL CIRCUITRY MEDIATING REACTIVE AGGRESSION

Of the three distinct forms of aggression that have been distinguished at a neurobiological level through work with animals (predatory, intermale, and reactive), reactive aggression is the one that is likely to be relevant to the study of human irritability.[34] Reactive aggression, like human irritability, involves unplanned, "enraged" attacks on the object perceived to be the source of threat/ frustration. Considerable work has been conducted characterizing the subcortical neural circuitry involved in reactive aggression in nonhuman mammals.[34,35] A circuit has been identified that runs from medial amygdaloidal areas downward, largely via the stria terminalis to the medial hypothalamus, and from there to the dorsal half of the periaqueductal gray (PAG). This system is organized in a hierarchical manner such that aggression evoked from the amygdala is dependent on functional integrity of the medial hypothalamus and PAG, but aggression evoked from the PAG is not dependent on the functional integrity of the amygdala.[34–36]

While the medial hypothalamus and the dorsal half of the PAG mediate reactive aggression, the amygdala, orbital, and medial frontal cortex play a more modulatory role.[37] With respect to the amygdala, stimulation of the medial amygdala elicits reactive aggression,[34,35] but lesions of the amygdala may lead to either increases or decreases in the incidence of reactive aggression in both humans[38,39] and animals.[40, 41] This apparent inconsistency might be explained by recent data on the functioning of the amygdala. While much work has concentrated on the response of the amygdala to aversive stimuli,[42,43] it is now clear that the amygdala is also responsive to reinforcing stimuli.[44] This suggests that the amygdala could either upgrade (in response to an aversive stimulus) or downgrade (in response to reinforcement) the reactivity of systems to threat.[37]

Orbital and medial frontal cortex also modulate the brainstem systems mediating reactive aggression. Damage to medial frontal and orbitofrontal cortex is associated with increased risk for the display of reactive aggression in humans, whether the lesion occurs in childhood[45,46] or adulthood.[47] Moreover, neuroimaging work indicates that individuals with high levels of reactive aggression have reduced frontal lobe activity.[48,50] Indeed, Raine has demonstrated that it is only those violent individuals exhibiting reactive aggression who show reduced prefrontal cortex functioning, while violent individuals with goal-directed instrumental aggression show appropriate frontal activity.[48] Whereas most neuroimaging studies do not distinguish regions of frontal cortex, a PET study by Goyer *et al.*[49] did so and found that lower normalized cerebral blood flow in lateral orbitofrontal cortex (BA 47) was associated with a history of reactive aggression.

This finding of Goyer and colleagues (1994)[49] implicating BA 47 is of particular interest because BA 47 mediates two psychological processes that may be important in regulating reactive aggression: response reversal and social response reversal.[37] Frustration occurs when a behavior is not followed by an expected reward. Orbitofrontal cortex (and BA 47 in particular) is crucially involved in the computation of expectations of reward, identifying if expectations have been violated, and reversing responses in order to adapt to the changing contingencies.[50,51] Thus, these regions may be important in mediating reactive aggression in response to frustration.

With regard to social-response reversal, it has been suggested that, in addition to mediating reward expectancy, BA 47 may be involved in modulating behavior in response to social cues.[52,53] In nonhuman primates and adult humans without impulse-control disorders, angry expressions exhibited by authority figures (i.e., individuals high in the dominance hierarchy) curtail behavior that might violate social rules or expectations.[54,55] Individuals who exhibit extreme behavior in response to frustration or other negative emotional stimuli may have a deficit in recognizing, or responding to, such social cues. Neuroimaging work has shown that BA 47 is activated by negative emotional expressions, including anger, fear, and disgust.[56–58] Patients with lesions in this area are impaired in the ability to recognize facial expressions, particularly anger, and may display heightened levels of reactive aggression.[54,59] Patients with impulsive aggressive disorder, who display marked levels of reactive aggression, present with impairments in expression recognition that are particularly marked for angry expressions and with deficits in response reversal.[60] Finally, both alcohol and diazepam, two pharmacological agents associated with increased risk for reactive aggression,[61] selectively impair the ability of healthy individuals to process angry expressions,[62, 63] and this effect appears to be due to suppression of the response of BA 47 to angry expressions.[37]

STUDYING THE NEUROPHYSIOLOGY OF IRRITABILITY

If investigators are to study the pathophysiology of irritability in general and pediatric BPD in particular, it is important to develop behavioral paradigms that can be used to study the symptom in the laboratory and during functional MRI scanning. As described in the section on neural circuitry, paradigms assessing individuals' ability to execute response reversal and to recognize angry faces may have relevance to the pathophysiology of irritability. Indeed, we have evidence indicating that, compared to control subjects and to anxious or depressed children, children with BPD tend to misidentify anger in peers' faces, specifically, misidentifying other expressions (happy, fearful, or sad) as angry.[64] In this same data set, children with BPD were unimpaired in their ability to identify emotion on adult faces. These results differ, therefore, from those in adults with impulse-control disorders (see earlier), because the deficit appears in response to peers', but not authority figures', faces, and because the children with BPD overidentify anger, whereas the adults with impulse-control disorders underidentify anger. However, our results in children with BPD resemble those reported by Dodge and colleagues in aggressive children.[65,66] These data indicate that behavioral paradigms testing subjects' responses to angry faces may be important in understanding the pathophysiology of irritability. In addition, the data once again indicate the importance of describing subtypes of irritability, and the fact that the pathophysiology of irritability may vary developmentally and across diagnoses.

In addition to facial emotion recognition and paradigms testing response reversal, four other types of paradigms may be relevant to the study of irritability: those inducing a state of frustration, as well as those assessing the ability to regulate emotional responses, the ability to maintain attention, and the ability to inhibit a prepotent motor response. Studies using these paradigms in irritable children are just beginning, so data are not yet available to ascertain whether these children perform differently than do their unaffected peers. The paradigms are described briefly here in order to suggest possible avenues for future research and to encourage future task development.

Paradigms inducing frustration are relevant to the study of irritability because frustration is a common precipitant of disruptive behavior in irritable children. The development of frustrating paradigms is difficult because the reward (or punishment) must be sufficiently motivating while remaining ethically acceptable. In addition, the degree to which a task is frustrating may differ by age, gender, diagnosis, or other variables, complicating attempts to develop a generalizable paradigm. While paradigms have been developed to measure young children's ability to tolerate frustration and defer gratification,[20,67] these paradigms are not appropriate for older children. Koraly-Perez and Fox created a frustrating task suitable for use in older children by adapting the "affective Posner" task of Derryberry and Reed.[68,69] Derryberry and Reed modified the attentional cuing Posner task[70] by adding monetary rewards for correct responses (and monetary punishments for incorrect responses). Koraly-Perez et al. further adapted the task by "rigging" it so that children received feedback that their answers were too slow or incorrect, regardless of their actual performance. In our work with children with BPD, we have hypothesized that frustration will elicit more marked behavioral responses (refusal to complete the task, decreased reaction time, and decreased accuracy including greater anticipatory errors) in patients than in controls.

Since irritability can be viewed as a deficit in emotion regulation, other potentially relevant behavioral paradigms assess an individual's ability to dampen negative affect. For example, Davidson and colleagues showed subjects emotionally evocative pictures from the IAPS series and instructed them to increase or decrease their emotional response. Using this paradigm, they demonstrated that the augmentation of startle response by negatively valenced pictures was more marked when subjects increased their emotional response, compared to when they did not regulate their response.[71] Collaborating researchers then used fMRI to demonstrate that maintaining the emotional response after the offset of a negative picture (versus passively viewing the picture) was associated with prolonged amygdala activation, and that this activation correlated with subjects' self-reported negative affect.[72] Working along similar lines, we are developing a paradigm in which children are asked to regulate their response to IAPS pictures. While we anticipate that this paradigm will facilitate our study of emotion regulation in control and ill populations, its relevance to irritability may depend on the degree to which irritability is associated with deficits in the regulation of emotions other than anger, since the IAPS pictures are generally thought to evoke sadness, anxiety, fear, and happiness, but not anger.

Studies of interindividual differences in the ability to maintain attention (as measured, for example, by the Continuous Performance Test) may also be relevant to the study of irritability. Mischel *et al.*,[67] as well as Posner and Rothbart,[73] have suggested that, as children develop, their ability to tolerate frustration increases, in part because they are better able to maintain their focus on a relatively distal goal in the face of immediately frustrating stimuli. The role that attentional deficits may play in the pathophysiology of irritability is particularly germane to the study of children with BPD, given the high comorbidity of ADHD with pediatric BPD;[5,6] the observation that ADHD is frequently the first evident psychopathology in children with BPD and in children at risk for BPD;[74,75] and the fact that attentional deficits have been documented in adults with BPD.[76–78] In particular, research is needed that examines interactions between attention and variations in context or in the emotional content of stimuli.

A final type of behavioral paradigm that may further the study of irritability assesses an individual's ability to inhibit a prepotent motor response. The relevance of this type of paradigm, which includes continuous performance tests (CPT), go-no-go tasks, and the stop signal task,[79,80] rests on the hypothesis that the irritable behavior of some children (e.g., storming out of the room, punching the wall, assaultiveness) results from their inability to inhibit a motor response when emotionally aroused. Thus, whereas a control child would be able to control their motor impulse to hit a peer when rejected, an irritable child would not, resulting in an act of reactive aggression. Go-no-go or CPT and stop tasks, while related, actually engage subtly different psychological processes. While go-no-go and CPT tasks examine the degree to which prepotent responses can be inhibited very early in the process of motor execution, the stop task examines inhibition of responses that are in later stages of execution. We are currently testing whether children with BPD, like those with ADHD and other disruptive behavior disorders,[80] are slower on the stop task than controls in inhibiting a prepotent motor response. Recently, we added conditions to the stop task in which children are rewarded (with money) or punished (with money or airpuff) for their success or failure in inhibiting a motor response. Our goal is to test motor inhibition under conditions with and without these emotionally arousing features, comparing the behavior of children with BPD to that of children with ADHD and to unaffected children. Thus, as with tests of attention, it is important to develop paradigms that test motor inhibition in the context of emotionally arousing stimuli.

THE NEUROPHARMACOLOGY AND TREATMENT OF IRRITABILITY

Any discussion of the pharmacological treatment of irritability must begin by acknowledging the overriding importance of nonpharmacologic approaches in the treatment of irritability in children. Such approaches include cognitive–behavioral treatment, family education about underlying psychiatric illnesses, and other techniques.[81,82] Regarding the neuropharmacology of aggression, this has been studied in rodents, cats, nonhuman primates, and humans. Animal studies have documented the role of a number of neurotransmitters, including glutamate (acting via NMDA receptors), peptides (substance P and cholecystokinin), norepinepherine (acting via alpha-2 adrenergic receptors), dopamine (acting via the D-2 receptor), GABA, and serotonin (5-HT) in regulating reactive aggression [for a review, see Siegel *et al.* (1999)].[83] With few exceptions (noted below), clinical trials have included adults, not children.

In considering the treatment of irritability in children with BPD, it is important to consider studies examining the impact of lithium and sodium valproate on irritability, since these mood stabilizers are commonly used in the treatment of both pediatric and adult BPD. Several studies in adults indicate that sodium valproate may be more effective than lithium in treating hostility in adults with mixed mania.[84] However, lithium is still more effective than placebo, and the differences between the two active treatments may reflect Type II error.[85] In addition to these data in BPD, the efficacy of lithium and sodium valproate in treating irritability has been examined in children with diagnoses other than BPD. A series of double-blind, placebo-controlled studies by Campbell and collaborators indicate that lithium is effective in the treatment of aggression in youth with conduct disorder (CD).[86,87] There also have been two negative studies of lithium in CD, although one only involved two weeks of treatment.[88,89] With regard to sodium valproate, a crossover study in adolescents with aggressive behavior found that active treatment was more effective than placebo in reducing such behavior.[90]

An extensive literature implicates 5-HT in the regulation of impulsive, aggressive behavior. This literature, which includes a few studies of children[91,92] and many more of adults[93,95] demonstrates that impulsive patients have reduced central 5-HT function. In addition, considerable evidence suggests that the relationship between 5-HT and aggression varies meaningfully as a function of developmental level.[96,97] Such variations appear to occur most consistently among children living in conditions of social adversity.[98] In addition, there is evidence in adults of a possible association between polymorphisms in serotonergic genes and impulsivity and/or aggression [for a review, see Lesch and Merschdorf (2000)].[99] Serotonergic knockout mice differ from controls in aggressive behavior and, in nonhuman primates, an interaction between 5-HT transporter genotype and rearing history may influence central 5-HT levels.[99] However, as with studies in children, other research suggests that the effects of molecular manipulations on the 5-HT system vary as a function of development.[100]

Building on this basic research, clinical investigators have studied the efficacy of serotonin reuptake inhibitors (SRIs) in decreasing irritability and aggressive behavior in adults with and without histories of depression. In a double-blind, placebo-controlled trial, Coccaro and Kavoussi[101] demonstrated that fluoxetine had an anti-aggressive effect in nondepressed individuals diagnosed with personality disorder. In a series of open and controlled studies, Fava and colleagues found that fluoxetine, sertraline, and imipramine decreased anger attacks in depressed individuals.[102] Large-scale trials of SRIs in children have tended to focus more on symptoms of anxiety or depression than on symptoms of irritability, targeting children who generally display higher levels of the former than of the latter. Studies specifically targeting the symptom of irritability may be warranted. Given the known antianxiety efficacy of SRIs in children, it might be interesting to test these agents in children whose irritable behavior is precipitated by separation or other loss. In children with BPD, SRI monotherapy is complicated by the potential of these agents to induce mania. However, it may be important to study the effect on aggressive behavior of SRIs in combination with mood-stabilizing agents.

ADHD and autism are two childhood-onset conditions that are often associated with irritability and aggressive behavior. Given the role of dopamine in mediating reactive aggression in animals, and the clinical association between ADHD and conditions characterized by aggressive behavior (such as ODD, CD, and BPD), the antiaggressive properties of stimulant medications have been studied. In general, studies of children with comorbid ADHD and CD find that such treatment decreases physical and verbal aggression.[103-105] As with SRIs, stimulant monotherapy in children with BPD must be approached with caution because of possible activating effects, but the careful use of stimulants combined with mood stabilizers may be appropriate.[106] With regard to autism, a recent study demonstrated the efficacy of risperodone, an atypical antipsychotic with both serotonin- and dopamine-blocking properties, in decreasing aggressive behavior in children with autism.[107]

In sum, considerably more research is needed to provide clinicians with guidance regarding the treatment of irritability in children. In cases where irritable behavior is associated with a diagnosis for which there are known, effective treatments, the clinician should begin with the treatment of the underlying illness. Thus, if the child's irritability is part of the clinical presentation of an anxiety disorder or depression, treatment with an SRI would be indicated. If the irritability is associated with ADHD, a trial of stimulants would be reasonable. Although there are as yet no placebo-controlled, double-blind studies of mood stabilizers in childhood BPD, open studies do indicate that these medications are effective in children, as in adults. Therefore, the clinician could treat BPD with mood stabilizers and monitor the treatment's effects on irritability and other symptoms. Indeed, when treating irritability, it is most important to operationalize the target symptom clearly and monitor systematically the treatment's effects.

CONCLUSION

As this review demonstrates, there is a significant disparity between the importance of irritability as a clinical symptom and the amount of research that has been devoted to it. Fundamental questions of definition and measurement must be addressed so that investigators can measure the prevalence of irritability in children with and without psychopathology. The development of appropriate behavioral paradigms will enable researchers to use neuroimaging and psychophysiological techniques to explore the neural circuitry underlying irritable, angry behavior. In this way, researchers working with humans will be able to build on the rich animal literature concerning the circuitry underlying reactive aggression. Such pathophysiological studies, coupled with clinical trials, should result ultimately in improved treatments for this important symptom in children.

REFERENCES

1. AMERICAN PSYCHIATRIC ASSOCIATION. 2000. Diagnostic and Statistical Manual of Mental Disorders, 4th ed., Text Revision (DSM-IV-TR). American Psychiatric Association Press. Washington, DC.
2. FEIGHNER, J.P., E. ROBINS, S.B. GUZE, et al. 1972. Diagnostic criteria for use in psychiatric research. Arch. Gen. Psychiatry 26: 57–63.
3. BIEDERMAN, J., R.G. KLEIN, D.S. PINE & D.F. KLEIN. 1998. Resolved: mania is mistaken for ADHD in prepubertal children. J. Am. Acad. Child Adolesc. Psychiatry 37: 1091–1096; discussion 1096–1099.
4. CARLSON, G.A. 1998. Mania and ADHD: comorbidity or confusion. J. Affective Disord. 51: 177–187.
5. GELLER, B., M. WILLIAMS, B. ZIMERMAN, et al. 1998. Prepubertal and early adolescent bipolarity differentiate from ADHD by manic symptoms, grandiose delusions, ultrarapid or ultradian cycling. J. Affective Disord. 51: 81–91.
6. WOZNIAK, J., J. BIEDERMAN, K. KIELY, et al. 1995. Mania-like symptoms suggestive of childhood-onset bipolar disorder in clinically referred children. J. Am. Acad. Child Adolesc. Psychiatry 34: 867–876.
7. LEIBENLUFT, E., D.S. CHARNEY, K.E. TOWBIN, et al. 2003. Defining clinical phenotypes of juvenile mania. Am. J. Psychiatry 160: 430–437.
8. BIEDERMAN, J., E. MICK, S.V. FARAONE, et al. 2000. Parsing the association between bipolar, conduct, and substance use disorders: a familial risk analysis. Biol. Psychiatry 48: 1037–1044.
9. KAUFMAN, J., B. BIRMAHER, D.A. BRENT, et al. 2000. K-SADS-PL. J. Am. Acad. Child Adolesc. Psychiatry 39: 1208.
10. COSTELLO, E.J., C.S. EDELBROCK & A.J. COSTELLO. 1985. Validity of the NIMH Diagnostic Interview Schedule for Children: a comparison between psychiatric and pediatric referrals. J. Abnorm. Child Psychol. 13: 579–595.
11. POZNANSKI, E.I. & H.B. MOKROS. 1985. Children's depression rating scale-revised. Psychopharmacol. Bull. 21: 979–989.
12. GELLER, B., B. ZIMERMAN, M. WILLIAMS, et al. 2001. Reliability of the Washington University in St. Louis Kiddie Schedule for Affective Disorders and Schizophrenia (WASH-U-KSADS) mania and rapid cycling sections. J. Am. Acad. Child Adolesc. Psychiatry 40: 450–455.
13. LEIBENLUFT, E., P. COHEN, J.S. BROOK & D.S. PINE. Irritability in youth: a community-based, longitudinal study of diagnostic associations and clinical course. Unpublished.
14. COHEN, P., J. COHEN & J. BROOK. 1993. An epidemiological study of disorders in late childhood and adolescence—II. Persistence of disorders. J. Child Psychol. Psychiatry 34: 869–877.
15. PINE, D.S., P. COHEN, D. GURLEY, et al. 1998. The risk for early-adulthood anxiety and depressive disorders in adolescents with anxiety and depressive disorders. Arch. Gen. Psychiatry 55: 56–64.
16. MOFFITT, T.E., A. CASPI, H. HARRINGTON & B.J. MILNE. 2002. Males on the life-course-persistent and adolescence-limited antisocial pathways: follow-up at age 26 years. Dev. Psychopathol. 14: 179–207.
17. ANGOLD, A., E.J. COSTELLO & C.M. WORTHMAN. 1998. Puberty and depression: the roles of age, pubertal status and pubertal timing. Psychol. Med. 28: 51–61.
18. ACHENBACH, T. 1991. Manual for the Child Behavior Checklist/4-18 and 1991 Profile. University of Vermont, Department of Psychiatry. Burlington, VT.
19. ACHENBACH, T.M. 1966. The classification of children's psychiatric symptoms: a factor-analytic study. Psychol. Monogr. 80: 1–37.
20. KOCHANSKA, G., K.T. MURRAY & E.T. HARLAN. 2000. Effortful control in early childhood: continuity and change, antecedents, and implications for social development. Dev. Psychol. 36: 220–232.
21. ROTHBART, M.K., S.A. AHADI & D.E. EVANS. 2000. Temperament and personality: origins and outcomes. J. Pers. Soc. Psychol. 78: 122–135.
22. LARSON, R.W., G. MONETA, M.H. RICHARDS & S. WILSON. 2002. Continuity, stability, and change in daily emotional experience across adolescence. Child Dev. 73: 1151–1165.

23. SHINER, R. & A. CASPI. 2003. Personality differences in childhood and adolescence: measurement, development, and consequences. J. Child Psychol. Psychiatry **44:** 2–32.
24. YOUNG, R.C., J.T. BIGGS, V.E. ZIEGLER & D.A. MEYER. 1978. A rating scale for mania: reliability, validity and sensitivity. Br. J. Psychiatry **133:** 429–435.
25. AXELSON, D., B. BIRMAHER, D. BRENT, *et al.* A preliminary study of the KSADS mania rating scale for childen and adolescents. J. Child Adolesc. Psychopharm. In press.
26. VITIELLO, B. & D.M. STOFF. 1997. Subtypes of aggression and their relevance to child psychiatry. J. Am. Acad. Child Adolesc. Psychiatry **36:** 307–315.
27. MARSHBURN, E.C. & M.G. AMAN. 1992. Factor validity and norms for the aberrant behavior checklist in a community sample of children with mental retardation. J. Autism Dev. Disord. **22:** 357–373.
28. DAVIDSON, R. 1998. Affective style and affective disorders: perspectives from affective neuroscience. Cogn. Emotion **12:** 307–330.
29. DAVIDSON, R.J. & W. IRWIN. 1999. The functional neuroanatomy of emotion and affective style. Trends Cogn. Sci. **3:** 11–21.
30. LANG, P.J., M.M. BRADLEY & B.N. CUTHBERT. 1998. Emotion, motivation, and anxiety: brain mechanisms and psychophysiology. Biol. Psychiatry **44:** 248–263.
31. HARMON-JONES, E. & J. SIGELMAN. 2001. State anger and prefrontal brain activity: evidence that insult-related relative left-prefrontal activation is associated with experienced anger and aggression. J. Pers. Soc. Psychol. **80:** 797–803.
32. COCCARO, E.F., C.S. BERGEMAN & G.E. MCCLEARN. 1993. Heritability of irritable impulsiveness: a study of twins reared together and apart. Psychiatry Res. **48:** 229–242.
33. COCCARO, E.F. & R.J. KAVOUSSI. 1997. Heritability of aggression and irritability: a twin study of the Buss-Durkee aggression scales in adult male subjects. Biol. Psychiatry **41:** 273–284.
34. PANKSEPP, J. 1998. Affective Neuroscience: The Foundations of Human and Animal Emotions. Oxford University Press. New York.
35. GREGG, T.R. & A. SIEGEL. 2001. Brain structures and neurotransmitters regulating aggression in cats: implications for human aggression. Prog. Neuropsychopharmacol. Biol. Psychiatry **25:** 91–140.
36. BANDLER, R. 1988. Brain mechanisms of aggression as revealed by electrical and chemical stimulation: suggestion of a central role for the midbrain periaqueductal gray region. *In* Progress in Psychobiology and Physiological Psychology, Vol. 14. A. R. Morrison, Ed.: 135–233. Academic Press. San Diego.
37. BLAIR, R.J.R. & D. CHARNEY. 2003. Emotion regulation: an affective neuroscience approach. *In* Neurobiology of Aggression: Understanding and Preventing Violence. M. Mattson, Ed. Humana Press. Totowa, NJ. In Press
38. RAMAMURTHI, B. 1988. Stereotactic operation in behaviour disorders. Amygdalotomy and hypothalamotomy. Acta Neurochir. Suppl. (Wien) **44:** 152–157.
39. VAN ELST, L.T., L. LEMIEUX, P.J. THOMPSON & M.R. TRIMBLE. 2000. Affective aggression in patients with temporal lobe epilepsy: a quantitative MRI study of the amygdala. Brain **123**(Pt. 2): 234–243.
40. LILLY, R., J.L. CUMMINGS, D.F. BENSON & M. FRANKEL. 1983. The human Kluver-Bucy syndrome. Neurology **33:** 1141–1145.
41. ZAGRODZKA, J., C.E. HEDBERG, G.L. MANN & A.R. MORRISON. 1998. Contrasting expressions of aggressive behavior released by lesions of the central nucleus of the amygdala during wakefulness and rapid eye movement sleep without atonia in cats. Behav. Neurosci. **112:** 589–602.
42. DAVIS, M. 2000. The role of the amygdala in conditioned and unconditioned fear and anxiety. *In* The Amygdala: A Functional Analysis. J.P. Aggleton, Ed.: 289–310. Oxford University Press. Oxford.
43. LEDOUX, J.E. 2000. The amygdala and emotion: A view through fear. *In* The Amygdala: A Functional Analysis. J.P. Aggleton, Ed.: 289–310. Oxford University Press. Oxford.
44. BAXTER, M.G. & E.A. MURRAY. 2002. The amygdala and reward. Nat. Rev. Neurosci. **3:** 563–573.
45. ANDERSON, S.W., A. BECHARA, H. DAMASIO, *et al.* 1999. Impairment of social and moral behaviour related to early damage in human prefrontal cortex. Nature Neurosci. **2:** 1032–1037.

46. PENNINGTON, B.F. & L. BENNETTO. 1993. Main effects or interaction in the neuropsychology of conduct disorder? Commentary on "The neuropsychology of conduct disorder." Dev. Psychopathol. **5:** 153–164.
47. GRAFMAN, J., K. SCHWAB, D. WARDEN, *et al.* 1996. Frontal lobe injuries, violence, and aggression: a report of the Vietnam head injury study. Neurology **46:** 1231–1238.
48. RAINE, A., J.R. MELOY, S. BIHRLE, *et al.* 1998. Reduced prefrontal and increased subcortical brain functioning assessed using positron emission tomography in predatory and affective murderers. Behav. Sci. Law **16:** 319–332.
49. GOYER, P.F., P.J. ANDREASON, W.E. SEMPLE, *et al.* 1994. Positron-emission tomography and personality disorders. Neuropsychopharmacology **10:** 21-8.
50. COOLS, R., L. CLARK, A.M. OWEN & T.W. ROBBINS. 2002. Defining the neural mechanisms of probabilistic reversal learning using event-related functional magnetic resonance imaging. J. Neurosci. **22:** 4563–4567.
51. ROLLS, E.T. 2000. The orbitofrontal cortex and reward. Cereb. Cortex **10:** 284–294.
52. BLAIR, R.J. 2001. Neurocognitive models of aggression, the antisocial personality disorders, and psychopathy. J. Neurol. Neurosurg. Psychiatry **71:** 727–731.
53. BLAIR, R.J. & L. CIPOLOTTI. 2000. Impaired social response reversal. A case of 'acquired sociopathy.' Brain **123**(Pt. 6): 1122–1141.
54. ALEXANDER, M. & A.A. PERACHIO. 1973. The influence of target sex and dominance on evoked attack in Rhesus monkeys. Am. J. Phys. Anthropol. **38:** 543–547.
55. AVERILL, J. 1982. Anger and Aggression: An Essay on Emotion. Springer-Verlag. New York.
56. BLAIR, R.J., J.S. MORRIS, C.D. FRITH, *et al.* 1999. Dissociable neural responses to facial expressions of sadness and anger. Brain **122**(Pt. 5): 883–893.
57. SPRENGELMEYER, R., M. RAUSCH, U.T. EYSEL & H. PRZUNTEK. 1998. Neural structures associated with recognition of facial expressions of basic emotions. Proc. R. Soc. Lond. B Biol. Sci. **265:** 1927–1931.
58. KESLER-WEST, M.L., A.H. ANDERSEN, C.D. SMITH, *et al.* 2001. Neural substrates of facial emotion processing using fMRI. Brain Res. Cogn. Brain Res. **11:** 213–226.
59. HORNAK, J., E.T. ROLLS & D. WADE. 1996. Face and voice expression identification in patients with emotional and behavioural changes following ventral frontal lobe damage. Neuropsychologia **34:** 247–261.
60. BEST, M., J.M. WILLIAMS & E.F. COCCARO. 2002. Evidence for a dysfunctional prefrontal circuit in patients with an impulsive aggressive disorder. Proc. Natl. Acad. Sci. USA **99:** 8448–8453.
61. BOND, A.J., H.V. CURRAN, M.S. BRUCE, *et al.* 1995. Behavioural aggression in panic disorder after 8 weeks' treatment with alprazolam. J. Affective Disord. **35:** 117–123.
62. BLAIR, R.J. & H.V. CURRAN. 1999. Selective impairment in the recognition of anger induced by diazepam. Psychopharmacology (Berl.) **147:** 335–338.
63. BORRILL, J.A., B.K. ROSEN & A.B. SUMMERFIELD. 1987. The influence of alcohol on judgement of facial expression of emotion. Br. J. Med. Psychol. **60**(Pt. 1): 71–77.
64. MCCLURE, E.B., K. POPE, A.J. HOBERMAN, *et al.* 2003. Facial expression recognition in adolescents with mood and anxiety disorders. Am. J. Psychiatry In Press.
65. LOCHMAN, J.E. & K.A. DODGE. 1998. Distorted perceptions in dyadic interactions of aggressive and nonaggressive boys: effects of prior expectations, context, and boys' age. Dev. Psychopathol. **10:** 495–512.
66. CRICK, N.R. & K.A. DODGE. 1996. Social information-processing mechanisms in reactive and proactive aggression. Child Dev. **67:** 993–1002.
67. MISCHEL, W., Y. SHODA & M.I. RODRIGUEZ. 1989. Delay of gratification in children. Science **244:** 933–938.
68. PEREZ-EDGAR, K.A. Children's performance in the traditional and affective Posner as a function of temperamental shyness. Unpublished.
69. DERRYBERRY, D. & M.A. REED. 1994. Temperament and attention: orienting toward and away from positive and negative signals. J. Pers. Soc. Psychol. **66:** 1128–1139.
70. POSNER, M.I. 1978. Chronometric Explorations of Mind. Erlbaum. Hillsdale, NJ.
71. JACKSON, D.C., J.R. MALMSTADT, C.L. LARSON & R.J. DAVIDSON. 2000. Suppression and enhancement of emotional responses to unpleasant pictures. Psychophysiology **37:** 515–522.

72. SCHAEFER, S.M., D.C. JACKSON, R.J. DAVIDSON, *et al.* 2002. Modulation of amygdalar activity by the conscious regulation of negative emotion. J. Cogn. Neurosci. **14:** 913–921.
73. POSNER, M.I. & M.K. ROTHBART. 1998. Attention, self-regulation and consciousness. Philos. Trans. R. Soc. Lond. B Biol. Sci. **353:** 1915–1927.
74. CHANG, K.D., H. STEINER & T.A. KETTER. 2000. Psychiatric phenomenology of child and adolescent bipolar offspring. J. Am. Acad. Child Adolesc. Psychiatry **39:** 453–460.
75. DELBELLO, M.P. & B. GELLER. 2001. Review of studies of child and adolescent offspring of bipolar parents. Bipolar Disord. **3:** 325–334.
76. SAX, K.W., S.M. STRAKOWSKI, S.L. MCELROY, *et al.* 1995. Attention and formal thought disorder in mixed and pure mania. Biol. Psychiatry **37:** 420–423.
77. CLARK, L., S.D. IVERSEN & G.M. GOODWIN. 2001. A neuropsychological investigation of prefrontal cortex involvement in acute mania. Am. J. Psychiatry **158:** 1605–1611.
78. SWANN, A.C., P. PAZZAGLIA, A. NICHOLLS, *et al.* 2003. Impulsivity and phase of illness in bipolar disorder. J. Affective Disord. **73:** 105–111.
79. LOGAN, G.D., W.B. COWAN & K.A. DAVIS. 1984. On the ability to inhibit simple and choice reaction time responses: a model and a method. J. Exp. Psychol. Hum. Percept. Perform. **10:** 276–291.
80. OOSTERLAAN, J., G.D. LOGAN & J.A. SERGEANT. 1998. Response inhibition in AD/HD, CD, comorbid AD/HD + CD, anxious, and control children: a meta-analysis of studies with the stop task. J. Child Psychol. Psychiatry **39:** 411–425.
81. FRISTAD, M.A., J.S. GOLDBERG-ARNOLD & S.M. GAVAZZI. 2002. Multifamily psychoeducation groups (MFPG) for families of children with bipolar disorder. Bipolar Disord. **4:** 254–262.
82. CRAIGHEAD, W.E. & D.J. MIKLOWITZ. 2000. Psychosocial interventions for bipolar disorder. J. Clin. Psychiatry **61**(Suppl. 13): 58–64.
83. SIEGEL, A., T.A. ROELING, T.R. GREGG & M.R. KRUK. 1999. Neuropharmacology of brain-stimulation-evoked aggression. Neurosci. Biobehav. Rev. **23:** 359–389.
84. BOWDEN, C.L., A.M. BRUGGER, A.C. SWANN, *et al.* 1994. Efficacy of divalproex vs lithium and placebo in the treatment of mania. The Depakote Mania Study Group. JAMA **271:** 918-24.
85. SWANN, A.C., C.L. BOWDEN, J.R. CALABRESE, *et al.* 2002. Pattern of response to divalproex, lithium, or placebo in four naturalistic subtypes of mania. Neuropsychopharmacology. **26:** 530–536.
86. MALONE, R.P., R.P. MALONE, M.A. DELANEY, *et al.* 2000. A double-blind placebo-controlled study of lithium in hospitalized aggressive children and adolescents with conduct disorder. Arch. Gen. Psychiatry **57:** 649–654.
87. CAMPBELL, M., P.B. ADAMS, A.M. SMALL, *et al.* 1995. Lithium in hospitalized aggressive children with conduct disorder: a double-blind and placebo-controlled study. J. Am. Acad. Child Adolesc. Psychiatry **34:** 445–453.
88. RIFKIN, A., B. KARAJGI, R. DICKER, *et al.* 1997. Lithium treatment of conduct disorders in adolescents. Am. J. Psychiatry **154:** 554–555.
89. KLEIN, R.G. 1991. Preliminary results: lithium effects in conduct disorders. *In* CMR Syllabus and Proceedings Summary, Symposium 2. The 144th Annual Meeting of the American Psychiatric Association: 199–220. New Orleans, LA.
90. DONOVAN, S.J., J.W. STEWART, E.V. NUNES, *et al.* 2000. Divalproex treatment for youth with explosive temper and mood lability: a double-blind, placebo-controlled crossover design. Am. J. Psychiatry **157:** 818–820.
91. BIRMAHER, B. 1990. Platelet imipramine binding in children and adolescents with impulsive behavior. J. Am. Acad. Child Adolesc. Psychiatry **29:** 914–918.
92. STOFF, D.M., L. POLLOCK, B. VITIELLO, *et al.* 1987. Reduction of (3H)-imipramine binding sites on platelets of conduct-disordered children. Neuropsychopharmacology **1:** 55–62.
93. FILLEY, C.M., G.H. PRICE, V. NELL, *et al.* 2001. Toward an understanding of violence: neurobehavioral aspects of unwarranted physical aggression: Aspen Neurobehavioral Conference consensus statement. Neuropsychiatry Neuropsychol. Behav. Neurol. **14:** 1–14.
94. LINNOILA, M., M. VIRKKUNEN, M. SCHEININ, *et al.* 1983. Low cerebrospinal fluid 5-hydroxyindoleacetic acid concentration differentiates impulsive from nonimpulsive violent behavior. Life Sci. **33:** 2609–2614.

95. COCCARO, E.F., J.M. SILVERMAN, H.M. KLAR, et al. 1994. Familial correlates of reduced central serotonergic system function in patients with personality disorders. Arch. Gen. Psychiatry **51:** 318–324.
96. HALPERIN, J.M., J.H. NEWCORN, S.T. SCHWARTZ, et al. 1997. Age-related changes in the association between serotonergic function and aggression in boys with ADHD. Biol. Psychiatry **41:** 682–689.
97. PINE, D.S., G. WASSERMAN, J. COPLAN, et al. 1996. Serotonergic and cardiac correlates of aggression in children. Ann. N.Y. Acad. Sci. **794:** 391–393.
98. KAUFMAN, J., B. BIRMAHER, J. PEREL, et al. 1998. Serotonergic functioning in depressed abused children: clinical and familial correlates. Biol. Psychiatry **44:** 973–981.
99. LESCH, K.P. & U. MERSCHDORF. 2000. Impulsivity, aggression, and serotonin: a molecular psychobiological perspective. Behav. Sci. Law **18:** 581–604.
100. GROSS, C., X. ZHUANG, K. STARK, et al. 2002. Serotonin1A receptor acts during development to establish normal anxiety-like behaviour in the adult. Nature **416:** 396–400.
101. COCCARO, E.F. & R.J. KAVOUSSI. 1997. Fluoxetine and impulsive aggressive behavior in personality disordered subjects. Arch. Gen. Psychiatry **54:** 1081–1088.
102. FAVA, M. & J.F. ROSENBAUM. 1999. Anger attacks in patients with depression. J. Clin. Psychiatry **60**(Suppl. 15): 21–24.
103. KLEIN, R.G., H. ABIKOFF, E. KLASS, et al. 1997. Clinical efficacy of methylphenidate in conduct disorder with and without attention deficit hyperactivity disorder. Arch. Gen. Psychiatry **54:** 1073–1080.
104. SPENCER, T., J. BIEDERMAN, T. WILENS, et al. 1996. Pharmacotherapy of attention-deficit hyperactivity disorder across the life cycle. J. Am. Acad. Child Adolesc. Psychiatry **35:** 409–432.
105. CONNOR, D.F., S.J. GLATT, I.D. LOPEZ, et al. 2002. Psychopharmacology and aggression. I: A meta-analysis of stimulant effects on overt/covert aggression-related behaviors in ADHD. J. Am. Acad. Child Adolesc. Psychiatry **41:** 253–261.
106. CARLSON, G.A., J. LONEY, H. SALISBURY, et al. 2000. Stimulant treatment in young boys with symptoms suggesting childhood mania: a report from a longitudinal study. J. Child Adolesc. Psychopharmacol. **10:** 175–184.
107. MCCRACKEN, J.T., J. MCGOUGH, B. SHAH, et al. 2002. Risperidone in children with autism and serious behavioral problems. N. Engl. J. Med. **347:** 314–321.
108. LEIBENLUFT, E., D.S. CHARNEY & D.S. PINE. 2003. Researching the pathophysiology of pediatric bipolar disorder. Bio. Psychiatry **53:** 1009–1020.

Brain Imaging Studies of the Anatomical and Functional Consequences of Preterm Birth for Human Brain Development

BRADLEY S. PETERSON

Columbia College of Physicians & Surgeons and the New York State Psychiatric Institute, New York, New York 10032, USA

ABSTRACT: Premature birth can have devastating effects on brain development and long-term functional outcome. Rates of psychiatric illness and learning difficulties are high, and intelligence on average is lower than population means. Brain imaging studies of infants born prematurely have demonstrated reduced volumes of parietal and sensorimotor cortical gray matter regions. Studies of school-aged children have demonstrated reduced volumes of these same regions, as well as in temporal and premotor regions, in both gray and white matter. The degrees of these anatomical abnormalities have been shown to correlate with cognitive outcome and with the degree of fetal immaturity at birth. Functional imaging studies have shown that these anatomical abnormalities are associated with severe disturbances in the organization and use of neural systems subserving language, particularly for school-aged children who have low verbal IQs. Animal models suggest that hypoxia-ischemia may be responsible at least in part for some of the anatomical and functional abnormalities. Increasing evidence suggests that a host of mediators for hypoxic-ischemic insults likely contribute to the disturbances in brain development in preterm infants, including increased apoptosis, free-radical formation, glutamatergic excitotoxicity, and alterations in the expression of a large number of genes that regulate brain maturation, particularly those involved in the development of postsynaptic neurons and the stabilization of synapses. The collaboration of both basic neuroscientists and clinical researchers is needed to understand how normal brain development is derailed by preterm birth and to develop effective prevention and early interventions for these often devastating conditions.

KEYWORDS: magnetic resonance imaging; children; prematurity; cognition; outcome

INTRODUCTION

The public health ramifications of premature birth are profound. Infants weighing less than 1500 g at birth now represent nearly 2% of all live births in the United

Address for correspondence: Bradley S. Peterson, M.D., Columbia College of Physicians & Surgeons and New York State Psychiatric Institute, Unit 74, 1051 Riverside Drive, New York, NY 10032. Voice: 212-543-5330; fax: 212-543-0522.
PetersoB@childpsych.columbia.edu

Ann. N.Y. Acad. Sci. 1008: 219–237 (2003). © 2003 New York Academy of Sciences.
doi: 10.1196/annals.1301.023

States,[1,2] and survival rates for these infants approach 85%.[3] The numbers of prematurely born infants surviving into later childhood, adolescence, and adulthood are staggering.

Functional Outcome

The adverse consequences of preterm birth have been increasingly well appreciated by medical professionals and researchers, but they have not been widely recognized yet by the lay public. The prevalence in this population of major neurodevelopmental handicaps, such as cerebral palsy and mental retardation, ranges from 12% to 32%, depending on the particular cohort and study.[4–8] The prevalence of less devastating and less obvious adverse neurodevelopmental outcomes is even higher. IQ scores in this population average 85, or one standard deviation below the population mean.[9] Even those with uncomplicated neonatal courses frequently have serious cognitive and educational difficulties,[10,11] and more than half require special assistance in school or education in full-time special education classrooms. By 8 years of age, nearly 20% have repeated at least one grade in school[12,13] and, frequently, more fail in school later as educational demands increase.[14,15] Rates of attention-deficit hyperactivity disorder, various anxiety disorders, disturbances in thought processes, schizophrenia,[16] and learning disabilities in this population are several times higher than in the general population.[8,10]

Preterm Birth and Brain Development

Fetuses born as young as 24 weeks gestational age, or in the late second trimester of pregnancy, are now routinely viable. The brains of these children must develop in an environment that differs vastly from its normally protective intrauterine environment. These babies frequently have serious respiratory illnesses and hypoxia that require intubation and mechanical ventilation, a variety of infections and sepsis, blood pressure abnormalities, intravenous feeding and malnutrition, growth retardation, intracranial hemorrhages, metabolic disturbances, hyperbilirubinemia, and they are placed in a noxious intensive care environment that isolates the infant from maternal tactile stimulation while exposing them to painful needle sticks and sensory stimulation that is far in excess of that experienced by term infants *in utero.*

Brain development during the late second and early third trimesters is normally a smoothly orchestrated series of complex and interrelated neurodevelopmental events. These events include neuronal migration, glial cell proliferation, axonal and dendritic spine elaboration, synapse formation, myelination, programmed cell death, and stabilization of cortical connectivity.[17–22] In a healthy intrauterine environment, this maturational program is presumed to be largely under genetic control. When the environment in which this brain is developing is sufficiently stressed, however, the unfolding of the maturational program can be seriously disrupted.

Regional Specificity

Because the pace of brain maturation varies by brain region,[23–25] the range of available adaptive responses to these stresses is thought to be regionally specific and to depend critically upon the nature and timing of the insult.[18,26–30] Birth early in or prior to the third trimester of gestation might therefore be expected to disrupt this maturational program in a regionally specific manner, and the resulting abnormalities in regional brain structure presumably would contribute to the long-term cognitive, behavioral, and emotional problems experienced by these children.

QUALITATIVE BRAIN IMAGING STUDIES

Early neuroimaging studies of prematurely born children were most often qualitative and poorly controlled. Published reports did consistently seem to indicate that children and infants born prematurely have elevated rates of anatomical brain abnormalities than children in the general population. These reported abnormalities included white matter damage[31–33] (particularly periventricular leukomalacia, or "PVL"),[34,35] cysts,[34] hemorrhage,[34] delayed myelination,[36,37] thinning of the corpus callosum,[33,38] ventricular enlargement[33] (especially of occipital horns[32]), basal ganglia hemorrhage,[34,39] thalamic lesions,[39] and brainstem abnormalities.[39] Several of these retrospective, qualitative studies suggested that these brain lesions might predict poor neurodevelopemental outcome.[7,31–33,36]

QUANTITATIVE BRAIN IMAGING STUDIES

Anatomic Abnormalities at Birth

Early quantitative measurements of brain volume in term and preterm infants came primarily from one investigative group.[40–42] In one study of 10 preterm infants with PVL, 10 preterm infants without PVL, and 14 term controls, these investigators found reduced cortical gray matter only in the preterm infants who had PVL.[41] White matter volumes, however, did not differ across any of the diagnostic groups. CSF volumes were greater in preterm infants, whether or not they had PVL. In a subsequent study, 11 preterm infants unexposed to postnatal steroid treatment did not differ significantly from 14 term infants in volumes of total cortical gray matter or ventricular CSF.[42] The 7 preterm infants who had been treated with dexamethasone had reduced cortical gray matter volumes compared with volumes in the other groups.[42] Methods for tracking white matter fibers using diffusion tensor imaging suggested the presence of disturbed structural organization of these myelinated fibers in preterm infants.[43] These initial studies also suggested that cortical gray matter volumes in the absence of white matter injury did not differ in preterm infants from values in term controls.

We subsequently measured regional brain volumes in 10 preterm and 14 term infants scanned as close as possible to their term due dates.[44] In contrast to the earlier studies of preterm infants, we were able to subdivide gray and white matter into anatomically distinct subregions (FIG. 1). Cortical gray matter volumes in the preterm group were reduced primarily in the parieto-occipital regions and, to a lesser extent, in sensorimotor cortices bilaterally. Few differences were found in white matter volumes. Volumes of the occipital and temporal horns of the lateral ventricles, however, were increased by 300% in the preterm infants. Volumes of the sensorimotor and temporal regions correlated significantly with measures of cognitive development at

20 months corrected age (FIG. 2). These findings suggest that morphological abnormalities that are specific to tissue type and to brain region are present soon after preterm infants are born. Volume reductions are most prominent in gray matter and in the parietal cortices, with concomitant enlargement of the occipital horns of the lateral ventricles. These structural abnormalities could be predictors of long-term out-

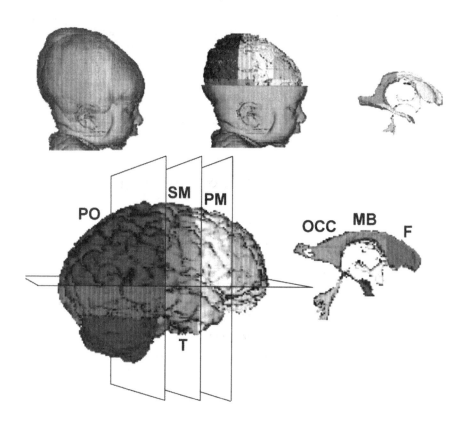

FIGURE 1. Top Row: Regional volumes in infant brains The subdivided cortical surface of an infant brain is visible on the left beneath the scalp, which is peeled away in the *top middle figure*. The subdivided ventricular system of the infant brain is shown on the *top right*. **Bottom Row:** Regional brain volumes in school-aged children. The subdivided cerebral cortex is seen, fully exposed, on the *bottom left*. Subdivisions are defined using four 2-dimensional planes: three coronal planes (one each positioned through the anterior commissure, posterior commissure, and anteriormost extent of the genu of the corpus callosum) and one axial plane (containing the anterior and posterior commissures). The cerebral hemispheres are separated using a curvilinear (cubic splines) plane positioned through standard midline landmarks. The subdivided ventricular system of the school-aged child is seen on the *bottom right*. PO = parieto-occipital; SM = sensorimotor; PM = premotor; T = temporal; OCC = occipital horn; MB = midbody of lateral ventricles; F = frontal horn.

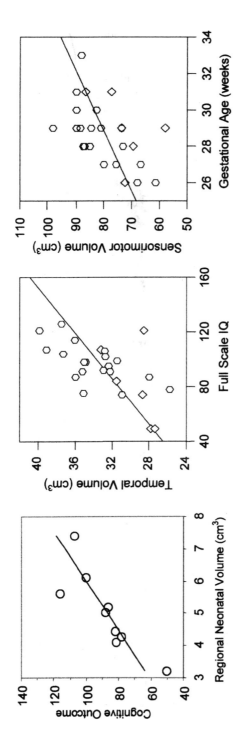

FIGURE 2. Regional volumes and IQ. Volumes are adjusted for height and sex. **Left:** Regional brain volumes in preterm infants at birth predicted mental developmental indices at 20 months corrected age. **Middle:** Full-scale IQ correlated positively with volumes of the right temporal regional in school-age children who were born prematurely. **Right:** Gestational age correlated positively with volumes of the right sensorimotor cortex of prematurely born, 8-year-old children.

come, and they may be good candidates for identifying infants who could be targeted for early therapeutic intervention.

Functional Abnormalities at Birth

Imaging studies of brain metabolism in newborn term infants suggest that resting metabolism is not uniform across the brain. Metabolism is generally low in the cortex at term, with the exception of relatively high metabolic rates in sensorimotor cortex. By 3 months postnatal age, metabolism increases in parietal, temporal, and occipital cortices. The frontal cortex is the latest cortical region to increase in its metabolism, not reaching the levels of other cortical regions until approximately 8 months of age.[4-47]

Substantial evidence has suggested that overall cerebral blood flow (CBF) may be reduced in preterm compared with term infants[48,49] and that the lowest blood flow values may be present in preterm infants who are mechanically ventilated.[48] In the context of this overall reduction in CBF, regional flow was found to be relatively greatest in the sensorimotor cortices of 12 preterm infants[50] studied with 99mTc-HMPAO single-photon computed tomography, similar to findings in term infants.[45-47] In contrast, measurement of blood flow velocities in the middle cerebral artery of 17 normoxemic, preterm infants and in 51 normal fetuses studied *in utero*, with both groups studied at 28 weeks gestational age, demonstrated a significantly greater *increase* in blood flow velocity in the preterm infants over the first 4 weeks of life than in same-age normal fetuses over the same time frame.[51] An increase in some aspects of the blood flow measure (viz., velocity at the end of diastole) was noted prominently even within the first day of life of the preterm infants.[51-53]

Thus, even though the overall *volume* of blood moving into and out of the brain per unit time may be reduced in preterm infants, certain features of the *velocity* of flow may actually be increased early in the postnatal life of preterm infants relative to same-age fetuses who remain *in utero*. These hemodynamic differences, in conjunction with the relative immaturity and fragility of the cerebral vessels in the brains of preterm infants, is thought to contribute to hemorrhages in the germinal matrix surrounding the cerebral ventricles.[51,54,55]

Many,[56,57] but not all,[58] studies have found that cerebral blood flow in preterm infants is passively dependent on systemic blood pressure. In mechanically ventilated preterm infants, a greater variability in cerebral blood flow soon after birth has been associated with a greater likelihood of sustaining an intraventricular hemorrhage (IVH),[59] and reducing this variability in CBF by inducing muscular paralysis has been shown to reduce the incidence of IVH.[60] Presumably, the variability in CBF that is induced by motoric activity is attributable at least in part to the passive dependence of CBF on systemic blood pressure.

Conversely, the passive dependence of CBF on systemic blood pressure in immature brains is thought by some investigators to place the brains of preterm infants at risk for hypoxia-ischemia during episodes of decreased systemic blood pressure,[61-66] and sustained hypotension has been shown to predict brain damage and a poor neurodevelopmental outcome in preterm infants.[67,68] Furthermore, if hypoxia-ischemia complicates preterm birth, reduced concentrations of adenosine triphosphate and other high-energy phosphate compounds necessary for brain metabolism have been shown to predict both reduced head circumference[69] and poor neurodevelopmental outcome later in childhood.[69-72]

Anatomic Abnormalities in School-Aged Children

We measured regional brain volumes from the MRI scans of 25 prematurely born 8-year-old children and 39 term control subjects group-matched on age, sex, race, and socioeconomic status. Brain volumes in preterm children were markedly reduced in comparison with term controls throughout many brain regions, but not all regions, after controlling for overall scaling effects that could accompany an overall reduced size of the body, head, and brain in the preterm children. Cortical abnormalities centered around the sensorimotor region of the brain but also affected the adjacent premotor, parieto-occipital, and midtemporal cortices, as well as the cerebellum (FIG. 1). The occipital and temporal horns of the lateral ventricles were increased in volume by 300–400%, whereas the rest of the ventricular system did not differ significantly from values in term control subjects.

Volumes of the amygdala and hippocampus were reduced by as much as 30%. Volumes of the basal ganglia, particularly in their predominantly motor portions (the putamen and globus pallidus) were reduced by 12%. Subregions of the corpus callosum, measured as representatives of pure white matter in this well-defined anatomical structure, were reduced in size by as much as 35%. Reductions were greatest in the midbody and isthmus of the corpus callosum, which interconnect motor cortices of each cerebral hemisphere. We speculated that the greatly elevated risk of developing cerebral palsy in preterm children could be explained by the findings that the greatest degrees of abnormality in cortical, basal ganglia, and corpus callosum all involve primarily motor subregions of those structures.

In brain regions of the preterm group where the greatest abnormalities in volume were detected, the degree of anatomical abnormalitiy correlated with IQ (FIG. 2), suggesting that the morphological abnormalities did indeed contribute to the cognitive disturbances in this population. Regional volumes also correlated significantly with gestational age at birth, with smaller volumes accompanying younger gestational ages when these infants were born. This association argues for the presence of a dose-response effect, with a greater duration of development outside of the protective intrauterine environment, producing progressively greater disturbances in anatomical brain development. Thus, the younger these babies were born, the greater were their anatomical abnormalities, and the greater their anatomical abnormalities, the greater their degree cognitive impairment, consistent with reports that the degree of long-term neurodevelopmental impairment in preterm infants is associated with gestational age at birth.[4,13,73] Taken together with our findings that volumes in preterm infants correlate with IQ 20 months later, these findings suggest that volumes of brain regions in preterm neonates may prove to be a useful marker to identify infants at risk for cognitive impairment if they are followed into later childhood. If the predictive utility of neonatal brain volumes for later functional outcome is confirmed, then the regional abnormalities detected at birth may help to direct efforts to develop prevention and early intervention strategies that are based on the purported functional correlates of the brain regions where these anatomical abnormalities are found.

Of the many correlations of obstetrical complications with regional brain volumes that were assessed, only the degree of anatomical abnormality of basal ganglia volumes with 5-minute Apgar scores and with the presence of intraventricular hemorrhage (IVH) within 6 hours of birth were statistically significant. The presence of IVH at birth accentuated the pattern of abnormalities that were detected across the

Phonologic

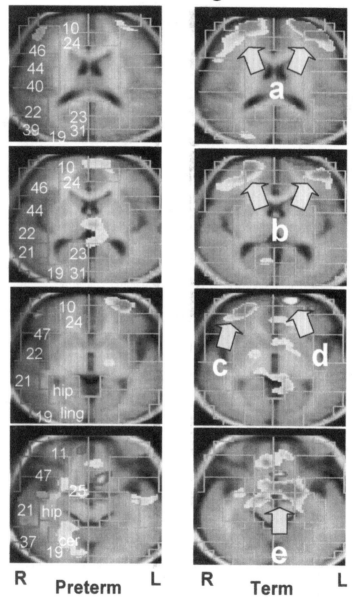

FIGURE 3. Brain activity during a language listening task in preterm children. Group activation maps for semantic and phonological processing for term and preterm 8-year-old children are shown. These are axial slices, with slices lower in the brain positioned below slices that are higher in the brain. The numbers in the left column of brain slices represent Brodmann's areas (BA's). The *large letters* and *arrows* refer to regional activations that were most similar across the semantic processing maps for the preterm children and phonological

Semantic

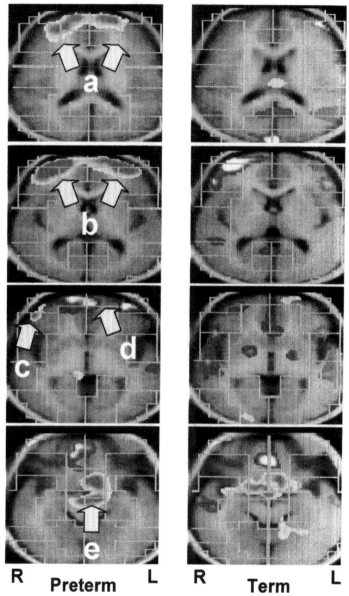

processing maps for the terms controls. The figures show that preterm children processed meaningful (i.e., semantic) speech using neural systems that are normally engaged in the processing of meaningless (i.e., phonological) speech sounds. a = Prefrontal cortex deactivation (BA 10); b = prefrontal cortex deactivation (BAs 10 and 46); c = prefrontal cortex deactivation (BA 47); d = prefrontal cortex activation (BA 10); e = ventral anterior cingulate deactivation (BA 25); R = right; L = left.

brain in the entire sample of preterm children, but it did not account for those same abnormalities in preterm children without IVH. This accentuation of the pattern of regional abnormality across the cerebrum suggests that perhaps morphological disturbances (even in children without a history of IVH) could have at least in part a vascular etiology. The correlation of basal ganglia volumes with Apgar scores 5 minutes after birth further support this possibility, as these structures are known to be endartery watershed territories that are highly susceptible to perfusion deficits, and poor perfusion together with hypoxia is probably the most important determinant of the 5-minute Apgar score.

Functional Abnormalities in School-Aged Children

To assess whether the anatomical disturbances detected in school-aged children have consequences for neural functioning, we examined brain activation during a language-listening task using functional MRI (fMRI) in 26 preterm children at 8 years of age and in 13 comparably matched, term community control children. Children listened to a pleasant children's story and then to the same story in which the syllables of each word were scrambled in time. These conditions were designed to assess brain activity associated, respectively, with understanding the meaning of speech and with the processing of phonemes, the elemental sounds of speech. The term infants during meaningful speech activated prototypical language areas, including frontal and temperoparietal regions bilaterally (FIG. 3). Preterm infants did not demonstrate this normal pattern of activation during normal speech. Instead, they activated the same brain regions during meaningful speech as were activated by the term children listening to the nonsensical, phonemic sounds. The more the preterm children activated their brains in this unusual way during meaningful speech, the lower was their verbal IQ and the poorer was their comprehension of the meaningful story (FIG. 3).

These findings demonstrated that the preterm children tended to use the same neural pathways for processing of meaning speech that are normally used for processing nonsensical, elemental speech sounds. The findings also suggested that these preterm children may have tended to hear meaningful speech as meaningless sounds. The more this was true, the lower was their verbal IQ. Because verbal IQ is a stable intellectual trait, the findings also suggest that aberrant language processing in preterm children has far-reaching and enduring consequences, in that preterm children may process normal, meaningful speech in a similar way throughout their daily activities, whether at school, at home with family, or at play with peers. If this language processing is in fact disrupted throughout their daily activities, it could well help to explain the common thought disturbances and emotional illnesses that have been reported in this population.

PATHOPHYSIOLOGY

The causes of the anatomical and functional disturbances in the brains of prematurely born infants and children are unknown. Given the many differences in environmental and physiological differences in the intra- and extrauterine milieus of these infants during the second and third trimesters of fetal development, potential candidates are legion. These include acute or chronic hypoxia or ischemia[51,56,67,74–77] that are unrecognized,[57,78,79] medication effects,[80–83] nutritional abnormalities,[84] the absence of unidentified maternally derived growth factors, stress,[85–87] differences in handling[88] and other mediators of stress and reactivity,[89,90] physical positioning,[91] activity,[60,92–94] infection,[95–98] and other mechanical factors related to the neonatal intensive care unit.[99,100]

The bulk of evidence thus far suggests that some component of ischemia contributes to the genesis of gross white matter lesions that are common in preterm infants, such as PVL, IVH, and cystic lesions,[101] and these white matter lesions could conceivably disrupt the development and function of overlying cortical gray matter. In our own studies, however, the morphological abnormalities in the cortex were present even when children with these white matter lesions were excluded from statistical analyses, thus suggesting that these white matter lesions are not necessary for the presence of gray and white matter volumetric abnormalities. Furthermore, the similar locations of regional volume abnormalities in infants and children born prematurely were specific to gray matter in the infants, suggesting that the cortical abnormalities develop before and are independent of the presence of white matter lesions. Disturbances in development of white matter could share a common etiology with disturbances in development of cortical gray matter, but simply develop later. Alternatively, disturbances in development of cortical gray matter could themselves disrupt the later development of white matter axons that extend from anatomically abnormal cortical gray matter.

The pattern of regional morphological abnormalities in prematurely born infants and children—reduced volumes of sensorimotor, parieto-occipital, and temporal regions, as well as enlargement of the occipital and temporal horns of the lateral ventricles—bears some resemblance to the pattern of lesions associated with asphyxia[102,103] or IVH[104] in term infants. In fact, in our own data, IVH was associated with an exaggeration of this characteristic pattern of morphological abnormality, suggesting that the causes of the morphological abnormalities in preterm infants and children without IVH may be the same as or similar to the causes of the morphological abnormalities in preterm infants and children with IVH. Morphological abnormalities associated with IVH or hypoxia-ischemia has been hypothesized by some to be due to disruptions in blood flow and oxygen delivery to regions where metabolism is highest.[102,105,106] As we have seen, the region where metabolism is highest in term and preterm newborns is the sensorimotor cortex.[45,46,107]

Perhaps their relatively greater metabolic demands places these sensorimotor regions at particularly high risk for even subtle deficits in prematurely born infants.[55,61–66,108] Furthermore, these subtle perfusion deficits could be caused by the failure of autoregulation of cerebral blood flow which, as we have seen, is common in preterm infants.[56,57,63,64,66,109] Impaired autoregulation itself could be established in the brains of preterm infants by the immaturity of the walls of cerebral vessels,[109] which lack the smooth muscle layers present in the vessel walls of term infants.[55,108] Autoregulation of cerebral perfusion will only be further compromised by the presence of hypoxia, hypercarbia, malnutrition, infection, inflammatory mediators, and a host of other currently unidentified influences on vascular reactivity that are commonly present in preterm infants.[110] The reduced flow, which presumably contributes to ischemia, when combined with exaggerated fluctuations in velocity, could predispose to hemorrhage superimposed on areas of ischemia,[101] thus possibly accounting for the exaggerated morphological abnormalities in children with a history of perinatal IVH that we detected in children without a history of IVH. Poor elaboration of the distal vessels in the long and short penetrating arteries and poor collateral flow in vessels supplying the superficial and deep white matter[111,112] likely compound ischemia in the presence of impaired autoregulation, hypoperfusion, and regionally greater metabolic demands.

Whether or not the disturbances in development of brain structure in preterm infants have a vascular etiology, the ultimate molecular mediators of the developmental disturbances are unknown. Deficient delivery of oxygen to developing cerebral tissues, whether it is caused by chronic perfusion problems or by the more generalized and chronic respiratory insufficiency that commonly afflicts preterm newborns, can have profound effects on brain development. The reported effects of chronic hypoxia on brain development in animal models include an increase in the numbers and density of cortical neurons, possibly the consequence of a reduction in the programmed cell death of neurons in the developing cortex,[113] as well as increased angiogenesis and a disruption in the normal temporal and spatial expression of vascular endothelial growth factor.[114] Chronic, sublethal hypoxia also produces smaller brains, decreased white matter volumes, decreased size of the corpus callosum, reduced volume of cortical gray matter, and ventriculomegaly,[115] all of which are abnormalities detected in preterm infants and children.

Animal models of ischemia suggest disturbances that are further reminiscent of those reported in preterm infants, suggesting additional molecular and cellular mediators. Bilateral ligation of the uterine arteries of pregnant rats, for example, produces in the fetus neuronal cell loss, disturbances in stratification of parietal cortex,[116] white matter rarefaction, reduced numbers of oligodendrocytes, and macrophage activation.[117] Prenatal hypoxia-ischemia in rats disturbs expression of nitric oxide synthase, the enzyme responsible for synthesizing nitric oxide, an important paracrine modulator of cerebral blood flow and neurotransmitter release.[118,119] Experimentally induced placental ischemia in pregnant sheep produces severe gliosis in the cortex, white matter injury, and reduced Purkinje cell numbers in the cerebellum of the offspring.[120] Moderate ischemia tends to produce cell death in immature piglets by enhanced apoptosis, rather than by necrosis,[121] an effect that may be mediated in part by the molecular consequences of cerebral ischemia, such as glutamate excitotoxicity[122–125] or increases in the cellular mediators of apoptosis.[126] Extreme hypercapnia seems to worsen brain damage associated with hypoxia-ischemia, probably by depressing cardiovascular functioning and thereby exacerbating the degree of ischemia that is otherwise already present.[127]

One rat model of brain development during chronic, sublethal hypoxia has suggested that hypoxia alters expression of a large number of genes throughout the brain.[128] In an analysis of gene microchip arrays, genes that promote development of presynaptic neurons were induced, whereas genes that promote development of postsynaptic neurons and receptors were suppressed. Moreover, genes controlling synaptogenesis and apoptosis were generally up-regulated. Chronic, sublethal hypoxia in this same model also increased levels of fibroblast growth factor, which in turn increase the numbers of radial glial cells,[129] the cellular elements that constitute the cellular scaffolding upon which neurons migrate from the ventricular zone to the cerebral cortex. These findings were in general interpreted as indicating a dysynchrony of the extraordinarily complex unfolding of brain maturation during chronic hypoxia.[128]

Immature oligodenroglia are exquisitely sensitive to ischemic injury, probably mediated at least in part by the abundant production of free radicals during hypoxia-ischemia.[130,131] Because myelin deposition begins in earnest only late in fetal development and continues long after birth,[132–136] injury to immature oligodendroglia may not manifest in macroscopic volume measurements until later in infancy or childhood. This delayed manifestation of early white matter injury, if present, could explain our detection of cortical gray matter abnormalities in preterm neonates but white matter abnormalities only in older prematurely born children.

CONCLUSION

We do not yet know the pathophysiology or molecular mediators of the anatomical and functional brain disturbances of preterm birth. Hypoxia-ischemia likely plays a prominent role in generating brain abnormalities in at least some of these children, probably by disrupting the timing and complex orchestration of brain maturational events variably across brain regions. Not all brain regions seem to be equally vulnerable to the effects of premature birth. Sensorimotor, parietal, and temporal brain regions seem to be particularly vulnerable. These effects are detectable in cortical gray matter soon after birth, and are only later observed in white matter. The magnitude of the anatomical disturbances in school-aged children is proportional to the degree of prematurity. We have some evidence that the magnitude of these anatomical disturbances at birth may predict long-term cognitive outcome, although long-term follow-up studies of infants imaged at birth will be necessary to demonstrate the predictive value of neonatal brain volumes. Functional imaging studies have shown promise not only in demonstrating disturbances in brain function in preterm children, but also in identifying the neural circuits that are unusually engaged in preterm children who have the greatest cognitive dysfunction.

Knowledge of the location of anatomical disturbances in the brains of preterm infants may suggest new therapeutic strategies to help prevent the development of these anatomical disturbances and preserve the functional capacities that those regions presumably subserve. However, identification of the physiological and molecular mediators of these disturbances will be necessary if we are ever to develop fully effective prevention or early intervention strategies for the adverse consequences of preterm birth on human brain development. Early attempts at prevention and intervention strategies have been suggested in animal models of hypoxia-ischemia. Neonatal handling and administration of brain-derived neurotrophic factor, for instance, have been shown to reduce some of the anatomical and behavioral deficits following hypoxia-ischemia of the developing rat brain.[137,138] Developing safe and better preventions for the anatomical, functional, and behavioral abnormalities of preterm birth will require further improvements in our animal models for prematurity, better knowledge of the molecular mediators that produce these abnormalities, and careful monitoring of the effects of our interventions on those molecular pathways throughout the brain. This program of translational research will require a concerted, close collaboration of basic scientists and clinicians who will take knowledge from the bench to the bedside and back again.

ACKNOWLEDGMENTS

This work was supported in part by NIMH grants MH01232 and MH59139, the Thomas D. Klingenstein & Nancy D. Perlman Family Fund, and the Suzanne Crosby Murphy Endowment at Columbia University. I am grateful to Drs. Laura Ment and Betty Vohr for their scientific collaboration and guidance on several of the studies described in this paper.

REFERENCES

1. HACK, M. *et al.* 1995. Very-low-birth-weight outcomes of the National Institute of Child Health and Human Development Neonatal Network, November 1989 to October 1990. Am. J. Obstet. Gynecol. **172**: 457–464.
2. JOSEPH, K.S. *et al.* 1998. Determinants of preterm birth rates in Canada from 1981 through 1983 and from 1992 through 1994. N. Engl. J. Med. **339**: 1434–1439.
3. RICHARDSON, D.K. *et al.* 1998. Declining severity adjusted mortality: evidence of improving neonatal intensive care. Pediatrics **102**: 893–899.
4. HACK, M., H. FRIEDMAN & A.A. FANAROFF. 1996. Outcomes of extremely low birth weight infants. Pediatrics **98**: 931–937.
5. HALL, A. *et al.* 1995. School attainment, cognitive ability and motor function in a total Scottish very-low-birth weight population at eight years: a controlled study. Dev. Med. Child Neurol. **37**: 1037–1050.
6. PIECUCH, R. *et al.* 1997. Outcome of extremely low birth weight infants (500-999 grams) over a 12-year period. Pediatrics **100**: 633–639.
7. STEWART, A. & V. KIRKBRIDE. 1996. Very preterm infants at fourteen years: relationship with neonatal ultrasound brain scans and neurodevelopmental status at one year. Acta Paediatr. Suppl. **416**: 44–47.
8. WHITAKER, A.H. *et al.* 1997. Psychiatric outcomes in low-birth-weight children at age 6 years: relation to neonatal cranial ultrasound abnormalities. Arch. Gen. Psychiatry **54**: 847–856.
9. WOLKE, D. 1991. Annotation: supporting the development of low birthweight infants. J. Child Psychol. Psychiatry **32**: 723–741.
10. SYKES, D.H. *et al.* 1997. Behavioral adjustment in school of very low birthweight children. J. Child Psychol. Psychiatry **38**: 315–325.
11. BOTTING, N. *et al.* 1998. Cognitive and educational outcome of very-low-birthweight children in early adolescence. Dev. Med. Child Neurol. **40**: 652–660.
12. KLEBANOV, P. *et al.* 1994. Classroom behavior of very low birth weight elementary school children. Pediatrics **94**: 700–708.
13. MCCORMICK, M., K. WORKMAN-DANIELS & J. BROOKS-GUNN. 1996. The behavioral and emotional well-being of school-age children with different birth weights. Pediatrics **97**: 18–25.
14. D'ANGIO, C.T. *et al.* 2002. Longitudinal, 15-year follow-up of children born at less than 29 weeks' gestation after introduction of surfactant therapy into a region: neurologic, cognitive, and educational outcomes. Pediatrics **110**: 1094–1102.
15. MSALL, M.E. & M.R. TREMONT. 2002. Measuring functional outcomes after prematurity: developmental impact of very low birth weight and extremely low birth weight status on childhood disability. Ment. Retard. Dev. Disabil. Res. Rev. **8**: 258–272.
16. ICHIKI, M. *et al.* 2000. Intra-uterine physical growth in schizophrenia: evidence confirming excess of premature birth. Psychol. Med. **30**: 597–604.
17. RAKIC, P. & K.P. RILEY. 1983. Overproduction and elimination of retinal axons in the fetal rhesus monkey. Science **209**: 1441–1444.
18. RAKIC, P. 1988. Specification of cerebral cortical areas. Science. **241**: 170–176.
19. DOBBING, J. & J. SANDS. 1973. Quantitative growth and development of human brain. Arch. Dis. Child. **48**: 757–767.

20. NELIGAN, G.A. 1974. The human brain growth spurt. Dev. Med. Child Neurol. **16:** 677–678.
21. BOURGEOIS, J.-P. & P. RAKIC. 1993. Changing of synaptic density in the primary visual cortex of the rhesus monkey from fetal to adult stage. J. Neurosci. **13:** 2801–2820.
22. CHANGEUX, J.-P. 1993. A critical view of neuronal models of learning and memory. *In* Memory Concepts. P. Anderson, Ed.: 413–433. Elsevier. Amsterdam.
23. BECKER, L.E. *et al.* 1984. Dendritic development in human occipital cortical neurons. Brain Res. **315:** 117–124.
24. MRZLJAK, L. *et al.* 1990. Neuronal development in human prefrontal cortex in prenatal and postnatal stages. Prog. Brain Res. **85:** 185–222.
25. HUTTENLOCHER, P.R. & A.S. DABHOLKAR. 1997. Regional differences in synaptogenesis in human cerebral cortex. J. Comp. Neurol. **387:** 167–178.
26. KATZ, L.C. & C.J. SHATZ. 1996. Synaptic activity and the constuction of cortical circuits. Science **274:** 1133–1138.
27. SIMONATI, A., T. ROSSO & N. RIZZUTO. 1997. DNA fragmentation in normal development of the human central nervous system: a morphological study during corticogenesis. Neuropathol. Appl. Neurobiol. **23:** 203–211.
28. BUONOMANO, D.V. & M.M. MERZENICH. 1998. Cortical plasticity: from synapses to maps. Annu. Rev. Neurosci. **21:** 149–186.
29. FELDMAN, D.E. & E.I. KNUDSEN. 1998. Experience-dependent plasticity and the maturation of glutamatergic synapses. Neuron **20:** 1067–1071.
30. PHAM, T.A. *et al.* 1999. CRE-mediated gene transcription in neocortical neuronal plasticity during the developmental critical period. Neuron **22:** 63–72.
31. OLSÉN, P. *et al.* 1997. Magnetic resonance imaging of periventricular leukomalacia and its clinical correlation in children. Ann. Neurol. **41:** 754–761.
32. OLSÉN, P. *et al.* 1998. Psychological findings in preterm children related to neurologic status and magnetic resonance imaging. Pediatrics **102:** 329–336.
33. STEWART, A.L. *et al.* 1999. Brain structure and neurocognitive and behavioral function in adolescents who were born very preterm. Lancet **353:** 1653–1657.
34. KEENEY, S.E., E.W. ADCOCK & C.B. MCARDLE. 1991. Prospective observations of 100 high-risk neonates by high-field (1.5 Tesla) magnetic resonance imaging of the central nervous system. II. Lesions associated with hypoxic-ischemic encephalopathy. Pediatrics **87:** 431–438.
35. DE VRIES, L.S. *et al.* 1993. Correlation between the degree of periventricular leukomalacia diagnosed using cranial ultrasound and MRI later in infancy in children with cerebral palsy. Neuropediatric **24:** 263–268.
36. GUIT, G.L. *et al.* 1990. Prediction of neurodevelopmental outcome in the preterm infant: MR-staged myelination compared with cranial US. Pediatric Radiology. **175:** 107–109.
37. HÜPPI, P.S. *et al.* 1996. Structural and neurobehavioral delay in postnatal brain development of preterm infants. Pediatr. Res. **39:** 895–901.
38. COOKE, R.W.I. & L.J. ABERNETHY. 1999. Cranial magnetic resonance imaging and school performance in very low birth weight infants in adolescence. Arch. Dis. Child Fetal Neonatal Ed. **81:** F116–F121.
39. BARKOVICH, A.J. & S.K. SARGENT. 1995. Profound asphyxia in the premature infant: Imaging findings. AJNR **16:** 1837–1846.
40. HÜPPI, P.S. *et al.* 1998. Quantitative magnetic resonance imaging of brain development in premature and mature newborns. Ann. Neurol. **43:** 224–235.
41. INDER, T.E. *et al.* 1999. Periventricular white matter injury in the premature infant is followed by reduced cerebral cortical gray matter volume at term. Ann. Neurol. **46:** 755–760.
42. MURPHY, B.P. *et al.* 2001. Impaired cerebral cortical gray matter growth following treatment with dexamethasone for neonatal chronic lung disease. Pediatrics **107:** 217–221.
43. HÜPPI, P.S. *et al.* 1998. Microstructural development of human newborn cerebral white matter assessed in vivo by diffusion tensor magnetic resonance imaging. Pediatr. Res. **44:** 584–590.
44. PETERSON, B.S. *et al.* 2003. Regional brain volumes and their later neurodevelopmental correlates in term and preterm infants. Pediatrics **111:** 938–948.

45. CHUGANI, H.T. & M.E. PHELPS. 1986. Maturational changes in cerebral function in infants determined by [18]FDG positron emission tomography. Science **231:** 840–843.
46. CHUGANI, H.T., M.E. PHELPS & J.C. MAZIOTTA. 1987. Positron emission tomography study of human brain functional development. Ann. Neurol. **22:** 487–497.
47. CHUGANI, H.T. & M.E. PHELPS. 1991. Imaging human brain development with positron emission tomography. J. Nucl. Med. **32:** 23–26.
48. GREISEN, G. 1986. Cerebral blood flow in preterm infants during the first week of life. Acta Paediatr. Scand. **75:** 43–51.
49. KEHRER, M. *et al.* 2002. Measurement of volume of cerebral blood flow in healthy preterm and term neonates with ultrasound. Lancet **360:** 1749–1750.
50. BORCH, K. & G. GREISEN. 1998. Blood flow distribution in the normal human preterm brain. Pediatr. Res. **43:** 28–33.
51. KURMANAVICHIUS, J. *et al.* 1991. Fetal and preterm newborn cerebral blood flow velocity. Early Hum. Dev. **26:** 113–120.
52. ANDO, Y., S. TAKASHIMA & K. TAKESHITA. 1985. Cerebral blood flow velocity in preterm neonates. Brain Dev. **7:** 385–391.
53. PEZZATI, M. *et al.* 2002. Early postnatal doppler assessment of cerebral blood flow velocity in healthy preterm and term infants. Dev. Med. Child Neurol. **44:** 745–752.
54. HAMBLETON, G. & J. WIGGLESWORTH. 1976. Origin of intraventricular haemorrhage in the preterm infant. Arch. Dis. Child. **51:** 651–659.
55. KUBAN, K.C.K. & F.H. GILLES. 1985. Human telencephalic angiogenesis. Ann. Neurol. **17:** 539–548.
56. VAN DE BOR, M. & F.J. WALTHER. 1991. Cerebral blood flow velocity regulation in preterm infants. Biol. Neonate **59:** 329–235.
57. COUGHTREY, H., J.M. RENNIE & D.H. EVANS. 1997. Variability in cerebral blood flow velocity: observations over one minute in preterm babies. Early Hum. Dev. **47:** 63–70.
58. TYSZCZUK, L. *et al.* 1998. Cerebral blood flow is independent of mean arterial blood pressure in preterm infants undergoing intensive care. Pediatrics **102:** 337–341.
59. PERLMAN, J.M., J.B. MCMENAMIN & J.J. VOLPE. 1983. Fluctuating cerebral blood flow velocity in respiratory distress syndrome. N. Engl. J. Med. **309:** 204–209.
60. PERLMAN, J.M. *et al.* 1985. Reduction in intraventricular hemorrhage by elimination of fluctuating cerebral blood-flow velocity in preterm infants with respiratory distress syndrome. N. Engl. J. Med. **312:** 1353–1357.
61. TUOR, U.I. & D. GREWAL. 1994. Autoregulation of cerebral blood flow: influence of local brain development and postnatal age. Am. J. Physiol. **267:** H2220–H2228.
62. PRYDS, O. *et al.* 1990. Vasoparalysis associated with brain damage in asphyxiated term infants. J. Pediatr. **117:** 119–125.
63. RAMAEKERS, V.T. *et al.* 1990. Upper limits of brain blood flow autoregulation in stable infants of various conceptional age. Early Hum. Dev. **24:** 249–258.
64. JORCH, G. & N. JORCH. 1987. Failure of autoregulation of cerebral blood flow in neonates studied by pulsed Doppler ultrasound of the internal carotid artery. Eur. J. Pediatr. **146:** 468–472.
65. PRYDS, O. 1991. Control of cerebral circulation in the high-risk neonate. Ann. Neurol. **30:** 321–329.
66. LOU, H.C., N.A. LASSEN & B. FRIIS-HANSEN. 1979. Impaired autoregulation of cerebral blood flow in the distressed newborn infant. J. Pediatr. **94:** 118–121.
67. LOW, J.A. *et al.* 1993. The association between newborn hypotension and hypoxemia and outcome during the first year. Acta Paediatr. **82:** 433–437.
68. LOU, H.C., H. SKOV & H. PEDERSEN. 1979. Low cerebral blood flow: a risk factor in the neonate. J. Pediatr. **95:** 606–609.
69. ROTH, S.C. *et al.* 1997. Relation of deranged neonatal cerebral oxidative metabolism with neurodevelopmental outcome and head circumference at 4 years. Dev. Med. Child Neurol. **39:** 718–725.
70. HOPE, P.L. *et al.* 1984. Cerebral energy metabolism studied with phosphorus NMR spectroscopy in normal and birth-asphyxiated infants. Lancet **2:** 366–370.
71. AZZOPARDI, D. *et al.* 1989. Prognosis of newborn infants with hypoxic-ischemic brain injury assessed by phosphorus magnetic resonance spectroscopy. Pediatr. Res. **25:** 445–451.

72. MARTIN, E. *et al.* 1996. Diagnostic and prognostic value of cerebral 31P magnetic resonance spectroscopy in neonates with perinatal asphyxia. Pediatr. Res. **40:** 749–758.
73. BHUTTA, A.T. *et al.* 2002. Cognitive and behavioral outcomes of school-aged children who were born preterm: a meta-analysis. JAMA **288:** 728–737.
74. MULLER, A.M. *et al.* 1997. Loss of CO_2 reactivity of cerebral blood flow is associated with severe brain damage in mechanically ventilated very low birth weight infants. Eur. J. Paediatr. Neurol. **1:** 157–163.
75. BAENZIGER, O. *et al.* 1999. Cerebral blood flow and neurological outcome in the preterm infant. Eur. J. Pediatr. **158:** 138–143.
76. BAENZIGER, O. *et al.* 1995. Regional differences of cerebral blood flow in the preterm infant. Eur. J. Pediatr. **154:** 919–924.
77. MEEK, J.H. *et al.* 1998. Cerebral blood flow increases over the first three days of life in extremely preterm neonates. Arch. Dis. Child Fetal. Neonatal Ed. **78:** F33–F37.
78. KLUCKOW, M. & N. EVANS. 2001. Low systemic blood flow in the preterm infant. Semin. Neonatal. **6:** 75–84.
79. WINBERG, P., S.E. SONESSON & B.P. LUNDELL. 1990. Postnatal changes in intracranial blood flow velocity in preterm infants. Acta Paediatr. Scand. **79:** 1150–1155.
80. RANTONEN, T. *et al.* 2001. Maternal magnesium sulfate treatment is associated with reduced brain-blood flow perfusion in preterm infants. Crit. Care Med. **29:** 1460–1465.
81. AUSTIN, N.C. *et al.* 1992. Regional cerebral blood flow velocity changes after indomethacin infusion in preterm infants. Arch. Dis. Child. **67:** 851–854.
82. VAN DE BOR, M., E.J. MA & F.J. WALTHER. 1991. Cerebral blood flow velocity after surfactant instillation in preterm infants. J. Pediatr. **118:** 285–287.
83. LUNDSTROM, K.E. *et al.* 1995. Cerebral blood flow and left ventricular output in spontaneously breathing, newborn preterm infants treated with caffeine or aminophylline. Acta Paediatr. **84:** 6–9.
84. BOEHM, G. & N.C. RAIHA. 1993. Postmenstrual age correlates to indices of protein metabolism in very low birth weight infants. J. Pediatr. Gastroenterol. Nutr. **16:** 306–310.
85. PHAM, K. *et al.* 2003. Repeated restraint stress suppresses neurogenesis and induces biphasic PSA-NCAM expression in the adult rat dentate gyrus. Eur. J. Neurosci. **17:** 879–886.
86. MAGARINOS, A.M., J.M. VERDUGO & B.S. MCEWEN. 1997. Chronic stress alters synaptic terminal structure in hippocampus. Proc. Natl. Acad. Sci. USA **94:** 14002–14008.
87. MCEWEN, B.S. 2001. Plasticity of the hippocampus: adaptation to chronic stress and allostatic load. Ann. N.Y. Acad. Sci. **933:** 265–277.
88. CHOU, I.C. *et al.* 2001. Behavioral/environmental intervention improves learning after cerebral hypoxia-ischemia in rats. Stroke **32:** 2192–2197.
89. WEAVER, I.C., R.J. GRANT & M.J. MEANEY. 2002. Maternal behavior regulates long-term hippocampal expression of BAX and apoptosis in the offspring. J. Neurochem. **82:** 998–1002.
90. ANISMAN, H. *et al.* 1998. Do early-life events permanently alter behavioral and hormonal responses to stressors? Int. J. Dev. Neurosci. **16:** 149–164.
91. EICHLER, F. *et al.* 2001. Position dependent changes of cerebral blood flow velocities in premature infants. Eur. J. Pediatr. **160:** 633–639.
92. RAMAEKERS, V.T. & P. CASAER. 1987. Influence of behavioral states on cerebral blood flow velocity patterns in preterm infants. J. Pediatr. **111:** 795.
93. MULLAART, R.A. *et al.* 1992. Cerebral blood flow fluctuation in low-risk preterm newborns. Early Hum. Dev. **30:** 41–48.
94. BRACEWELL, M. & N. MARLOW. 2002. Patterns of motor disability in very preterm children. Ment. Retard. Dev. Disabil. Res. Rev. **8:** 241–248.
95. ADINOLFI, M. 1993. Infectious diseases in pregnancy, cytokines and neurological impairment: an hypothesis. Dev. Med. Child Neurol. **35:** 549–558.
96. PATRICK, L.A. & G.N. SMITH. 2002. Proinflammatory cytokines: a link between chorioamnionitis and fetal brain injury. J. Obstet. Gynaecol. Can. **24:** 705–709.
97. ANDREWS, W.W., J.C. HAUTH & R.L. GOLDENBERG. 2000. Infection and preterm birth. Am. J. Perinatol. **17:** 357–365.
98. GONCALVES, L.F., T. CHAIWORAPONGSA & R. ROMERO. 2002. Intrauterine infection and prematurity. Ment. Retard. Dev. Disabil. Res. Rev. **8:** 3–13.

99. BAERTS, W., R.A. VALENTIN & P.J. SAUER. 1992. Ophthalmic and cerebral blood flow velocities in preterm infants: influence of ambient lighting conditions. J. Clin. Ultrasound **20:** 43–48.

100. PERLMAN, J.M. & J.J. VOLPE. 1983. Suctioning in the preterm infant: effects on cerebral blood flow velocity, intracranial pressure, and arterial blood pressure. Pediatrics **72:** 329–334.

101. VOLPE, J.J. 2001. Neurobiology of periventricular leukomalacia in the premature infant. Pediatr. Res. **50:** 553–562.

102. RADEMAKERS, R.P. *et al.* 1995. Central cortico-subcortical involvement: a distinct pattern of brain damage caused by perinatal and postnatal asphyxia in term infants. J. Comput. Assisted Tomogr. **19:** 256–263.

103. VOLPE, J.J. *et al.* 1985. Positron emission tomography in the asphyxiated term newborn: parasagittal impairment of cerebral blood flow. Ann. Neurol. **17:** 287–296.

104. VOLPE, J.J. *et al.* 1983. Positron emission tomography in the newborn: extensive impairment of regional cerebral blood flow with intraventricular hemorrhage and hemorrhagic intracerebral involvement. Pediatrics **72:** 589–601.

105. DAVISON, A.N. & J. DOBBING. 1966. Myelination as a vulnerable period in brain development. Br. Med. Bull. **22:** 40–44.

106. AZZARELLI, B., P. MEADE & J. MULLER. 1980. Hypoxic lesions in areas of primary myelination. A distinct pattern in cerebral palsy. Child's Brain **7:** 132–145.

107. BØRCH, K. & G. GREISEN. 1998. Blood flow distribution in the normal human preterm brain. Pediatr. Res. **43:** 28–33.

108. NELSON, M.D.J., I. GONZALEZ-GOMEZ & F.H. GILLES. 1991. The search for human telencephalic ventriculofugal arteries. AJNR. **12:** 215–222.

109. HARUDA, F.D. 2001. The structure of blood vessels in the germinal matrix and the autoregulation of cerebral blood flow in premature infants. Pediatrics **108:** 1050–1051.

110. SALIBA, E. & A. HENROT. 2001. Inflammatory mediators and neonatal brain damage. Biol. Neonate **79:** 224–227.

111. TAKSHIMA, S. & K. TANAKA. 1978. Development of cerebrovascular architecture and its relationship to periventricular leukomalacia. Arch. Neurol. **35:** 11–16.

112. RORKE, L.B. 1992. Anatomical features of the developing brain implicated in pathogenesis of hypoxic-ischemic injury. Brain Pathol. **2:** 211–221.

113. STEWART, W.B., L.R. MENT & M. SCHWARTZ. 1997. Chronic postnatal hypoxia increases the numbers of cortical neurons. Brain Res. **760:** 17–21.

114. OGUNSHOLA, O.O. *et al.* 2000. Neuronal VEGF expression correlates with angiogenesis in postnatal developing rat brain. Brain Res. Dev. Brain Res. **119:** 139–153.

115. MENT, L.R. *et al.* 1998. Association of chronic sublethal hypoxia with ventriculomegaly in the developing rat. Dev. Brain Res. **111:** 197–203.

116. TASHIMA, L. *et al.* 2001. Prenatal influence of ischemia-hypoxia-induced intrauterine growth retardation on brain development and behavioral activity in rats. Biol. Neonate. **80:** 81–87.

117. CAI, Z. *et al.* 2001. Chronic ischemia preferentially causes white matter injury in the neonatal rat brain. Brain Res. **898:** 126–135.

118. GIDDAY, J.M. *et al.* 1999. Nitric oxide mediates cerebral ischemic tolerance in a neonatal rat model of hypoxic preconditioning. J. Cereb. Blood Flow Metab. **19:** 331–340.

119. CAI, Z. *et al.* 1999. Prenatal hypoxia-ischemia alters expression and activity of nitric oxide synthase in the young rat brain and causes learning deficits. Brain Res. Bull. **49:** 359–365.

120. MALLARD, E.C. *et al.* 1998. Effects of chronic placental insufficiency on brain development in fetal sheep. Ped. Res. **43:** 262–270.

121. YUE, X. *et al.* 1997. Apoptosis and necrosis in the newborn piglet brain following transient cerebral hypoxia-ischemia. Neuropath. Appl. Neurobiol. **23:** 16–25.

122. BONFOCO, E. *et al.* 1995. Apoptosis and necrosis: two distinct events induced, respectively, by mild and intense insults with N-methyl-D-aspartate or nitric oxide/superoxide in cortical cell cultures. Proc. Natl. Acad. Sci. USA **92:** 7162–7166.

123. FOLLETT, P.L. *et al.* 2000. NBQX attenuates excitotoxic injury in developing white matter. J. Neurosci. **20:** 9235–9241.

124. YOSHIOKA, A., B. BACSKAI & D. PLEASURE. 1996. Pathophysiology of oligodendro-glial excitotoxicity. J. Neurosci. Res. **46:** 427–438.
125. MCDONALD, J.W. *et al.* 1998. Oligodendrocytes from forebrain are highly vulnerable to AMPA/kainate receptor-mediated excitotoxicity. Nat. Med. **4:** 291–297.
126. GILL, R. *et al.* 2002. Role of caspase-3 activation in cerebral ischemia-induced neuro-degeneration in adult and neonatal brain. J. Cereb. Blood Flow Metab. **22:** 420–430.
127. VANNUCCI, R.C. *et al.* 2001. Effect of extreme hypercapnia on hypoxic-ischemic brain damage in the immature rat. Pediatr. Res. **49:** 799–803.
128. CURRISTIN, S.M. *et al.* 2002. Disrupted synaptic development in the hypoxic newborn brain. Proc. Natl. Acad. Sci. USA **99:** 15729–15734.
129. GANAT, Y. *et al.* 2002. Chronic hypoxia up-regulates fibroblast growth factor ligands in the perinatal brain and induces fibroblast growth factor-responsive radial glial cells in the sub-ependymal zone. Neuroscience **112:** 977–991.
130. BACK, S.A. *et al.* 1998. Maturation-dependent vulnerability of oligodendrocytes to oxidative stress-induced death caused by glutathione depletion. J. Neurosci. **18:** 6241–6253.
131. SANCHEZ-ALVAREZ, R., A. ALMEIDA & J.M. MEDINA. 2002. Oxidative stress in pre-term rat brain is due to mitochondrial dysfunction. Pediatr. Res. **51:** 34–39.
132. MCARDLE, C.B. *et al.* 1987. Developmental features of the neonatal brain: MR imag-ing. Part I. Gray-white matter differentiation and myelination. Pediatr. Radiol. **162:** 223–229.
133. DIETRICH, R.B. *et al.* 1988. MRI evaluation of early myelination patterns in normal and developmentally delayed infants. AJNR **150:** 889–896.
134. DIETRICH, R.B. 1999. Maturation, myelination, and dysmyelination. *In* Magnetic Res-onance Imaging, Vol. III. E. Corra, Ed.: 1425–1447. Mosby. St. Louis.
135. VAN DER KNAAP, M.S. & J. VALK. 1990. MR imaging of the various stages of normal myelination during the first year of life. Neuroradiology **31:** 459–470.
136. PETERSON, B.S. *et al.* 2001. Automated measurement of latent morphological features in the human corpus callosum. Hum. Brain Map. **12:** 232–245.
137. CHENG, Y. *et al.* 1997. Marked age-dependent neuroprotection by BDNF against neo-natal hypoxic-ischemic brain injury. Ann. Neurol. **41:** 521–529.
138. ALMLI, C.R. *et al.* 2000. BDNF protects against spatial memory deficits following neonatal hypoxia-ischemia. Exp. Neurol. **166:** 99–114.

Integrating Neuroscience and Psychological Approaches in the Study of Early Experiences

MEGAN R. GUNNAR

Institute of Child Development, University of Minnesota, Minneapolis, Minnesota 55455, USA

ABSTRACT: Rodent maternal separation and primate rearing environment paradigms demonstrate that early disturbances in caregiving that sensitize stress-responsive neurocircuits may play a role in the etiology of mood disorders. Psychosocial studies document the importance of adverse early experiences in the risk for psychopathology. The time is ripe for integrating the animal neuroscience and human psychosocial research on early experiences and stress. Based on work by the National Institute of Mental Health Early Experience, Stress Neurobiology & Prevention Science research network, findings in the human literature that are consistent with those in animal models are reviewed. In addition, however, anomalous findings and the challenge they pose in translating the basic neuroscience findings to human development are also discussed.

KEYWORDS: stress; glucocorticoids; early experience; caregiving; adverse environments; negative emotionality; translational research

INTRODUCTION

A large body of literature confirms an important biological basis of mood disorders.[1] Likewise, stressful events are common in the life histories of adults and youth who develop anxiety and depressive disorders.[2] Alterations in stress-sensitive neurobiological systems are believed to link stressful experiences and the development of affective pathology in genetically vulnerable individuals.[3] Considerable research has focused on alterations in functioning of the limbic hypothalamic-pituitary-adrenocortical (L-HPA) system and its primary releasing hormone, corticotropin-releasing hormone (CRH).[4] Abundant evidence shows that disrupting normal caregiver-infant interactions in rodents and nonhuman primates alters the activity of the developing L-HPA system, producing potentially maladaptive glucocorticoid (GC) responses.[5] This animal research may serve as a model of how early psychosocial adversity in humans creates vulnerability to affective disorders.

Bringing this body of basic research to bear on our understanding of human psychopathology, however, requires that a number of challenging problems be addressed. In 1999, to stimulate translational research on affective disorders, the National Institute of Mental Health funded three networks. Our network, the Early

Address for correspondence: Megan R. Gunnar, Ph.D., Institute of Child Development, University of Minnesota, Minneapolis, MN 55455. Voice: 612-624-4351; fax: 612-624-6373.
gunnar@umn.edu

Ann. N.Y. Acad. Sci. 1008: 238–247 (2003). © 2003 New York Academy of Sciences.
doi: 10.1196/annals.1301.024

Experience, Stress Neurobiology & Prevention Science network, brought basic scientists together with researchers in pediatrics, developmental psychology, and prevention/intervention science in an attempt to integrate neuroscience and psychosocial research on early experiences. We sought to determine where the findings were consistent, where there were discrepancies and, most critically, where we lacked the evidence needed to foster the translation. The following chapter summarizes some of our work to date.

COMPARABILITY OF THE EMERGING HUMAN LITERATURE

The chapter by Plotsky (this volume) reviews the rodent literature, key findings from which served as points of departure in our examination of the human data (see also Ref. 5). First, in rodents, early experiences shape heightened vulnerability to later stressful stimulation. Consistent with this, the neural systems affected are the ones that are believed to regulate physiological, behavioral, and emotional responses to novelty, uncertainty, and potential threat. In most cases, maternal behavior seems capable of mediating the effects of these early experiences. In the rodent, there appears to be a sensitive period for shaping regulation of the L-HPA system that extends from the prenatal period (at least partially via effects that elevate maternal GCs) through the first few postnatal weeks. The sensitive postnatal period roughly corresponds to the relative stress hyporesponsive period (SHRP) observed in pups between postnatal days (PNDs) 4 and 12. In the rodent, the SHRP is characterized by low basal GC levels and relative hyporesponsivity at the adrenal and, to some extent, pituitary levels of the L-HPA axis. Aspects of maternal behavior, especially licking and grooming, appear to maintain the SRHP in rodents. These aspects of maternal behavior, along with latency to retrieve pups and the amount of time spent nursing, appear to mediate early experience manipulations. While the SHRP is defined by this period of low GC responsivity, perturbations during this period may produce marked increases in hypothalamic and extrahypothalamic CRH. There is increasing evidence that early experience manipulations that have an impact on later vulnerability to stress may operate, at least in part, through regulation of central CRH activity.[6]

Using the rodent findings as a point of departure, we asked the following questions of the emerging human psychoneuroendocrine literature: (1) Is there a period in human development that may be comparable to the rodent SHRP? (2) If so, is there evidence that GCs are regulated during this period by interactions with the mother and other caregivers? (3) Is there evidence that disturbances in caregiving during this period are associated with heightened vulnerability to stressors? (4) Is there evidence of developing individual set points for GCs and do these set points appear to be sensitive to variations in caregiving? (5) Is negative emotionality associated with individual differences in basal or response parameters of the L-HPA system during early childhood? (6) Finally, is there any evidence that disturbances in the caregiving environment produce long-lasting effects on L-HPA activity in children?

THE SHRP AND SOCIAL BUFFERING

The evidence on whether there is a period of relative hyporesponsivity of GCs to stressors in human development is equivocal (see Ref. 7 for a review). Several lines of evidence converge on the conclusion that GCs are quite responsive to perturbations early in the postnatal period (roughly up to 3–4 months), but then become increasingly difficult to elevate over the course of the first year. Tentatively, the period between 6 and 12 months marks the transition into a human functional equivalent of the rodent SHRP. By 12 months, even stimuli such as inoculations and brief maternal separations fail to elevate GCs over home baseline levels in many family-reared children. However, GC responsivity to stressors by the end of the first year is highly dependent on the psychosocial context. As in nonhuman primates, what appears to be a period of GC hyporesponsivity may be better characterized as a period of intense psychosocial buffering of the L-HPA axis.[8]

In the rodent, licking and grooming appear to be critical in regulating GC responsivity during the SHRP. In humans and other primates, the parameters of parental care associated with the development of secure attachment relationships are likely to be the ones regulating GC activity (see Ref. 7 for a review). Between 6 and 12 months the human infant begins to organize her security-seeking behavior around one, or a few, familiar adults, and individual differences in patterns of secure-base behavior begin to be discerned that vary by relationships more so than by child (see Zeanah, this volume). In the presence of adults with whom secure patterns of attachment are evident, children explore new situations and recover rapidly from perturbations. Sensitive and responsive caregiving supports the development of secure attachment relationships, disturbances of which are associated with behavioral and emotional problems in young children. It is now well documented that GC buffering is pronounced in the presence of an adult with whom the child has formed a secure attachment relationship. It is not clear, however, whether the child needs to have formed an attachment relationship with the caregiver in order to benefit from sensitive, supportive care. During brief, 30-minute, separations, even an unfamiliar substitute caregiver programmed to be sensitive and responsive is able to inhibit GC increases in infants. In family-based child care, care providers who give stimulating and supportive care prevent afternoon elevations in cortisol, particularly in children with negative emotional temperaments.

The flip side of social buffering is vulnerability to stressors when adult support is insufficient (see Ref. 7 for a review). How long this period of vulnerability to GC elevations may last is not determined. Thus far, the largest GC increases to mild stressors (brief separations, long days at child care, strange people/events) have been noted among toddlers and young preschoolers. Maturation of the neurobiology of the L-HPA system as well as potentially related changes in cognitive and behavioral competence likely underlie the developmental changes in GC responsivity just described. Explication of these changes and their interrelations will be an important target of translational research in this area.

INDIVIDUAL DIFFERENCES IN SET POINTS

If early experiences in interaction with genetic factors shape activity of stress-sensitive neural systems, we might expect to observe individual differences in the tone or set point of the L-HPA system that become more entrenched over development and more reflective of the child's psychosocial history. This is a needed focus of future translational efforts. Nonetheless, based on the data available to date, individual set points in GC activity have been noted in early childhood. Several studies have examined rank-order stability in GC levels across contexts (e.g., home vs laboratory). Modest correlations typically have been reported in the 0.4–0.6 range when samples are taken at the same time of day (e.g., Ref. 9). Cross-age stability has also been reported to emerge around 4–6 months, although associations decrease with the time in between sampling.[9,10] One of the challenges of interpreting these data is that GC estimates are based on only one or a few samples. In a dynamic system like the L-HPA system, single measures are unlikely to be reliable indices of individual set points. For example, in preschool settings we found that aggregates of 5 or more measures are needed to obtain stable individual estimates (unpublished). Similar evidence is available for adults.[11]

While individual differences in GC set points may be emerging over the first years of life, clearly there is also considerable plasticity in the L-HPA system. Changing the care context can dramatically affect typical GC activity. This was noted both in a small study of children adopted from orphanages into homes in the United States and in a larger study of children placed in therapeutic foster care.[12,13] Overall, studies of the effects of changing care quality on L-HPA activity have been too few to describe the potential for recovery of this system following early adverse experiences.

THE L-HPA AXIS AND NEGATIVE EMOTIONALITY

The relation between L-HPA axis activity and negative emotionality is complex. In infants and young children, GC increases and behavioral responses to stressors correlate only modestly, if at all (see Ref. 14 for a review). Early in infancy, manipulations that reduce crying (e.g., providing pacifiers) often do not buffer cortisol increases to stressors such as heel lances or physical examinations. As social buffering of the axis develops, research findings more often reveal evidence of behavioral distress in the absence of GC increases than the reverse. Fussing, crying, and seeking proximity to caregivers are measures of distress, but at the same time they are behaviors that solicit adult protection. By the end of the first year of life, the buffering potential of sensitive, responsive caregiving appears to moderate associations between behavioral distress and GC responsivity.[15,16]

This analysis suggests that the study of concurrent relations between behavioral and cortisol responses to stressors is the study of coping behaviors and their effectiveness in regulating GC activity. Of perhaps more importance in understanding the etiology of affective disorders is the study of negative emotional dispositions or temperaments and stress responding.[48]

Because activation of neural circuits supporting fear and anxiety should produce elevations in GCs, young children who are temperamentally prone to be shy, anxious, and inhibited are expected to produce more marked GC responses to situations that evoke shy, inhibited behavior.[17] Socially fearful infants and toddlers do show larger increases in cortisol over the child care day, as do preschool boys with similar emotional dispositions.[18–20] In preliminary data from my laboratory, shy, cautious preschoolers compared to exuberant, extroverted preschoolers also exhibit a larger GC response (area under the curve, AUC) when exposed to a room filled with the opportunity for "risky" behavior.[21] Finally, GC levels near the time of awakening have been reported to be higher in extremely inhibited children.[22] Thus, these findings are consistent with predictions. Against these findings, however, are studies of children during the first weeks of a new school year, showing that under these conditions shy, cautious children may exhibit smaller GC increases than exuberant, extroverted children.[23,24]

The results are more consistent for negative emotionality, a temperament dimension consisting of nonsocial fearfulness, sadness, discomfort, anger proneness, and problems in soothing or calming.[25] Negative emotionality has frequently been found to correlate with higher GC levels, particularly when GCs are measured in the home or in other situations that are familiar to the child.[26–28] Higher GC levels in preschoolers under familiar conditions have also been shown to be predictive of social withdrawal several months later in kindergarten and heightened teacher-reported behavior problems over a year later in first grade.[29,30] Negative emotionality has been shown to correlate with greater right than left frontal electroencephalographic (EEG) activity in children and adults.[48] In monkeys (see Kalin, this volume), greater right than left frontal EEG activity correlates with higher GC levels. While there is a great deal of complexity that still needs to be understood, the extant evidence does point to potentially important associations between GC set points early in life and the development of negative emotional dispositions.

EARLY ADVERSITY AND LATER L-HPA ACTIVITY

Evidence that early adverse life conditions produce long-term changes in activity of the L-HPA system is meager, but suggestive. Physical and sexual maltreatment early in life as well as severe neglect has been associated with higher GC levels and/ or larger L-HPA responses to stressors several years post-rescue.[31–33] However, the clearest effects have been obtained in individuals who, in addition to early maltreatment, also suffer concurrent mood disorders.[31,33] Additionally, in some studies evidence of hypo-GC rather than hyper-GC responsivity has been observed (see Ref. 34 for a review). Evidence that less drastic variations in early experience predict later GC activity is not as available, but is compelling. In one large-scale study, home GC levels in children at 4.5 years were associated with maternal stress and family socioeconomic status; however, this was true only if both the concurrent home environment was stressful and the environment had been stressful in the child's infancy.[29] These data would suggest that early adverse care may sensitize the L-HPA system to later stressful conditions, similar to the evidence in rodents and nonhuman primates. Likewise, a study of maternal depression, which should be a significant stressor for young children, showed that controlling for concurrent maternal depression, maternal depression in infancy predicted higher home GC levels among 3-year-old children.[35] Data such as those reviewed in this section should encourage further examination of the role of early experiences in shaping responsivity of the neural circuits regulating stress and negative emotionality in children.

ANOMALOUS FINDINGS

The data reviewed herein have led our network to believe that there is considerable consistency between basic animal and human developmental findings. Nonetheless, we also have uncovered several distinctly anomalous findings that beg explanation. The first of these anomalous findings involves one of the most consistent results in the human literature on early GC responses to challenge. In animals, bringing them into a new situation or altering their home environment stimulates increased L-HPA activity.[36] Novelty, uncertainty, and unpredictability are also salient stimulators of the L-HPA axis for human adults.[37] Among adults, coming into the laboratory for testing may also be a stressor exemplifying preparatory responses of the L-HPA system. By at least 9 years of age, children may show this kind of preparatory response, as noted by Tottenham and colleagues[38] who found that laboratory baselines averaged 40% higher than home baselines at the same time of day. By contrast, nearly every study of infants, toddlers, and preschoolers that has examined laboratory versus comparable home baselines has reported significant *decreases* in cortisol levels in response to coming into the novel laboratory setting. When observed in infants, the effect was attributed to the potential soporific effect of the car ride to the laboratory.[39] However, this hypothesis is less tenable now, as similar findings have now been obtained for 4-year-old children.[21]

A recent study by Goldberg and colleagues, who also noted a drop from home to laboratory, demonstrated that laboratory rather than home baselines were more likely to reveal stable individual differences in GC responsivity among toddlers.[9] This was a small study ($n < 30$ children), and needs replication. Even if we can ignore home baselines in examining individual differences in GC responsivity in children, we may need to attend to them in interpreting and designing studies. For example, if in laboratory testing young children's baselines are lower than home levels, can we adequately examine the efficacy of negative feedback regulation of the axis? Presumably, such regulation should require that elevations in GCs lead to occupation of the glucocorticoid receptor (GR). But if the laboratory elevations we see are in ranges that are below home baseline levels, it is unlikely that they lead to significant GR occupation. Another reason we may need to understand the mechanisms that produce this suppression of GCs to novelty in young children is that they may be sensitive to early disturbances in caregiving. For example, in a study of infants and toddlers in foster care, Dozier and colleagues[40] found that the foster care infants did not show the decrease in GCs from home to laboratory, whereas their community comparison group did.

The second of these anomalous findings concerns the sensitivity of the daytime diurnal pattern of cortisol production to variations in psychosocial context. Disturbances in diurnal rhythms have been reported in adults and some adolescents with mood disorders; however, these are due to elevated later afternoon and evening GCs (e.g., depression)[41] or extremely low afternoon and evening levels (e.g., PTSD).[42] However, Heim and colleagues[43] have noted that the lack of a daytime diurnal rhythm due more to low early morning than altered afternoon and evening levels is sometimes observed in adults and may be coupled with hypo-GC rather than hyper-GC responses to acute stressors. Young children living under conditions of neglect and relationship disruption also have been noted to exhibit a similar, low and flat pattern of GC production over the daytime hours.[34] In young children, at least, this low, flat diurnal GC pattern does not appear to be permanent, but rather varies with the caregiving environment. Randomly assigning children to foster care placements where parents have ongoing support and training relative to community foster care results in improvement in GC daily rhythms over a 6-month period.[13] Pilot studies supported by our network have shown that both an unpredictable separation paradigm and naturally occurring maternal maltreatment result in similar blunted patterns of diurnal GC production in rhesus monkeys. The availability of a non-human primate model allows examination of the neurobiological and molecular mechanism mediating the susceptibility of diurnal GC rhythm in young primates to disturbances in caregiving. We suspect that these effects may be related to other diurnal changes, such as alterations in the quality of nighttime sleep.

Finally, there is the anomaly of developmental timing. As noted, the sensitive period for shaping the L-HPA system in the rodent is described as early, during the first 2 postnatal weeks. Given differences in neural maturity at birth between rodents and primates, the equivalent period of brain development in humans should be primarily prenatal.[5] Yet, the data just reviewed for children deals with development over a number of postnatal years. There are at least two ways that this apparent discrepancy may be resolved. First, the sensitive period in rodents may be wider than originally believed. With development, the pup becomes less dependent on the dam for stimulation and more dependent on what is provided by the nonmaternal social and physical environment. Manipulations that disturb dam–pup interaction may become less important in shaping the developing neural circuits involved in stress reactivity and regulation, but this may not necessarily mean that experience becomes less important. Indeed, recent evidence that early licking/grooming effects can be largely reversed (except for GR number) by placing pups in complex social and physical environments at weaning argues for a period of developmental plasticity in the rodent stress system that extends into at least the early postweaning period.[44]

The second, and not mutually exclusive, possibility is that species differences in the organization of the L-HPA system and in the distribution of its family of neuropeptides and receptors shifts or widens the developmental window for early experience effects in nonhuman primates and humans. Recent anatomical studies indicate that marked species differences exist in the distribution of GC and CRH receptors, particularly in limbic regions.[45,46] Relative to the rodent, humans and some Old World primates may have far fewer GRs in the hippocampus. Furthermore, distributions of both MRs and GRs, and CRH receptors in primates suggest considerable reliance on corticolimbic circuits, particularly circuits involving the medial prefrontal area, in the regulation of stress and emotion responses to perturbations.[46] Interestingly, social buffering of the L-HPA system appears to emerge strongly between 12 and 24 months in humans, and this corresponds to the period of rapid development of the prefrontal cortex and the organization of self-regulatory behavior.[47] It seems possible that in humans, early environmental regulation of the developing stress-emotion system encompasses those processes that heavily target the organization of corticolimbic circuits. If so, this presents another challenge to translation of the rodent early experience story. Specifically, a strong developmental focus needs to be encouraged in the nascent field of affective neuroscience that would support adequate identification and examination of the corticolimbic circuits impacted by early experiences and involved in the regulation of stress and emotion in human development.

SUMMARY AND CONCLUSIONS

Review of the human literature suggests that, as in rodents, early experiences affect the development of the L-HPA system. However, although a number of findings are strikingly comparable in humans to those noted in basic, preclinical studies, evidence also suggests that the human early experience story will have uniquely human components. Translating the basic neuroscience findings to enhance our understanding of the roots of mental illness in children will require attention to data that are inconsistent as well as those that are consistent with the animal models.

ACKNOWLEDGMENTS

This work was supported by a K05 award (MH 66208) and a network grant (MH 65046) to the author. The author wishes to thank the members of the National Institute of Mental Health Early Experience, Stress Neurobiology & Prevention Science Network for their helpful comments and critiques: R.G. Barr, J. Black, M. Dozier, P. Fisher, N. Fox, C. Neal, P. Plotsky, S. Pollak, S. Levine, M. Sanchez, S. Suomi, and D. Vazquez.

REFERENCES

1. GOLD, P.W. et al. 1988. Clinical and biochemical manifestations of depression: relations to the neurobiology of stress. N. Engl. J. Med. **319:** 348–353.
2. GOODYER, I.M. & P.M.E. ALTHAM. 1991. Lifetime exit events and recent social and family adversities in anxious and depressed school-age children and adolescents. J. Affect. Dis. **21:** 219–228.
3. ROSEN, J.B. & J. SCHULKIN. 1998. From normal fear to pathological anxiety. Psychol. Rev. **105:** 325–350.
4. NEMEROFF, C.B. 1996. The corticotropin-releasing factor (CRF) hypothesis of depression. Mol. Psychiatry **1:** 336–342.
5. SANCHEZ, M.M. et al. 2001. Early adverse experience as a developmental risk factor for later psychopathology: evidence from rodent and primate models. Dev. Psychopathol. **13:** 419–450.
6. BRUNSON, K.L. et al. 2002. Corticotropin-releasing hormone (CRH) downregulates the function of its receptor (CRF1) and induces CRF1 expression in hippocampal and cortical regions of the immature rat brain. Exp. Neurol. **176:** 75–86.
7. GUNNAR, M.R. & B. DONZELLA. 2002. Social regulation of the LHPA axis in early human development. Psychoneuroendocrinology **27:** 199–220.
8. MENDOZA, S.P. et al. 1980. Functional consequences of attachment: a comparison of two species. In Maternal Influences and Early Behavior. R.W. Bell and W.P. Smotherman, Eds.: 235–252. Spectrum Press. New York.
9. GOLDBERG, S. et al. 2003. Cortisol concentrations in 12-18-month-old infants: stability over time, location, and stressor. Biol Psychiatry **54:** 719–726.
10. LEWIS, M. & D. RAMSAY. 1995. Stability and change in cortisol and behavioral responses to stress during the first 18 months of life. Dev. Psychobiol. **28:** 419–428.
11. PRUESSNER, J.C. et al. 1997. Increasing correlations between personality traits and cortisol stress responses obtained by data aggregation. Psychoneuroendocrinology **22:** 615–625.
12. BRUCE, J. et al. 2000. The relationships between cortisol patterns, growth retardation, and developmental delays in post-institutionalized children. In International Conference on Infant Studies. Brighton, England.
13. FISHER, P.A. et al. 2003. Impact of a Psychosocial Intervention on Foster Children's Problem Behavior and Daytime Diurnal HPA Axis Activity. Under review.
14. GUNNAR, M. et al. 1988. Coping with uncertainty: new models of the relations between hormonal, behavioral and cognitive processes. In Coping with Uncertainty. D. Palermo, Ed.: 101–130. Erlbaum. Hillsdale, N.J.

15. GUNNAR, M. *et al.* 1992. The stressfulness of separation among 9-month-old infants: effects of social context variables and infant temperament. Child Dev. **63:** 290–303.
16. SPANGLER, G. & M. SCHIECHE. 1998. Emotional and adrenocortical responses of infants to the strange situation: the differential function of emotional expression. Int. J. Behav. Dev. **22:** 681–706.
17. KAGAN, J. *et al.* 1987. The physiology and psychology of behavioral inhibition in children. Child Dev. **58:** 1459–1473.
18. GRANGER, D. *et al.* 1994. Preschoolers' behavioral and neuroendocrine responses to social challenge. Merrill-Palmer Q. **40:** 20–41.
19. TOUT, K. *et al.* 1998. Social behavior correlates of adrenocortical activity in daycare: gender differences and time-of-day effects. Child Dev. **69:** 1247–1262.
20. WATAMURA, S. *et al.* 2003. Morning to afternoon increases in cortisol concentrations for infants and toddlers at childcare. Child Dev. **74:** 1006–1020.
21. TALGE, N. *et al.* 2003. Cortisol and behavioral responses to laboratory tasks designed to elicit behavioral inhibition in preschool-aged children. In preparation.
22. SCHMIDT, L.A. *et al.* 1997. Behavioral and neuroendocrine responses in shy children. Dev. Psychobiol. **30:** 127–140.
23. BRUCE, J. *et al.* 2002. Individual differences in children's cortisol response to the beginning of a new school year. Psychoneuroendocrinology **27:** 635–650.
24. DAVIS, E.P. *et al.* 1999. The start of a new school year: individual differences in salivary cortisol response in relation to child temperament. Dev. Psychobiol. **35:** 188–196.
25. AHADI, S. *et al.* 1993. Children's temperament in the U.S. and China: similiarities and differences. Eur. J. Pers. **7:** 359–377.
26. GUNNAR, M.R. *et al.* 1997. Temperament, social competence, and adrenocortical activity in preschoolers. Dev. Psychobiol. **31:** 65–85.
27. DETTLING, A. *et al.* 1999. Cortisol levels of young children in full-day childcare centers: relations with age and temperament. Psychoneuroendocrinology **24:** 505–518.
28. DETTLING, A. *et al.* 2000. Quality of care and temperament determine whether cortisol levels rise over the day for children in full-day child care. Psychoneuroendocrinology **25:** 819–36.
29. ESSEX, M.J. *et al.* 2002. Maternal stress beginning in infancy may sensitize children to later stress exposure: effects on cortisol and behavior. Biol. Psychiatry **52:** 776–784.
30. SMIDER, N. *et al.* 2002. Salivary cortisol as a apredictor of socioemotional adjustment during kindergarten: a prospective study. Child Dev. **73:** 75–92.
31. DE BELLIS, M.D. *et al.* 1999. Developmental traumatology. Part 1: Biological stress systems. Biol. Psychiatry **9:** 1259–1270.
32. GUNNAR, M. *et al.* 2001. Salivary cortisol levels in children adopted from Romanian orphanages. Dev. Psychopathol. **13:** 611–628.
33. HEIM, C. *et al.* 2000. Pituitary-adrenal and autonomic responses to stress in women after sexual and physical abuse in childhood. J. Am. Med. Assoc. **284:** 592–597.
34. GUNNAR, M. & D.M. Vazquez. 2001. Low cortisol and a flattening of the expected daytime rhythm: potential indices of risk in human development. Dev. Psychopathol. **13:** 516–538.
35. HESSL, D. *et al.* 1998. A longitudinal study of children of depressed mothers: psychobiological findings related to stress. *In* Advancing Research on Developmental Plasticity: Integrating the Behavioral Sciences and the Neurosciences of Mental Health. D.M. HANN *et al.*, Eds. National Institutes of Mental Health. Bethesda, MD.
36. HENNESSY, M.B. & S. LEVINE. 1978. Sensitive pituitary–adrenal responsiveness to varying intensities of psychological stimulation. Phys. Behav. **21:** 295–297.
37. KIRSCHBAUM, C. & D.H. HELLHAMMER. 1994. Salivary cortisol in psychoneuroendocrine research: recent developments and application. Psychoneuroendocrinology **19:** 313–333.
38. TOTTENHAM, N. *et al.* 2003. Temperament, autonomic activity, and cortisol elevations to the Trier Social Stress Test among 9-year-old girls. In preparation.
39. LARSON, M. *et al.* 1991. The effects of morning naps, car trips, and maternal separation on adrenocortical activity in human infants. Child Dev. **62:** 362–372.
40. DOZIER, M. *et al.* 2003. Foster children's stability of care and diurnal production of cortisol. Under review.

41. DAHL, R. *et al.* 1991. 24-Hour cortisol measures in adolescents with major depression: a controlled study. Biol. Psychiatry **30:** 25–36.

42. YEHUDA, R. 2000. Biology of posttraumatic stress disorder. J. Clin. Psychiatry **61:** 12–21.

43. HEIM, C. *et al.* 2000. The potential role of hypocortisolism in the pathophysiology of stress-related bodily disorders. Psychoneuroendocrinology **25:** 1–35.

44. FRANCIS, D. *et al.* 2002. Environmental enrichment reverses the effects of maternal separation on stress reactivity. J. Neurosci. **22:** 7840–7843.

45. SÁNCHEZ, M.M. *et al.* 1999. Autoradiographic and in situ hybridization localization of CRF1 and CRF2 receptors in non-human primate brain. J. Comp. Neurol. **408:** 365–377.

46. SANCHEZ, M.M. *et al.* 2000. Distribution of corticosteroid receptors in the Rhesus brain: relative absence of glucocorticoid receptors in the hippocampal formation. J. Neurosci. **20:** 4657–4668.

47. DAWSON, G. *et al.* 1992. The role of frontal lobe functioning in the development of infant self-regulatory behavior. Brain Cognit. **20:** 152–175.

48. DAVIDSON, R.J. 2003. The neural substrates of affective style across development. Paper presented at Conference on Roots of Mental Illness in Children. The Rockefeller University, New York.

The Serotonin Transporter Gene in Aggressive Children with and without ADHD and Nonaggressive Matched Controls

JOSEPH H. BEITCHMAN,[a,b] KRISTEN M. DAVIDGE, [a,b] JAMES L. KENNEDY,[b] LESLIE ATKINSON,[b] VIVIEN LEE,[b] SOLOMON SHAPIRO, [b] AND LORI DOUGLAS[b]

[a]Hospital for Sick Children, Department of Psychiatry, and

[b]Centre for Addiction and Mental Health, Clarke Division, Toronto, Ontario, Canada

ABSTRACT: Using an ethnically homogeneous sample of highly aggressive Caucasian children and their matched controls, we report differential associations of the 5HTTLPR and VNTR polymorphisms with ADHD and aggression, respectively. Given the small sample size and the peliminary nature of our findings, replication is necessary.

KEYWORDS: serotonin transporter gene; aggression; children; attention deficit hyperactivity disorder (ADHD)

INTRODUCTION

Considerable evidence indicates that serotonin system dysfunction is related to aggressive behavior in animals[1,2] and human adults.[3,4] However, studies examining this relationship in children have yielded mixed results, with some reporting a positive correlation between 5HT function and aggression,[5,6] and others reporting an inverse association[7] or none at all.[8,9] To explain these discrepancies, researchers have pointed to the heterogeneous nature of aggressive behavior in children, with some evidence that low 5HT functioning may be specifically associated with childhood aggression that is extreme and persistent.[7,9,10] Inconsistent findings among child studies have also been posited to stem from differences in comorbid conditions across samples, specifically in the proportion of participants with a diagnosis of attention deficit hyperactivity disorder (ADHD).[11] The aforementioned studies that reported an inverse or no association between central 5HT function and aggression were conducted in samples that contained fewer cases of ADHD than those that reported a positive correlation. Accordingly, it has been suggested that the presence of ADHD may influence the relationship between serotonin and aggression.

Address for correspondence: Dr. Joseph H Beitchman, Centre for Addiction and Mental Health, Clarke Division, 250 College Street, Toronto, Ontario M5T 1R8, Canada.
Joe_Beitchman@camh.net

Ann. N.Y. Acad. Sci. 1008: 248–251 (2003). © 2003 New York Academy of Sciences.
doi: 10.1196/annals.1301.025

METHODS

In this case-control study, we investigated whether the serotonin transporter (5HTT) gene, which encodes the protein responsible for reuptake of serotonin from the synaptic cleft, is a susceptibility factor for extreme, persistent, and pervasive aggressive behavior in children. Two polymorphisms of the 5HTT gene were examined, a 44-bp insertion/deletion in the promoter region and a variable number of tandem repeats (VNTR) in intron 2. The VNTR polymorphism consists of 9, 10, or 12 copies of a 16–17-bp repeat element that may influence transcription of the 5HTT gene.[12] The promoter polymorphism (5HTTLPR) has long (l) and short (s) alleles that differ in transcriptional efficiencies, with approximately twofold greater expression of the 5HTT gene for the l/l genotype than the l/s or s/s genotypes.[13] We hypothesized a significant difference in allele and/or genotype frequencies between aggressive children and nonaggressive matched controls for one or both of these polymorphisms. To further examine the role of the serotonin transporter, we divided our sample of cases into an aggressive ADHD group and an aggressive non-ADHD group.

Families were recruited through mailed advertisements to schools, pediatricians, and mental health agencies. Conditions for inclusion in the study included scores above the nintieth percentile on the aggression subscales of both the Child Behavior Checklist and the Teacher's Report Form, and a minimum 2-year history of aggression according to the Diagnostic Interview Schedule for Children (DISC) administered to the primary caretaker. The DISC was also administered to establish concurrent diagnoses of ADHD. A two-subtest short form of the Wechsler Intelligence Scale for Children—3rd Edition (WISC-III; Information and Similarities) was used to assess subject IQ. Any children scoring lower than 80 were excluded. Other exclusion criteria included chronic medical illness, diagnosed neurological disorder, and diagnoses of schizophrenia, mania, autism, Tourette's, or pervasive developmental disorder. To reduce ethnic stratification effects and thereby simplify the interpretation of findings, this sample was restricted to Caucasians. Genotyping was completed for 41 Caucasian children classified as aggressive (33 males and 8 females; mean age 10.3 years) and 41 controls of the same ethnic origin who were recruited via local advertisements and matched to probands on the basis of gender. Differences in allele and genotype frequencies were analyzed via chi square or Fisher's exact tests (two-tailed) where appropriate.

RESULTS

The 10R allele of the 5HTT VNTR polymorphism was significantly less frequent among cases than controls ($\chi^2 = 5.959$, $P = .015$). Recent studies have shown increased levels of 5HTT expression in embryonic stem cell constructs having the 12R allele as compared to the 10R allele.[12] Since higher levels of the serotonin transporter protein could result in decreased synaptic serotonin via faster reuptake, conceivably either the 12R allele confers risk for or the 10R allele confers protection from the reduced serotonergic activity associated with aggressive behavior.

No significant association was found between the second serotonin transporter polymorphism, 5HTTLPR, and aggression in our sample; however, there was a significant link between 5HTTLPR and ADHD. Aggressive children with ADHD ($n = 29$) were significantly more likely to have either one or two copies of the 'l' allele than were those without ADHD ($n = 9$) (89.7% vs. 55.6%; Fisher's exact test, $P = .041$). This finding provides support for a role for the serotonin promoter polymorphism in ADHD, along with several recent studies that have demonstrated either increased frequency of the "l" allele and/or decreased prevalence of the "s/s" genotype among individuals with ADHD.[14–16] By contrast, the 5HTT VNTR polymorphism has not been implicated in susceptibility to ADHD in our sample or previous studies.

CONCLUSION

Using an ethnically homogeneous sample of highly aggressive Caucasian children and their matched controls, results presented here suggest differential associations of the 5HTT LPR and VNTR polymorphisms with ADHD and aggression. Given the small sample size and the preliminary nature of our findings, replication is necessary.

REFERENCES

1. GINGRICH, J.A. & R. HEN. 2001. Dissecting the role of the serotonin system in neuropsychiatric disorders using knockout mice. Psychopharmacology 155: 1–10.
2. MEHLMAN, P.T. et al. 1994. Low CSF 5-HIAA concentrations and severe aggression and impaired impulse control in nonhuman primates. Am. J. Psychiatry 151: 1485–1491.
3. DAVIDSON, R.J., K.M. PUTNAM & C.L. LARSON. 2000. Dysfunction in the neural circuitry of emotion regulation: a possible prelude to violence. Science 289: 591–594.
4. LEE, R. & E. COCCARO. 2001. The neuropsychopharmacology of criminality and aggression. Can. J. Psychiatry 46: 35–44.
5. HALPERIN, J.M. et al. 1994. Serotonergic function in aggressive and nonaggressive boys with attention deificit hyperactivity disorder. Am. J. Psychiatry 151: 243–248.
6. PINE, D.S. et al. 1997. Neuroendocrine response to fenfluramine challenge in boys. Arch. Gen. Psychiatry 54: 839–846.
7. KRUESI, M.J.P. et al. 1992. A 2-year prospective follow-up study of children and adolescents with disruptive behavior disorders. Arch. Gen. Psychiatry 49: 429–435.
8. STOFF, D.M. et al. 1992. Neuroendocrine responses to challenge with D,L-fenfluramine and aggression in disruptive behavior disorders of children and adolescents. Psychiatry Res. 43: 263–276.
9. HALPERIN, J.M. et al. 1997. Serotonin, aggression and parental psychopathology in children with attention-deficit hyperactivity disorder. Am. J. Psychiatry 151: 243–248.
10. NEWCORN, J.H. et al. 1996. Emotionality and serotonergic function in aggressive and non-aggressive ADHD children. Sci. Proc. Ann. Meet. Am. Acad. Child Adolesc. Psychiatry 12: 94.
11. SCHULZ, K.P. et al. 2001. Relationship between central serotonergic function and aggression in prepubertal boys: effect of age and attention-deficit/hyperactivity disorder. Psychiatry Res. 101: 1–10.
12. MACKENZIE, A. & J. QUINN. 1999. A serotonin transporter gene intron 2 polymorphic region, correlated with affective disorders, has allele-dependent differential enhancer-like properties in the mouse embryo. Proc. Natl. Acad. Sci. USA 96: 15251–15255.
13. HEILS, A. et al. 1996. Allelic variation of human serotonin transporter gene expression. J. Neurochem. 66: 2621–2624.

14. MANOR, I. *et al.* 2001. Family-based association study of the serotonin transporter promoter region polymorphism (5-HTTLPR) in attention deficit hyperactivity disorder. Am. J. Med. Genet. **105:** 91–95.
15. KENT, L. *et al.* 2002. Evidence that variation at the serotonin transporter gene influences susceptibility to attention deficit hyperactivity disorder (ADHD): analysis and pooled analysis. Mol. Psychiatry **7:** 908–912.
16. ZOROGLU, S.S. *et al.* 2002. Significance of serotonin transporter gene 5-HTTLPR and variable number of tandem repeat polymorphism in attention deficit hyperactivity disorder. Neuropsychobiology **45:** 176–181.

Effortful Control, Attention, and Aggressive Behavior in Preschoolers at Risk for Conduct Problems

TRACY A. DENNIS AND LAURIE MILLER BROTMAN

New York University Child Study Center, New York, New York 10016, USA

ABSTRACT: This work examines distinct aspects of effortful control and attention predicted aggression in a group of children at elevated risk for the development of conduct problems. Results suggested that behavioral inhibition, rather than attentional control, best predicted maternal reports of child aggressive behaviors.

KEYWORDS: effortful control; attention; preschoolers; aggressive behavior; conduct problems

INTRODUCTION

Aggressive behavior in young children is multiply determined. Individual, family, and contextual factors have been implicated in the development of aggression. Children who have problems inhibiting behavior are at elevated risk for the development of aggressive behavior, as are children who are inattentive and impulsive.[1] Studies of the ability to voluntarily inhibit behavior, or Effortful Control (EC), have been carried out with normally developing low-risk children. In these studies, EC has been reliably measured with behavioral tasks and yields three distinct subcomponents: motor control, inhibition in response to a signal, and delay.[1] The relations among EC, attention, and the development of aggressive behavior remain poorly understood.

The present study assessed EC, attention, and aggressive behavior in young children at risk for the development of conduct problems. Study aims were to (1) evaluate the psychometric properties of the EC measure in a high-risk sample, and (2) examine the relations among the three components of EC, attention, and aggressive behavior. We hypothesized that of the three EC components, inhibition would be most strongly related to parent-reported aggression and that attention and inhibition would make independent contributions to the prediction of aggressive behavior.

METHOD

Participants. Participants were 37 of 99 children participating in a larger prevention trial. Inclusion criteria for the larger trial required that children be the younger

Address for correspondence: Tracy A. Dennis, Ph.D., Department of Psychology, Hunter College, 695 Park Avenue, New York, NY 10021. Voice: 212-650-3878; fax: 212-650-3931.
tden@hunter.cuny.edu

Ann. N.Y. Acad. Sci. 1008: 252–255 (2003). © 2003 New York Academy of Sciences.
doi: 10.1196/annals.1301.026

TABLE 1. Descriptive statistics for EC, Attention, and Aggression scores

Variables	Total	Males	Females	Younger (4–5)	Older (6–7)
EC-Motor	−0.03 (0.89)	0.06 (0.96)	−0.13 (0.82)	−0.31 (0.85)	0.22 (0.88))
EC-Inhibition	0.00 (0.75)	−0.21 (0.67)	0.21 (0.75)	−0.41 (0.83)	0.38 (0.30)
EC-Delay	0.00 (0.85)	−0.05 (0.93)	0.05 (0.80)	−0.03 (0.94)	0.03 (0.78)
K-CPT-Inattention	12.6 (10.2)	16.8 (11.9)	8.2 (5.6)	13.0 (12.8)	12.3 (7.3)
K-CPT-Impulsivity	48.1 (24.5)	47.1 (23.6)	49.3 (26.1)	56.2 (28.4)	40.5 (17.7)
CBCL-Aggression t Score	54.1 (06.2)	53.5 (5.6)	55.8 (7.0)	54.6 (6.7)	54.7 (5.8)

NOTE: Values are means and standard deviations, in parentheses.

siblings of youth adjudicated through the New York City Family Court. The vast majority of children were from low-income families. The subsample in the current study was above the age of 4 years at the assessment phase of interest and had complete EC, attention, and aggression data. The sample included 19 males and 18 females, with a mean age of 71.8 months (SD = 8.9, range = 53–90). Twenty-seven were African-American and 10 were Latino.

Effortful Control. The Effortful Control Battery consists of a series of nine tasks requiring the child to control, inhibit, and delay responses (see TABLE 2 for examples).[2] Scores were standardized and averaged across tasks and yielded Motor Control, Inhibition, and Delay subscales.

Attention. The Continuous Performance Test–Kiddie Version (K-CPT) is a computerized test that requires children to inhibit a prepotent response by pressing a space bar only at the appearance of target pictures.[3] Children received approximately 200 trials over 7 minutes. Percent errors of omission reflect inattention, and percent errors of commission reflect impulsivity.

Aggression. Aggression was assessed with the aggression subscale of the parent report version of the Child Behavior Checklist (CBCL) (e.g., fights, argues, teases, and bullies).[4] Raw scores were transformed to *t* scores based on age and gender-based norms.

RESULTS

TABLE 1 presents descriptive statistics for all variables: three subscales of EC, two measures of K-CPT attention, and aggression. Males showed greater inattention than females, $t(35) = 2.77$, $P < .05$, and older children showed greater EC Inhibition than younger children, $t(35) = 3.89$, $P < .01$.

The overall construct of EC and two of the three subscales (Motor Control and inhibition) yielded moderate to high internal consistencies. The internal consistency of the Delay subscale was low relative to the other scales and compared to findings from previous studies with low-risk children (TABLE 2).

Zero-order correlations among all variables showed that both the EC Inhibition and Motor Control subscales were negatively correlated with K-CPT impulsivity

TABLE 2. Reliability statistics for subscales of effortful control

Subscale	β or R	Tasks from the EC Battery
Motor Control	$R = .65$	Walking a line slowly
		Tracing stars and circles slowly
Inhibition	$\beta = .78$	Simon Says
		Whispering on demand
		Taking turns while building a block tower
		Matching game with distracters
Delay	$\beta = .38$	Delay eating food
		Delay touching a toy
		Delay touching a wrapped present
Total scale	$\beta = .77$	

($R = -.41$ and -52, respectively; $P < .001$), but were unrelated to K-CPT inattention. EC inhibition was significantly negatively correlated with aggression ($R = -.37$, $P < .01$). Of the two attention measures, only K-CPT impulsivity was marginally positively associated with aggression ($R = .25$, $P < .07$).

Next, in a hierarchical multiple regression, age was entered in the first step and K-CPT impulsivity and EC Inhibition in the second step (stepwise forward method). Only EC Inhibition accounted for significant variance in aggression t scores: $r2 = .14$, $Fch = 5.85$, $P < .05$, and $\beta = -.48$.

DISCUSSION

The overall psychometric properties of the EC battery were adequate when applied to this high-risk sample. There was strong internal consistency for the Total scale and for the Motor Control and Inhibition subscales of EC, although internal consistency was modest for the Delay subscale. The Inhibition and Motor Control subscales were negatively correlated with K-CPT impulsivity, but not with K-CPT inattention. EC Inhibition was significantly negatively associated with aggression.

The modest internal consistency for the Delay subscale might reflect less consolidation of this capacity in early school age and might account for low correlations between Delay and aggression. The fact that EC (Inhibition and Motor Control) was associated with K-CPT impulsivity but not K-CPT inattention suggests that these measures are overlapping and may be tapping into a similar construct of inhibition. This construct, and not inattention *per se*, might be related to parent-reported aggressive behavior.

Despite associations between EC Inhibition and K-CPT impulsivity, only EC Inhibition accounted for significant variance in aggression scores. Therefore, children who are aggressive may have specific deficits in the ability to *inhibit* behavior rather than in attending effectively to their environment. This finding requires replication with larger samples. If the finding is replicated, then intervention programs for children at risk for conduct problems might increase effectiveness by focusing on the promotion of inhibitory skills.

In conclusion, although limited by a small sample size, this study of children exposed to multiple risk factors for conduct problems provides suggestive evidence of the multifaceted nature of EC and its distinct associations with aggressive behavior.

REFERENCES

1. KOCHANSKA, G., K.T. MURRAY & E.T. HARLAN. 2000. Effortful control in early childhood: continuity and change, antecedents, and implications for social development. Dev. Psychol. **36:** 220–232.
2. KOCHANSKA, G. & K.T. MURRAY. The Effortful Control Battery. Unpublished Manual. University of Iowa, Iowa City.
3. ACHENBACH, T.M. 1991. Manual for the Child Behavior Checklist/4-18 and 1991 Profile. Department of Psychiatry, University of Vermont. Burlington, VT.
4. CONNERS, C.K. & MHS STAFF. 2001. Conners' K-CPT Manual. Multi-Health Systems, Inc. North Towanda, NY.

Functional Neuroimaging of Social Cognition in Pervasive Developmental Disorders

A Brief Review

ADRIANA DI MARTINO AND F. XAVIER CASTELLANOS

New York University Child Study Center, New York, New York 10016, USA

ABSTRACT: An emerging literature on the neuroanatomical correlates of social cognition in pervasive developmental disorders is reviewed. Studies conducted with high-functioning adults with autism or Asperger's syndrome highlight patterns of decreased activation in ventromedial prefrontal cortex, temporoparietal junction, amygdala, and periamygdaloid cortex, along with aberrantly increased activation in primary sensory cortices. Future studies should extend these important initial results to younger and more severely affected subjects.

KEYWORDS: social cognition; pervasive developmental disorders; functional neuroimaging

INTRODUCTION

Social cognition is the ability to interpret and predict another's behavior in terms of beliefs, intentions, and desires and to use flexibly the representation of the relations between oneself and others to guide social behavior.[1] Impairment in social cognition has been hypothesized to be one of the principal roots in the pathogenesis of Pervasive Developmental Disorders (PDD), which are early-onset neurodevelopmental disorders characterized by impairments in social functioning, verbal and nonverbal communication, and restricted patterns of interests and activities. Postmortem brain studies have shown some neurobiological abnormalities in PDD, but it has been difficult to relate such anatomic findings to behavioral impairments. By contrast, functional brain imaging studies can provide information on the neuronal substrates of social cognition in healthy subjects and in patients with PDD, thus contributing to the delineation of brain-behavior relationships and to a more neurobiologically informed dissection of the various phenotypes. This review, focusing on functional neuroimaging studies of PDD as they relate to two aspects of social cognition, mentalizing and face processing tasks, was conducted after a Medline search using the words "functional imaging" matched with "autism" and/or "PDD" and "social cognition" and/or "theory of mind."

Address for correspondence: F. Xavier Castellanos, M.D., NYU Child Study Center, 577 First Avenue, CSC Room 204, New York, NY 10016-6404. Voice: 212-263-3697; fax: 212-263-8662. castef01@med.nyu.edu

Ann. N.Y. Acad. Sci. 1008: 256–260 (2003). © 2003 New York Academy of Sciences.
doi: 10.1196/annals.1301.027

SOCIAL COGNITION IN NORMAL ADULTS

The current consensus model of the neuronal circuits underlying social cognition in normal adults is described in detail in several recent comprehensive reviews.[1-3] Briefly, this circuit includes ventromedial prefrontal cortex, amygdala with adjacent temporal pole, and temporoparietal junction. More specifically, mentalizing, defined as the ability to represent the mental states of others and self, is associated with activations of paracingulate cortex, temporoparietal junction (particularly the right superior temporal gyrus), and periamygdaloid temporal cortex.[2] Ventromedial, orbitofrontal, and cingulate cortex are also engaged by emotional experiences in complex situations and underlie volitional control of behavior as well as executive function.[3] The role of the amygdala in threat recognition, whether from faces, eye gaze, or nonbiological motions, is established,[4] but its function in other social behaviors, which had been suggested by early studies,[5] has not been confirmed by recent animal or human lesion studies.[6] Additionally, the fusiform gyrus, a visual association area in the temporal cortex, is a key region for processing social stimuli such as faces.

IMAGING OF SOCIAL COGNITION IN ADULTS WITH PDD

The studies that have explored the neuronal correlates of social cognition in PDD along with their main design characteristics and results are summarized in TABLE 1. As shown in the table, there is now sufficient convergence of results and methods to begin testing regionally specific hypotheses regarding brain abnormalities in PDD and their relation to behavioral abnormalities in social cognition.

Decreased activation of medial prefrontal cortex during different mentalizing tasks has been detected in subjects with high-functioning autism and/or Asperger's syndrome in two studies using different imaging modalities.[7,8] Other frontal regions (inferior frontal gyrus and dorsolateral prefrontal cortex) were underactivated in a study exploring the ability to infer mental states from pictures of eyes.[9] Absent or decreased activation of the left amygdala was reported during the same and a similar task[9,10] and also while processing neutral facial expressions versus inanimate shapes.[11] Decreased activation was also observed in periamygdaloid cortex as well as inferior temporal gyrus and superior temporal sulcus during mentalizing tasks.[7,10]

Hypoactivation of the face area in the right fusiform gyrus has consistently been reported[10-12] in PDD adults looking at faces. This pattern of decreased activation has been accompanied by excessive activation of auxiliary areas such as inferior temporal gyrus (implicated in processing objects)[12] and frontal, occipital, and anterior fusiform gyrus.[11] Abnormally increased activation in PDD subjects than in controls was also observed in primary auditory cortex (superior temporal gyrus)[9,10] and in primary visual cortex[10] during visual processing of emotions in faces. Underactivation of lateral cerebellum, a region not typically considered a component of social cognition circuits, was seen during implicit processing of emotional faces.[10]

In the Castelli et al. study,[7] during a mentalizing task using animations of geometric shapes, medial prefrontal, periamygdaloid, and superior temporal sulcus cortices, but not extrastriate cortex, were underactivated. Connectivity between extrastriate cortex and superior temporal sulcus was significantly weaker in PDD subjects. The authors suggested that this weaker connectivity resulted from a lack of

TABLE 1. Functional neuroimaging studies of social cognition in pervasive developmental disorders

Ref.	Method	PDD Dx/N	PDD Mean (SD) Age	Control n	Control Mean (SD) Age	Task(s)	Differences in PDD Ss	Comments
7	PET	AS/10	33 (7.6)	10	25 (4.8)	Viewing animations of shapes that elicit mental states	↓ basal temporal area (ITG, FG, TP/AMY); STS and MPFC	No difference in extrastriate occipital cortex but reduced connectivity with STS
8	PET	AS/5	24–27 (age range)	6	26–45 (age range)	Attribution of mental state to story	↓ Left MPFC (BA8/9), ↑ in more ventral area (BA9/10)	Same control group as a previous study.[19]
9	fMRI	Aut or AS/6	26.3 (2.1)	12	25.5 (2.8)	Inferring mental states from pictures of eyes	No activation in left AMY; ↓ frontal areas (IFG, DLPFC); ↑ in STG	Judging expression of an extended range of mental states, not only emotional (i.e., interest, reflecting, ignoring).
10	fMRI	AS/7, Aut/2	37 (7)	9	27 (7)	Explicit and implicit processing of emotional facial expressions	↓ in AMY & L cerebellum for implicit task; ↓ right FG across tasks; no activation in left MTG in explicit task; ↑ in left STG and lingual/FG across tasks	
11	FMRI	Aut/7	29.5 (8)	8	20–42 (age range)	Face perception (neutral expression) versus shape perception	↓ Bilaterally in FG and left AMY, ↑ in aberrant and individual specific neural sites (frontal, occipital cortex, anterior FG)	Anatomical study found statistically significant decreased amygdala volume.
12	FMRI	Aut/6, AS/14	23.8 (12.4)	2 groups of 14 Ss.	21.5 (10.6) 23.8 (12.4), respectively	Face versus object discrimination	↓ Bilaterally in FG and left AMY, ↑ in aberrant and individual specific neural sites (frontal, occipital cortex, anterior FG)	Anatomical study found statistically significant decreased amygdala volume.

ABBREVIATIONS: AMY, amygdala; AS, Asperger's syndrome; Aut, autism disorder; BA, Brodmann Area; DLPFC, dorsolateral prefrontal cortex; FG, fusiform gyrus; IFG, inferior frontal gyrus; ITG, inferior temporal gyrus; MPFC, medial prefrontal cortex; MTG, medial temporal gyrus; NC, normal control group; Ss, subjects; STG, superior temporal gyrus; STS, superior temporal sulcus; TP/AMY, temporal pole adjacent to amygdala.

top-down modulation from anterior regions (medial prefrontal cortex, amygdala, and periamygdala) to superior temporal sulcus that normally allows the recognition of the social significance of visual stimuli.

DISCUSSION AND PRELIMINARY CONCLUSIONS

In summary, there is substantial convergence of findings from neuroimaging studies that individuals with PDD do not activate the typical regions associated with social cognition in normal subjects, including ventromedial prefrontal cortex,[7–9] temporoparietal junction, amygdala,[9–11] and periamygdaloid cortex.[7,10] Interestingly, patients with PDD also exhibit abnormally greater activation in atypical regions, including primary visual[10] and auditory[9,10] cortices. Additionally, although such patients show hypoactivation of the fusiform face area,[10–12] they overactivate nearby regions that have been linked to perception and discrimination of objects as opposed to faces.[12] This would appear to confirm that social stimuli such as faces are instead perceived more like objects.

Fusiform gyrus activity was recently shown to be modulated by experience,[13] raising the question of whether decreased activation of the fusiform gyrus in PDD is a primary deficit or merely reflects a lack of expertise in looking at people's faces.[14] A recent study in normal adults showed that perceiving a face meeting the viewer's eyes increases neuronal activity in the ventral striatum, a region that is implicated in reward.[15] Future studies in PDD should investigate whether activation of ventral striatum is related to making eye contact or to joint attention.

Finally, the amygdala appears to be the key region in the social impairments intrinsic to PDD by virtue of its functional location in the brain as the integrator of stimuli from the environment and from prefrontal and other cortical regions.[16–18] This remarkable convergence does not seem to fit with recent results in monkeys with neonatal lesions of the amygdala.[6] In that study, lesioned monkeys showed a decrease in their natural reluctance to engage in novel social relations with conspecifics, that is, they were more social than the nonoperated controls. This paradoxical result at least confirms that the amygdala influences social relatedness and indirectly supports amygdala theories of autism and PDD.

These intriguing results remain preliminary for several reasons. Because of the necessity of performing behavioral tasks inside a scanner, all these studies have focused on adults with PDD who have normal IQ and who therefore are not representative of PDD in general. Although PDD is, by definition, a disorder of development, limiting studies to adults has made it impossible to examine the development of the neuronal bases for dysfunction in social cognition. As neuroimaging techniques continue to improve, we can anticipate being able to study younger and more representative children and adolescents with autistic spectrum disorders and continuing the process of uncovering the roots of these profoundly impairing conditions.

REFERENCES

1. ADOLPHS, R. 2001. The neurobiology of social cognition. Curr. Opin. Neurobiol. **11:** 231–239.
2. FRITH, U. 2001. Mind blindness and the brain in autism. Neuron **32:** 969–979.

3. ADOLPHS, R. 1999. Social cognition and the human brain. Trends Cogn. Sci. **3:** 469–479.
4. AGGLETON, J. 2000. The Amygdala: A Functional Analysis. Oxford University Press. New York.
5. BACHEVALIER, J. 1996. Brief report: medial temporal lobe and autism: a putative animal model in primates. J. Autism Dev. Disord. **26:** 217–220.
6. AMARAL, D.G. et al. 2003. The amygdala: is it an essential component of the neural network for social cognition? Neuropsychologia **41:** 517–522.
7. CASTELLI, F. et al. 2002. Autism, Asperger syndrome and brain mechanisms for the attribution of mental states to animated shapes. Brain **125:** 1839–1849.
8. HAPPE, F. et al. 1996. 'Theory of mind' in the brain. Evidence from a PET scan study of Asperger syndrome. Neuroreport **8:** 197–201.
9. BARON-COHEN, S. et al. 1999. Social intelligence in the normal and autistic brain: an fMRI study. Eur. J. Neurosci. **11:** 1891–1898.
10. CRITCHLEY, H.D. et al. 2000. The functional neuroanatomy of social behaviour: changes in cerebral blood flow when people with autistic disorder process facial expressions. Brain **123**(Pt 11): 2203–2212.
11. PIERCE, K. et al. 2001. Face processing occurs outside the fusiform 'face area' in autism: evidence from functional MRI. Brain **124:** 2059–2073.
12. SCHULTZ, R.T. et al. 2000. Abnormal ventral temporal cortical activity during face discrimination among individuals with autism and Asperger syndrome. Arch. Gen. Psychiatry **57:** 331–340.
13. GAUTHIER, I. et al. 2000. Expertise for cars and birds recruits brain areas involved in face recognition. Nat. Neurosci. **3:** 191–197
14. GRELOTTI, D.J. et al. 2002. Social interest and the development of cortical face specialization: what autism teaches us about face processing. Dev. Psychobiol. **40:** 213–225.
15. KAMPE, K.K. et al. 2001. Reward value of attractiveness and gaze. Nature **413:** 589.
16. BARON-COHEN, S. et al. 2000. The amygdala theory of autism. Neurosci. Behav. Rev. **24:** 355–364.
17. STONE, V.E. et al. 2003. Acquired theory of mind impairments in individuals with bilateral amygdala lesions. Neuropsychologia **41:** 209–220.
18. SWEETEN T.L. et al. 2002. The amygdala and related structures in the pathophysiology of autism. Pharmacol. Biochem. Behav. **71:** 449–455.
19. FLETCHER, P.C. et al. 1995. Other minds in the brain: a functional imaging study of "theory of mind" in story comprehension. Cognition **57:** 109–128.

Hallucinations in Nonpsychotic Children

Findings from a Psychiatric Emergency Service

GAIL A. EDELSOHN, HARRIS RABINOVICH, AND RUBEN PORTNOY

*Department of Psychiatry and Human Behavior, Thomas Jefferson University,
Philadelphia, Pennsylvania 19107, USA*

ABSTRACT: Sixty-two cases of children with hallucinations but without psychosis were identified in a psychiatric emergency service. Auditory hallucinations were more frequent than visual ones. There were positive trends between the content of auditory hallucinations and diagnosis. Recognition of this clinical phenomenon of hallucinations in children in the absence of psychosis and awareness of underlying psychopathology and precipitating factors is necessary in evaluating hallucinations in nonpsychotic children. Children with such presentations run the risk of being misdiagnosed as having psychosis or schizophrenia and being subjected to the inherent risks of treatment with antipsychotics.

KEYWORDS: hallucinations; nonpsychotic; children

INTRODUCTION

Historically there has been an interest in understanding the continuity or discontinuity between childhood and adult psychiatric disorders. This focus certainly had been applied to the area of schizophrenia, with emphasis on the longitudinal study of children at high risk for schizophrenia and tracking the course of childhood onset of psychosis. However, the literature with regard to hallucinations in nonpsychotic children is fairly limited. Published articles include case reports, case series, and few follow-up studies with differences in methods and treatment settings. The prognostic significance of hallucinations in children remains unclear. The National Institute of Mental Health Epidemiologic Catchment Study found 2.8% adults reported hallucinating before age 21. Garralda[1] reported that 1.1% of nonpsychotic children had hallucinations (inpatients and outpatients) over 14 years. The rates of hallucinations vary with the setting, with inpatient units estimated at 5% to state hospital rates estimated at 63%. Garralda conducted a 17-year follow-up, with 50% of youth continuing to have hallucinations but with little prognostic significance;[2] however, Del Beccaro et al.[3] reported that follow-up study of 25 inpatients with hallucinations revealed a poor outcome. The development of hallucinations has been associated with child psychopathology and social/family environmental adver-

Address for correspondence: Gail A. Edelsohn, Department of Psychiatry and Human Behavior, Thomas Jefferson University, 833 Chestnut Street, Suite 210-D, Philadelphia, PA 19107. Voice: 215-955-8180; fax: 215-503-2852.

Gail.Edelsohn@mail.tju.edu

Ann. N.Y. Acad. Sci. 1008: 261–264 (2003). © 2003 New York Academy of Sciences.
doi: 10.1196/annals.1301.028

sity;[4] with the death of a parent in the face of limited emotional availability of the surviving parent;[5] and with anxious low-functioning children at bedtime.[6] None of the studies reviewed drew upon children who presented in a psychiatric emergency setting nor did they detail both demographic and diagnostic variables.

OBJECTIVE

This study seeks to clinically characterize a poorly recognized clinical phenomenon and to test hypotheses involving the content of the hallucinations and underlying psychopathology. The specific hypotheses are: (1) auditory hallucinations are more frequent than visual ones; (2) auditory hallucinations with voices telling you to do bad things will more frequently have associated diagnoses of Attention Deficit Hyperactivity Disorder (ADHD) and Disruptive Behavior Disorders (DBD) than will other diagnostic categories; (3) auditory hallucinations of deceased individuals will more frequently have associated diagnoses of depression; and (4) auditory hallucinations to kill yourself will more likely be associated with the diagnosis of depression.

METHODS

All charts from a 2-month time period in children under 18 years of age who were evaluated in an urban psychiatric emergency service were reviewed for the presence of hallucinations without psychosis. Age, ethnicity, gender, DSM-IV diagnoses, and disposition were recorded. Nonpsychotic children were defined as not delusional, not having disturbances in the production of language, with no evidence of decreased motor activity, without signs of incongruous mood, lacking bizarre behavior. and without social withdrawal. Hallucinations were categorized as auditory, visual, or tactile. Content of auditory and visual hallucinations was recorded verbatim and then categorized. Descriptive statistics were obtained for demographic and clinical variables. The relation between the content of auditory hallucination and diagnoses as well as the relation between content of auditory hallucination and age were tested with Fisher's exact test.

RESULTS

Sixty-two children with hallucinations (mean age 11.4 years) but without psychosis were identified. Thirty-five children were 12 years and under, while 27 children were between 13 and 17 years of age. Males accounted for 56.5% of the sample. Ethnicity was distributed as: African-American (66%), Latino (21%), and Caucasian (13%). The prevalence of the diagnoses was: Depression (34%), ADHD (22%), Disruptive Behavior Disorder (21%), and Other (23%). Sixty-two percent of the cases had two or more diagnoses. Dispositions were as follows: hospitalization (43.5%), outpatient treatment (38.7%), discharged against medical advice (3.2%), and missing (14.5%). Six children had only visual hallucinations, 32 had only auditory hallucinations, and 24 had both auditory and visual hallucinations ($P < .001$). There were positive trends between content of the auditory hallucination and diagnosis.

TABLE 1. Auditory hallucinations (AH): do bad things

	Do bad things	Other AH
ADHD or DBD	11 (68.8 %)	19 (47.5 %)
Other diagnoses	5 (31.3 %)	21 (52.5 %)

NOTE: *P* value ns.

TABLE 2. Auditory hallucinations (AH): voices of the deceased

	Voices of deceased	Other AH
Depression	4 (100%)	
Other diagnoses		23 (44.2 %)

NOTE: *P* value ns.

TABLE 3. Auditory hallucinations (AH): suicidal voice

	Suicidal voice	Other AH
Depression	9 (81.8%)	28 (54.9%)
Other diagnoses	2 (18.2%)	23 (45.1%)

NOTE: *P* value ns.

TABLE 4. Gender and suicidal voice

	Female	Male
Voice to kill self	8 (29.6%)	3 (8.6%)
No voice to kill self	19 (70.4%)	32 (91.4%)

NOTE: *P* value ns.

TABLE 5. Age and AH content

	12 years and under	13–17 years	Total
Voice to do bad things	13 (37.1%)	3 (11.1%)	16 (25.8%)
Other AH	22 (62.9%)	24 (88.9%)	46 (74.2%)
Total	35 (100%)	27 (100%)	62 (100%)

NOTE: *P* value < .05.

Being 12 years old or younger was significantly associated with hearing voices telling you to do bad things ($P < .05$) (TABLES 1–5).

CONCLUSIONS

Given our detection of 62 cases in a 2-month period (study ongoing), we are confident that nonpsychotic hallucinations are more common than generally appreciated. We found positive trends for the association between the content of the auditory hallucination and a specific diagnostic category. These results did not reach statistical significance, likely due to the small cell size. However, they do appear clinically significant and suggest that the content of hallucinations can be relevant to the underlying psychopathology. Awareness of underlying psychopathology and precipitating factors is necessary in evaluating hallucinations in nonpsychotic children. Children such as those in our sample are at risk of being diagnosed as having psychosis not otherwise specified (NOS) or schizophrenia, and hence subjected to a course of antipsychotic medications with their inherent risks. Future research with an enlarged sample size will permit sufficient power to repeat these preliminary analyses and investigate other questions. Longitudinal follow-up of the sample and neuroimaging studies are research avenues to be pursued with regard to differentiating nonpsychotic hallucinating children from those who develop a psychotic illness.

REFERENCES

1. GARRALDA, M.E. 1982. Hallucinations in psychiatrically disordered children: preliminary communication. J. R. Soc. Med. **75:** 181–184.
2. GARRALDA, M.E. 1984. Hallucinations in children with conduct and emotional disorders: I. The clinical phenomena. Psychol. Med. **14:** 589–596.
3. DEL BECARRO, M.A. 1988. Hallucinations in children: a follow-up study. J. Am. Acad. Child Adolesc. Psychiatry **27:** 462–465.
4. WILKING, V.N. & C. PAOLI. 1966. The hallucinatory experience: psychodynamic classification and diagnostic significance. J. Am. Acad. Child Psychiatry **5:** 431–440.
5. YATES, T. & J.R. BANNARD. 1988. The "haunted" child: grief, hallucinations, and family dynamics. J. Am. Acad. Child Adolesc. Psychiatry **275:** 573–581.
6. KOTSOPOULOS, S., J. KANISBERG, A. COTE, et al. 1987. Hallucinatory experiences in nonpsychotic children. J. Am. Acad. Child Adolesc. **26:** 375–380.

Subanalysis of the Location of White Matter Hyperintensities and Their Association with Suicidality in Children and Youth

STEFAN EHRLICH,[a] GIL G. NOAM,[a] IN KYOON LYOO,[a] BAE J. KWON,[b] MEGAN A. CLARK,[a] AND PERRY F. RENSHAW[a]

[a]McLean Hospital, Harvard Medical School, Belmont, Massachusetts 02478, USA

[b]Department of Radiology, Seoul National University Hospital, Seoul, Korea

ABSTRACT: Our previous research with psychiatrically hospitalized children and youth indicates that white matter hyperintensities (WMH) on T2-weighted MRI images are associated with a history of suicide attempt. This subanalysis of the specific locations of the WMH suggests that youth with deep WMH in the parietal lobe but not in the frontal lobe have a significantly higher prevalence of reported past suicide attempt.

KEYWORDS: hyperintensities; parietal lobe; suicidality; children; youth; brain; white matter

BACKGROUND

As the third leading cause of death among youth and adolescents, suicide is a major health problem in the United States.[1] Despite extensive research, the prediction of suicide attempts and preventive therapeutic intervention remain extraordinarily difficult. We and others have evidence to suggest that the development of much improved brain-imaging techniques can be used to identify biological markers of suicidality.[2] In our previous work, we found that white matter hyperintensities (WMHs) in unipolar depressed children and adolescents were strongly associated with a history of suicide attempt, having controlled for age, gender, Axis II and III diagnosis, substance abuse, head injury, and cerebral hypoxia (Ehrlich et al., submitted for publication).

WMHs can be visualized by T2-weighted MRI scans and then classified into either Deep White Matter Hyperintensities (DWMHs) or Periventricular Hyperintensities (PVHs). Both represent areas of increased water density due to ependymal loss or differing degrees of myelination.[3] Because WMHs probably reflect disruptions of neuroanatomic pathways essential for the maintenance of normal mood,[4] the exact location of WMHs is of great interest and was the focus of the current study.

Address for correspondence: Stefan Ehrlich and Dr. Gil G. Noam, McLean Hospital, West Cottage, 115 Mill Street, Belmont, MA 02478. Voice: 617-855-3513; fax: 617-855-3777. mail@stefanehrlich.de

Ann. N.Y. Acad. Sci. 1008: 265–268 (2003). © 2003 New York Academy of Sciences. doi: 10.1196/annals.1301.029

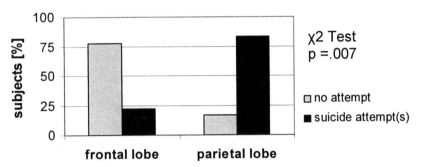

FIGURE 1. Location of Deep White Matter Hyperintensities and their relationship to suicidality.

DESIGN

Dual Echo, proton density, and T2-weighted MRI images of 153 child and adolescent psychiatry inpatients (mean age 14.6 ± 3.4; 74.2% male; 52.1%, unipolar depression; 28.1%, history of suicide attempt) used for our previous study were reexamined for locations of DWMH and PVH. Complete DSM-IV discharge diagnosis, history of suicide attempt, and control variables were obtained from medical records.

RESULTS

The relations of side and location of DWMHs (26 patients) and PVHs (22 patients) to suicidality were investigated. DWMHs in the parietal lobes were most significantly associated with a history of suicide attempt (χ^2 Test, $P = .007$; FIG. 1). This relationship was even stronger in the group of unipolar patients. A logistic regression analysis predicting suicidality showed that subjects with DWMHs in the parietal lobe had 8.6 (1.3–59.0, 95% CI) higher estimated odds for a history of suicide attempt compared to those who had no parietal DWMHs. This finding was not confounded by any of the aforementioned control variables. All suicidal subjects with DWMHs had these lesions in the right posterior parietal lobe (FIG. 2). The prevalence and location of PVHs only played a role in the subgroup of unipolar patients. Among those, a parietal PVH was more often related to a history of suicide attempt. Because of small cell sizes. this finding was not significant.

SUMMARY

Taken together, our preliminary data indicate that children and youth with DWMHs in the right parietal lobe are at the highest risk for a history of suicide attempt. The posterior parietal lobe is considered to be critical for spatial cognition, attentional orienting, task switching, and consciousness.[5] Disturbances in the parietal lobes

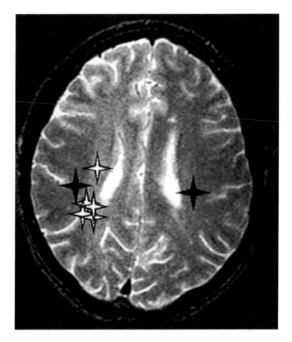

FIGURE 2. Location of parietal Deep White Matter Hyperintensities in the brain. Location lesions associated with suicidality are indicated with a *white cross*.

were shown to be associated with neglect as well as with unipolar and bipolar disorder.[6,7] Thus, the identified location in the white matter of the right posterior parietal lobe, which is tied to high suicide risk, could be of great interest for further studies striving for a larger sample size.

Biological markers investigated in this study can lead to a better understanding of the risk factors of suicidality in children and youth.

ACKNOWLEDGMENTS

This work was supported by the American Foundation for Suicide Prevention, John Alden Trust, Klingenstein Third Generation Foundation, and Studienstiftung des Deutschen Volkes.

REFERENCES

1. MacDorman, M.F. *et al.* 2001. Annual summary of vital statistics–2001. Pediatrics **110:** 1037–1052.
2. Ahearn, E.P. *et al.* 2001. MRI correlates of suicide attempt history in unipolar depression. Biol. Psychiatry **50:** 266–270.
3. Thomas, A.J. *et al.* 2002. Pathologies and pathological mechanisms for white matter hyperintensities in depression. Ann. N.Y. Acad. Sci. **977:** 333–339.

4. Steffens, D.C. & K.R. Krishnan. 1998. Structural neuroimaging and mood disorders: recent findings, implications for classification, and future directions. Biol. Psychiatry **43:** 705–712.
5. Taylor, J.G. 2001. The central role of the parietal lobes in consciousness. Conscious Cognit. **10:** 379–417.
6. Biver, F. *et al.* 1994. Frontal and parietal metabolic disturbances in unipolar depression. Biol. Psychiatry **36:** 381–388.
7. Berns, G.S., M. Martin & S.M. Proper. 2002. Limbic hyperreactivity in bipolar II disorder. Am. J. Psychiatry **159:** 304–306.

Obstetric Complications Correlate with Neurobehavioral and Brain Structural Alterations in Young Relatives at Risk for Schizophrenia

ANDREW R. GILBERT, DEBRA M. MONTROSE, SARAH D. SAHNI, VAIBHAV A. DIWADKAR, AND MATCHERI S. KESHAVAN

Western Psychiatric Institute and Clinic, Department of Psychiatry, University of Pittsburgh School of Medicine, Pittsburgh, Pennsylvania 15213, USA

ABSTRACT: As complications of pregnancy and birth may be important risk factors for the development of schizophrenia, studying the "roots" of schizophrenia in high-risk offspring may better elucidate the interface between biology, environment, and susceptibility to illness. Using magnetic resonance imaging (MRI), neurobehavioral assessments and obstetric histories, we found several significant correlations between these multiple factors, suggesting that birth complications may be a nonspecific etiopathogenic risk factor for psychopathology in young relatives at risk for schizophrenia.

KEYWORDS: schizophrenia; obstetrics; pregnancy; brain; magnetic resonance imaging (MRI)

INTRODUCTION

There is growing evidence that complications of pregnancy and birth are risk factors for schizophrenia and may contribute to the emergence of illness by interacting with a genetic liability.[1–4] Studies of young relatives at high risk for schizophrenia may further implicate perinatal and obstetric complications in the premorbid pathogenesis of the illness.[5–8]

As the concordance for schizophrenia in monozygotic twins is only about 50%, genetic liability alone cannot account for the clinical manifestation of the disorder.[9] Genetic susceptibility for schizophrenia is apparently complex, and additional, nongenetic factors may be necessary for the inherited risk to become evident.

A variety of environmental events, especially during early development, have been associated with an increased risk of schizophrenia.[6] Individuals with schizophrenia have a greater frequency of adverse in utero events, such as severe maternal malnutrition during the first trimester or maternal influenza or rubella during mid-

Address for correspondence: Andrew R. Gilbert, M.D., Western Psychiatric Institute and Clinic, University of Pittsburgh School of Medicine, Department of Psychiatry, 3811 O'Hara Street, Pittsburgh, PA 15213. Voice: 412-586-9108; fax: 412-586-9011.

gilbertar@msx.upmc.edu

Ann. N.Y. Acad. Sci. 1008: 269–275 (2003). © 2003 New York Academy of Sciences.
doi: 10.1196/annals.1301.030

pregnancy.[1] Additionally, complications during labor or delivery may increase the risk for schizophrenia.[3, 4]

To assess the effects of perinatal and obstetric factors on the risk of developing schizophrenia, we recruited several high-risk offspring of schizophrenic patients and healthy comparison subjects. Using magnetic resonance imaging (MRI), we measured total brain and total gray matter volumes. We evaluated the degree of perinatal and birth complications using maternal reports and hospital records whenever available. We also measured schizotypal symptom ratings, conducted neurocognitive and neurological soft sign tests, and assessed other clinical characteristics that may be important risk factors for illness.

METHODS

Subjects

Subjects included consecutively recruited offspring of a parent with schizophrenia ($n = 42$; age 6–21 years) and age- and sex-matched healthy comparison subjects ($n = 36$; age 6–25 years) without psychiatric history in self or first-degree relatives. The parental diagnosis of schizophrenia was confirmed by SCID interviews.[10] The healthy comparison subjects were recruited by advertisements in the same communities from which the high-risk offspring were recruited. The offspring and healthy comparison subjects were clinically evaluated using the schedule for Affective Disorders and Schizophrenia–Child Version (K-SADS)[11] or Structured Clinical Interview for DSM-IV Schizophrenia (SCID);[10] subjects with neurological or medical illness or an IQ < 75 were excluded. We also excluded high-risk subjects who had any lifetime evidence of psychotic disorders.

Clinical Assessments

Perinatal and birth complications were assessed using a modified version of the Pregnancy History Instrument (PHI).[2] Hospital records, wherever available, were used to verify maternal reports. All subjects were assessed for schizotypal symptoms using the Chapman Perceptual Aberration and Magical Ideation Scales, which were combined to yield a composite schizotypy score.[12,13] Neurological soft signs were assessed using a modified version of the Neurological Evaluation Scale (NES).[14] Cognitive deficits were measured by assessing for perseverative errors on the Wisconsin Card Sorting Test (WCST).[15] IQ scores were based on the highest score on either the Ammons or the Peabody test.[16,17]

Magnetic Resonance Imaging Studies

All volumetric MRI scans were conducted at the University of Pittsburgh Medical Center (1.5-T Signa Whole Body Scanner, G.E. Medical Systems, Milwaukee, WI). Intracranial volume was measured with a three-dimensional spoiled gradient recalled acquisition (SPGR) in the steady-state pulse sequence that obtained 124 1.5-mm thick contiguous coronal images (echo time, 5 ms; repetition time, 25 ms; acquisition matrix, 256×192; field of view, 24 cm; flip angle, 10 degrees). In order to facilitate image orientation, coronal slices were obtained perpendicular to the

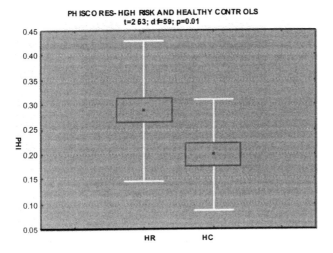

FIGURE 1.

anterior commissure–posterior commissure line. National Institutes of Health (NIH) image software (version 1.56) was used to measure anatomic data.[18]

Statistical Analysis

Comparison of PHI scores between high-risk offspring and healthy controls was assessed using paired *t* tests (*P* < .05). Correlational analyses were conducted using Spearman's rank correlation coefficient (*P* < .05).

RESULTS

The high-risk offspring had a significantly higher frequency of birth complications as compared to controls (*P* = .01) (FIG. 1). When all subjects were included, significant negative correlations were noted between PHI scores and gray matter volume (*n* = 42; *P* = .04) (FIG. 2) as well as IQ (*n* = 51; *P* = .005). Also, significant positive correlations were found between PHI scores and perseverative errors on the WCST (*n* = 58; *P* = .005) (FIG. 3). When only the high-risk subjects were included, the correlations between PHI and both IQ (*n* = 26; *P* = .03) (FIG. 4) and neurological soft signs (*n* = 34; *P* = .03) (FIG. 5) remained significant. Significant positive-correlations between PHI scores and schizotypal ratings in high-risk subjects (*n* = 32; *P* = .02) (FIG. 6) were also seen.

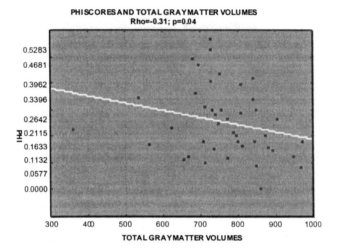

FIGURE 2.

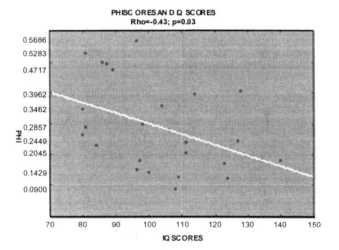

FIGURE 3.

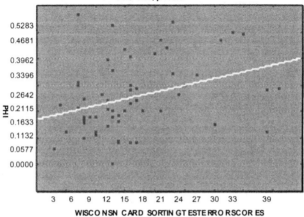

FIGURE 4.

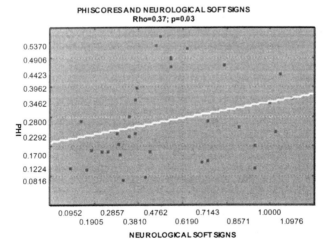

FIGURE 5.

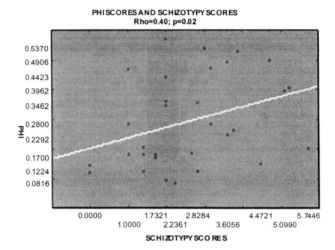

FIGURE 6.

CONCLUSIONS

These findings suggest that perinatal and birth complications may be a non-specific etiopathogenic risk factor for psychopathology among young relatives at risk for schizophrenia. Whether high-risk individuals are more vulnerable to these complications or whether the complications make them more susceptible to schizophrenia remains to be fully elucidated. Future studies examining individual obstetric complications and their relation to the development of schizophrenia will improve our understanding of this environmental association.

REFERENCES

1. BROWN, A.S. & E.S. SUSSER. 2002. In utero infection and adult schizophrenia. Ment. Retard Dev. Disabil. Res. Rev. **8:** 51–57.
2. BUKA, S.L., J.M. GOLDSTEIN & M.T. TSUANG. 1989. The measurement of fetal events in schizophrenia research. Paper presented at the American Psychiatric Association Symposium on Fetal Brain Development in Schizophrenia, San Francisco, CA.
3. CANNON, M., P.B. JONES & R.M. MURRAY. 2002. Obstetric complications and schizophrenia: historical and meta-analytic review. Am. J. Psychiatry **159:** 1080–1092.
4. JONES, P.B. et al. 1998. Schizophrenia as a long-term outcome of pregnancy, delivery, and perinatal complications: a 28–year follow-up of the 1966 North Finland general population birth cohort. Am. J. Psychiatry **155:** 355–364.
5. KESHAVAN, M.S. et al. 2002. Decreased left amygdala and hippocampal volumes in young offspring at risk for schizophrenia. Schizophr. Res. **58:** 173–183.
6. KESHAVAN, M.S. & G.E. HOGARTY. 1999. Brain maturational processes and delayed onset in schizophrenia. Dev. Psychopathol. **11:** 525–543
7. KESHAVAN, M.S. et al. 1998. Superior temporal gyrus and the course of early schizophrenia: progressive, static, or reversible? J. Psychiatr. Res. **32:** 161–167.

8. LAWRIE, S.M. *et al.* 2001. Brain structure, genetic liability, and psychotic symptoms in subjects at high risk of developing schizophrenia. Biol. Psychiatry **49:** 811–823.

9. GOTTESMAN, I.I. 1991. Schizophrenia Genesis: The Origins of Madness. Freeman. New York.

10. FIRST, M.D., R.L. SPITZER, M. GIBBON & J.B.W. WILLIAMS. 1995. Structured Clinical Interview for DSM-IV Axis I Disorders–Patient Edition. Biometrics Research Department, NYSPI. New York.

11. CHAMBERS, E.J. *et al.* 1985. The assessment of affective disorders in children and adolescents by semi-structured interview. Arch. Gen. Psychiatry **42:** 696–702.

12. CHAPMAN, L.J., J.P. CHAPMAN & M.L. RAULIN. 1978. Body-image aberration in schizophrenia. J. Abnorm. Psychol. **87:** 399–407.

13. ECKBLAD, M. & L.J. CHAPMAN. 1983. Magical ideation as an indicator of schizotypy. J. Consult. Clin. Psychol. **51:** 215–225.

14. BUCHANAN, R.W. & D.W. HEINRICHS. 1989. The neurological evaluation scale (NES): a structured instrument for the assessment of neurological signs in schizophrenia. Psychiatry Res. **27:** 335–350.

15. HEATON, R. 1981. The Wisconsin Card Sorting Test Manual. Psychological Assessment Resources. Odessa, FL.

16. AMMONS, R.B. & C.H. AMMONS. 1958. Quick Test Manual. Southern University Press . Psychological Test Specialists (now Birmingham Publishing Co.). Birmingham, AL.

17. DUNN, L.M., L.M. DUNN, G.J. ROBERTSON & J.L. EISENBERG. 1981. Peaboldy Picture Vocabulary Test–Revised. American Guidance Service. Circle Pines, MN.

18. RASBAND, W. 1993. NIH Image Manual. National Institutes of Health. Bethesda, MD.

Longitudinal Assessment of Callous/Impulsive Traits, Substance Abuse, and Symptoms of Depression in Adolescents

A Latent Variable Approach

CRAIG S. NEUMANN,[a] MICHAEL VITACCO,[a,b] ANGELA ROBERTSON,[c] AND KENNETH SEWELL[a]

[a]Department of Psychology, University of North Texas, Denton, Texas 76203, USA

[b]Mendota Mental Health Institute, Madison, Wisconsin 53704, USA

[c]Social Science Research Center, Mississippi State University, Starkville, Mississippi 39762, USA

ABSTRACT: Latent variable structural modeling was used to examine the associations among callous/impulsive personality traits, substance abuse, and symptoms of depression in a sample of 156 adjudicated male adolescents. Assessments were conducted at baseline and 6-month follow-up. The results highlight an unfolding of interrelationships among disturbances in personality, substance use, and mood over time.

KEYWORDS: adolescents; substance abuse; longitudinal; structural equation modeling; personality

INTRODUCTION

Comorbidity exists between substance abuse/dependence (SUB) and other psychopathology (e.g., anxiety, depression) among adults and adolescents.[1-4] Among males, a strong relationship exists between SUB and antisocial personality traits,[5-7] and psychopathy and SUB.[8] Two critical antisocial psychopathic traits are callousness and impulsivity.[9]

Further understanding of comorbidity comes from longitudinal studies. Kandell *et al.* found that adolescents reporting previous SUB were at increased risk for mood and conduct disorders.[1] A longitudinal study using latent variable modeling, found baseline depression predicted *decreased* subsequent SUB among males, but SUB at first follow-up predicted *increased* depression at second follow-up.[4] Kushner *et al.* reported a reciprocal association between negative affect and SUB in young adults.[2] Clearly, the link between SUB and other psychopathology is complex.

Address for correspondence: Craig S. Neumann, Department of Psychology, P.O. Box 311280, University of North Texas, Denton, TX 76203-1280. Voice: 940-565-2671; fax: 940-565-4682.
csn0001@unt.edu

Ann. N.Y. Acad. Sci. 1008: 276–280 (2003). © 2003 New York Academy of Sciences.
doi: 10.1196/annals.1301.031

TABLE 1. Structural equation model: standardized item-to-factor parameters

Manifest variables	Substance abuse	Symptoms of depression	Callous/ impulsive	Error
Time 1 (baseline)				
Frequency alcohol/drug	.652			.758
Alcohol/drug behaviors	.785			.619
Alcohol/drug effects	.938			.347
Depressed		.892		.452
Suicidal		.557		.831
Forceful			.657	.754
Impulsive			.848	.531
(poor) Social tolerance			.722	.692
Time 2 (6-month follow-up)				
Frequency alcohol/drug	.654			.757
Alcohol/drug behaviors	.785			.619
Alcohol/drug effects	.938			.348
Depressed		.892		.452
Suicidal		.551		.835
Forceful			.658	.753
Impulsive			.848	.530
(poor) Social tolerance			.722	.692

Latent variables header spans Substance abuse, Symptoms of depression, and Callous/impulsive columns.

Other studies have examined the longitudinal relationship between personality disorders (PDs) and Axis I disorders (other than SUB). Daley *et al.* found PD symptoms predicted increased depression over a two-year period, but also that depression predicted increased PD symptoms.[10] Cross-sectional studies also suggest links between negative affect and psychopathy.[9,11]

Thus, adolescent studies reveal comorbidity, with interrelationships between personality, mood, and SUB disorders.[12]

METHOD

There were 156 male participants (age range, 11–17 years; grade level, approximately eigth grade), comprising 100 African-Americans and 56 Caucasians. The adolescents had been adjudicated in a youth court system prior to volunteering for the study: 13% had committed a minor offense, 24% a moderate offense, and 63% a serious or very serious offense. The current study reports on baseline and 6-month follow-up assessments.

Three scales from the Millon Adolescent Personality Inventory[13] were used as indicators for a callous/impulsive latent variable (LV). The callousness scales were Forceful and (poor) Social Tolerance. The third scale was Impulse Control. The Personal Experience Screening Questionnaire (PESQ)[14] is a 40-item screen for sub-

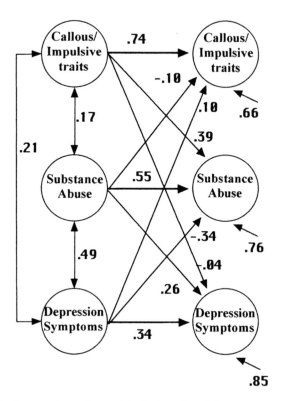

FIGURE 1. Structural equation model of callous/impulsive, substance use, and depression latent variables: baseline and six-month follow-up.

stance abuse and psychopathology in adolescents. Three subscales were used as indicators of a SUB LV: frequency of SUB, behaviors related to SUB use, and negative effects of SUB. The PESQ has two dichotomous items ($0 = $ no, $1 = $ yes) assessing symptoms of depression (feeling depressed and suicidal), which were used as indicators for a depression (DEP) LV.

RESULTS

EQS was used for structural equation modeling (SEM) analyses.[15] The statistical theory implemented in EQS for estimating parameters from categorical and continuous variables was used.[16] The SEM results were excellent ($\chi^2(100) = 143$; NNFI = .976; CFI = .980; ACFI = .999; mean absolute standardized residuals = .08). All factor loadings and structural parameters were significant ($P < .01-.001$) (see TABLE and FIG. 1). The SUB and callous/impulsive LVs were stable over time, while the DEP LV showed modest stability. The SUB LV at baseline predicted increased DEP at follow-up, and DEP at baseline predicted increased callous/impulsive traits but decreased SUB at follow-up. Callous/impulsive personality traits at baseline predicted increased SUB at follow-up. The SEM accounted for 56, 42, and 28% of the variance in the follow-up callous/impulsive, SUB and DEP LVs, respectively (see FIG. 1).

CONCLUSIONS

The SEM results were excellent and map onto the studies cited above. The SUB LV at baseline predicted increased depression (DEP) at follow-up, consistent with other studies.[1,4] Moreover, baseline DEP predicted decreased SUB, consistent with other research.[4] These longitudinal patterns may help explain the biphasic process that has been documented in other research on depression and alcohol abuse. The current study and other research indicates initial negative mood co-occurs with SUB, but that baseline DEP is associated with subsequent decreases in SUB.[4,17]

Nonetheless, additional factors promote increased SUB in adolescents. Our results showed that callous/impulsive personality traits significantly predicted increased SUB. While links between antisocial personality features (e.g., callousness and impulsivity) and SUB have been shown previously,[6,8] a critical finding in our study was that callous/impulsive traits predicted increased SUB, rather than the reverse. This asymmetrical pattern between antisocial traits and SUB is consistent with other studies in adolescents.[18,19]

Other research with adolescents has showed that DEP predicted increased personality disorder (PD) symptoms.[10] Recent longitudinal research with adolescents reported DEP increased the odds of antisocial PD at follow-up tenfold.[20] The current results revealed that DEP predicts increased callous/impulsive traits. Thus, negative mood disrupts the development of personality in adolescents. Taken together, our results are consistent with the documented comorbidity among adolescents,[12] and they highlight unfolding interrelationships among PD symptoms, SUB, and DEP.

REFERENCES

1. KANDEL, D.B. *et al.* 1997. Psychiatric disorders associated with substance use among children and adolescents: findings from the methods for the epidemiology of child and adolescent disorders (MECA) study. J. Abnorm. Child Psychol. **25:** 121–132.
2. KUSHNER, M.G. *et al.* 1999. Prospective analysis of the relation between DSM-III anxiety disorders and alcohol use disorders. Am. J. Psychiatry **156:** 723–732.
3. PRESCOTT, C.A. *et al.* 1997. Predictors of problem drinking and alcohol dependence in a population-based sample of female twins. J. Stud. Alcohol **58:** 167–181.
4. SCHUTTE, K.K. *et al.* 1997. Gender differences in the relations between depressive symptoms and drinking behavior problem drinkers: a three-wave study. J. Consult. Clin. Psychol. **65:** 392–404.
5. CLONINGER, C.R. *et al.* 1988. Genetic heterogeneity and the classification of alcoholism. Adv. Alcohol Subst. Abuse **7:** 3–16.
6. HELZER, J.E. & T.R. PRYZBECK. 1988. The co-occurrence of alcoholism with other psychiatric disorders in the general population and its impact on treatment. J. Stud. Alcohol **49:** 219–224.
7. KESSLER, R.C. *et al.* 1997. Lifetime co-occurrence of DSM-III-R alcohol abuse and dependence with other psychiatric disorders in the National Comorbidity Survey. Arch. Gen. Psychiatry **54:** 313–321.

8. SMITH, S.S. & J.P. NEWMAN. 1990. Alcohol and drug abuse/dependence disorders in psychopathic and nonpsychopathic offenders. J. Abnorm. Psychol. **99:** 430–439.
9. KOSSON, D.S. *et al.* 2002. The reliability and validity of the psychopathy checklist: youth version in non-incarcerated adolescent males. Psychol. Assessment **14:** 97–109.
10. DALEY, S.E. *et al.* 1999. Depression and axis II symptomology in an adolescent community sample: concurrent and longitudinal associations. J. Personality Dis. **13:** 47–59.
11. SCHMITT, W.A. & J.P. NEWMAN. 1999. Are all psychopathic individuals low-anxious? J. Abnorm. Psych. **108:** 353–358.
12. ANGOLD, A. *et al.* 1999. Comorbidity. J. Child Psychol. Psychiatry **40:** 57–87.
13. MILLON, T., C.J. GREEN & R.B. MEAGHER. 1982. Millon Adolescent Personality Inventory Manual. Interpretive Scoring Systems. National Computer Systems. Minneapolis, MN.
14. WINTERS, K.C. 1992. Development of an adolescent alcohol and other drug abuse screening scale: Personal Experience Screening Questionnaire. Addict. Behav. **17:** 479– 490.
15. BENTLER, P.M. 1995. EQS structural equations program manual. Multivariate Software, Inc. Encino, CA.
16. LEE, S.Y. *et al.* 1992. Structural equation models with continuous and polytomous variable. Psychometrika **57:** 89–105.
17. CRUM, R.M. *et al.* 2001. The association of depression and problem drinking: analyses from the Baltimore ECA follow-up study. Addict. Behav. **26:** 765.
18. ADALBJARNARDOTTIR, A. *et al.* 2002. Adolescent antisocial behavior and substance use: longitudinal analyses. Addict. Behav. **27:** 227–240.
19. KUPERMAN, S. *et al.* 2002. Developmental sequence from disruptive behavior diagnosis to adolescent alcohol dependence. Am. J. Psychiatry **158:** 2022–2026.
20. KASEN, S *et al.* 2001. Childhood depression and adult personality disorder: alternative pathways of continuity. Arch. Gen. Psychiatry **58:** 237–238.

Sex Differences and Hormonal Effects in a Model of Preterm Infant Brain Injury

JOSEPH L. NUÑEZ AND MARGARET M. McCARTHY

Department of Physiology, University of Maryland, Baltimore, Baltimore, Maryland 21201, USA

ABSTRACT: Premature infants are at an exceptionally high risk for brain injury, with damage resulting in permanent behavioral deficits. A contributing factor to the severity of brain injury is gender, with males more sensitive to insult than females. The role of gender and early hormonal environment in addressed in our novel model of prenatal brain damage.

KEYWORDS: estradiol; gamma-aminobutyric acid (GABA); hippocampus; hypoxia-ischemia (H-I); muscimol

Premature infants are prone to pathological brain damage resulting from umbilical cord strangulation, stroke, preeclampsia, maternal diabetes, iron deficiency, and numerous other events that result in acute or prolonged periods of hypoxia-ischemia (H-1).[1,2] With the high incidence of insult (greater in premature than in newborn and post-term human infants), and the persistence of pathological and behavioral deficits,[3] it is of major concern that no clinically effective methods of treatment exist. Current therapies rely upon treatments that work in adults (i.e., GABAergic agonists, steroid hormones, and glutamatergic antagonists). We discuss our recently developed model of preterm human infant H-I, and give evidence as to why steroid hormones such as estradiol and agonists of the GABAergic system are not only ineffective methods of treatment, but also significantly exacerbate damage.

A point of concern in the establishment of an animal model is developmental age equivalency to humans. The developmental state of the newborn human, based on brain growth rate, acetylcholinesterase activity, and reflex ontogeny is thought to be equivalent to the postnatal day 5–7 rat.[4] More recent work documenting synapse formation, glutamate decarboxylase activity, choline acetyltransferase activity, and electrical activity in the rat cerebral cortex has suggested a later age equivalency, with the postnatal day 12–13 rat being equivalent to the newborn human.[5] Regardless, it can be assumed that the newborn rat is analogous to the preterm human infant.

Address for correspondence: Joseph L. Nuñez, Department of Physiology, University of Maryland, Baltimore, Baltimore, MD 21201. Voice: 410-706-2654; fax: 410-706-8341.
jnune001@umaryland.edu

Ann. N.Y. Acad. Sci. 1008: 281–284 (2003). © 2003 New York Academy of Sciences.
doi: 10.1196/annals.1301.032

Another issue is the relevance of the animal model to an actual pathological condition. Following an hypoxic-ischemic event, there is a dramatic elevation in the extracellular levels of neurotransmitters such as GABA and glutamate.[6] Elevated levels persist for 30 min to 2 h following insult.[6] Therefore, exogenous administration of glutamate receptor agonists to induce excitotoxicity is a commonly accepted model of H-I.[7] However, exogenous glutamate receptor agonists do not induce appreciable damage in the newborn rat brain,[8] while H-I induces damage in the preterm human infant brain.[1] We hypothesized that the activation of $GABA_A$ receptors may mediate brain injury in preterm infants, and we have developed an animal model involving exogenous administration of muscimol to newborn rat pups to test this hypothesis.

Finally, there is a growing body of literature that neonatal males are more sensitive to brain injury than females. Studies in both humans and animals have documented that an equivalent insult in both sexes produces not only greater damage, but also poorer functional recovery in males.[9] It appears that the steroid hormone environment, which differs during development and in adulthood between males and females,[10] may play an integral role. Therefore, we investigated the effect of sex and

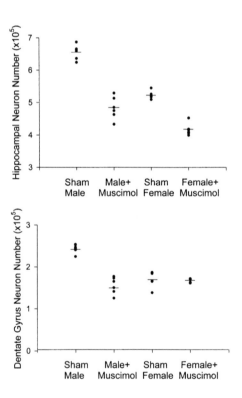

FIGURE 1. Neonatal muscimol treatment induces a loss of hippocampal and dentate gyrus neurons in male and female rats. Stereological estimates of neuron number ($n = 6$/ group) are shown for each animal, along with the group mean.

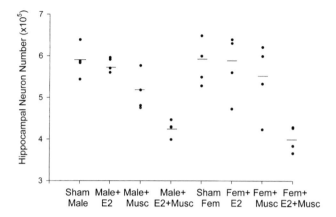

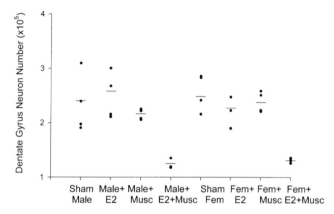

FIGURE 2. Neonatal estradiol pretreatment exacerbates muscimol-induced neuronal loss in the hippocampus and dentate gyrus of both male and female rats. Stereological estimates of neuron number ($n = 4$/group) are shown for each animal, along with the group mean.

steroid hormones on $GABA_A$ receptor agonist-induced damage to the newborn rat brain.

We documented that administration of the specific $GABA_A$ receptor agonist muscimol is damaging to the hippocampal formation of newborn male and female rats (FIG. 1). There is a sex difference in response to this insult, with males more susceptible to injury than females. Exogenous administration of estradiol to both males and females exacerbated muscimol-induced neuronal loss (FIG. 2). Therefore, we propose that the elevated intracerebral estradiol levels during development in males[10] predispose them to increased susceptibility to brain injury.

Muscimol-induced damage in the newborn rat hippocampus is due to $GABA_A$ receptor-mediated excitation. During early development, $GABA_A$ receptor activation leads to chloride efflux and membrane depolarization sufficient to open L-type voltage sensitive calcium channels (VSCCs).[11] Muscimol-induced calcium influx is responsible for injury, given that damage is completely blocked by pretreatment with diltiazem (L-type VSCC blocker) (data not shown).

In summary, we have documented that muscimol induces damage in the newborn rat hippocampus and that sex and hormonal milieux affect response to this early insult. We propose that estradiol, which is elevated during early development in males, is an important component in determining why males are more sensitive to many forms of neonatal insult than females. Therefore, as opposed to the adult rat in which estradiol attenuates damage following stroke and H-I, estradiol exacerbates damage in our model of preterm infant brain injury.

REFERENCES

1. SIE, L.T. *et al.* 2000. MR patterns of hypoxic-ischemic brain damage after prenatal, perinatal and postnatal asphyxia. Neuropediatrics **31:** 128–136.
2. YAGER, R.G.Y. 1999. Pathophysiology of perinatal brain damage. Brain Res. Rev. **30:** 107–134.
3. SIMON, N.P. 1999. Long-term neurodevelopmental outcome of asphyxiated newborns. Clin. Perinatol. **26:** 767-778.
4. ADLARD, B.P.F., J. DOBBING & J.L. SMART. 1973. An alternative animal model for the full-term small-for-dates human baby. Biol. Neonate **23:** 95–108.
5. ROMINJ, H.J. *et al.* 1991. At what age is the developing cerebral cortex of the rat comparable to that of the full-term newborn human baby? Early Hum. Dev. **26:** 61–67.
6. ANDINE, P. *et al.* 1991. Changes in extracellular amino acids and spontaneous neuronal activity during ischemia and extended reflow in CA1 of rat hippocampus. J. Neurochem. **57:** 222–229.
7. CHOI, D.W. & S.M. ROTHMAN. 1990. The role of glutamate neurotoxicity in hypoxic-ischemic neuronal death. Annu. Rev. Neurosci. **13:** 171–182.
8. MCDONALD, J.W. & M.V. JOHNSON. 1990. Physiological and pathophysiological roles of excitatory amino acids during central nervous system development. Brain Res. Rev. **15:** 41–70.
9. LAUTERBACH, M.D., S. RAZ & C.J. SANDER. 2001. Neonatal hypoxic risk in preterm birth infants: the influence of sex and severity of respiratory distress on cognitive recovery. Neuropsychology **15:** 411–420.
10. WEISZ, J. & I.L. WARD. 1984. Plasma testosterone and progesterone titers of pregnant rats, their male and female fetuses, and neonatal offspring. Endocrinology **106:** 306–316.
11. LEINEKUGEL, X. *et al.* 1999. GABA is the principal fast-acting excitatory transmitter in the neonatal brain. Adv. Neurol. **79:** 189–201.

Coping Strategies Moderate the Relation of Hypothalamus–Pituitary–Adrenal Axis Reactivity to Self-Injurious Behavior

SALLY I. POWERS[a] AND ELIZA T. MCARDLE[b]

[a]Department of Psychology, University of Massachusetts, Amherst, Massachusetts 01003, USA

[b]Department of Psychiatry, Harvard Medical School, Massachusetts Mental Health Center, Boston, Massachusetts 02115, USA

ABSTRACT: An alarming proportion of adolescents engage in purposefully self-injurious behavior (SIB). SIB is a maladaptive strategy for coping with extreme tension generated in response to stress, particularly interpersonal stress. This study investigated the relation of older adolescents' SIB to the reactivity of the body's major physiological system for responding to stress, the hypothalamus–pituitary–adrenal (HPA) axis, after interpersonal stress. Adolescents' behavioral, cognitive, and emotional coping strategies were shown to alter the relation between SIB and HPA reactivity after conflict with a romantic partner.

KEYWORDS: self-injury; cortisol; HPA axis; coping; interpersonal conflict

INTRODUCTION

Self-injurious behavior (SIB) is a highly disturbing and poorly understood phenomenon that includes body cutting or scratching, self-inflicted burns, intentional self-bruising, and intentional ingestion of poisonous substances. These behaviors cause mild to moderate physical damage, are unacceptable within our society, and are performed in a state of psychic crisis. SIB occurs in several psychiatric disorders and also in the general population, reaching up to 12% in older adolescent populations.[1]

SIB is considered a maladaptive strategy for coping with extreme tension generated in response to stress, particularly interpersonal stress.[2,3] Evidence suggests that self-injurious behaviors reduce physiological arousal after a stress event.[4] Prior to an act of self-injury, individuals report experiencing internal agitation, anxiety, rage, or despair.[3] As the tension increases, the individual may begin to feel a sense of emptiness and isolation followed by an inability to verbalize or to tolerate the extreme feelings. The act of self-injury is often impulsive and has the effect of releasing the tension quickly.

Address for correspondence: Sally I. Powers, University of Massachusetts, Department of Psychology, Tobin Hall, 135 Hicks Way, Amherst, MA 01003. Voice: 413-545-3307; fax: 413-545-0996.

powers@psych.umass.edu; emcardle@psych.umass.edu

Ann. N.Y. Acad. Sci. 1008: 285–288 (2003). © 2003 New York Academy of Sciences.
doi: 10.1196/annals.1301.033

The body's major system for responding to stress, the hypothalamus–pituitary–adrenal (HPA) axis, functions primarily to mobilize physiological arousal, alertness, vigilance, and appropriate aggression to deal with stress.[5] The relation of human SIB with dysregulation of the HPA axis response to interpersonal stress has only recently been documented.[6] The current study investigates whether use of specific behavioral, cognitive, and emotional coping strategies alter the relation of SIB to HPA reactivity to conflict in romantic relationships.

METHODS

Subjects

Subjects were 170 older adolescents and young adults (85 males, 85 females) engaged in heterosexual romantic relationships for at least two months. Ages ranged from 18 to 20 years with a mean age of 19.3 years (SD = .87). Ethnicity was representative of the western Massachusetts community from which the sample was drawn, with 80.6% (137) European American.

Procedure

After subjects gave an initial salivary cortisol sample (a baseline sample), they were given a detailed description of the conflict task and asked to name a recent source of disagreement with their romantic partner. Fifteen minutes later, subjects gave a second salivary cortisol sample, which served as a measure of anticipatory anxiety about the conflict task.

Couples were then taken to a soundproofed room, seated at a couch, and instructed to spend 15 min to try to come to a resolution of one of the issues (chosen by a coin toss) that they had provided earlier. Researchers were not present in the room during the videotaped discussion. After the conflict negotiation task, couples completed a questionnaire packet and provided five additional saliva samples at 10, 20, 30, 45, and 60 min post-task.

Measures

Symptoms of post-traumatic stress disorder (PTSD) and depression were assessed because these disorders are empirically associated with self-injury and HPA dysregulation.[6] Depressive symptoms were assessed with the Center for Epidemiological Studies Depression Scale,[7] and PTSD symptoms were measured with the Trauma Symptom Checklist.[8] The frequency, timing, and severity of SIB were assessed with the Self-Injurious Behavior Questionnaire.[6] Subjects' use of 14 coping strategies was measured by the Brief COPE.[9] Salivary cortisol was used as a noninvasive indicator of HPA axis functioning and is widely recognized as sensitive to experimental conditions in which stress is induced.[10] In the last decade, researchers have emphasized the advantages of assessing HPA reactivity to social stressors, suggesting that this yields information about the function of HPA dysregulation in disorders associated with social stress.[10] Two measures of HPA functioning were used in these analyses: (1) salivary cortisol sampled in anticipation of the conflict task and (2) the change in salivary cortisol from the first pretask sample to the maximum level after the conflict.

RESULTS

Multiple regression analyses examining coping as a moderator of the relation of self-injury to HPA functioning were run separately for males and for females because of documented gender differences in PTSD, depression, and HPA reactivity to social stress, and to ameliorate the issue of interdependence in data from couples. In separate sets of analyses, HPA functioning in anticipation of conflict and in reaction to an actual conflict discussion were regressed on the control variables of PTSD and depression symptoms, SIB, coping strategies, and the interaction of SIB and coping strategies.

Coping strategies of these older adolescents significantly moderated the associations between SIB and HPA reactivity to interpersonal conflict. Additionally, different coping strategies altered the SIB-HPA associations for men than for women. SIB in young men was associated with heightened cortisol release in anticipation of romantic conflict when they typically used three coping strategies that are considered to interfere with effective coping, denial ($\beta = .57$, $P < .01$), behavioral disengagement ($\beta = .62$, $P < .05$), and self-blame ($\beta = .85$, $P < .00$), as well as one problem-focused strategy, instrumental support ($\beta = .88$, $P < .02$). SIB in men was associated with higher HPA reactivity to the actual conflict discussion when they relied more on religious ($\beta = .33$, $P < .05$) and self-blaming ($\beta = .56$, $P < .03$) coping strategies.

SIB of young women was positively associated with heightened cortisol release in anticipation of romantic conflict when their typical coping strategies were characterized by low active coping ($\beta = -.42$, $P < .05$), low positive reframing ($\beta = -.63$, $P < .05$), and high use of planning ($\beta = .30$, $P < .05$). In contrast, SIB of women showed lowered HPA reactions to actual conflict with their boyfriends when they typically used the strategy of seeking emotional support to cope with stress ($\beta = -.72$, $P < .03$.).

CONCLUSIONS

SIB of older adolescents was related to HPA functioning as they anticipated conflict with their romantic partners and also in reaction to an actual conflict discussion with their partners. Moreover, different coping strategies moderated the relations between self-injury and HPA functioning for men than for women. These contrasting patterns in how coping strategies alter the relation of SIB to HPA reactivity for men and women suggest the need for further examination of differences in the reasons that older adolescent men and women engage in self-injurious behavior.

REFERENCES

1. FAVAZZA, A.R. & K. CONTERIO. 1989. Female habitual self-mutilators. Acta Psychiatr. Scand. **79:** 283–289.
2. WINCHEL, R.M. & M. STANLEY. 1991. Self-injurious behavior: a review of the behavior and biology of self-mutilation. Am. J. Psychiatry **148:** 306–317.
3. HERPERTZ, S. 1995. Self-injurious behavior: psychopathological and nosological characteristics in subtypes of self-injurers. Acta Psychiatr. Scand. **91:** 57–68.
4. BRAIN, K.L., J. HAINES & C.L.WILLIAMS. 1998. The psychophysiology of self-mutilation: evidence of tension reduction. Arch. Suicide Res. **4:** 227–242.

5. CHROUSOS, G.P. & P.W. GOLD. 1992. The concepts of stress and stress system disorders: overview of physical and behavioral homeostasis. J. Am. Med. Assoc. **267:** 1244–1252.
6. MCARDLE, E.T. & S.I. POWERS. 2003. Self-injurious behaviors and hypothalamus-pituitary-adrenal axis reactivity after interpersonal conflict. Submitted.
7. RADLOFF, L.S. 1977. The CES-D Scale: a self-report depression scale for research in the general population. Appl. Psychol. Measurement **1:** 385–401.
8. BRIERE, J. & E. GIL. 1998. Self-mutilation in clinical and general population samples: prevalence, correlates, and functions. Am. J. Orthopsychiatry **68:** 609–620.
9. CARVER, C.S. 1997. You want to measure coping but your protocol's too long: consider the Brief COPE. Int. J. Behav. Med. **4:** 92–100.
10. SCHWARTZ, E., D. GRANGER, E. SUSMAN, *et al.* 1998. Assessing salivary cortisol in studies of child development. Child Dev. **69:** 1503–1513.

Prenatal Nicotine Exposure and Behavior

V. ROSSI, T. MESSENGER, D. PETERS, C. FERRIS, AND J. KING

Department of Psychiatry, University of Massachusetts Medical Center,
55 Lake Avenue North, Worcester, Massachusetts 01655, USA

ABSTRACT: Prenatal exposure to nicotine has been associated with changes in behavioral indices in offspring. Flank marking, a scent-marking behavior in golden hamsters, appears to be controlled by arginine vasopressin (AVP) neurons in the hypothalamus. The present study examines the effects of prenatal exposure to nicotine on the vasopressinergic system associated with flank marking behavior.

KEYWORDS: nicotine; vasopressin; behavior; gender

INTRODUCTION

Nicotine is the main chemical constituent in tobacco. Various animal and human studies have indicated that prenatal exposure to nicotine is associated with altered neural structures, cognitive deficits, and behavioral problems in the offspring. Prenatal exposure to nicotine is also associated with decreased learning efficiency, inattention, impulsivity, and motor hyperactivity.

Flank marking is a scent-marking behavior that golden hamsters display for species recognition, individual discrimination, social status, and agonistic behavior.[1] Flank marking appears to be controlled by arginine vasopressin (AVP) neurons in the hypothalamus.

By postnatal day 18 (P18), the vasopressinergic system is comparable to that of adult golden hamsters. However, flank-marking behavior has been found to begin around P20. This observation indicates that perhaps this short period during development (between P18 and P20) is associated with activation of the vasopressinergic system in golden hamsters.

The present study was conducted to examine the effects of prenatal exposure to nicotine on the vasopressinergic system associated with flank-marking behavior and their gender specificity in golden hamsters. Golden hamsters have been shown to voluntarily consume nicotine as chewing tobacco.[2] It was hypothesized that both male and female golden hamsters prenatally exposed to nicotine would display decreased flank-marking behavior as a result of delayed development of the vasopressinergic system.

Address for correspondence: Jean King, Ph.D., Department of Psychiatry, University of Massachusetts Medical Center, 55 Lake Avenue North, Worcester, MA 01655. Voice: 508-856-4979; fax: 508-856-6426.

Jean.King@umassmed.edu

Ann. N.Y. Acad. Sci. 1008: 289–292 (2003). © 2003 New York Academy of Sciences.
doi: 10.1196/annals.1301.034

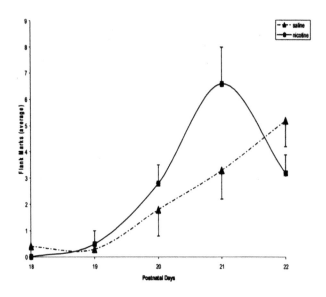

FIGURE 1. Data on the average daily flank marking for developmental period of postnatal days 18–22 (P18–P22) for male golden hamsters ($n = 28$) prenatally exposed to nicotine and saline.

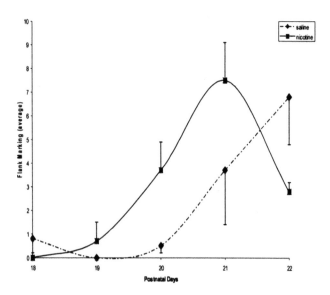

FIGURE 2. Data on the average daily flank marking for developmental period of postnatal days 18–22 (P18–P22) for female golden hamsters ($n = 16$) prenatally exposed to nicotine and saline.

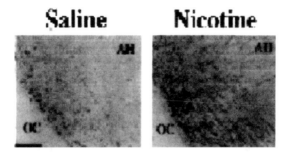

FIGURE 3. The difference in arginine vasopressin (AVP) cell bodies and fibers leading to the anterior hypothalamus of saline and nicotine exposed golden hamsters. AH, anterior hypothalamus; OC, optic chiasm.

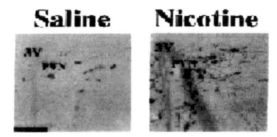

FIGURE 4. A comparison of arginine vasopressin (AVP) cell bodies and fibers in the hypothalamus proximal to the third ventricle of saline and nicotine exposed golden hamsters. 3V, third ventricle; PVN, paraventricular nucleus.

METHODS

Six female adult hamsters were lightly anesthetized using nembutal, and Alzet osmotic pumps containing either nicotine (1.05 mg nicotine/mL dH_2O) or saline (0.9% saline) was subcutaneously implanted in each hamster. The six female hamsters were mated one day after implantation of the pumps. Male and female pups from these dams were followed for their flank-marking behavior (see FIGS. 1 and 2).

Beginning on P18 and continuing through P22, flank-marking behavior tests were conducted. In the laboratory, flank marking can be induced by the odors of other hamsters. The pups were placed in the recently vacated cage of another hamster for 10 min each day, and the number of flank markings were recorded. On P22 the female pups were sacrificed and their flank glands were measured. Their brains were extracted, fixed in a 10% acrolein solution, and immunocytochemistry (ICC) for AVP was performed (see FIGS. 3 and 4).

SUMMARY AND CONCLUSIONS

Prenatal nicotine causes golden hamsters to display significantly increased flank marking at an earlier age; it causes flank-marking behavior to peak at P 21 and then decline on P22. Prenatal nicotine increases the number of AVP cell bodies and fibers in the hypothalamus of the golden hamster's brain.

The effects of prenatal nicotine exposure are not gender specific in golden hamsters. Contrary to the stated hypothesis, prenatal nicotine accelerates development of the vasopressinergic system. These data are significant because past studies in our laboratory have shown that vasopressin-sensitive neurons in the anterior hypothalamus are involved in the control of intraspecific aggression in male hamsters.[3]

REFERENCES

1. FERRIS, C.F., L. GOLD, G.J. DE VRIES, *et al.* 1990. Evidence for a functional and anatomical relationship between the lateral septum and the hypothalamus in the control of flank marking behavior in Golden hamsters. J. Comp. Neurol. **293:** 476–485.
2. KSIR, C. 1983. Taste and nicotine as determinants of voluntary tobacco use by hamsters. Pharmacol. Biochem. Behav. **19:** 605–608.
3. FERRIS, C.F. & M. POTEGAL. 1988. Vasopressin receptor blockade in the anterior hypothalamus suppresses aggression in hamsters. Physiol. Behav. **44:** 235–239.

Familial Psychiatric Disorders in Child DSM-IV ADHD: Moderation by Child Gender

JULIEANN STAWICKI AND JOEL T. NIGG

Department of Psychology, Michigan State University,
East Lansing, Michigan 48824, USA

ABSTRACT: Examined selected psychiatric disorders in parents of boys and girls with DSM-IV ADHD and control children. Excess parent psychopathology was observed for parents of boys—primarily due to psychopathology in fathers—score potential gender differences in development of ADHD.

KEYWORDS: parent psychopathology; ADHD; gender; family study; DSM-IV

INTRODUCTION

Family psychiatric studies of attention-deficit/hyperactivity disorder (ADHD) are still relatively few, especially for the DSM-IV syndrome.[1] Yet parental psychopathology data are important to genetic and family process models. With regard to the latter, parental psychiatric problems may degrade parenting ability, lower the family's SES by interfering with work achievement, and disrupt marital relationships.[2]

Past studies established familial transmission of earlier definitions of ADHD itself.[3,4] However, little is known about the transmission of *other* psychiatric disorders in the families of children with ADHD, especially using contemporary definitions of the syndrome. The few extant studies have yielded somewhat inconsistent results with regard to whether or not non-ADHD disorders are more common in relatives of children with ADHD, once ADHD is distinguished from antisocial behavior and conduct problems.[4,5]

In addition, prior family studies of ADHD have emphasized male probands, leaving it unclear whether specific familial patterns may exist that are moderated by child gender. Although gender differences in ADHD expression is beginning to be elaborated and appreciated,[6] the investigation of possible gender moderation of etiological risk factors has been limited. We aimed to clarify gender moderation of parent psychopathology effects in DSM-IV ADHD.

Address for correspondence: Julieann Stawicki, 4700 E. Hagadorn Road, Suite 110, East Lansing, MI 48824. Voice: 517-353-9800; fax: 517-432-1938.
stawick1@msu.edu

Ann. N.Y. Acad. Sci. 1008: 293–296 (2003). © 2003 New York Academy of Sciences.
doi: 10.1196/annals.1301.035

METHODS

Participants were $n = 176$ community-recruited children and their biological parents. Following an extensive multistage screening and diagnostic process that made use of parent and teacher ratings and parent structured interviews (the widely used Diagnostic Interview Schedule for DSM-IV for Child Disorders), children were placed into two groups: (1) $n = 114$ (81 boys; 33 girls) children diagnosed with ADHD (any DSM-IV subtype) and (2) $n = 62$ (37 boys; 25 girls) non-ADHD control children. Mothers and fathers completed the structured NIMH Diagnostic Interview Schedule for DSM-IV[7] to assess their lifetime psychiatric disorders for generalized anxiety disorder (GAD), major depression disorder (MDD), antisocial personality disorder (ASPD), alcohol use disorder, and drug use disorder. We report elsewhere on ADHD subtypes transmission within this sample, and focus here on parent non-ADHD psychiatric disorders among all ADHD versus non-ADHD children.

RESULTS

Data are presented in TABLE 1. Parents of boys with ADHD had more disorders than control parents ($F[1] = 6.84$, $P = .009$). This was due to more GAD ($\chi^2(1) = 5.71$, $P = .017$), ASPD ($\chi^2(1) = 6.84$, $P = .009$), and alcohol abuse disorder ($\chi^2(1) = 4.02$, $P .045$) in those parents. Effects were carried by GAD in mothers, $\chi^2(1) = 5.07$, $P= .02$, and by ASPD ($\chi^2(1) = 16.85$, $P = .01$) and alcohol use disorder ($\chi^2(1) = 6.49$, $P = .01$) in fathers. There were no omnibus between-group differences in rates of individual disorders or total number of disorders for parents of girls, although univariate within-parent tests revealed higher rates of drug use disorder in mothers of girls with ADHD ($\chi^2(1) = 4.41$, $P = .04$) compared to control mothers. There were no differences between the fathers of ADHD and control girls.

DISCUSSION

These are among the first data to examine rates of parent psychiatric disorders in boys and girls separately, with ADHD defined by DSM-IV. It was striking that results for boys were consistent with expectations from the earlier (DSM-III and DSM-III-R) ADHD literature, whereas results for girls failed to clearly reflect this pattern. The latter negative findings were generally not attributable to the lower power for girls; effect magnitudes were for the most part sharply smaller for parents of girls than boys. However, mothers of girls with ADHD were at increased risk of drug use disorder. If taken at face value, these gender-specific findings could be consistent with other evidence that molecular genetic correlates of ADHD are better understood when gender-specific transmission is considered.[8] They could also imply greater psychosocial risk for boys than for girls with ADHD.

Overall, this suggestion in an early study of DSM-IV ADHD of distinct gender-specific familial risk profiles requires replication, but is provocative. Family psychiatric studies lay the foundation for exploring family context for development of ADHD in children, as well as providing converging evidence for genetic theories. These results may help to explain differences in gender expression of ADHD symp-

TABLE 1. Prevalence of parent non-ADHD disorder by child ADHD status and gender

	Control girls (%)	Girls with ADHD (%)	$\chi^2(2) =$	P	Control boys (%)	Boys with ADHD (%)	$\chi^2(2) =$	P
All parents combined	(N = 43)	(N = 48)			(N = 61)	(N = 119)		
GAD	14.0	14.6	0.01	.93	3.3	15.1	5.73	.02*
MDD	20.9	35.4	2.33	.13	26.2	31.1	0.63	.43
Antisocial PD	39.0	39.6	0.00	.96	16.3	37.3	6.84	.01*
Drug use disorder	4.7	17.0	3.48	.06	1.6	8.9	3.52	.06
Alcohol use disorder	18.6	21.7	0.14	.71	18.0	32.2	4.02	.045
Total number			F(1) = .25	P = .62			F(1) = 4.10	P = .045*
Mothers	(N = 24)	(N = 30)			(N = 34)	(N = 73)		
GAD	12.5	20.0	0.54	.46	2.9	19.1	5.07	.02*
MDD	29.2	43.3	1.15	.28	29.4	40.5	1.24	.27
Antisocial PD	26.1	26.7	0.00	.96	17.9	30.8	1.66	.20
Drug use disorder	0	16.7	4.41	.04*	2.9	13.9	0.39	.39
Alcohol use disorder	4.2	6.7	0.16	.69	8.8	7.1	0.55	.46
Total number			F(1) = 2.70	P = .15			F(1) = 2.91	P = .09
Fathers	(N = 19)	(N = 18)			(N = 27)	(N = 46)		
GAD	15.8	5.6	1.00	.32	3.7	8.7	0.65	.42
MDD	10.5	22.2	0.93	.34	22.2	17.8	0.21	.65
Antisocial PD	55.5	61.1	0.11	.74	14.3	48.6	16.85	.01*
Drug use disorder	10.5	17.6	0.38	.54	0	11.9	3.47	.06
Alcohol use disorder	31.6	37.5	0.14	.74	14.8	44.2	6.49	.01
Total number			F(1) = .03	P = .86			F(1) = 5.52	P = .02*

*P < .5.

toms and comorbid profiles. Therefore, these data underscore the importance of understanding in more depth gender-based effects in ADHD.

REFERENCES

1. CANTWELL, D.P. 1997. The scientific study of child and adolescent psychopathology: the attention deficit disorder syndrome. J. Am. Acad. Child Adolesc. Psychiatry **36:** 1033–1035.
2. BIEDERMAN, J., S. MILBERGER, S.V. FARAONE, *et al.* 1995. Impact of adversity on functioning and comorbidity in children with attention-deficit hyperactivity disorder. J. Am. Acad. Child Adolesc. Psychiatry **34:** 1495–1503.
3. FRICK, P.J., B.B. LAHEY, M.A.G. CHRIST, *et al.* 1991. History of childhood behavior problems in biological relatives of boys with attention-deficit hyperactivity disorder and conduct disorder. J. Clin. Child Psychology **20:** 445–451.
4. NIGG, J.T. & S.P. HINSHAW. 1998. Parent personality traits and psychopathology associated with antisocial behaviors in childhood attention-deficit hyperactivity disorder. J. Child Psychol. Psychiatry **31:** 145–159.
5. STEWART, M.A., S. DEBLOIS & C. CUMMINGS. 1980. Psychiatric disorder in the parents of hyperactive boys and those with conduct disorder. J. Child Psychol. Psychiatry **21:** 263–291.
6. BIEDERMAN, J., E. MICK, S.V. FARAONE, *et al.* 2002. Influence of gender on attention deficit hyperactivity disorder in children referred to a psychiatric clinic. Am. J. Psychiatry **159:** 36–42.
7. ROBINS, L.N., L.B. COTTLER, K.K. BUCHOLZ, *et al.* 1995. The Diagnostic Interview for DSM-IV (DIS-IV). Washington University. St. Louis, MO.
8. SMALLEY, S.L., J.J. MCGOUGH, M. DEL'HOMME, *et al.* 2000. Familial clustering of symptoms and disruptive behaviors in multiplex families with attention-deficit/ hyperactivity disorder. J. Am. Acad. Child Adolesc. Psychiatry **39:** 1135–1143.

Reorganization of Unresolved Childhood Traumatic Memories Following Exposure Therapy

K. CHASE STOVALL-McCLOUGH AND MARYLENE CLOITRE

University School of Medicine, Child Study Center, Institute for Trauma and Stress, New York, New York 10016, USA

ABSTRACT: As part of an ongoing randomized clinical trial for childhood-abuse-related PTSD, this study examined the association between PTSD and unresolved attachment as measured by the Adult Attachment Interview in a sample of 52 female childhood-abuse survivors. Results revealed that 55% of the sample was classified as preoccupied and almsot 75% was classified as unresolved with regard to trauma. In a preliminary sample of 18 women who completed treatment, 13 were unresolved before treatment and 8 lost their unresolved status following treatment. This effect was significantly more pronounced in the exposure condition compared to the skills training condition.

KEYWORDS: attachment; exposure therapy; childhood abuse; PTSD

REORGANIZATION OF UNRESOLVED CHILDHOOD TRAUMATIC MEMORIES FOLLOWING EXPOSURE THERAPY

Childhood trauma is associated with dysregulation of behavioral, memory, and physiological systems, often culminating in significant disturbances consistent with posttraumatic stress disorder (PTSD). Both the trauma and attachment literatures agree that a failure to complete a process of memory consolidation following a traumatic event underlies both the development of PTSD and the uniquely incoherent speech seen in "unresolved attachment states of mind." This study sought to examine the distribution of attachment states of mind in a preliminary sample of women seeking treatment for childhood-abuse-related (CA) symptoms (Aim I). Second, we examined the impact of a cognitive behavior treatment for CA-related PTSD on unresolved attachment states of mind in a pilot sample of 18 women (Aim 2).

Aim 1

Although mounting research indicates that psychiatric disorders are characterized by insecure and unresolved attachment states of mind,[1] no studies have examined attachment representations among those diagnosed with the one psychiatric disorder that is most commonly associated with trauma and that is believed to best characterize the symptom sequelea of childhood trauma: PTSD. Thus, under Aim 1

Address for correspondence: K. Chase Stovall-McClough, NYU Child Study Center, 215 Lexington Avenue, 16th Floor, New York, NY 10016. Voice: 212-263-2473; fax: 212-263-2476.
stovak01@med.nyu.edu

Ann. N.Y. Acad. Sci. 1008: 297–299 (2003). © 2003 New York Academy of Sciences.
doi: 10.1196/annals.1301.036

we examined the distribution of unresolved states of mind among three treatment-seeking groups of women: women with CA-related PTSD only ($N = 34$), women with both CA-related PTSD and borderline personality disorder (BPD; $N = 13$), and women with histories of childhood abuse with no trauma-related diagnosis ($N = 5$). We hypothesized that women diagnosed with CA-related PTSD and BPD would have higher rates of unresolved classifications in the AAI compared to women with abuse histories without CA-related diagnosis. Furthermore, based on a previous study with borderline patients,[2] we were particularly interested in the relative rates of preoccupied and secure attachment states of mind among these groups.

Method

In an ongoing randomized clinical trial for CA-related PTSD, we included the AAI[3] as part of the pretreatment evaluation package. We also administered the SCID-I and -II as well as the Clinician Administered PTSD Scale to determine psychiatric status. AAI classifications were made by outside consultants who were trained, reliable coders. Each coder has met the 85% reliability criterion with Mary Main and Eric Hesse and was blind to all other data. When an unresolved classification was made, a secondary classification of preoccupied, secure, or dismissing was also made, as is standard protocol for AAI classifications.

Results

Demographic breakdown of the sample was as follows: 33% Caucasion, 28% African-American, and 26% Hispanic. Thirty-seven percent of the sample made less than $15,000/year, 33% made between $15 and 30,000/year, and 24% made over $30,000/year. The mean age of the sample was 30 years. Over half the sample (51%) had a history of physical abuse before the age of 18, and 89% had a history of sexual abuse.

There were only three cases of dismissing states of mind in the sample. Both the psychiatric (PTSD and PTSD/BPD) groups showed unusually high rates of unresolved trauma (67% and 72%, respectively) compared to the trauma controls (40%). Collapsing across the unresolved category, rates of preoccupied attachment were lowest in the control group (20%), somewhat higher in the PTSD group (33%), and highest in the comorbid PTSD/BPD group (39%). Rates of secure attachment also covaried with psychiatric status. The control group showed the highest rates of secure attachment (80%), followed by the PTSD group (50%), and the comorbid PTSD/BPD group (30%). Continuous scores on the SCID-II measure of BPD positively correlated with continuous scores of unresolved trauma ($R = .44, P < .01$), but not with continuous scores of PTSD symptoms.

Aim 2

Our second aim was to investigate whether a PTSD treatment involving emotion regulation skills training and prolonged exposure (STAIR/MPE)[4] impacted rates of unresolved trauma in a preliminary sample ($N = 18$) of women with CA-related PTSD (no women diagnosed with BPD in this sample). We were specifically interested in whether prolonged exposure was superior in reducing rates of unresolved attachment compared to skills training.

Method

As part of a randomized clinical trial,[4] participants were randomly selected to receive a 16-session, manualized treatment that either contained prolonged exposure ($N = 12$) or skills training in affect and interpersonal regulation ($N = 6$). AAIs were administered pretreatment and treatment for three months following the end of treatment (approximately 7 months following the initial AAI).

Results

Results from a preliminary sample of 18 women with CA-related PTSD indicated that 13 of the 18 women (72%) were unresolved on the AAI before treatment. Of the 13 women who were unresolved before treatment, 8 lost their unresolved status following treatment (62%). In addition, 11% of the sample was classified as secure at pretreatment and 50% were classified as secure at posttreatment. In addition, there was a trend for those who lost their PTSD status following treatment, to show greater decreases in unresolved trauma scores compared to those who maintained their PTSD status following treatment, ($t = 2.02$; $P = .06$). Also consistent with our hypotheses, unresolved scores were significantly lower for those who received exposure condition ($M = 2.8$) compared to those who received the skills-training condition ($M = 5.4$), after controlling for pretreatment unresolved scores ($F = 7.86$; $P < .05$).

CONCLUSIONS

These data support our hypothesis that unresolved trauma on the AAI is strongly associated with CA-related diagnoses of PTSD and BPD. In addition, we see in a small preliminary sample that prolonged exposure to traumatic memories of childhood abuse results in a reorganization and increased coherence of traumatic memory resulting in reduced rates of PTSD and unresolved attachment on the AAI. In addition, these data suggest that exposure therapy is superior to skills training in this regard. We hope that these findings will provide the empirical basis for the development of a treatment program aimed at changing traumatized mothers' internal representations of trauma and abuse and improving parent–child attachment relationships.

REFERENCES

1. DOZIER, M. *et al.* 1999. Attachment and psychopathology in adulthood. *In* Handbook of Attachment Theory and Research. J. Cassidy and P.R. Shaver, Eds. Guilford Press. New York.
2. FONAGY, P. *et al.* 1996. The relation of attachment status psychiatric classification, and response to psychotherapy. J. Consult. Clin. Psychol. **64:** 22–31.
3. GEORGE, C. *et al.* 1985. Attachment interview for adults. Unpublished manuscript. University of California. Berkeley.
4. CLOITRE, M. *et al.* 2002. Skills training in affective and interpersonal regulation followed by exposure: a phase-based treatment for PTSD related to childhood abuse. J. Consult. Clin. Psychol. **70:** 1067–1074.

Ineffective Parenting: A Precursor to Psychopathic Traits and Delinquency in Hispanic Females

MICHAEL J. VITACCO,[a] CRAIG S. NEUMANN,[b] VINCENT RAMOS,[b] AND MARY K. ROBERTS[b]

[a]University of Massachusetts Medical School, Worcester, MA 01655, USA

[b]University of North Texas, Denton, TX 76203, USA

ABSTRACT: Research studies with antisocial children have posited that multiple etiologies, including ineffective parenting, can produce psychopathic traits. The current study evaluated 136 Hispanic females and found that poor parenting predicted psychopathology and poor behavioral controls. Effective clinical interventions with antisocial children should focus on improving quality of parenting.

KEYWORDS: psychopathy; parenting; Hispanic females

Research has consistently linked poor parenting practices to the development of disruptive and antisocial behaviors in children and adolescents. For instance, Stormshak et al.[1] studied 631 first-graders and found that children who were disciplined with physical aggression were more oppositional and aggressive in classrooms. Moreover, children receiving harsh and inconsistent parenting are more likely to bully children outside of classrooms.[2] Longitudinally, poor parental monitoring predicts unruly behavior in children; however, exposure to parental negativity and low emotional responsiveness are associated with childhood internalizing disorders, including depression and anxiety.[3] Likewise, Seifer et al.[4] discovered children were at higher risk to develop psychopathology if their parents were highly critical and unsupportive. In developing integrative programmatic research on parenting and delinquency, Paul Frick and his colleagues[5,6] elucidated a pathway model wherein ineffective parenting was a precursor to conduct disturbances in children. Notably, there was a subgroup of children with a combination of callous traits and conduct problems whose delinquency was not affected by the type of parenting received. These children are labeled "psychopathic" and demonstrate greater conduct problems, have higher numbers of police contacts, an earlier onset to their antisocial behavior,[7] and once institutionalized, are more disruptive.[8]

Address for correspondence: Michael J. Vitacco, Ph.D., Mendota Mental Health Institute, 301 Troy Drive, Madison, WI 53704. Voice: 608-301-1518.
vitacmj@dhfs.state.wi.us

Ann. N.Y. Acad. Sci. 1008: 300–303 (2003). © 2003 New York Academy of Sciences.
doi: 10.1196/annals.1301.037

The current study evaluates poor parental discipline strategies and their relationship to both psychopathology and psychopathy in Hispanic females, a traditionally understudied population. The use of understudied populations in research is consistent with recent research recommendations to examine the theoretical underpinnings and etiology of psychopathy in understudied, nonadjudicated samples.[10]

METHOD

Participants

Participants consisted of 136 Hispanic adolescent females ranging in age from 10 to 15 years (M = 12.94; SD = 1.05) who were assessed in their schools in South Texas as part of a pilot study on the efficacy of a female support group.

Measures

(1) Behavior Assessment System for Children-Self Report[10] (BASC-SRP-A) is a 186-item multiscale inventory measuring a variety of personality and behavioral traits, including sensation seeking, depression, and anxiety.
(2) Antisocial Process Screening Device[11] (APSD) is a 20-item, self-report inventory measuring three dimensions of psychopathic traits. The three dimensions consist of Callous/Unemotional Temperament, Narcissism, and Impulsivity. The children are marked "0" if the trait did not apply to them, "1" if it represented them somewhat, or "2" if it highly represented them.
(3) Alabama Parenting Questionnaire[12] (APQ) is a 42-item, 5-point Likert Scale given to assess parenting strategies the child experienced. The current study utilized the constructs of Poor Parental Monitoring and Inconsistent Discipline.

Procedure

The adolescents were assessed at baseline at their respective schools in South Texas as part of a pilot study on the efficacy of a female support group. The purpose of these groups is to improve self-esteem, academic performance, and communication skills in Hispanic females. The groups were developed to serve adolescent females in the sixth, seventh, and eighth grades. At baseline, the measures were given in a counterbalanced order to minimize potential response bias.

RESULTS

The current sample possessed a reasonably low level of psychopathic traits (M = 16.51; SD = 5.39), which is not surprising given that they are an nonadjudicated sample. In order to test our hypotheses regarding parenting behavior and psychopathy, we ran three separate regressions with parenting strategies (i.e., poor monitoring and inconsistent parenting) as our predictive variables regressing onto three dimensions of psychopathy (i.e., narcissism, impulsivity, and callous traits). TABLE 1 presents the regression analyses for each aspect of psychopathy, indicating poor parenting was associated with impulsivity and narcissistic traits, but not callousness.

TABLE 1. Regression analyses for psychopathic traits

Criterion	Predictor	Beta	Adjusted R^2	F	P
Narcissism	Poor monitoring	.15	.14	10.31	<.001
	Inconsistent parenting	.29			
Impulsivity	Poor monitoring	.20	.21	17.40	<.001
	Inconsistent parenting	.35			
Callous	Poor monitoring	.04	−.01	.23	.80
	Inconsistent parenting	−.07			

Further exploring the interrelationships between our variables, we also examined the correlations between psychopathic traits and aspects of psychopathology. Interestingly, callous traits were not significantly related to sensation seeking, depression, or anxiety. In contrast, impulsivity was significantly related to sensation seeking ($R = .38$, $P < .001$), depression ($R = .24$, $P < .01$), and anxiety ($R = .20$, $P < .05$). Moreover, narcissist traits also evidenced relationships with sensation seeking ($R = .38$, $P < .001$), depression ($R = .25$, $P < .01$), and anxiety ($R = .18$, $P < .05$).

DISCUSSION

This study adds to previous knowledge regarding the etiology of delinquency as a function of parenting and presents several important theoretical findings. First, our results indicate that failure to properly monitor and supervise children's behavior leads to impulsivity and behavioral dysregulation in a nonadjudicated sample of Hispanic females. Additionally, impulsivity and narcissism were associated with symptoms of depression and anxiety, suggesting that poor quality of parental supervision has far-reaching consequences for the mental health of Hispanic females. Specifically, adolescents who develop behavioral prolems in the absence of callous traits are more likely to be depressed and anxious.

A second, and equally important theoretical finding from this study, is that parenting style was unrelated to the presence of callousness, suggesting that these traits have a unique developmental pathway independent from quality of parenting. The etiology of callous traits may be heavily influenced by physiological factors[13] as opposed to environmental ones. The construct of callousness is critical to psychopathy, as it is considered its most important developmental precursor. Additionally, it has been hypothesized that callous traits may be the critical link explaining the continuity between adolescent and adult antisocial behavior.[14]

Finally, our results suggest directions for the development of treatment programs that target antisocial behavior in youth. First, when treating delinquency, strategies not involving parenting would leave an important developmental facet of antisocial behavior untouched, and thus may limit treatment success. On the other hand, when callous traits are present, therapeutic techniques should focus on developing empathy and decreasing callousness. Our results suggest that the presence of callousness may suppress anxiety, and may ultimately have a negative impact on treatment modalities. Unfortunately, treatment strategies have not been systematically evaluated with children and adolescents manifesting psychopathic traits. For this reason, treatment strategies with children should focus on pinpointing various psychopathic traits and evaluate the effectiveness of such strategies on subtypes (e.g., with or without callous traits) of antisocial behavior.

REFERENCES

1. STORMSHAK, E.A., K.L. BIERMAN, R.J. MCMAHON & L.J. LENGUA. 2000. Parenting practices and child disruptive behavior in early elementary school. J. Clin. Child Psychol. **29:** 17–29.
2. SMITH, P.K. & R. MYRON-WILSON. 1998. Parenting and school bullying. Clin. Child Psychol. Psychiatry **3:** 405–417.
3. BERG-NIELSEN, T.S. A. VIKAN & A.A. DAHL. 2002. Parenting related to child and parental psychopathology: a descriptive review of the literature. Clin. Child Psychol. Psychiatry **7:** 529–552.
4. LOEBER, R., D.P. FARRINGTON, M. STOUTHAMER-LOEBER & W.B. VAN KAMMEN. 1998. Antisocial Behavior and Mental Health Problems: Explanatory Factors in Childhood and Adolescence. Erlbaum. Mahwah, NJ.
5. WOOTTON, J.M., P.J. FRICK, K.K. SHELTON & P. SILVERTHORN. 1997. Ineffective parenting and childhood conduct problems: the moderating role of callous-unemotional traits. J. Consult. Clin. Psychol. **65:** 301–308.
6. MCCOY, M.G., P.J. FRICK, B.R. LONEY & M.L. ELLIS. 1999. The potential mediating role of parenting practices in the development of conduct problems in a clinic-referred sample. J. Child Fam. Stud. **8:** 477–494.
7. CHRISTIAN, R.E., P.J. FRICK, N. HILL & L. TYLER. 1997. Psychopathy and conduct problems in children II: implications for subtyping children with conduct problems. J. Am. Acad. Child Adolesc. Psychol. **36:** 233–241.
8. HICKS, M., R. ROGERS & M.L. CASHEL. 2000. Predictions of violent and total infractions among institutionalized male juvenile offenders. J. Am. Acad. Psychiatry Law **28:** 183–190.
9. KIRKMAN, C.A. 2002. Non-incarcerated psychopaths: why we need to know more about the psychopaths who live amongst us. J. Psychiatr. Men Health Nurs. **9:** 155–160.
10. REYNOLDS, C.R. & R.W. KAMPHAUS. 1992. Behavior Assessment System for Children (BASC). American Guidance Services. Circle Pines, MN.
11. FRICK, P.J. & R.D. HARE. 2001. The Antisocial Process Screening Device (APSD). Multihealth Systems. Toronto, Ont., Canada.
12. FRICK, P.J. 1991. The Alabama Parenting Questionnaire (APQ). Unpublished rating scales. The University of Alabama. Tuscaloosa.
13. BLAIR, J.R. 2003. Neurological basis of psychopathy. Br. J. Psychiatry **182:** 5–7.
14. VITACCO, M.J., R. ROGERS & C.S. NEUMANN. 2003. The Antisocial Process Screening Device: An Examination of its Construct and Criterion-Related Validity. Assessment **10:** 143–150.

Mother Lowers Glucocorticoid Levels of Preweaning Rats After Acute Threat

CHRISTOPH P. WIEDENMAYER,[a,d] ANA M. MAGARINOS,[b]
BRUCE S. McEWEN,[b] AND GORDON A. BARR[c,d]

[a]Department of Psychiatry, Columbia University, New York,
New York 10032, USA

[b]Laboratory of Neuroendocrinology, Rockefeller University, New York,
New York 10021, USA

[c]Department of Psychology, Hunter College, New York, New York 10021, USA

[d]Developmental Psychobiology, New York State Psychiatric Institute, New York,
New York 10032, USA

ABSTRACT: Exposure to a deadly threat, an adult male rat, induced the release of corticosterone in 14-day-old rat pups. The endocrine stress response was decreased when the pups were reunited with their mother immediately after exposure. These findings demonstrate that social variables can reduce the consequences of an aversive experience.

KEYWORDS: HPA axis; anxiety disorders; aversive stimulation; social buffering

The experience of extremely aversive events in childhood is associated with an increased risk for mood and anxiety disorders such as depression and posttraumatic stress disorder later in life.[1,2] Interventions after an acute exposure, however, may be effective in reducing the long-term consequences of the aversive experience.

In young animals, aversive stimulation induces endocrine and behavioral changes that can affect neurobehavioral development.[3] The aim of this study was to examine if the endocrine response can be modulated by social variables after the aversive stimulation has occurred. For preweaning rats, an unfamiliar unrelated adult male rat poses a deadly threat because adult males are infanticidal. In the absence of the mother, the adult male induces in the pups an acute defensive response[4] and an endocrine activation that persists after the male exposure.[5] We hypothesized that the male-induced endocrine stress response in young rats is reduced when the pups are reunited with their mother after the aversive exposure.

Address for correspondence: Christoph Wiedenmayer, Ph.D., Department of Psychiatry, Columbia University, 1051 Riverside Drive, Unit 40, New York, NY 10032. Voice: 212-543-5973; fax: 212-543-5467.
cpw14@columbia.edu

Ann. N.Y. Acad. Sci. 1008: 304–307 (2003). © 2003 New York Academy of Sciences.
doi: 10.1196/annals.1301.038

METHOD

A huddle of three 14-day-old rats was exposed for 5 min to an unfamiliar adult male rat behind a screen. Littermate controls were tested without the male present. Immediately after exposure, half of the male-exposed and control litters were reunited with the mother. The other half of each group were left alone as a group. Thirty min after exposure, trunk blood was collected from one male pup from each of the four experimental groups. In addition to the rats from the four groups, an unexposed male pup from each litter was taken from the home cage for basal measurements. Trunk blood was collected in chilled EDTA-coated tubes (Sherwood, St. Louis, MO) and centrifuged (4000 rpm) at 4°C for 15 min. Plasma was stored at –30°C until assayed. Corticosterone levels were determined by solid-phase radio immunoassay (DPC, Los Angeles, CA). Assay sensitivity was 0.6 µg/dL. Intra-assay and inter-assay variability were 4.0–12.2% and 4.8–14.9%, respectively.

RESULTS

Male-exposed rats were significantly more immobile than controls (FIG. 1, t test, $t = -18.5$, $P < .001$). Thirty minutes after exposure, corticosterone levels differed between conditions (FIG. 2, ANOVA, F = 7.01, $P < .01$). Experimental animals had higher corticosterone levels than undisturbed pups from the home cage (Newman-Keuls test, $P < .05$). Male-exposed pups without the mother had significantly higher corticosterone levels than controls ($P < .01$). The male-exposed pups that were re-

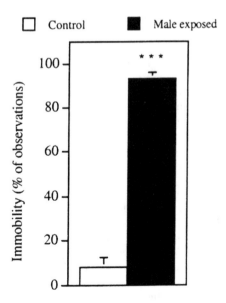

FIGURE 1. Immobility of 14-day-old rats during 5-min exposure to an adult male rat. Controls were not exposed to the male. ***$P < .001$.

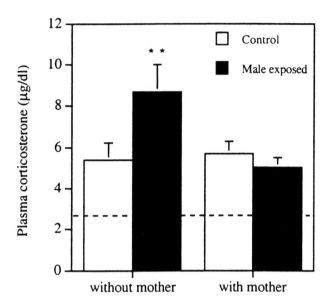

FIGURE 2. Corticosterone levels in undisturbed 14-day-old rats from home cage (*dashed line*) and experimental rats (*control, male exposed*) 30-min after exposure. [**]$P < .01$.

united with the mother had significantly lower corticosterone levels than male-exposed pups without the mother ($P < .01$) and did not differ from controls.

DISCUSSION

The proximity of a deadly threat, the male, elicited an acute immobility response in young rats separated from their mother. Immobility is a defensive behavior that may help conceal the pups from detection. The testing procedure alone activated the hypothalamic–pituitary–adrenal (HPA) axis and induced corticosterone release in all experimental animals. Male exposure, however, increased corticosterone secretion even further. Increased corticosterone levels after male exposure were selectively prevented when the pups were reunited with their mother.

The HPA axis in preweaning rats is regulated through interactions with the dam.[6] Contact with a lactating, anesthetized dam prevented the corticosterone increase in 20- and 24-day-old but not 16-day-old rats that were isolated in a novel environment.[7] The presence of an anesthetized dam or tactile stimulation were effective to suppress the increase of corticosterone in 10-day-old pups that were kept as a group in isolation.[8] Our results extend these findings and demonstrate that maternal cues modulate HPA axis activity even after the actual exposure to an aversive situation. Contact with the mother could either reduce activity of the HPA axis, resulting in decreased corticosterone secretion, or actively remove already released corticosterone from circulation.

In conclusion, social variables can regulate the endocrine response in the developing organism and reduce the consequences of an individual's exposure to aversive events.

ACKNOWLEDGMENT

This research was supported by MH01975, MH41256, and DA00325.

REFERENCES

1. HEIM, C. & C.B. NEMEROFF. 1999. The impact of early adverse experiences on brain systems involved in the pathophysiology of anxiety and affective disorders. Biol. Psychiatry **46:** 1509–1522.
2. BREMNER, J.D. & E. VERMETTEN. 2001. Stress and development: behavioral and biological consequences. Dev. Psychopathol. **13:** 473–489.
3. SÁNCHEZ, M.M., C.O. LADD & P.M. PLOTSKY. 2001. Early adverse experience as a developmental risk factor for later psychopathology: evidence from rodent and primate models. Dev. Psychopathol. **13:** 419–449.
4. WIEDENMAYER, C.P. & G.A. BARR. 1998. Ontogeny of defensive behavior and analgesia in rat pups exposed to an adult male rat. Physiol. Behav. **63:** 261–269.
5. WIEDENMAYER, C.P., A.M. MAGARINOS, B.S. MCEWEN & G.A. BARR. 2001. Young rats respond differentially to adult male and cat odor exposure. Society for Neuroscience Annual Meeting, San Diego, CA.
6. LEVINE, S. 1994. The ontogeny of the hypothalamic-pituitary-adrenal axis. Ann. N.Y. Acad. Sci. **746:** 275–288.
7. STANTON, M.E. & S. LEVINE. 1988. Maternal modulation of infant glucocorticoid stress responses: role of age and maternal deprivation. Psychobiology **16:** 223–228.
8. KUHN, C.M., J. PAUK & S.M. SCHANBERG. 1990. Endocrine responses to mother-infant separation in developing rats. Dev. Psychobiol. **23:** 395–410.

Early Deprivation Alters the Vocalization Behavior of Neonates Directing Maternal Attention in a Rat Model of Child Neglect

BETTY ZIMMERBERG, JU H. KIM, ABIGAIL N. DAVIDSON, AND ABIGAIL J. ROSENTHAL

Department of Psychology, Williams College, Williamstown, Massachusetts 01267, USA

ABSTRACT: Animal models of child neglect (known as maternal separation or early deprivation) have suggested a causal link to subsequent depression and/ or anxiety in children. In this experiment, the acoustical features of the ultrasonic calls emitted by a rat pup when separated from its dam were analyzed as well as the maternal behavior when the dam was allowed to retrieve the pup. Bout structure and harmonic double shifts did differ between controls and "neglected" pups, as did maternal attention. This model will be used to determine neural mechanisms underlying deficits in attachment behavior.

KEYWORDS: ultrasonic vocalizations; maternal separation; maternal behavior; isolation; distress calls; neglect; early experience; stress

INTRODUCTION

Since the Harlows' pioneering work on maternal separation in rhesus monkeys,[1] developmental psychobiologists have used animal models to support the hypothesis that early stressful life experiences can have long-term psychological effects. Interactions between mother and infant are integral to the normal growth and development of mammalian young. Numerous studies using rats have demonstrated that disruption of the maternal–infant bond is a profound stressor to pups, producing diverse changes in behavioral functioning, including alterations in activity, stress response, cognition, and fearfulness.[2–8]

Contributing to the formation of the maternal–infant bond is communication; infant mammals vocalize when separated from their dams in order to elicit protection, nourishment, and warmth. When separated from its dam, the infant rat produces ultrasonic vocalizations (USVs) in the range of 30–90 kHz, which direct maternal care.[9] The pattern of vocalizations corresponds directly to cycles of maternal care, with few vocalizations when pups are undisturbed in the nest. When pups are isolated from both the dam and littermates, there is an increase in vocalization, as well as a corresponding increase in activity.[10] While this increase in activity rapidly habituates, USVs do not.[11]

Address for correspondence: Betty Zimmerberg, Department of Psychology, Williams College, Williamstown, MA 02167. Voice: 413-597-2446; fax: 413-597-2085.
bzimmerb@williams.edu

Ann. N.Y. Acad. Sci. 1008: 308–313 (2003). © 2003 New York Academy of Sciences.
doi: 10.1196/annals.1301.039

Using an animal model of early social isolation that focuses on stressing the pup, not the dam, we have recently examined the effects of "early deprivation" on the production of USVs after brief maternal separation.[12] Pups at 7 or 12 days of age with 5 days of prior individual isolation vocalized less than control pups in the standard testing paradigm of brief maternal separation. Despite the lower rate, dams spent more time with, and licked and groomed more frequently and for a longer time, previously isolated pups compared to control pups. These results suggested that maternal behavior was somehow differentially sensitive to the prior experiences of her offspring, but not simply a function of the *rate* of their USVs.

In this experiment, we asked whether the pups with a prior history of early deprivation, although calling less frequently, might be differing from controls in some other acoustical features of their calls that cued their dams to provide greater maternal attention. We therefore repeated the previous experiment, this time examining the sonographic structure of the USVs emitted during the test.

MATERIALS AND METHODS

Subjects

Subjects were bred in this laboratory from Long-Evans hooded rats (Harlan Sprague Dawley, Indianapolis, IN). Pregnant females were individually housed in an isolated nursery on a 0700–1900-h LD cycle. Litters were culled to 12 pups on the day following their birth (postnatal day (PN) 1). On PN 2, litters were randomly assigned to one of two postnatal treatment groups: early deprivation or control.

In early deprivation litters, starting at PN 2, all but four pups were removed from the home nest ("chronic isolates"). Four pups were always left with the dam to ensure continued lactation during the isolation period ("stay-at-home" subjects). Isolated pups were placed individually in plastic containers (11.5 cm diameter) floating in a circulating, heated water bath (99 cm × 74 cm) maintained at 34°C. This procedure maintains rectal temperatures at 34°C.[12] After 6 hours of isolation, the pups were returned to the home cage. Control litters were left undisturbed except for standard cage changing. Early deprivation was conducted for five consecutive days.

Vocalization and Maternal Choice Test

The Maternal Choice Test apparatus has been previously described.[12] Suspended over each arm of the T-maze, with the microphone slightly below the level of the maze, were bat detectors with microphones (Ultrasound Advice, S-25) with connectors to both tape recorders and headphones. The bat detectors were connected to Mac G3 computers; sounds were recorded into SoundEdit (Macromedia).

On PN 7, each dam was tested once, with her own pups. The dam was placed in the start box and two of her pups were chosen for baiting each of the arms. In the case of the early deprivation litters, one pup had been isolated daily for the previous five days (chronic isolate) and the other pup (same gender) had always remained with that dam (stay-at-home). In the case of the control litters, one pup had been isolated on the day of testing ("acute isolate") and the other pup (same gender) had always remained with that dam (stay-at-home). The chronic and acute isolates had been removed from the home nest and isolated for 4 h on the day of testing. The experimenter was not aware of the treatment condition of the litter. The test consisted of 2 min with the dam confined to the start box and then free access for 5 min. The latency to enter each arm and retrieve each pup was recorded.

The sonograms were printed out and the following characteristics scored by hand by an investigator blind to conditions: the numbers of USVs, bouts, USVs per bout, interbout intervals, USVs with double shifts, and USVs with suppressed harmonics. A bout was defined as any group of calls that was separated from the next group of calls by at least 0.33 s (3 cm on sonogram).

RESULTS

Isolate pups that had been separated either acutely or chronically made significantly fewer calls (83.7 ± 29.9) than stay-at-home controls (275. 7 ± 22.0), $F(1,10) = 16.83, P < .01$. Similarly, the number of bouts was fewer in the isolates (19.0 ± 4.0) than stay-at-homes (38.0 ± 1.0), $F(1,10) = 28.34, P < .001$, and there was a significant interaction between litter condition and test condition, $F(1,10) = 7.84, P < .02$, seen in FIGURE 1A. The number of calls per bout were then also fewer in the Isolates (3.5 ± 0.5) than stay-at-homes (7.2 ± 0.6), $F(1,10) = 28.34, P < .001$. Interbout intervals were conversely increased in the isolates (4,4 ± 1.2 s) compared to stay-at-homes (1.4 ± 0.1 s), $F(1,10) = 7.88, P < .02$, and there was a trend toward an interaction between litter condition and test condition, $P = .10$, seen in FIGURE 1B.

The two main acoustic characteristics detected in the sonograms were calls with double shifts and calls with suppressed harmonics. There were no differences between groups in the number of suppressed harmonics, but there were fewer calls with double shifts in the isolates (34.1 ± 13.1) compared to stay-at-homes (110.5 ± 13.5), $F(1,10) = 8.78, P < .02$.

During free access, all the dams first entered the stay-at-home pups' arms. The latency to first enter the arm of the isolate pups was slower (0.39 ± 0.02 s) than entering stay-at-homes (0.16 ± 0.02 s), $F(1,10) = 65.7, P < .001$. However, all but one dam retrieved the isolate pup to the start box before retrieving the stay-at-home pup. There was a significant interaction between litter condition and test condition, $F(1,10) = 13.28, P < .01$, on the retrieval latency, as seen in FIGURE 1C.

DISCUSSION

It may be surprising, but rat dams can distinguish between a pup that has been separated from the nest and exhibit altered maternal behavior toward that pup compared to a littermate. Pups with a history of early deprivation of 6 h/day for 5 days were retrieved more quickly than acute isolates or controls. Their sonograms revealed the longest interbout intervals and the fewest number of call bouts. Certain other characteristics of the ultrasonic vocalizations emitted to call the dam were different in both acutely and chronically separated pups: a lower rate of calling, fewer calls per bout, and fewer calls with double shifts. Although the dam went first to the control pup calling more frequently, it then turned toward the previously isolated pup, retrieving that pup and then spending more time licking, grooming, and nursing

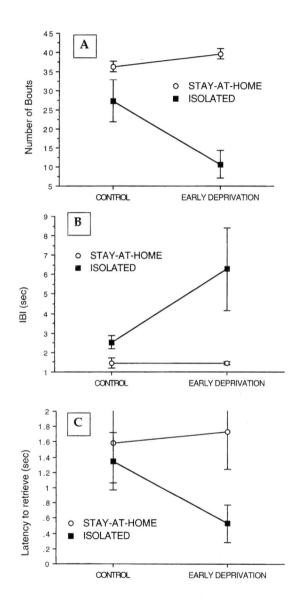

FIGURE 1. The effects of litter condition (control versus early deprivation) on vocalization patterns in pups that had been isolated or that had only stayed in the home nest (*Panel A*: number of call bouts, and *Panel B*: interbout intervals). In *Panel C*, the effect of litter condition on retrieval time for pups who had been isolated or stayed in the home nest.

those pups.[12] Most likely the factors that modulate this differential maternal behavior are multimodal, including odors and taste, although body temperatures were not different.

There are a few reports of maternal behavior being sensitive to individual differences within the litter. Dams engage in more ano-genital licking of males versus female pups.[13] Dams have also been reported to retrieve pups in order of descending body weight and neuromotor skills.[14] Pups who had received injections regardless of content also receive increased nonspecific maternal licking.[15] There are also some examples of altered maternal behavior toward a whole litter exposed to different experiences. Handling pups, which typically involves removing the pups briefly (<15 min) from the nest, leads to an increase in maternal behaviors like licking and arch-backed nursing.[3] The presence of a shocked or handled pup leads to increased maternal responsiveness to the entire litter.[16] When pups are subjected to a mild stressor (2 min of cold), the dam responds with increased maternal attention; with a more severe stressor (5 min of cold), maternal attention decreases.[17-19] Fostering studies have also shown pup-specific alterations in maternal behavior.[20-22]

Differential maternal behavior has consequences for later life. Female pups whose dams (either biological or foster) engaged in high rates of licking and grooming and arched back nursing show higher rates of this behavior when they are dams, as well as reduced fearfulness.[3] Pups that are licked less as pups show less exploration as juveniles.[23] Since the repercussions of differential maternal behavior continue into adulthood, greater understanding of this differentiation may help explain some of the long-term effects of early disruption of maternal–infant interactions. Analyses of USVs after brief maternal separation in the early deprivation paradigm may provide a good model system to determine neural mechanisms underlying deficits in attachment behavior and possibly depression in children with histories of neglect.

ACKNOWLEDGMENT

This work was supported by the National Science Foundation under Grant No. 0074627.

REFERENCES

1. HARLOW, H.F. & M.K. HARLOW. 1965. The affectional systems. *In* Behavior of nonhuman Primates. A.M. Schrier, H.F. Harlow, and F. Stollnitz, Eds.: 287–334. Academic Press. London.
2. CALDJI, C., B. TANNENBAUM, S. SHARMA, *et al.* 1998. Maternal care during infancy regulates the development of neural systems mediating the expression of fearfulness in the rat. Proc. Natl. Acad. Sci. USA **95**: 5335–5340.
3. FRANCIS, D.D., C. CALDJI, F. CALDJI, *et al.* 1999. The role of corticotropin-releasing factor-norepinephrine systems in mediating the effects of early experience on the development of behavioral and endocrine responses to stress. Biol. Psychiatry **46**: 1153–1166.
4. KEHOE, P., W.J. SHOEMAKER, L. TRIANO, *et al.* 1998. Adult rats stressed as neonates show exaggerated behavioral responses to both pharmacological and environmental challenges. Behav. Neurosci. **112**: 116–125.
5. LADD, C.O., M.J. OWENS & C.B. NEMEROFF. 1996. Persistent changes in corticotropin-releasing factor neuronal systems induced by maternal deprivation. Endocrinology **137**: 1212–1218.

6. LEHMANN, J., T. STOHR & J. FELDON. 2000. Long-term effects of prenatal stress experience and postnatal maternal separation on emotionality and attentional processes. Behav. Brain Res. **107**: 133–144.

7. ZIMMERBERG, B. & A.M. SHARTRAND. 1992. Temperature-dependent effects of maternal separation on growth, activity, and amphetamine sensitivity in the rat. Dev. Psychobiol. **25**: 213–226.

8. ZIMMERBERG, B., S.H. RACKOW & K.P. GEORGE-FRIEDMAN. 1999. Sex-dependent behavioral effects of the neurosteroid allopregnanolone 3α,5α-THP in neonatal and adult rats after postnatal stress. Pharmacol. Biochem. Behav. **64**: 717–724.

9. NOIROT, E. 1972. Ultrasounds and maternal behavior in small rodents. Dev. Psychobiol. **5**: 371–387.

10. HOFER, M.A. & H.N. SHAIR. 1978. Ultrasonic vocalization during social interaction and isolation in 2-week-old rats. Dev. Psychobiol. **11**: 495–504.

11. HOFER, M.A. & H.N. SHAIR. 1980. Sensory processes in the control of isolation-induced ultrasonic vocalization by 2-week-old rats. J. Comp. Physiol. Psychol. **94**: 271–279.

12. ZIMMERBERG, B., A.J ROSENTHAL & A.C. STARK. 2003. Neonatal social isolation alters both maternal and pup behaviors in rats. Dev. Psychobiol. **42**: 52–63.

13. MOORE, C.L. & G.A. MORELLI. 1979. Mother rats interact differently with male and female offspring. J. Comp. Physiol. Psychol. **93**: 677–684.

14. DEVITERNE, D. & D. DESOR. 1990. Selective pup retrieving by mother rats: sex and early characteristics as discrimination factors. Dev. Psychobiol. **23**: 361–368.

15. MOORE, C.L. 1982. Maternal behavior of rats is affected by hormonal condition of pups. J. Comp. Physiol. Psychol. **96**: 123–129.

16. BROWN, C.P., W.P. SMOTHERMAN & S. LEVINE. 1977. Interaction-induced reduction in differential maternal responsiveness: an effect of cue-reduction or behavior? Dev. Psychobiol. **10**: 273–280.

17. BELL, R.W. 1979. Ultrasonic control of maternal behavior: developmental implications. Am. Zool. **19**: 413–148.

18. BELL, R.W., W. NITSCHKE, T.H. GORRY & T.A. ZACHMAN. 1971. Infantile stimulation and ultrasonic signaling: a possible mediator of early handling phenomena. Dev. Psychobiol. **4**: 181–191.

19. BELL, R.W., W. NITSCHKE, N.J. BELL & T.A. ZACHMAN. 1974. Early experience, ultrasonic vocalizations, and maternal responsiveness in rats. Dev. Psychobiol. **7**: 235–242.

20. MOORE, C.L., L. WONG, M.C. DAUM & O.U. LECLAIR. 1997. Mother-infant interactions in two strains of rats: implications for dissociating mechanism and function of a maternal pattern. Dev. Psychobiol. **30**: 301–312.

21. BARBAZANGES, A., M. VALLEE, W. MAYO, *et al.* 1996. Early and later adoptions have different long-term effects on male rat offspring. J. Neurosci. **16**: 7783–7790.

22. MACCARI, S., P.V. PIAZZA, M. KABBAJ, *et al.* 1995. Adoption reverses the long-term impairment in glucocorticoid feedback induced by prenatal stress. J. Neurosci. **15**: 110–116.

23. BIRKE, L.I.A. & D. SADLER. 1987. Differences in maternal behavior of rats and the sociosexual development of the offspring. Dev. Psychobiol. **20**: 85–99.

Index of Contributors

Atkinson, L., 248–251

Barr, G.A., 304–307
Beitchman, J.H., 248–251
Blair, R.J.R., 201–218
Brotman, L.M., 252–255
Burdick, S., 160–169

Castellanos, F.X., 256–260
Charney, D.S., 201–218
Clark, M.A., 265–268
Cloitre, M., 297–299
Colamussi, L., 160–169
Connor, D.F., 79–90

Dahl, R.E., 183–188
Davidge, K.M., 248–251
Davidson, A.N., 308–313
Davis, M., 112–121
Dennis, T.A., 252–255
Di Martino, A., 256–260
Diwadkar, V.A., 269–275
Doerfler, L.A., 79–90
Douglas, L., 248–251

Edelsohn, G.A., 261–264
Ehrlich, S., 265–268

Ferris, C.F., 69–78, 289–292

Gilbert, A.R., 269–275
Guessous, O., 55–68
Gunnar, M.R., 238–247

Heron, S., 55–68
Hinshaw, S.P., 149–159
Hoagwood, K., 140–148

Jones, C., 55–68

Kalin, N.H., 189–200
Kaslow, N.J., 55–68
Kennedy, J.L., 248–251
Keshavan, M.S., 269–275
Keyes, A., 22–30
Kim, J.H., 308–313
King, J.A., ix, 160–169, 289–292
Kwon, B.J., 265–268

Lawrence, K., 91–101
Lederhendler, I.I., 1–10
Lee, V., 248–251
Leibenluft, E., 201–218
Lyoo, I.K., 265–268

Magarinos, A.M., 304–307
McArdle, E.T., 285–288
McCarthy, M.M., 281–284
McEwen, B.S., 304–307
Melloni, R.H., Jr., 79–90
Messenger, T., 289–292
Montrose, D.M., 269–275
Morris, J., 91–101

Nelson, C.A., 48–54
Neumann, C.S., 276–280, 300–303
Nigg, J.T., 170–182, 293–296
Noam, G.G., 265–268
Nuñez, J.L., 281–284

Peters, D., 289–292
Peterson, B.S., 219–237
Pine, D.S., 201–218
Pollak, S.D., 102–111
Porges, S.W., 31–47
Portnoy, R., 261–264
Powers, S.I., 285–288

Rabinovich, H., 261–264
Ramos, V., 300–303
Renshaw, P.F., 265–268
Roberts, D.K., 55–68, 300–303

Robertson, A., 276–280
Rosenthal, A.J., 308–313
Rossi, V., 160–169, 289–292
Rothbaum, B.O., 112–121
Rutter, M., 11–21

Sahni, S.D., 269–275
Settles, L., 22–30
Sewell, K., 276–280
Shapiro, S., 248–251
Shelton, S.E., 189–200
Skuse, D., 91–101
Stawicki, J., 293–296
Steingard, R.J., 79–90
Stovall-McClough, K.C., 297–299

Sullivan, R.M., 122–131
Suomi, S.J., 132–139

Tenney, J., 160–169
Thompson, M., 55–68

Vitacco, M.J., 276–280, 300–303
Volungis, A.M., 79–90

Wiedenmayer, C.P., 304–307

Zeanah, C.H., 22–30
Zimmerberg, B., 308–313